Texts and Monographs in Computer Science

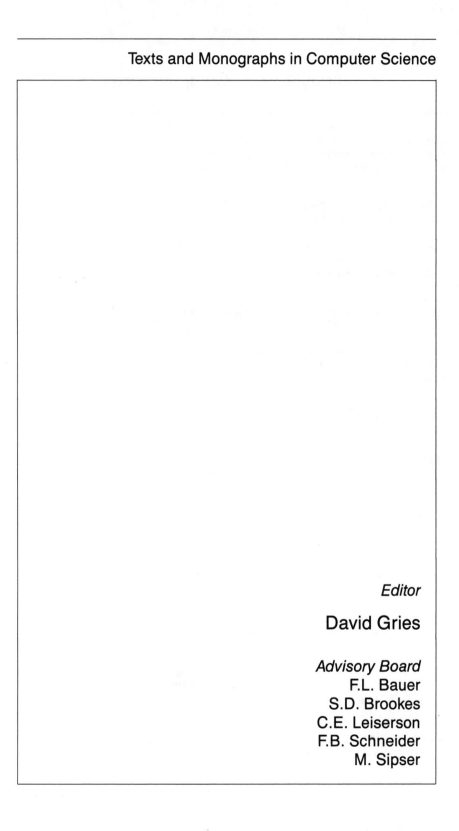

Editor

David Gries

Advisory Board
F.L. Bauer
S.D. Brookes
C.E. Leiserson
F.B. Schneider
M. Sipser

Texts and Monographs in Computer Science

Suad Alagic
Object-Oriented Database Programming
1989. XV, 320 pages, 84 illus.

Suad Alagic
Relational Database Technology
1986. XI, 259 pages, 114 illus.

Suad Alagic and Michael A. Arbib
The Design of Well-Structured and Correct Programs
1978. X, 292 pages, 68 illus.

S. Thomas Alexander
Adaptive Signal Processing: Theory and Applications
1986. IX, 179 pages, 42 illus.

Krzysztof R. Apt and Ernst-Rüdiger Olderog
Verification of Sequential and Concurrent Programs
1991. XVI, 441 pages

Michael A. Arbib, A.J. Kfoury, and Robert N. Moll
A Basis for Theoretical Computer Science
1981. VIII, 220 pages, 49 illus.

Friedrich L. Bauer and Hans Wössner
Algorithmic Language and Program Development
1982. XVI, 497 pages, 109 illus.

Kaare Christian
A Guide to Modula-2
1986. XIX, 436 pages, 46 illus.

Edsger W. Dijkstra
Selected Writings on Computing: A Personal Perspective
1982. XVII, 362 pages, 13 illus.

Edsger W. Dijkstra and Carel S. Scholten
Predicate Calculus and Program Semantics
1990. XII, 220 pages

W.H.J. Feijen, A.J.M. van Gasteren, D. Gries, and J. Misra, Eds.
Beauty Is Our Business: A Birthday Salute to Edsger W. Dijkstra
1990. XX, 453 pages, 21 illus.

P.A. Fejer and D.A. Simovici
Mathematical Foundations of Computer Science, Volume I:
Sets, Relations, and Induction
1990. X, 425 pages, 36 illus.

continued after index

The Design and Analysis of Algorithms

Dexter C. Kozen

With 72 Illustrations

Springer-Verlag
New York Berlin Heidelberg London Paris
Tokyo Hong Kong Barcelona Budapest

Dexter C. Kozen
Department of Computer Science
Cornell University
Upson Hall
Ithaca, NY 14853-7501
USA

Series Editor:
David Gries
Department of Computer Science
Cornell University
Upson Hall
Ithaca, NY 14853-7501
USA

Library of Congress Cataloging-in-Publication Data
Kozen, Dexter, 1951–
    The design and analysis of algorithms / Dexter C. Kozen.
      p.   cm.
    Includes bibliographical references and index.
    ISBN 0-387-97687-6
    1. Computer algorithms.   I. Title.
QA76.9.A43K69   1991
005.1—dc20   91-38759

Printed on acid-free paper.

Production managed by Bill Imbornoni; manufacturing supervised by Jacqui Ashri.
Photocomposed from a LaTeX file.
Printed and bound by R.R. Donnelley & Sons, Inc., Harrisonburg, VA.
Printed in the United States of America.

9 8 7 6 5 4 3 2

ISBN 0-387-97687-6 Springer-Verlag New York Berlin Heidelberg
ISBN 3-540-97687-6 Springer-Verlag Berlin Heidelberg New York

*To my wife Frances
and my sons Alexander, Geoffrey, and Timothy*

Preface

These are my lecture notes from **CS681: Design and Analysis of Algorithms**, a one-semester graduate course I taught at Cornell for three consecutive fall semesters from '88 to '90. The course serves a dual purpose: to cover core material in algorithms for graduate students in computer science preparing for their PhD qualifying exams, and to introduce theory students to some advanced topics in the design and analysis of algorithms. The material is thus a mixture of core and advanced topics.

At first I meant these notes to supplement and not supplant a textbook, but over the three years they gradually took on a life of their own. In addition to the notes, I depended heavily on the texts

- A. V. Aho, J. E. Hopcroft, and J. D. Ullman, *The Design and Analysis of Computer Algorithms*. Addison-Wesley, 1975.

- M. R. Garey and D. S. Johnson, *Computers and Intractibility: A Guide to the Theory of NP-Completeness*. W. H. Freeman, 1979.

- R. E. Tarjan, *Data Structures and Network Algorithms*. SIAM Regional Conference Series in Applied Mathematics 44, 1983.

and still recommend them as excellent references.

The course consists of 40 lectures. The notes from these lectures were prepared using scribes. At the beginning of each lecture, I would assign a scribe who would take notes for the entire class and prepare a raw LaTeX source, which I would then doctor and distribute. In addition to the 40 lectures, I have included 10 homework sets and several miscellaneous homework exercises, all with complete solutions. The notes that were distributed are essentially as they appear here; no major reorganization has been attempted.

There is a wealth of interesting topics, both classical and current, that I would like to have touched on but could not for lack of time. Many of these, such as computational geometry and factoring algorithms, could fill an entire semester. Indeed, one of the most difficult tasks was deciding how best to spend a scant 40 lectures.

I wish to thank all the students who helped prepare these notes and who kept me honest: Mark Aagaard, Mary Ann Branch, Karl-Friedrich Böhringer, Thomas Bressoud, Suresh Chari, Sofoklis Efremidis, Ronen Feldman, Ted

Fischer, Richard Huff, Michael Kalantar, Steve Kautz, Dani Lischinski, Peter Bro Miltersen, Marc Parmet, David Pearson, Dan Proskauer, Uday Rao, Mike Reiter, Gene Ressler, Alex Russell, Laura Sabel, Aravind Srinivasan, Sridhar Sundaram, Ida Szafranska, Filippo Tampieri, and Sam Weber. I am especially indebted to my teaching assistants Mark Novick (fall '88), Alessandro Panconesi (fall '89), and Kjartan Stefánsson (fall '90) for their help with proofreading, preparation of solution sets, and occasional lecturing. I am also indebted to my colleagues László Babai, Gianfranco Bilardi, Michael Luby, Keith Marzullo, Erik Meineche Schmidt, Bernd Sturmfels, Éva Tardos, Steve Vavasis, Sue Whitesides, and Rich Zippel for valuable comments and interesting exercises. Finally, I wish to express my sincerest gratitude to my colleague Vijay Vazirani, who taught the course in fall '87 and who was an invaluable source of help.

I would be most grateful for any suggestions or criticism from readers.

Cornell University   Dexter Kozen
Ithaca, NY   December 1990

Contents

I Lectures

Lecture 1   Algorithms and Their Complexity

This is a course on the design and analysis of algorithms intended for first-year graduate students in computer science. Its purposes are mixed: on the one hand, we wish to cover some fairly advanced topics in order to provide a glimpse of current research for the benefit of those who might wish to specialize in this area; on the other, we wish to introduce some core results and techniques which will undoubtedly prove useful to those planning to specialize in other areas.

We will assume that the student is familiar with the classical material normally taught in upper-level undergraduate courses in the design and analysis of algorithms. In particular, we will assume familiarity with:

- sequential machine models, including Turing machines and random access machines (RAMs)
- discrete mathematical structures, including graphs, trees, and dags, and their common representations (adjacency lists and matrices)
- fundamental data structures, including lists, stacks, queues, arrays, balanced trees
- fundamentals of asymptotic analysis, including $O(\cdot)$, $o(\cdot)$, and $\Omega(\cdot)$ notation, and techniques for the solution of recurrences
- fundamental programming techniques, such as recursion, divide-and-conquer, dynamic programming
- basic sorting and searching algorithms.

These notions are covered in the early chapters of [3, 39, 100].

3

Familiarity with elementary algebra, number theory, and discrete probability theory will be helpful. In particular, we will be making occasional use of the following concepts: linear independence, basis, determinant, eigenvalue, polynomial, prime, modulus, Euclidean algorithm, greatest common divisor, group, ring, field, random variable, expectation, conditional probability, conditional expectation. Some excellent classical references are [69, 49, 33].

The main emphasis will be on *asymptotic worst-case complexity*. This measures how the worst-case time or space complexity of a problem grows with the size of the input. We will also spend some time on probabilistic algorithms and analysis.

1.1 Asymptotic Complexity

Let f and g be functions $\mathcal{N} \to \mathcal{N}$, where $\mathcal{N}$ denotes the natural numbers $\{0, 1, \ldots\}$. Formally,

- f is $O(g)$ if

$$\exists c \in \mathcal{N} \; \overset{\infty}{\forall} n \; f(n) \leq c \cdot g(n) .$$

  The notation $\overset{\infty}{\forall}$ means "for almost all" or "for all but finitely many". Intuitively, f grows no faster asymptotically than g to within a constant multiple.

- f is $o(g)$ if

$$\forall c \in \mathcal{N} \; \overset{\infty}{\forall} n \; f(n) \leq \frac{1}{c} \cdot g(n) .$$

  This is a stronger statement. Intuitively, f grows strictly more slowly than any arbitrarily small positive constant multiple of g. For example, n^{347} is $o(2^{(\log n)^2})$.

- f is $\Omega(g)$ if g is $O(f)$. In other words, f is $\Omega(g)$ if

$$\exists c \in \mathcal{N} \; \overset{\infty}{\forall} n \; f(n) \geq \frac{1}{c} \cdot g(n) .$$

- f is $\Theta(g)$ if f is both $O(g)$ and $\Omega(g)$.

There is one cardinal rule:

Always use O and o for upper bounds and Ω for lower bounds. *Never* use O for lower bounds.

There is some disagreement about the definition of Ω. Some authors (such as [43]) prefer the definition as given above. Others (such as [108]) prefer: f is $\Omega(g)$ if g is not $o(f)$; in other words, f is $\Omega(g)$ if

$$\exists c \in \mathcal{N} \; \overset{\infty}{\exists} \, n \; f(n) > \frac{1}{c} \cdot g(n) \, .$$

(The notation $\overset{\infty}{\exists}$ means "there exist infinitely many".) The latter is weaker and presumably easier to establish, but the former gives sharper results. We won't get into the fray here, but just comment that neither definition precludes algorithms from taking less than the stated bound on certain inputs. For example, the assertion, "The running time of mergesort is $\Omega(n \log n)$" says that there is a c such that for all but finitely many n, there is some input sequence of length n on which mergesort makes at least $\frac{1}{c} n \log n$ comparisons. There is nothing to prevent mergesort from taking less time on some other input of length n.

The exact interpretation of statements involving O, o, and Ω depends on assumptions about the underlying model of computation, how the input is presented, how the size of the input is determined, and what constitutes a single step of the computation. In practice, authors often do not bother to write these down. For example, "The running time of mergesort is $O(n \log n)$" means that there is a fixed constant c such that for any n elements drawn from a totally ordered set, at most $cn \log n$ comparisons are needed to produce a sorted array. Here nothing is counted in the running time except the number of comparisons between individual elements, and each comparison is assumed to take one step; other operations are ignored. Similarly, nothing is counted in the input size except the number of elements; the size of each element (whatever that may mean) is ignored.

It is important to be aware of these unstated assumptions and understand how to make them explicit and formal when reading papers in the field. When making such statements yourself, always have your underlying assumptions in mind. Although many authors don't bother, it is a good habit to state any assumptions about the model of computation explicitly in any papers you write.

The question of what assumptions are reasonable is more often than not a matter of esthetics. You will become familiar with the standard models and assumptions from reading the literature; beyond that, you must depend on your own conscience.

1.2 Models of Computation

Our principal model of computation will be the unit-cost random access machine (RAM). Other models, such as uniform circuits and PRAMs, will be introduced when needed. The RAM model allows random access and the use of arrays, as well as unit-cost arithmetic and bit-vector operations on arbitrarily large integers; see [3].

For graph algorithms, arithmetic is often unnecessary. Of the two main representations of graphs, namely *adjacency matrices* and *adjacency lists*, the former requires random access and $\Omega(n^2)$ array storage; the latter, only linear storage and no random access. (For graphs, *linear* means $O(n + m)$, where n is the number of vertices of the graph and m is the number of edges.) The most esthetically pure graph algorithms are those that use the adjacency list representation and only manipulate pointers. To express such algorithms one can formulate a very weak model of computation with primitive operators equivalent to **car**, **cdr**, **cons**, **eq**, and **nil** of pure LISP; see also [99].

1.3   A Grain of Salt

No mathematical model can reflect reality with perfect accuracy. Mathematical models are abstractions; as such, they are necessarily flawed.

For example, it is well known that it is possible to abuse the power of unit-cost RAMs by encoding horrendously complicated computations in large integers and solving intractible problems in polynomial time [50]. However, this violates the unwritten rules of good taste. One possible preventative measure is to use the log-cost model; but when used as intended, the unit-cost model reflects experimental observation more accurately for data of moderate size (since multiplication really does take one unit of time), besides making the mathematical analysis a lot simpler.

Some theoreticians consider asymptotically optimal results as a kind of Holy Grail, and pursue them with a relentless frenzy (present company not necessarily excluded). This often leads to contrived and arcane solutions that may be superior by the measure of asymptotic complexity, but whose constants are so large or whose implementation would be so cumbersome that no improvement in technology would ever make them feasible. What is the value of such results? Sometimes they give rise to new data structures or new techniques of analysis that are useful over a range of problems, but more often than not they are of strictly mathematical interest. Some practitioners take this activity as an indictment of asymptotic complexity itself and refuse to admit that asymptotics have anything at all to say of interest in practical software engineering.

Nowhere is the argument more vociferous than in the theory of parallel computation. There are those who argue that many of the models of computation in common use, such as uniform circuits and PRAMs, are so inaccurate as to render theoretical results useless. We will return to this controversy later on when we talk about parallel machine models.

Such extreme attitudes on either side are unfortunate and counterproductive. By now asymptotic complexity occupies an unshakable position in our computer science consciousness, and has probably done more to guide us in improving technology in the design and analysis of algorithms than any other mathematical abstraction. On the other hand, one should be aware of its limitations and realize that an asymptotically optimal solution is not necessarily the best one.

A good rule of thumb in the design and analysis of algorithms, as in life, is to use common sense, exercise good taste, and always listen to your conscience.

1.4 Strassen's Matrix Multiplication Algorithm

Probably the single most important technique in the design of asymptotically fast algorithms is *divide-and-conquer*. Just to refresh our understanding of this technique and the use of recurrences in the analysis of algorithms, let's take a look at Strassen's classical algorithm for matrix multiplication and some of its progeny. Some of these examples will also illustrate the questionable lengths to which asymptotic analysis can sometimes be taken.

The usual method of matrix multiplication takes 8 multiplications and 4 additions to multiply two 2×2 matrices, or in general $O(n^3)$ arithmetic operations to multiply two $n \times n$ matrices. However, the number of multiplications can be reduced. Strassen [97] published one such algorithm for multiplying 2×2 matrices using only 7 multiplications and 18 additions:

$$\begin{bmatrix} a & b \\ c & d \end{bmatrix} \cdot \begin{bmatrix} e & f \\ g & h \end{bmatrix} = \begin{bmatrix} s_1 + s_2 - s_4 + s_6 & s_4 + s_5 \\ s_6 + s_7 & s_2 - s_3 + s_5 - s_7 \end{bmatrix}$$

where

$$\begin{aligned} s_1 &= (b - d) \cdot (g + h) \\ s_2 &= (a + d) \cdot (e + h) \\ s_3 &= (a - c) \cdot (e + f) \\ s_4 &= h \cdot (a + b) \\ s_5 &= a \cdot (f - h) \\ s_6 &= d \cdot (g - e) \\ s_7 &= e \cdot (c + d) . \end{aligned}$$

Assume for simplicity that n is a power of 2. (This is not the last time you will hear that.) Apply the 2×2 algorithm recursively on a pair of $n \times n$ matrices by breaking each of them up into four square submatrices of size $\frac{n}{2} \times \frac{n}{2}$:

$$\begin{bmatrix} A & B \\ C & D \end{bmatrix} \cdot \begin{bmatrix} E & F \\ G & H \end{bmatrix} = \begin{bmatrix} S_1 + S_2 - S_4 + S_6 & S_4 + S_5 \\ S_6 + S_7 & S_2 - S_3 + S_5 - S_7 \end{bmatrix}$$

where

$$S_1 = (B - D) \cdot (G + H)$$

$$
\begin{aligned}
S_2 &= (A+D) \cdot (E+H) \\
S_3 &= (A-C) \cdot (E+F) \\
S_4 &= H \cdot (A+B) \\
S_5 &= A \cdot (F-H) \\
S_6 &= D \cdot (G-E) \\
S_7 &= E \cdot (C+D) \ .
\end{aligned}
$$

Everything is the same as in the 2×2 case, except now we are manipulating $\frac{n}{2} \times \frac{n}{2}$ matrices instead of scalars. (We have to be slightly cautious, since matrix multiplication is not commutative.) Ultimately, how many scalar operations $(+, -, \cdot)$ does this recursive algorithm perform in multiplying two $n \times n$ matrices? We get the recurrence

$$
T(n) = 7T(\frac{n}{2}) + dn^2
$$

with solution

$$
\begin{aligned}
T(n) &= (1 + \frac{4}{3}d)n^{\log_2 7} + O(n^2) \\
&= O(n^{\log_2 7}) \\
&= O(n^{2.81\ldots})
\end{aligned}
$$

which is $o(n^3)$. Here d is a fixed constant, and dn^2 represents the time for the matrix additions and subtractions.

This is already a significant asymptotic improvement over the naive algorithm, but can we do even better? In general, an algorithm that uses c multiplications to multiply two $d \times d$ matrices, used as the basis of such a recursive algorithm, will yield an $O(n^{\log_d c})$ algorithm. To beat Strassen's algorithm, we must have $c < d^{\log_2 7}$. For a 3×3 matrix, we need $c < 3^{\log_2 7} = 21.8\ldots$, but the best known algorithm uses 23 multiplications.

In 1978, Victor Pan [83, 84] showed how to multiply 70×70 matrices using 143640 multiplications. This gives an algorithm of approximately $O(n^{2.795\ldots})$. The asymptotically best algorithm known to date, which is achieved by entirely different methods, is $O(n^{2.376\ldots})$ [25]. Every algorithm must be $\Omega(n^2)$, since it has to look at all the entries of the matrices; no better lower bound is known.

Lecture 2   Topological Sort and MST

A recurring theme in asymptotic analysis is that it is often possible to get better asymptotic performance by maintaining extra information about the structure. Updating this extra information may slow down each individual step; this additional cost is sometimes called *overhead*. However, it is often the case that a small amount of overhead yields dramatic improvements in the asymptotic complexity of the algorithm.

To illustrate, let's look at *topological sort*. Let $G = (V, E)$ be a directed acyclic graph (dag). The edge set E of the dag G induces a *partial order* (a reflexive, antisymmetric, transitive binary relation) on V, which we denote by E^* and define by: uE^*v if there exists a directed E-path of length 0 or greater from u to v. The relation E^* is called the *reflexive transitive closure* of E.

Proposition 2.1 *Every partial order extends to a total order (a partial order in which every pair of elements is comparable).*

Proof. If R is a partial order that is not a total order, then there exist u, v such that neither uRv nor vRu. Extend R by setting

$$R := R \cup \{(x, y) \mid xRu \text{ and } vRy\} .$$

The new R is a partial order extending the old R, and in addition now uRv. Repeat until there are no more incomparable pairs.   □

In the case of a dag $G = (V, E)$ with associated partial order E^*, to say that a total order $\leq$ extends E^* is the same as saying that if uEv then $u \leq v$. Such a total order is called a *topological sort* of the dag G. A naive $O(n^3)$ algorithm to find a topological sort can be obtained from the proof of the above proposition.

Here is a faster algorithm, although still not optimal.

Algorithm 2.2 (Topological Sort II)

1. Start from any vertex and follow edges backwards until finding a vertex u with no incoming edges. Such a u must be encountered eventually, since there are no cycles and the dag is finite.

2. Make u the next vertex in the total order.

3. Delete u and all adjacent edges and go to step 1.

Using the adjacency list representation, the running time of this algorithm is $O(n)$ steps per iteration for n iterations, or $O(n^2)$.

The bottleneck here is step 1. A minor modification will allow us to perform this step in constant time. Assume the adjacency list representation of the graph associates with each vertex two separate lists, one for the incoming edges and one for the outgoing edges. If the representation is not already of this form, it can easily be put into this form in linear time. The algorithm will maintain a queue of vertices with no incoming edges. This will reduce the cost of finding a vertex with no incoming edges to constant time at a slight extra overhead for maintaining the queue.

Algorithm 2.3 (Topological Sort III)

1. Initialize the queue by traversing the graph and inserting each v whose list of incoming edges is empty.

2. Pick a vertex u off the queue and make u the next vertex in the total order.

3. Delete u and all outgoing edges (u, v). For each such v, if its list of incoming edges becomes empty, put v on the queue. Go to step 2.

Step 1 takes time $O(n)$. Step 2 takes constant time, thus $O(n)$ time over all iterations. Step 3 takes time $O(m)$ over all iterations, since each edge can be deleted at most once. The overall time is $O(m + n)$.

Later we will see a different approach involving depth first search.

2.1 Minimum Spanning Trees

Let $G = (V, E)$ be a connected undirected graph.

Definition 2.4 A *forest* in G is a subgraph $F = (V, E')$ with no cycles. Note that F has the same vertex set as G. A *spanning tree* in G is a forest with exactly one connected component. Given weights $w : E \rightarrow \mathcal{N}$ (edges are assigned weights over the natural numbers), a *minimum (weight) spanning tree (MST)* in G is a spanning tree T whose total weight (sum of the weights of the edges in T) is minimum over all spanning trees. □

Lemma 2.5 *Let* $F = (V, E)$ *be an undirected graph, c the number of connected components of F, $m = |E|$, and $n = |V|$. Then F has no cycles iff $c + m = n$.*

Proof.

($\rightarrow$) By induction on m. If $m = 0$, then there are n vertices and each forms a connected component, so $c = n$. If an edge is added without forming a cycle, then it must join two components. Thus m is increased by 1 and c is decreased by 1, so the equation $c + m = n$ is maintained.

($\leftarrow$) Suppose that F has at least one cycle. Pick an arbitrary cycle and remove an edge from that cycle. Then m decreases by 1, but c and n remain the same. Repeat until there are no more cycles. When done, the equation $c + m = n$ holds, by the preceding paragraph; but then it could not have held originally. □

We use a *greedy algorithm* to produce a minimum weight spanning tree. This algorithm is originally due to Kruskal [66].

Algorithm 2.6 (Greedy Algorithm for MST)

1. Sort the edges by weight.

2. For each edge on the list in order of increasing weight, include that edge in the spanning tree if it does not form a cycle with the edges already taken; otherwise discard it.

The algorithm can be halted as soon as $n - 1$ edges have been kept, since we know we have a spanning tree by Lemma 2.5.

Step 1 takes time $O(m \log m) = O(m \log n)$ using any one of a number of general sorting methods, but can be done faster in certain cases, for example if the weights are small integers so that bucket sort can be used.

Later on, we will give an almost linear time implementation of step 2, but for now we will settle for $O(n \log n)$. We will think of including an edge e in the spanning tree as taking the union of two disjoint sets of vertices, namely the vertices in the connected components of the two endpoints of e in the forest being built. We represent each connected component as a linked list. Each list element points to the next element and has a back pointer to the head of the list. Initially there are no edges, so we have n lists, each containing one vertex. When a new edge (u, v) is encountered, we check whether it would form a cycle, *i.e.* whether u and v are in the same connected component, by comparing back pointers to see if u and v are on the same list. If not, we add (u, v) to the spanning tree and take the union of the two connected components by merging the two lists. Note that the lists are always disjoint, so we don't have to check for duplicates.

Checking whether u and v are in the same connected component takes constant time. Each merge of two lists could take as much as linear time, since we have to traverse one list and change the back pointers, and there are $n - 1$ merges; this will give $O(n^2)$ if we are not careful. However, if we maintain counters containing the size of each component and always merge the smaller into the larger, then each vertex can have its back pointer changed at most $\log n$ times, since each time the size of its component at least doubles. If we charge the change of a back pointer to the vertex itself, then there are at most $\log n$ changes per vertex, or at most $n \log n$ in all. Thus the total time for all list merges is $O(n \log n)$.

2.2   The Blue and Red Rules

Here is a more general approach encompassing most of the known algorithms for the MST problem. For details and references, see [100, Chapter 6], which proves the correctness of the greedy algorithm as a special case of this more general approach. In the next lecture, we will give an even more general treatment.

Let $G = (V, E)$ be an undirected connected graph with edge weights $w : E \to \mathcal{N}$. Consider the following two rules for coloring the edges of G, which Tarjan [100] calls the *blue rule* and the *red rule*:

Blue Rule: Find a *cut* (a partition of V into two disjoint sets X and $V - X$) such that no blue edge crosses the cut. Pick an uncolored edge of minimum weight between X and $V - X$ and color it blue.

Red Rule: Find a *cycle* (a path in G starting and ending at the same vertex) containing no red edge. Pick an uncolored edge of maximum weight on that cycle and color it red.

The greedy algorithm is just a repeated application of a special case of the blue rule. We will show next time:

Theorem 2.7 *Starting with all edges uncolored, if the blue and red rules are applied in arbitrary order until neither applies, then the final set of blue edges forms a minimum spanning tree.*

Lecture 3 Matroids and Independence

Before we prove the correctness of the blue and red rules for MST, let's first discuss an abstract combinatorial structure called a *matroid*. We will show that the MST problem is a special case of the more general problem of finding a minimum-weight maximal independent set in a matroid. We will then generalize the blue and red rules to arbitrary matroids and prove their correctness in this more general setting. We will show that every matroid has a dual matroid, and that the blue and red rules of a matroid are the red and blue rules, respectively, of its dual. Thus, once we establish the correctness of the blue rule, we get the red rule for free.

We will also show that a structure is a matroid if and only if the greedy algorithm always produces a minimum-weight maximal independent set for any weighting.

Definition 3.1 A *matroid* is a pair $(S, \mathcal{I})$ where S is a finite set and $\mathcal{I}$ is a family of subsets of S such that

(i) if $J \in \mathcal{I}$ and $I \subseteq J$, then $I \in \mathcal{I}$;

(ii) if $I, J \in \mathcal{I}$ and $|I| < |J|$, then there exists an $x \in J - I$ such that $I \cup \{x\} \in \mathcal{I}$.

The elements of $\mathcal{I}$ are called *independent sets* and the subsets of S not in $\mathcal{I}$ are called *dependent sets*. □

This definition is supposed to capture the notion of *independence* in a general way. Here are some examples:

13

1. Let V be a vector space, let S be a finite subset of V, and let $\mathcal{I} \subseteq 2^S$ be the family of linearly independent subsets of S. This example justifies the term "independent".

2. Let A be a matrix over a field, let S be the set of rows of A, and let $\mathcal{I} \subseteq 2^S$ be the family of linearly independent subsets of S.

3. Let $G = (V, E)$ be a connected undirected graph. Let $S = E$ and let $\mathcal{I}$ be the set of forests in G. This example gives the MST problem of the previous lecture.

4. Let $G = (V, E)$ be a connected undirected graph. Let $S = E$ and let $\mathcal{I}$ be the set of subsets $E' \subseteq E$ such that the graph $(V, E - E')$ is connected.

5. Elements $\alpha_1, \ldots, \alpha_n$ of a field are said to be *algebraically independent* over a subfield k if there is no nontrivial polynomial $p(x_1, \ldots, x_n)$ with coefficients in k such that $p(\alpha_1, \ldots, \alpha_n) = 0$. Let S be a finite set of elements and let $\mathcal{I}$ be the set of subsets of S that are algebraically independent over k.

Definition 3.2 A *cycle* (or *circuit*) of a matroid $(S, \mathcal{I})$ is a setwise minimal (*i.e.*, minimal with respect to set inclusion) dependent set. A *cut* (or *cocircuit*) of $(S, \mathcal{I})$ is a setwise minimal subset of S intersecting all maximal independent sets.   □

The terms *circuit* and *cocircuit* are standard in matroid theory, but we will continue to use *cycle* and *cut* to maintain the intuitive connection with the special case of MST. However, be advised that cuts in graphs as defined in the last lecture are *unions* of cuts as defined here. For example, in the graph

the set $\{(s, u), (t, u)\}$ forms a cut in the sense of MST, but not a cut in the sense of the matroid, because it is not minimal. However, a moment's thought reveals that this difference is inconsequential as far as the blue rule is concerned.

Let the elements of S be weighted. We wish to find a setwise maximal independent set whose total weight is minimum among all setwise maximal independent sets. In this more general setting, the blue and red rules become:

Blue Rule: Find a cut with no blue element. Pick an uncolored element of the cut of minimum weight and color it blue.

Red Rule: Find a cycle with no red element. Pick an element of the cycle of maximum weight and color it red.

3.1   Matroid Duality

As the astute reader has probably noticed by now, there is some kind of duality afoot. The similarity between the blue and red rules is just too striking to be mere coincidence.

Definition 3.3 Let $(S, \mathcal{I})$ be a matroid. The *dual matroid* of $(S, \mathcal{I})$ is $(S, \mathcal{I}^*)$, where

$$\mathcal{I}^* = \{\text{subsets of } S \text{ disjoint from some maximal element of } \mathcal{I}\} .$$

In other words, the maximal elements of $\mathcal{I}^*$ are the complements in S of the maximal elements of $\mathcal{I}$.   □

The examples 3 and 4 above are duals. Note that $\mathcal{I}^{**} = \mathcal{I}$. Be careful: it is *not* the case that a set is independent in a matroid iff it is dependent in its dual. For example, except in trivial cases, $\emptyset$ is independent in both matroids.

Theorem 3.4

1. *Cuts in $(S, \mathcal{I})$ are cycles in $(S, \mathcal{I}^*)$.*

2. *The blue rule in $(S, \mathcal{I})$ is the red rule in $(S, \mathcal{I}^*)$ with the ordering of the weights reversed.*

3.2   Correctness of the Blue and Red Rules

Now we prove the correctness of the blue and red rules in arbitrary matroids. A proof for the special case of MST can be found in Tarjan's book [100, Chapter 6]; Lawler [70] states the blue and red rules for arbitrary matroids but omits a proof of correctness.

Definition 3.5 Let $(S, \mathcal{I})$ be a matroid with dual $(S, \mathcal{I}^*)$. An *acceptable coloring* is a pair of disjoint sets $B \in \mathcal{I}$ (the *blue elements*) and $R \in \mathcal{I}^*$ (the *red elements*). An acceptable coloring B, R is *total* if $B \cup R = S$, *i.e.* if B is a maximal independent set and R is a maximal independent set in the dual. An acceptable coloring B', R' *extends* or *is an extension of* an acceptable coloring B, R if $B \subseteq B'$ and $R \subseteq R'$.   □

Lemma 3.6 *Any acceptable coloring has a total acceptable extension.*

Proof. Let B, R be an acceptable coloring. Let U^* be a maximal element of $\mathcal{I}^*$ extending R, and let $U = S - U^*$. Then U is a maximal element of $\mathcal{I}$ disjoint from R. As long as $|B| < |U|$, select elements of U and add them to B, maintaining independence. This is possible by axiom (ii) of matroids. Let $\widehat{B}$ be the resulting set. Since all maximal independent sets have the same cardinality (Exercise 1a, Homework 1), $\widehat{B}$ is a maximal element of $\mathcal{I}$ containing B and disjoint from R. The desired total extension is $\widehat{B}, S - \widehat{B}$.   □

Lemma 3.7 *A cut and a cycle cannot intersect in exactly one element.*

Proof. Let C be a cut and D a cycle. Suppose that $C \cap D = \{x\}$. Then $D - \{x\}$ is independent and $C - \{x\}$ is independent in the dual. Color $D - \{x\}$ blue and $C - \{x\}$ red; by Lemma 3.6, this coloring extends to a total acceptable coloring. But depending on the color of x, either C is all red or D is all blue; this is impossible in an acceptable coloring, since D is dependent and C is dependent in the dual.　　　　□

Suppose B is independent and $B \cup \{x\}$ is dependent. Then $B \cup \{x\}$ contains a minimal dependent subset or cycle C, called the *fundamental cycle*[1] of x and B. The cycle C must contain x, because $C - \{x\}$ is contained in B and is therefore independent.

Lemma 3.8 (Exchange Lemma) *Let B, R be a total acceptable coloring.*

(i) Let $x \in R$ and let y lie on the fundamental cycle of x and B. If the colors of x and y are exchanged, the resulting coloring is acceptable.

(ii) Let $y \in B$ and let x lie on the fundamental cut of y and R (the fundamental cut of y and R is the fundamental cycle of y and R in the dual matroid). If the colors of x and y are exchanged, the resulting coloring is acceptable.

Proof. By duality, we need only prove (i). Let C be the fundamental cycle of x and B and let y lie on C. If $y = x$, there is nothing to prove. Otherwise $y \in B$. The set $C - \{y\}$ is independent since C is minimal. Extend $C - \{y\}$ by adding elements of $|B|$ as in the proof of Lemma 3.6 until achieving a maximal independent set B'. Then $B' = (B - \{y\}) \cup \{x\}$, and the total acceptable coloring $B', S - B'$ is obtained from B, R by switching the colors of x and y.　　　　□

A total acceptable coloring B, R is called *optimal* if B is of minimum weight among all maximal independent sets; equivalently, if R is of maximum weight among all maximal independent sets in the dual matroid.

Lemma 3.9 *If an acceptable coloring has an optimal total extension before execution of the blue or red rule, then so has the resulting coloring afterwards.*

Proof. We prove the case of the blue rule; the red rule follows by duality. Let B, R be an acceptable coloring with optimal total extension $\widehat{B}, \widehat{R}$. Let A be a cut containing no blue elements, and let x be an uncolored element of A of minimum weight. If $x \in \widehat{B}$, we are done, so assume that $x \in \widehat{R}$. Let C be the fundamental cycle of x and $\widehat{B}$. By Lemma 3.7, $A \cap C$ must contain

---

[1]We say "the" because it is unique (Exercise 1b, Homework 1), although we do not need to know this for our argument.

another element besides x, say y. Then $y \in \widehat{B}$, and $y \notin B$ because there are no blue elements of A. By Lemma 3.8, the colors of x and y in $\widehat{B}, \widehat{R}$ can be exchanged to obtain a total acceptable coloring $\widehat{B}', \widehat{R}'$ extending $B \cup \{x\}, R$. Moreover, $\widehat{B}'$ is of minimum weight, because the weight of x is no more than that of y. □

We also need to know

Lemma 3.10 *If an acceptable coloring is not total, then either the blue or red rule applies.*

Proof. Let B, R be an acceptable coloring with uncolored element x. By Lemma 3.6, B, R has a total extension $\widehat{B}, \widehat{R}$. By duality, assume without loss of generality that $x \in \widehat{B}$. Let C be the fundamental cut of x and $\widehat{R}$. Since all elements of C besides x are in $\widehat{R}$, none of them are blue in B. Thus the blue rule applies. □

Combining Lemmas 3.9 and 3.10, we have

Theorem 3.11 *If we start with an uncolored weighted matroid and apply the blue or red rules in any order until neither applies, then the resulting coloring is an optimal total acceptable coloring.*

What is really going on here is that all the subsets of the maximal independent sets of minimal weight form a submatroid of $(S, \mathcal{I})$, and the blue rule gives a method for implementing axiom (ii) for this matroid; see Miscellaneous Exercise 1.

3.3   Matroids and the Greedy Algorithm

We have shown that if $(S, \mathcal{I})$ is a matroid, then the greedy algorithm produces a maximal independent set of minimum weight. Here we show the converse: if $(S, \mathcal{I})$ is not a matroid, then the greedy algorithm fails for some choice of integer weights. Thus the abstract concept of matroid captures exactly when the greedy algorithm works.

Theorem 3.12 ([32]; see also [70]) *A system $(S, \mathcal{I})$ satisfying axiom (i) of matroids is a matroid (i.e., it satisfies (ii)) if and only if for all weight assignments $w : S \to \mathcal{N}$, the greedy algorithm gives a minimum-weight maximal independent set.*

Proof. The direction ($\rightarrow$) has already been shown. For ($\leftarrow$), let $(S, \mathcal{I})$ satisfy (i) but not (ii). There must be A, B such that $A, B \in \mathcal{I}$, $|A| < |B|$, but for no $x \in B - A$ is $A \cup \{x\} \in \mathcal{I}$.

Assume without loss of generality that B is a *maximal* independent set. If it is not, we can add elements to B maintaining the independence of B; for any element that we add to B that can also be added to A while preserving the independence of A, we do so. This process never changes the fact that $|A| < |B|$ and for no $x \in B - A$ is $A \cup \{x\} \in \mathcal{I}$.

Now we assign weights $w : S \to \mathcal{N}$. Let $a = |A - B|$ and $b = |B - A|$. Then $a < b$. Let h be a huge number, $h \gg a, b$. (Actually $h > b^2$ will do.)

Case 1　If A is a maximal independent set, assign

$$
\begin{aligned}
w(x) &= a + 1 \quad \text{for } x \in B - A \\
w(x) &= b + 1 \quad \text{for } x \in A - B \\
w(x) &= 0 \quad\quad\ \text{for } x \in A \cap B \\
w(x) &= h \quad\quad\ \text{for } x \notin A \cup B \ .
\end{aligned}
$$

Thus

$$
\begin{aligned}
w(A) &= a(b+1) &= ab + a \\
w(B) &= b(a+1) &= ab + b \ .
\end{aligned}
$$

This weight assignment forces the greedy algorithm to choose B when in fact A is a maximal independent set of smaller weight.

Case 2　If A is not a maximal independent set, assign

$$
\begin{aligned}
w(x) &= 0 \quad \text{for } x \in A \\
w(x) &= b \quad \text{for } x \in B - A \\
w(x) &= h \quad \text{for } x \notin A \cup B \ .
\end{aligned}
$$

All the elements of A will be chosen first, and then a huge element outside of $A \cup B$ must be chosen, since A is not maximal. Thus the minimum-weight maximal independent set B was not chosen.　　　　　　　　　　　　　□

Lecture 4   Depth-First and Breadth-First Search

Depth-first search (DFS) and breadth-first search (BFS) are two of the most useful subroutines in graph algorithms. They allow one to search a graph in linear time and compile information about the graph. They differ in that the former uses a stack (LIFO) discipline and the latter uses a queue (FIFO) discipline to choose the next edge to explore.

Undirected depth-first search produces in linear time a numbering of the vertices called the *depth-first numbering* and a particular spanning tree called the *depth-first spanning tree* of each connected component. This is done as follows. Choose an arbitrary vertex u, which will become the root of the tree. Push all edges $(u, v) \in E$ onto the stack. Assign u the DFS number 0 and set the DFS counter c to 1. Now repeat the following activity until the stack becomes empty. Let (x, y) be the top element of the stack. This is the next edge to explore. The vertex x has a DFS number already (this is an invariant of the loop). If y has no DFS number, assign it the DFS number c, increment c, push all edges $(y, z) \in E$ onto the stack, and make the (directed) edge (x, y) a *tree edge*. Otherwise, if y has a DFS number already, just pop (x, y) off the stack.

The tree edges form a directed spanning tree of the connected component of u rooted at u. It is a dag rooted at u, since tree edges (x, y) only go from lower numbered vertices to higher numbered vertices. It is a tree, since no vertex has indegree greater than one; this is because (x, y) becomes a tree edge only if y has no DFS number, and thereafter y has a DFS number. It is a spanning tree, since it is easily shown inductively that every vertex in the connected component of u eventually receives a DFS number. This spanning tree is called the *depth-first spanning tree*.

We can repeat the whole process with a new arbitrarily chosen unvisited vertex to search the other connected components.

The non-tree edges (x, y) are called *back edges* and are directed from higher numbered to lower numbered vertices. When we draw a DFS tree, we usually draw the root at the top, the tree edges pointing down (hence the term *depth-first*), and the back edges pointing up.

Back edges out of v can only go to ancestors of v in the DFS tree. There cannot be a back edge to a nonancestor, since that edge would have been explored earlier from the other direction and would have been a tree edge.

DFS takes time $O(m + n)$ where n is the number of vertices and m is the number of edges, since each edge is stacked at most once in each direction, and each edge and vertex requires a constant amount of processing.

See [3, 78] for an alternative treatment.

4.1 Biconnected Components

Let $G = (V, E)$ be a connected undirected graph.

Definition 4.1 A vertex v is an *articulation point* if its removal disconnects the graph. $\qquad\square$

Definition 4.2 A connected graph is called *biconnected* if any pair of distinct vertices u and v lie on a simple cycle (one with no repeated vertices). $\qquad\square$

Note that according to this definition, a graph with two vertices connected by a single edge is biconnected (no one said anything about not repeating edges).

If G is not biconnected, we define the *biconnected components* of G in terms of an equivalence relation on edges:

Definition 4.3 For $e, e' \in E$, define $e \equiv e'$ if e and e' lie on a simple cycle. $\qquad\square$

Lemma 4.4 *The relation $\equiv$ is an equivalence relation (reflexive, symmetric, and transitive).*

Proof. Reflexivity $e \equiv e$ follows from the fact that the edge e and its two endpoints constitute a simple cycle. The relation is symmetric, since e and e' can be interchanged in the definition of $\equiv$. The hard one is transitivity. Suppose $(u, v) \equiv (u', v')$ and $(u', v') \equiv (u'', v'')$. Let c and c' be the two simple cycles involved, respectively. Assume u, u', v', v occur in that order around c. Let x be the first vertex on the segment of c from u to u' that also lies in c'; x must exist since $u' \in c'$, at least. Let y be the first vertex on the segment of

c from v to v' that also lies in c'; y must exist since $v' \in c'$. Also, $x \neq y$ since c is simple. Let p be the path from x to y in c containing (u, v) and let p' be the path from x to y in c' containing (u'', v''). Then p and p' intersect only in x and y, and together form a simple cycle containing (u, v) and (u'', v''). □

Definition 4.5 The equivalence classes of $\equiv$ are called *biconnected components*. □

Lemma 4.6 *The vertex a is an articulation point iff a is contained in at least two biconnected components.*

Proof. Suppose the removal of a disconnects the graph. Then there exist u and v adjacent to a such that every path from u to v goes through a. Then the edges (u, a) and (a, v) cannot lie on a simple cycle, thus are in different biconnected components.

Conversely, suppose u and v are adjacent to a and $(u, a) \not\equiv (a, v)$. Then all paths between u and v must go through a. Thus if a is removed, there is no path between u and v, so G is disconnected. □

Below, when using the terms "descendant" and "ancestor" in a depth-first search tree, we will always consider a vertex u to be a descendant of itself and an ancestor of itself. In other words, we take the descendant and ancestor relations to be reflexive. If we want to exclude u, we do so explicitly by using the terms "proper descendant" and "proper ancestor".

Lemma 4.7 *Let (u, v) and (v, w) be two adjacent tree edges in a depth-first search tree of G. Then $(u, v) \equiv (v, w)$ if and only if there exists a back edge from some descendant of w to some ancestor of u.*

Proof.
($\rightarrow$) If there exists a back edge from some descendant w' of w to some ancestor u' of u, then (u, v) and (v, w) are edges in a simple cycle consisting of the back edge (w', u') along with the path of tree edges from u' to w'. Thus $(u, v) \equiv (v, w)$.

($\leftarrow$) Suppose $(u, v) \equiv (v, w)$. Then there must be a simple cycle containing them. This cycle must contain the edges (u, v) and (v, w) in this order, since it may only go through v once. Consider the subtree of the depth-first tree rooted at w. The simple cycle must contain a back edge (w', u') out of this subtree, since it must get back to u eventually. (Before coming out, the path inside the subtree can be quite complicated, since it can traverse tree and back edges in either direction—don't forget that the graph is undirected.) Then w' is a descendant of w and u' is an ancestor of w'. Since u' is not in the subtree rooted at w, it must be an ancestor of v. But it cannot be v because v cannot be used twice on the cycle. Therefore u' must be an ancestor of u. □

The biconnected components can be found from a DFS tree as follows. Assume the vertices are named by their DFS numbers. We compute a value for each vertex v, called $\textbf{low}(v)$, which gives the DFS number of the lowest numbered vertex x (*i.e.* the highest in the tree) such that there is a back edge from some descendant of v to x. By Lemmas 4.6 and 4.7, a vertex u will be an articulation point, and the biconnected component of the tree edge (u, v) will lie entirely in the subtree rooted at u, if $\textbf{low}(v) \geq u$. We can inductively compute $\textbf{low}(v)$ as follows:

$$
\begin{aligned}
x &:= \min\{\textbf{low}(w) \mid w \text{ is an immediate descendant of } v\} \\
y &:= \min\{z \mid z \text{ is reachable by a back edge from } v\} \\
\textbf{low}(v) &:= \min(x, y) \ .
\end{aligned}
$$

The values $\textbf{low}(v)$ can be computed simultaneously with the construction of the DFS tree in linear time. As soon as an articulation point u is discovered with (u, v) a tree edge such that $\textbf{low}(v) \geq u$, the biconnected component containing the edge (u, v) can be deleted from the graph. See [3, 78] for more details.

4.2 Directed DFS

The DFS procedure on directed graphs is similar to DFS on undirected graphs, except that we only follow edges from sources to sinks. Four types of edges can result:

- *tree edges* to a vertex not yet visited

- *back edges* to an ancestor

- *forward edges* to a descendant previously visited

- *cross edges* to a vertex previously visited that is neither an ancestor nor a descendant.

There can be no cross edges to a higher numbered vertex; such an edge would have been a tree edge. If we mark the vertex y when the tree edge (x, y) is popped to indicate that the subtree below y has been completely explored, we can recognize each of these four cases when we explore the edge (u, v) by checking marks and comparing DFS numbers:

(u, v) *is a*	*if*
tree edge	$\text{DFS}(v)$ does not exist
back edge	$\text{DFS}(v) < \text{DFS}(u)$ and v is not marked
forward edge	$\text{DFS}(v) > \text{DFS}(u)$
cross edge	$\text{DFS}(v) < \text{DFS}(u)$ and v is marked

The directed DFS tree can be constructed in linear time; see [3, 78] for details.
The first application of directed DFS is determining acyclicity:

Theorem 4.8 *A directed graph is acyclic iff its DFS forest has no back edges.*

Proof. If there is a back edge, the graph is surely cyclic. Conversely, if there are no back edges, consider the *postorder* numbering of the DFS forest: traverse the forest in depth-first order, but number the vertices in the order they are *last* seen. Then tree edges, forward edges, and cross edges all go from higher numbered to lower numbered vertices, so there can be no cycles. □

4.3 Strong Components

Definition 4.9 Let $G = (V, E)$ be a directed graph. For $u, v \in V$, define $u \equiv v$ if u and v lie on a directed cycle in G. This is an equivalence relation, and its equivalence classes are called *strongly connected components* or just *strong components*. A graph G is said to be *strongly connected* if for any pair of vertices u, v there is a directed cycle in G containing u and v; *i.e.*, if G has only one strong component. □

The strong components of a directed graph can be computed in linear time using directed depth-first search. The algorithm is similar to the algorithm for biconnected components in undirected graphs; see [3] for details.

4.4 Strong Components and Partial Orders

Strong components are important in the representation of partial orders. Finite partial orders are often represented as the reflexive transitive closures E^* of dags $G = (V, E)$ (recall $(u, v) \in E^*$ iff there exists an E-path from u to v of length 0 or greater). If G is not acyclic, then the relation E^* does not satisfy the antisymmetry law, and is thus not a partial order. However, it is still reflexive and transitive. Such a relation is called a *preorder* or sometimes a *quasiorder*.

Given an arbitrary preorder $(P, \preceq)$, define $x \approx y$ if $x \preceq y$ and $y \preceq x$. This is an equivalence relation, and we can collapse its equivalence classes into single points to get a partial order. This construction is called a *quotient construction*. Formally, let $[x]$ denote the $\approx$-class of x and let $P/\approx$ denote the set of all such classes; *i.e.*,

$$
\begin{aligned}
[x] &= \{y \mid y \approx x\} \\
P/\approx &= \{[x] \mid x \in P\} .
\end{aligned}
$$

The preorder $\preceq$ induces a preorder, also denoted $\preceq$, on $P/\approx$ in a natural way: $[x] \preceq [y]$ if $x \preceq y$ in P. (The choice of x and y in their respective equivalence classes doesn't matter.) It is easily shown that the preorder $\preceq$ is actually a partial order on $P/\approx$; intuitively, by collapsing equivalence classes, we identified those elements that caused antisymmetry to fail.

Forming the strong components of a directed (not necessarily acyclic) graph $G = (V, E)$ allows us to perform this operation effectively on the preorder (V, E^*). We form a quotient graph $G/\equiv$ by collapsing the strong components of G into single vertices:

$$
\begin{aligned}
[v] &= \{u \mid u \equiv v\} \text{ (the strong component of } v) \\
V/\equiv &= \{[v] \mid v \in V\} \\
E' &= \{([u], [v]) \mid (u, v) \in E\} \\
G/\equiv &= (V/\equiv, E') .
\end{aligned}
$$

It is not hard to show that $G/\equiv$ is acyclic. Moreover,

Theorem 4.10 *The partial orders $(V/\approx, E^*)$ and $(V/\equiv, (E')^*)$ are isomorphic.*

In other words, the partial order represented by the collapsed graph is the same as the collapse of the preorder represented by the original graph.

Lecture 5 Shortest Paths and Transitive Closure

5.1 Single-Source Shortest Paths

Let $G = (V, E)$ be an undirected graph and let ℓ be a function assigning a nonnegative length to each edge. Extend ℓ to domain $V \times V$ by defining $\ell(v, v) = 0$ and $\ell(u, v) = \infty$ if $(u, v) \notin E$. Define the *length*[2] of a path $p = e_1 e_2 \ldots e_n$ to be $\ell(p) = \sum_{i=1}^{n} \ell(e_i)$. For $u, v \in V$, define the *distance* $d(u, v)$ from u to v to be the length of a shortest path from u to v, or ∞ if no such path exists. The *single-source shortest path problem* is to find, given $s \in V$, the value of $d(s, u)$ for every other vertex u in the graph.

If the graph is unweighted (*i.e.*, all edge lengths are 1), we can solve the problem in linear time using BFS. For the more general case, here is an algorithm due to Dijkstra [28]. Later on we will give an $O(m + n \log n)$ implementation using Fibonacci heaps. The algorithm is a type of greedy algorithm: it builds a set X vertex by vertex, always taking vertices closest to X.

---

[2]In this context, the terms "length" and "shortest" applied to a path refer to ℓ, not the number of edges in the path.

Algorithm 5.1 (Dijkstra's Algorithm)

$X := \{s\}$;
$D(s) := 0$;
for each $u \in V - \{s\}$ do
        $D(u) := \ell(s, u)$;
while $X \neq V$ do
        let $u \in V - X$ such that $D(u)$ is minimum;
        $X := X \cup \{u\}$;
        for each edge (u, v) with $v \in V - X$ do
                $D(v) := \min(D(v), D(u) + \ell(u, v))$
end while

The final value of $D(u)$ is $d(s, u)$. This algorithm can be proved correct by showing that the following two invariants are maintained by the while loop:

- for any u, $D(u)$ is the distance from s to u along a shortest path through only vertices in X;

- for any $u \in X$, $v \notin X$, $D(u) \leq D(v)$.

5.2   Reflexive Transitive Closure

Let E denote the adjacency matrix of the directed graph $G = (V, E)$. Using Boolean matrix multiplication, the matrix E^2 has a 1 in position uv iff there is a path of length exactly 2 from vertex u to vertex v; *i.e.*, iff there exists a vertex w such that $(u, w), (w, v) \in E$. Similarly, one can prove by induction on k that $(E^k)_{uv} = 1$ iff there is a path of length exactly k from u to v.

The reflexive transitive closure of G is

$$
\begin{aligned}
E^* &= I \vee E \vee E^2 \vee \cdots \\
&= I \vee E \vee E^2 \vee \cdots \vee E^{n-1} \\
&= (I \vee E)^{n-1} .
\end{aligned}
$$

The infinite join is equal to the finite one because if there is a path connecting u and v, then there is one of length at most $n - 1$.

Suppose that two $n \times n$ Boolean matrices can be multiplied in time $M(n)$. Then $E^* = (I \vee E)^{n-1}$ can be calculated in time $O(M(n) \log n)$ by squaring $E \log n$ times. We will show below how to calculate E^* in time $O(M(n))$. Conversely, if there is an algorithm to compute E^* in time $T(n)$, then $M(n)$ is $O(T(n))$ (under the reasonable assumption that $M(3n)$ is $O(M(n))$): to multiply A and B, place them strategically into a $3n \times 3n$ matrix, then take its reflexive transitive closure:

$$
\begin{bmatrix} 0 & A & 0 \\ 0 & 0 & B \\ 0 & 0 & 0 \end{bmatrix}^* = \begin{bmatrix} I & A & AB \\ 0 & I & B \\ 0 & 0 & I \end{bmatrix} .
$$

The product AB can be read off from the upper right-hand block.

Here is a divide and conquer algorithm to find E^* in time $M(n)$.

Algorithm 5.2 (Reflexive Transitive Closure)

1. Divide E into 4 submatrices A, B, C, D of size roughly $\frac{n}{2} \times \frac{n}{2}$ such that A and D are square.

$$E = \left[\begin{array}{c|c} A & B \\ \hline C & D \end{array} \right]$$

2. Recursively compute D^*. Compute

$$F = A + BD^*C .$$

Recursively compute F^*.

3. Set

$$E^* = \left[\begin{array}{c|c} F^* & F^*BD^* \\ \hline D^*CF^* & D^* + D^*CF^*BD^* \end{array} \right] .$$

Essentially, we are partitioning the set of vertices into two disjoint sets U and V, where A describes the edges from U to U, B describes edges from U to V, C describes edges from V to U, and D describes edges from V to V. We compute reflexive transitive closures on these sets recursively and use this information to describe the reflexive transitive closure of E. Note that we compute two reflexive transitive closures, a few matrix multiplications (whose complexity is given by M) and a few matrix additions (whose complexity is assumed to be quadratic) of matrices of roughly half the size of E. This gives the recurrence

$$T(n) = 2T(\frac{n}{2}) + cM(\frac{n}{2}) + d(\frac{n}{2})^2$$

where c and d are constants. Under the quite reasonable assumption that $M(2n) \geq 4M(n)$, the solution to this recurrence is $O(M(n))$.

5.3   All-Pairs Shortest Paths

Let E denote the adjacency matrix of a directed graph with edge weights. Replace the 1's in E by the edge weights and the 0's by ∞. Apply Algorithm 5.2 to calculate E^*, except use $+$ instead of $\wedge$ and min instead of $\vee$. We will show next time that this solves the all-pairs shortest path problem.

Lecture 6   Kleene Algebra

Consider a binary relation on an n element set represented by an $n \times n$ Boolean matrix E. Recall from the last lecture that we can compute the reflexive transitive closure of E by divide-and-conquer as follows: partition E into four submatrices A, B, C, D of size roughly $\frac{n}{2} \times \frac{n}{2}$ such that A and D are square:

$$E \;=\; \left[\begin{array}{c|c} A & B \\ \hline C & D \end{array}\right].$$

By induction, construct the matrices D^*, $F = A + BD^*C$, and F^*, then take

$$E^* \;=\; \left[\begin{array}{c|c} F^* & F^*BD^* \\ \hline D^*CF^* & D^* + D^*CF^*BD^* \end{array}\right]. \tag{1}$$

We will prove that the matrix E^* as defined in (1) is indeed the reflexive transitive closure of E, but the proof will be carried out in a more abstract setting which will allow us to use the same construction in other applications. For example, we will be able to compute the lengths of the shortest paths between all pairs of points in a weighted directed graph using the same general algorithm, but with a different interpretation of the basic operations.

How did we come up with the expressions in (1)? This is best motivated by considering a simple finite-state automaton over the alphabet $\Sigma = \{a, b, c, d\}$ with states s, t and transitions $s \xrightarrow{a} s$, $s \xrightarrow{b} t$, $t \xrightarrow{c} s$, $t \xrightarrow{d} t$:

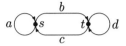

For each pair of states u, v, consider the set of input strings in Σ^* taking state u to state v in this automaton. Each such set is a regular subset of Σ^* and is represented by a regular expression corresponding to the expressions appearing in (1):

$$
\begin{aligned}
s \rightarrow s &: f^* \\
s \rightarrow t &: f^* b d^* \\
t \rightarrow s &: d^* c f^* \\
t \rightarrow t &: d^* + d^* c f^* b d^* \ ,
\end{aligned}
$$

where $f = a + b d^* c$. (See [3, §9.1, pp. 318-319] for more information on finite automata and regular expressions.)

6.1 Definition of Kleene Algebras

The appropriate level of abstraction we are seeking is *Kleene algebra*. This concept goes back to Kleene [61], but received significant impetus from the work of Conway [21]. The definition here is from [63].

Definition 6.1 A *(*-continuous) Kleene algebra* is any structure of the form

$$
\mathcal{K} = (S, +, \cdot, {}^*, 0, 1)
$$

where S is a set of elements, $+$ and $\cdot$ are binary operations $S \times S \rightarrow S$, * is a unary operation $S \rightarrow S$, and 0 and 1 are distinguished elements of S, satisfying the axioms

$$
\begin{aligned}
a + (b + c) &= (a + b) + c & \text{(+ is associative)} && (2) \\
a + b &= b + a & \text{(+ is commutative)} && (3) \\
a + a &= a & \text{(+ is idempotent)} && (4) \\
a + 0 &= 0 + a = a & \text{(0 is an a identity for +)} && (5) \\
a \cdot (b \cdot c) &= (a \cdot b) \cdot c & \text{($\cdot$ is associative)} && (6) \\
a \cdot 1 &= 1 \cdot a = a & \text{(1 is an a identity for $\cdot$)} && (7) \\
0 \cdot a &= a \cdot 0 = 0 & \text{(0 is an annihilator for $\cdot$)} && (8) \\
a \cdot (b + c) &= a \cdot b + a \cdot c & \text{($\cdot$ distributes over +)} && (9) \\
(b + c) \cdot a &= b \cdot a + c \cdot a & && (10)
\end{aligned}
$$

plus the following axiom to deal with the * operator, which will require further explanation:

$$
a b^* c = \sup_{n \geq 0} a b^n c \tag{11}
$$

where

$$b^0 = 1$$
$$b^{n+1} = b \cdot b^n .$$

$\square$

Axioms (2–5) say that the structure $(S, +, 0)$ is an *idempotent commutative monoid*. Axioms (6–7) say that $(S, \cdot, 1)$ is a *monoid*. Axioms (8–10) describe how these two monoid structures interact. Altogether, Axioms (2–10) say that $\mathcal{K}$ is an *idempotent semiring*.

The axiom (11) asserts the existence of the *supremum* or *least upper bound* of a certain set with respect to a certain partial order. In any idempotent semiring, there is a natural partial order defined by

$$a \leq b \quad \leftrightarrow \quad a + b = b . \tag{12}$$

It follows easily from the axioms (2–5) that $\leq$ is indeed a partial order; *i.e.*, it is

- reflexive: $a \leq a$

- antisymmetric: if $a \leq b$ and $b \leq a$ then $a = b$; and

- transitive: if $a \leq b$ and $b \leq c$ then $a \leq c$.

If A is a set of elements of a partially ordered set, the element y is said to be the *supremum* or *least upper bound* of the set A (notation: $y = \sup A$) if

- y is an upper bound for A; *i.e.*, $x \leq y$ for all $x \in A$;

- y is the least such upper bound; *i.e.*, for any other upper bound z for A, $y \leq z$.

The supremum of any pair of elements x, y exists and is equal to $x + y$. It follows that the supremum of any finite set $\{a_1, \ldots, a_n\}$ exists and is equal to $a_1 + \cdots + a_n$ (parentheses are not necessary because $+$ is associative). In general, the supremum of an infinite set need not exist, but if it exists then it is unique. The axiom (11) asserts that the supremum of the set $\{ab^n c \mid n \geq 0\}$ exists and is equal to $ab^* c$.

The postulate (11) captures axiomatically the behavior of reflexive transitive closure of a binary relation. It also captures the behavior of the Kleene * operator of formal language theory. In addition, there are many nonstandard examples of Kleene algebras that are useful in various contexts. We will give several examples below.

Instead of Kleene algebras, many authors (such as [3, 78]) use so-called *closed semirings*. These structures are strongly related to Kleene algebras, but are defined in terms of a countable summation operator $\sum$ instead of a supremum. In closed semirings, the * operator is not a primitive operator but is defined in terms of $\sum$ by

$$b^* = \sum_{n \geq 0} b^n .$$

The countable summation operator $\sum$, which sums a countably infinite sequence of elements, is postulated not to depend on the order of the elements in the sequence or their multiplicity, and thus is essentially a supremum. The operator $\sum$ is also postulated to satisfy an infinite distributivity property that we get for free for all suprema of interest by stating the axiom as we did in (11).

The main drawback with closed semirings is that the suprema of all countable sets are required to exist, which is too many. Although every closed semiring is a Kleene algebra, there are definitely Kleene algebras that are not closed semirings. The most important example of such a Kleene algebra is the family $\mathbf{Reg}_\Sigma$ of regular subsets of Σ^*, where Σ is a finite alphabet (Example 6.2 below). This example is important because it is the free Kleene algebra freely generated by Σ, which essentially says that an equation between regular expressions over Σ holds in all Kleene algebras if and only if it holds in $\mathbf{Reg}_\Sigma$. We will find this fact very useful in reducing arguments about Kleene algebras in general to arguments about regular subsets of Σ^*.

Kleene algebras were studied extensively in the monograph of Conway [21]. It is possible to axiomatize the equational theory of Kleene algebras in a purely finitary way [65]. The precise relationship between Kleene algebras and closed semirings is drawn in [64].

6.2 Examples of Kleene Algebras

Kleene algebras abound in computer science. Here are some examples.

Example 6.2 Let Σ be a finite alphabet and let $\mathbf{Reg}_\Sigma$ denote the family of regular sets over Σ with the following operations:

$$
\begin{aligned}
A + B &= A \cup B \\
A \cdot B &= \{xy \mid x \in A,\ y \in B\} \\
A^* &= \{x_1 x_2 \cdots x_n \mid n \geq 0 \text{ and } x_i \in A,\ 1 \leq i \leq n\} \\
&= \bigcup_{n \geq 0} A^n \\
0 &= \emptyset \\
1 &= \{\epsilon\}
\end{aligned}
$$

where A^n is defined inductively by

$$
\begin{aligned}
A^0 &= \{\epsilon\} \\
A^{n+1} &= A \cdot A^n
\end{aligned}
$$

and ϵ is the empty string. Under these operations, $\mathbf{Reg_\Sigma}$ is a Kleene algebra, and a very important one indeed: it is the *free Kleene algebra on free generators* Σ, which essentially means that any equation $\alpha = \beta$ between regular expressions holds in all Kleene algebras iff it holds in $\mathbf{Reg_\Sigma}$.   □

Example 6.3 Let X be a set and let $\mathcal{R}$ be any family of binary relations on X closed under the following operations:

$$
\begin{aligned}
R + S &= R \cup S \\
R \cdot S &= \{(x, z) \mid \exists y \in X \ (x, y) \in R \text{ and } (y, z) \in S\} \\
R^* &= \bigcup_{n \geq 0} R^n \\
&= \text{ the reflexive transitive closure of } R \\
0 &= \emptyset \\
1 &= \{(x, x) \mid x \in X\} \ .
\end{aligned}
$$

where R^n is defined inductively by

$$
\begin{aligned}
R^0 &= \{(x, x) \mid x \in X\} \\
R^{n+1} &= R \cdot R^n \ .
\end{aligned}
$$

Under these operations, $\mathcal{R}$ forms a Kleene algebra. Kleene algebras of binary relations are used to model programs in Dynamic Logic and other logics of programs.   □

Example 6.4 The set $\{0, 1\}$ of Boolean truth values forms a Kleene algebra under the operations

$$
\begin{aligned}
a + b &= a \vee b \\
a \cdot b &= a \wedge b \\
a^* &= 1
\end{aligned}
$$

and 0 and 1 as named. This is the smallest nontrivial Kleene algebra.   □

Example 6.5 The family of $n \times n$ Boolean matrices forms a Kleene algebra under the operations

$$
\begin{aligned}
A + B &= A \vee B \\
A \cdot B &= \text{ Boolean matrix product} \\
A^* &= \text{ reflexive transitive closure} \\
0 &= \text{ the zero matrix} \\
1 &= \text{ the identity matrix.}
\end{aligned}
$$

This is essentially the same as Example 6.3 above for an n-element set X.   □

Example 6.6 The following rather bizarre example will be useful in computing all-pairs shortest paths in a weighted graph. We will have to be a little
more explicit with notation than usual to avoid confusion.

Let $\mathcal{R}_+$ denote the family of nonnegative real numbers, and let ∞ be a
new element. Let $+_\mathcal{R}$ denote ordinary addition in $\mathcal{R}_+ \cup \{\infty\}$, where we define

$$a +_\mathcal{R} \infty \;=\; \infty +_\mathcal{R} a \;=\; \infty$$

for all $a \in \mathcal{R}_+ \cup \{\infty\}$. Let $\leq_\mathcal{R}$ denote the natural order in $\mathcal{R}_+ \cup \{\infty\}$, with
$a \leq_\mathcal{R} \infty$ for all $a \in \mathcal{R}_+$. Let $\min_\mathcal{R}\{a, b\}$ denote the minimum of a and b with
respect to this order. Let $0_\mathcal{R}$ denote the real number 0.

Define the Kleene algebra operations $+_\mathcal{K}$, $\cdot_\mathcal{K}$, $^{*\mathcal{K}}$, $0_\mathcal{K}$, and $1_\mathcal{K}$ on $\mathcal{R}_+ \cup \{\infty\}$
as follows:

$$
\begin{aligned}
a +_\mathcal{K} b \;&=\; \min_\mathcal{R}\{a, b\} \\
&=\; \begin{cases} a, & \text{if } a \leq_\mathcal{R} b \\ b, & \text{otherwise} \end{cases} \\
a \cdot_\mathcal{K} b \;&=\; a +_\mathcal{R} b \\
a^{*\mathcal{K}} \;&=\; 0_\mathcal{R} \\
0_\mathcal{K} \;&=\; \infty \\
1_\mathcal{K} \;&=\; 0_\mathcal{R} .
\end{aligned}
$$

If this appears confusing, don't worry, it really is. To make sense of it, just
keep in mind that the symbols on the left hand side of these equations refer to
the Kleene algebra operations being defined, whereas those on the right hand
side refer to the natural operations of $\mathcal{R}_+ \cup \{\infty\}$. Note that the zero element
of the Kleene algebra is ∞, the identity for $\min_\mathcal{R}$, and the multiplicative
identity 1 of the Kleene algebra is the real number 0, the identity for addition
in $\mathcal{R}_+ \cup \{\infty\}$ (which is multiplication in the Kleene algebra). The worst part
is that the natural partial order $\leq_\mathcal{K}$ in the Kleene algebra as defined by (12)
is the reverse of $\leq_\mathcal{R}$; that is, $a \leq_\mathcal{K} b$ iff $b \leq_\mathcal{R} a$.

This algebra is often called the min,+ Kleene algebra.   □

Lecture 7   More on Kleene Algebra

In this lecture we will see how Kleene algebra can be used in a variety of situations involving *-like operations. The key result that allows these applications is that the $n \times n$ matrices over a Kleene algebra again form a Kleene algebra. Along the way we will establish a central lemma that establishes the importance of the regular sets $\mathbf{Reg_\Sigma}$ over the finite alphabet Σ in reasoning about Kleene algebras in general.

Let

$$\mathcal{K} = (K, +_{\mathcal{K}}, \cdot_{\mathcal{K}}, *_{\mathcal{K}}, 0_{\mathcal{K}}, 1_{\mathcal{K}})$$

be a Kleene algebra. Let Σ a set and let $\mathbf{RExp_\Sigma}$ denote the family of regular expressions over Σ (see [3, §9.1, pp. 318-319]). An *interpretation* over $\mathcal{K}$ is a map

$$I : \Sigma \ \rightarrow \ \mathcal{K}$$

assigning an element of $\mathcal{K}$ to each element of Σ. An interpretation can be extended to domain $\mathbf{RExp_\Sigma}$ inductively as follows:

$$
\begin{aligned}
I(0) &= 0_{\mathcal{K}} \\
I(1) &= 1_{\mathcal{K}} \\
I(\alpha + \beta) &= I(\alpha) +_{\mathcal{K}} I(\beta) \\
I(\alpha \cdot \beta) &= I(\alpha) \cdot_{\mathcal{K}} I(\beta) \\
I(\alpha^*) &= I(\alpha)^{*_{\mathcal{K}}} \ .
\end{aligned}
$$

At the risk of confusing the operator symbols in regular expressions and the corresponding operations in $\mathcal{K}$, we henceforth drop the subscripts $\mathcal{K}$.

For example, the interpretation

$$R : \Sigma \;\to\; \mathbf{Reg}_\Sigma$$
$$a \;\mapsto\; \{a\}$$

over $\mathbf{Reg}_\Sigma$ extends to the map

$$R : \mathbf{RExp}_\Sigma \;\to\; \mathbf{Reg}_\Sigma$$

in which $R(\alpha)$ is the regular set denoted by the regular expression α in the usual sense. The interpretation R is called the *standard interpretation* over $\mathbf{Reg}_\Sigma$.

The following lemma generalizes (11).

Lemma 7.1 *Let $R : \Sigma \to \mathbf{Reg}_\Sigma$ be the standard interpretation over $\mathbf{Reg}_\Sigma$ and let $I : \Sigma \to \mathcal{K}$ be any interpretation over any Kleene algebra $\mathcal{K}$. For any regular expression α over Σ,*

$$I(\alpha) \;=\; \sup_{x \in R(\alpha)} I(x) \,. \tag{13}$$

Note that since $R(\alpha)$ is a regular set of strings over the alphabet Σ, the x in (13) denotes a string. Strings over Σ are themselves regular expressions over Σ, so the expression $I(x)$ makes sense. The equation (13) states that the supremum of the possibly infinite set

$$\{I(x) \mid x \in R(\alpha)\} \;\subseteq\; \mathcal{K}$$

exists and is equal to $I(\alpha)$. We leave the proof of Lemma 7.1 as an exercise (Homework 3, Exercise 2).

It follows that for any pair α, β of regular expressions over Σ, the equation $\alpha = \beta$ is a logical consequence of the axioms of Kleene algebra, *i.e.* it holds under all interpretations over all Kleene algebras, if and only if it holds under the standard interpretation R over $\mathbf{Reg}_\Sigma$. A fancy way of saying this is that $\mathbf{Reg}_\Sigma$ is the *free Kleene algebra on free generators* Σ.

Theorem 7.2 *Let α and β be regular expressions over Σ and let R be the standard interpretation over $\mathbf{Reg}_\Sigma$. Then*

$$I(\alpha) \;=\; I(\beta)$$

for all interpretations I over Kleene algebras if and only if

$$R(\alpha) \;=\; R(\beta) \,.$$

Proof. (→) This follows immediately from the fact that **Reg**$_\Sigma$ is a Kleene algebra and R is an interpretation over **Reg**$_\Sigma$.

(←) Suppose $R(\alpha) = R(\beta)$. Then

$$
\begin{aligned}
I(\alpha) &= \sup_{x \in R(\alpha)} I(x) \quad \text{by Lemma 7.1} \\
&= \sup_{x \in R(\beta)} I(x) \quad \text{by the assumption } R(\alpha) = R(\beta) \\
&= I(\beta) , \quad \text{again by Lemma 7.1.}
\end{aligned}
$$

□

7.1 Matrix Kleene Algebras

The collection $M(n, \mathcal{K})$ of $n \times n$ matrices with elements in a Kleene algebra $\mathcal{K}$ again forms a Kleene algebra, provided the Kleene algebra operators on $M(n, \mathcal{K})$ are defined appropriately. We always define $+$ as ordinary matrix addition, $\cdot$ as ordinary matrix multiplication, 0 as the zero matrix, 1 as the identity matrix, and * recursively by equation (1) of the previous lecture. We must show that all the axioms of Kleene algebra are satisfied by $M(n, \mathcal{K})$ under these definitions. For example, in $M(2, \mathcal{K})$ the identity elements for $+$ and $\cdot$ are

$$
\begin{bmatrix} 0 & 0 \\ 0 & 0 \end{bmatrix} \qquad \begin{bmatrix} 1 & 0 \\ 0 & 1 \end{bmatrix}
$$

respectively, and the operations $+$, $\cdot$, and * are given by

$$
\begin{bmatrix} a & b \\ c & d \end{bmatrix} + \begin{bmatrix} e & f \\ g & h \end{bmatrix} = \begin{bmatrix} a+e & b+f \\ c+g & d+h \end{bmatrix}
$$

$$
\begin{bmatrix} a & b \\ c & d \end{bmatrix} \cdot \begin{bmatrix} e & f \\ g & h \end{bmatrix} = \begin{bmatrix} ae+bg & af+bh \\ ce+dg & cf+dh \end{bmatrix}
$$

$$
\begin{bmatrix} a & b \\ c & d \end{bmatrix}^* = \begin{bmatrix} f^* & f^*bd^* \\ d^*cf^* & d^* + d^*cf^*bd^* \end{bmatrix}
$$

where $f = a + bd^*c$. Note that $A \leq B$ in the natural order on $M(n, \mathcal{K})$ defined by (12) if and only if $A_{ij} \leq B_{ij}$ for all $1 \leq i, j \leq n$.

Most of the Kleene algebra axioms are routine to verify for the structure $M(n, \mathcal{K})$. Let us verify (11) explicitly, assuming all the other axioms have been verified. First we will show that it is true for a particular choice of matrices over a particular Kleene algebra of regular sets, using a combinatorial argument; next we will use Theorem 7.2 to extend the result to all Kleene algebras.

Let $\mathbf{A}$, $\mathbf{B}$, and $\mathbf{C}$ be $n \times n$ symbolic matrices with ij^{th} elements $\mathbf{a}_{ij}$, $\mathbf{b}_{ij}$, and $\mathbf{c}_{ij}$, respectively, where the $\mathbf{a}_{ij}$, $\mathbf{b}_{ij}$, $\mathbf{c}_{ij}$ are distinct letters. Let

$$\Sigma = \{\mathbf{a}_{ij}, \mathbf{b}_{ij}, \mathbf{c}_{ij} \mid 1 \le i, j \le n\} .$$

Build an automaton $M_{\mathbf{B}}$ with n states and transition from state i to state j labeled with the letter $\mathbf{b}_{ij}$. The ij^{th} element of $\mathbf{B}^k$, the symbolic k^{th} power of $\mathbf{B}$, is a regular expression representing the set of strings of length k over Σ taking state i to state j in $M_{\mathbf{B}}$. Moreover, the ij^{th} element of $\mathbf{B}^*$ represents the set of all strings (of any length) taking state i to state j in $M_{\mathbf{B}}$. This follows from a purely combinatorial inductive argument, using the definition of $\mathbf{B}^*$ as given in (1); the partition in (1) corresponds to a partition of the states of $M_{\mathbf{B}}$ into two disjoint sets. We thus have

$$R((\mathbf{B}^*)_{ij}) = \bigcup_{k \ge 0} R((\mathbf{B}^k)_{ij})$$

where R is the standard interpretation.

Let $M_{\mathbf{A}}$ and $M_{\mathbf{C}}$ consist of n states each. Connect state i of $M_{\mathbf{A}}$ with state j of $M_{\mathbf{B}}$ and label the transition $\mathbf{a}_{ij}$. Similarly, connect state i of $M_{\mathbf{B}}$ with state j of $M_{\mathbf{C}}$ and label the transition $\mathbf{c}_{ij}$. Call this new automaton M. Then the regular set over Σ denoted by the ij^{th} element of $\mathbf{AB}^k\mathbf{C}$ is the set of strings of length $k + 2$ taking state i of $M_{\mathbf{A}}$ to state j of $M_{\mathbf{C}}$ in M, and the regular set denoted by the ij^{th} element of $\mathbf{AB}^*\mathbf{C}$ is the set of all strings (of any length) taking state i of $M_{\mathbf{A}}$ to state j of $M_{\mathbf{C}}$ in M. Therefore

$$R((\mathbf{AB}^*\mathbf{C})_{ij}) = \bigcup_{k \ge 0} R((\mathbf{AB}^k\mathbf{C})_{ij}) .$$

Now let A, B, C be arbitrary matrices over an arbitrary Kleene algebra $\mathcal{K}$. Let a_{ij}, b_{ij}, c_{ij} denote the ij^{th} elements of A, B, and C, respectively. Let I be the interpretation

$$I(\mathbf{a}_{ij}) = a_{ij}$$
$$I(\mathbf{b}_{ij}) = b_{ij}$$
$$I(\mathbf{c}_{ij}) = c_{ij} .$$

Then

$$
\begin{aligned}
(AB^*C)_{ij} &= I((\mathbf{AB}^*\mathbf{C})_{ij}) \\
&= \sup\{I(x) \mid x \in R((\mathbf{AB}^*\mathbf{C})_{ij})\} \quad \text{by Lemma 7.1} \\
&= \sup\{I(x) \mid x \in \bigcup_{k \ge 0} R((\mathbf{AB}^k\mathbf{C})_{ij})\} \\
&= \sup_{k \ge 0} \sup\{I(x) \mid x \in R((\mathbf{AB}^k\mathbf{C})_{ij})\} \\
&= \sup_{k \ge 0} I((\mathbf{AB}^k\mathbf{C})_{ij}) \\
&= \sup_{k \ge 0} (AB^kC)_{ij} ,
\end{aligned}
$$

therefore

$$AB^*C = \sup_{k \geq 0} AB^k C .$$

This establishes (11) for $M(n, \mathcal{K})$.

7.2 Applications

The obvious divide-and-conquer algorithm for computing E^* given by (1) yields the recurrence

$$T(n) = T(\frac{n}{2}) + O(M(n)) ,$$

where $M(n)$ is the number of basic operations needed to add or multiply two $n \times n$ matrices over $\mathcal{K}$. Under the quite reasonable assumption that $M(2n) \geq 4M(n)$, this recurrence has solution

$$T(n) = O(M(n)) .$$

For most applications, $M(n) = O(n^3)$. Better bounds can be obtained using Strassen's algorithm or other fast matrix multiplication algorithms when $\mathcal{K}$ is a ring.

Reflexive Transitive Closure

Using matrix Kleene algebras, we can prove the correctness of the algorithm for reflexive transitive closure presented in the last lecture. Let $\mathcal{B}$ denote the two-element Kleene algebra described in Example 6.4 above. Let E denote the adjacency matrix of a directed graph G with n vertices. Then $E \in M(n, \mathcal{B})$, and the ij^{th} element of E^k is 1 if and only if there exists a directed path in G from vertex i to vertex j of length exactly k. By the result of the last section, we know that

$$E^* = \sup_{k \geq 0} E^k ,$$

so the ij^{th} element of E^* is 1 iff there exists a path of *some* length from i to j. This is the reflexive transitive closure.

All-Pairs Shortest Paths

Here we use the same algorithm, but a different underlying Kleene algebra, namely the min,+ algebra of Example 6.6 above. Supremum in this order is infimum in the usual order on $\mathcal{R}_+ \cup \{\infty\}$. Thus a^* is the real number 0 for all a.

We apply this to the all-pairs shortest path problem. Let E be a matrix over the min,+ algebra containing the edge lengths of a weighted directed graph G. If (i, j) is not an edge in G, set $E_{ij} = \infty$. In E^2, the ij^{th} element will be the minimum over all vertices k of the sum of the lengths of (i, k) and (k, j). That is, it will contain the length of a shortest path of two edges from i to j. It follows by induction that the ij^{th} element of E^k is the length of a shortest path of k edges from i to j. Since

$$E^* \;=\; \sup_{k \geq 0} E^k$$

and supremum in the Kleene algebra is infimum in the natural order, E^* gives the length of a shortest path of any number of edges.

Lecture 8   Binomial Heaps

Binomial heaps were invented in 1978 by J. Vuillemin [106]. They give a data structure for maintaining a collection of elements, each of which has a *value* drawn from an ordered set, such that new elements can be added and the element of minimum value extracted efficiently. They admit the following operations:

makeheap(i)	return a new heap containing only element i
findmin(h)	return a pointer to the element of h of minimum value
insert(h, i)	add element i to heap h
deletemin(h)	delete the element of minimum value from h
meld(h, h')	combine heaps h and h' into one heap

Efficient searching for objects is not supported.

In the next lecture we will extend binomial heaps to *Fibonacci heaps* [35], which allow two additional operations:

decrement(h, i, Δ)	decrease the value of i by Δ
delete(h, i)	remove i from heap h

We will see that these operations have low *amortized* costs. This means that any particular operation may be expensive, but the costs average out so that over a sequence of operations, the number of steps per operation of each type is small. The amortized cost per operation of each type is given in the following table:

makeheap	$O(1)$
findmin	$O(1)$
insert	$O(1)$
deletemin	$O(\log n)$
meld	$O(1)$ for the lazy version
	$O(\log n)$ for the eager version
decrement	$O(1)$
delete	$O(\log n)$

where n is the number of elements in the heap.

Binomial heaps are collections of *binomial trees*, which are defined inductively: the ith binomial tree B_i consists of a root with i children $B_0, \ldots, B_{i-1}$.

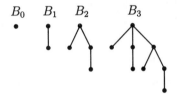

$B_0 \quad B_1 \quad B_2 \qquad B_3$

It is easy to prove by induction that $|B_i| = 2^i$.

If data elements are arranged as vertices in a tree, that tree is said to be *heap-ordered* if the minimum value among all vertices of any subtree is found at the root of that subtree. A *binomial heap* is a collection of heap-ordered binomial trees with a pointer **min** to the tree whose root has minimum value. We will assume that all children of any vertex are arranged in a circular doubly-linked list, so that we can link and unlink subtrees in constant time.

Definition 8.1 The *rank* of an element x, denoted rank (x), is the number of children of x. For instance, rank (root of B_i) $= i$. The *rank* of a tree is the rank of its root.   □

A basic operation on binomial trees is *linking*. Given two B_i's, we can combine them into a B_{i+1} by making the root of one B_i a child of the root of the other. We always make the B_i with the larger root value the child so as to preserve heap order. We never link two trees of different rank.

8.1 Operations on Binomial Heaps

In the "eager meld" version, the trees of the binomial heap are accessed through an array of pointers, where the ith pointer either points to a B_i or is **nil**. The operation **meld**(h, h'), which creates a new heap by combining h and h', is reminiscent of binary addition. We start with $i = 0$. If either h or h' has a B_0 and the other does not, we let this B_0 be the B_0 of **meld**(h, h'). If neither h nor h' have a B_0, then neither will **meld**(h, h'). If both h and h' have a B_0, then **meld**(h, h') will not; but the two B_0's are linked to form a

B_1, which is treated like a carry. We then move on to the B_1's. At stage i, we may have 0, 1, or 2 B_i's from h and h', plus a possible B_i carried from the previous stage. If there are at least two B_i's, then two of them are linked to give a B_{i+1} which is carried to the next stage; the remaining B_i, if it exists, becomes the B_i of **meld**(h, h'). The entire operation takes $O(\log n)$ time, because the size of the largest tree is exponential in the largest rank. We will modify the algorithm below to obtain a "lazy meld" version, which will take constant amortized time.

The operation **insert**(i, h) is just **meld**$(h, \mathbf{makeheap}(i))$.

For the operation **deletemin**(h), we examine the **min** pointer to x, the root of some B_k. Removing x creates new trees $B_0, \ldots, B_{k-1}$, the children of x, which are formed into a new heap h'. The tree B_k is removed from the old heap h. Now h and h' are melded to form a new heap. We also scan the new heap to determine the new **min** pointer. All this requires $O(\log n)$ time.

8.2   Amortization

The $O(\log n)$ bound on **meld** and **deletemin** is believable, but how on earth can we do **insert** operations in constant time? Any particular **insert** operation can take as much as $O(\log n)$ time because of the links and carries that must be done. However, intuition tells us that in order for a particular **insert** operation to take a long time, there must be a lot of trees already in the heap that are causing all these carries. We must have spent a lot of time in the past to create all these trees. *We will therefore charge the cost of performing these links and carries to the past operations that created these trees.* To the operations in the past that created the trees, this will appear as a constant extra overhead.

This type of analysis is known as *amortized analysis*, since the cost of a sequence of operations is spread over the entire sequence. Although the cost of any particular operation may be high, over the long run it averages out so that the cost per operation is low.

For our amortized analysis of binomial heaps, we will set up a savings account for each tree in the heap. When a tree is created, we will charge an extra credit to the instruction that created it and deposit that credit to the account of the tree for later use. (Another approach is to use a *potential function*; see [100].) We will maintain the following *credit invariant*:

> Each tree in the heap has one credit in its account.

Each **insert** instruction creates one new singleton tree, so it gets charged one extra credit, and that credit is deposited to the account of the tree that was created. The amount of extra time charged to the **insert** instruction is $O(1)$. The same goes for **makeheap**. The **deletemin** instruction exposes up to $\log n$ new trees (the subtrees of the deleted root), so we charge an extra

$\log n$ credits to this instruction and deposit them to the accounts of these newly exposed trees. The total time charged to the **deletemin** instruction is still $O(\log n)$.

We use these saved credits to pay for linking later on. When we link a tree into another tree, we pay for that operation with the credit associated with the root of the subordinate tree. The **insert** operation might cause a cascade of carries, but the time to perform all these carries is already paid for. We end up with a credit still on deposit for every exposed tree and only $O(1)$ time charged to the **insert** operation itself.

8.3 Lazy Melds

We can also perform **meld** operations in constant time with a slight modification of the data structure. Rather than using an array of pointers to trees, we use a doubly linked circular list. To **meld** two heaps, we just concatenate the two lists into one and update the **min** pointer, certainly an $O(1)$ operation. Then **insert**(h, i) is just **meld**$(h, \mathbf{makeheap}(i))$.

The problem now is that unlike before, we may have several trees of the same rank. This will not bother us until we need to do a **deletemin**. Since in a **deletemin** we will need $O(\log n)$ time anyway to find the minimum among the deleted vertex's children, we will take this opportunity to clean up the heap so that there will again be at most one tree of each rank. We create an array of empty pointers and go through the list of trees, inserting them one by one into the list, linking and carrying if necessary so as to have at most one tree of each rank. In the process, we search for the minimum.

We perform a constant amount of work for each tree in the list in addition to the linking. Thus if we start with m trees and do k links, then we spend $O(m + k)$ time in all. To pay for this, we have k saved credits from the links, plus an extra $\log n$ credits we can charge to the **deletemin** operation itself, so we will be in good shape provided $m + k$ is $O(k + \log n)$. But each link decreases the number of trees by one, so we end up with $m - k$ trees, and these trees all have distinct ranks, so there are at most $\log n$ of them; thus

$$
\begin{aligned}
m + k &= 2k + (m - k) \\
&\leq 2k + \log n \\
&= O(k + \log n) \ .
\end{aligned}
$$

Lecture 9   Fibonacci Heaps

Fibonacci heaps were developed by Fredman and Tarjan in 1984 [35] as a generalization of binomial heaps. The main intent was to improve Dijkstra's single-source shortest path algorithm to $O(m + n \log n)$, but they have many other applications as well. In addition to the binomial heap operations, Fibonacci heaps admit two additional operations:

$$\begin{aligned}
&\textbf{decrement}(h, i, \Delta) &&\text{decrease the value of } i \text{ by } \Delta \\
&\textbf{delete}(h, i) &&\text{remove } i \text{ from heap } h
\end{aligned}$$

These operations assume that a pointer to the element i in the heap h is given.

In this lecture we describe how to modify binomial heaps to admit **delete** and **decrement**. The resulting data structure is called a *Fibonacci heap*. The trees in Fibonacci heaps are no longer binomial trees, because we will be cutting subtrees out of them in a controlled way. We will still be doing links and melds as in binomial heaps. The *rank* of a tree is still defined in the same way, namely the number of children of the root, and as with binomial heaps we only link two trees if they have the same rank.

To perform a **delete**(i), we might cut out the subtree rooted at i, remove i, and **meld** in its newly freed subtrees. We must also search these newly freed subtrees for the minimum root value; this requires $O(\log n)$ time. In **decrement**(i, Δ), we decrement the value of i by Δ. The new value of i might violate the heap order, since it might now be less than the value of i's parent. If so, we might simply cut out the subtree rooted at i and **meld** it into the heap.

44

The problem here is that the $O(\log n)$ time bound on **deletemin** described in the last lecture was highly dependent on the fact that the size of B_k is exponential in k, *i.e.* the trees are bushy. With **delete** and **decrement** as described above, cutting out a lot of subtrees might make the tree scraggly, so that the analysis is no longer valid.

9.1   Cascading Cuts

The way around this problem is to limit the number of cuts among the children of any vertex to two. Although the trees will no longer be binomial trees, they will still be bushy in that their size will be exponential in their rank.

For this analysis, we will set up a savings account for every vertex. The first time a child is cut from vertex p, charge to the operation that caused the cut two extra credits and deposit them to the account of p. Not only does this give two extra credits to use later, it also marks p as having had one child cut already. When a second child is cut from p, cut p from its parent p' and **meld** p into the heap, paying for it with one of the extra credits that was deposited to the account of p when its first child was cut. The other credit is left in the account of p in order to maintain the invariant that each tree in the heap have a credit on deposit. If p was the second child cut from its parent p', then p' is cut from its parent; again, this is already paid for by the operation that cut the first child of p'. These cuts can continue arbitrarily far up the tree; this is called *cascading cuts*. However, all these cascading cuts are already paid for. Thus **decrement** is $O(1)$, and **delete** will still be $O(\log n)$ provided our precautions have guaranteed that the sizes of trees are still exponential in their rank.

Theorem 9.1 *The size of a tree with root r in a Fibonacci heap is exponential in* rank (r).

Proof. Fix a point in time. Let x be any vertex and let $y_1, \ldots, y_m$ be the children of x at that point, arranged in the order in which they were linked into x. We show that rank (y_i) is at least $i - 2$. At the time that y_i was linked into x, x had at least the $i - 1$ children $y_1, \ldots, y_{i-1}$ (it may have had more that have since been cut). Since only trees of equal rank are linked, y_i also had at least $i - 1$ children at that time. Since then, at most one child of y_i has been cut, or y_i itself would have been cut. Therefore the rank of y_i is at least $i - 2$.

We have shown that the ith child of any vertex has rank at least $i - 2$. Let F_n be the smallest possible tree of rank n satisfying this property. The first few F_n are illustrated below.

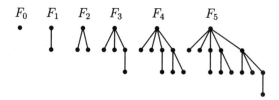

$$F_0 \quad F_1 \quad F_2 \quad F_3 \quad F_4 \quad\quad F_5$$

Observe that F_0, F_1, F_2, F_3, F_4, $F_5, \ldots$, are of size $1, 2, 3, 5, 8, 13 \ldots$, respectively. This sequence of numbers is called the *Fibonacci sequence*, in which each number is obtained by adding the previous two. It therefore suffices to show that the nth Fibonacci number $f_n = |F_n|$ is exponential in n.

Specifically, we show that $f_n \geq \varphi^n$, where $\varphi = \frac{1+\sqrt{5}}{2} \approx 1.618\ldots$, the positive root of the quadratic $x^2 - x - 1$. The proof proceeds by induction on n.

For the basis, $f_0 = 1 \geq \varphi^0$ and $f_1 = 2 \geq \varphi^1$. Now assume that $f_n \geq \varphi^n$ and $f_{n+1} \geq \varphi^{n+1}$. Then

$$
\begin{aligned}
f_{n+2} &= f_{n+1} + f_n \\
&\geq \varphi^{n+1} + \varphi^n \\
&= \varphi^n(\varphi + 1) \\
&= \varphi^n \cdot \varphi^2 \text{ since } \varphi^2 = \varphi + 1 \\
&= \varphi^{n+2} \,.
\end{aligned}
$$

$\square$

The real number φ is often called the *golden ratio*. It was considered the most perfect proportion for a rectangle by the ancient Greeks because it makes the ratio of the length of the longer side to the length of the shorter side equal to the ratio of the sum of the lengths to the length of the longer side.

$$\varphi = \frac{b}{a} = \frac{a+b}{b}$$

(with a labeling the shorter side and b the longer side of the rectangle)

(The picture is actually 81pt × 50pt, giving a ratio of 1.62. Apologies to the ancient Greeks.)

The golden ratio φ is more closely related to the Fibonacci sequence than is apparent from the proof of Theorem 9.1. Consider the linear system

$$
\begin{bmatrix} 0 & 1 \\ 1 & 1 \end{bmatrix}
\begin{bmatrix} f_n \\ f_{n+1} \end{bmatrix}
=
\begin{bmatrix} f_{n+1} \\ f_{n+2} \end{bmatrix}
\tag{14}
$$

which generates the Fibonacci sequence:

$$
\begin{bmatrix} 0 & 1 \\ 1 & 1 \end{bmatrix}^n
\begin{bmatrix} f_0 \\ f_1 \end{bmatrix}
=
\begin{bmatrix} f_n \\ f_{n+1} \end{bmatrix} .
$$

Let F denote the 2×2 matrix in (14). The eigenvalues of F are φ and $\varphi' = \frac{1-\sqrt{5}}{2}$, the two roots of its characteristic polynomial

$$\det (xI - F) \;=\; x^2 - x - 1 \;.$$

The eigenvectors associated with φ and φ' are

$$\begin{bmatrix} 1 \\ \varphi \end{bmatrix} \quad \text{and} \quad \begin{bmatrix} 1 \\ \varphi' \end{bmatrix} ,$$

respectively, of which the former is dominant. Successive applications of a matrix to a vector with a nonzero component in the direction of a dominant eigenvector, suitably scaled, will generate a sequence of vectors converging to that dominant eigenvector. Thus

$$\left(\varphi^{-1} \cdot \begin{bmatrix} 0 & 1 \\ 1 & 1 \end{bmatrix} \right)^n \begin{bmatrix} f_0 \\ f_1 \end{bmatrix} \;=\; \varphi^{-n} \cdot \begin{bmatrix} f_n \\ f_{n+1} \end{bmatrix} \;\rightarrow\; \begin{bmatrix} 1 \\ \varphi \end{bmatrix}$$

as $n \to \infty$; in other words, the ratio of successive Fibonacci numbers tends to φ.

9.2 Fibonacci Heaps and Dijkstra's Algorithm

We can use Fibonacci heaps to implement Dijkstra's single-source shortest-path algorithm (Algorithm 5.1) in $O(m + n \log n)$ time. We store the elements of $V - X$ in a Fibonacci heap. The value of the element v is $D(v)$. The initialization uses the **makeheap** operation and takes linear time. We use the **decrement** operation to implement the statement

$$D(v) := \min(D(v), D(u) + \ell(u, v)) \;.$$

This requires constant time for each edge, or $O(m)$ time in all. We use the **deletemin** operation to remove a vertex from the set of unreached vertices. This takes $O(\log n)$ time for each deletion, or $O(n \log n)$ time in all.

Another application of Fibonacci heaps is in Prim's algorithm for minimum spanning trees. We leave this application as an exercise (Homework 4, Exercise 1).

Lecture 10   Union-Find

The union-find data structure is motivated by Kruskal's minimum spanning tree algorithm (Algorithm 2.6), in which we needed two operations on disjoint sets of vertices:

- determine whether vertices u and v are in the same set;

- form the union of disjoint sets A and B.

The data structure provides two operations from which the above two operations can be implemented:

- **find**(v), which returns a canonical element of the set containing v. We ask if u and v are in the same set by asking if **find**$(u) =$ **find**(v).

- **union**(u, v), which merges the sets containing the canonical elements u and v.

To implement these operations efficiently, we represent each set as a tree with data elements at the vertices. Each element u has a pointer parent (u) to its parent in the tree. The root serves as the canonical element of the set.

To effect a **union**(u, v), we combine the two trees with roots u and v by making u a child of v or vice-versa. To do a **find**(u), we start at u and follow parent pointers, traversing the path up to the root of the tree containing u, which gives the canonical element.

To improve performance, we will use two heuristics:

- When merging two trees in a **union**, always make the root of the smaller tree a child of the root of the larger. We maintain with each vertex u the size of the subtree rooted at u, and update whenever we do a **union**.

- After finding the root v of the tree containing u in a **find**(u), we traverse the path from u to v one more time and change the parent pointers of all vertices along the path to point directly to v. This process is called *path compression*. It will pay off in subsequent **find** operations, since we will be traversing shorter paths.

Let us start with some basic observations about these heuristics. Let σ be a sequence of m **union** and **find** operations starting with n singleton sets. Consider the execution of σ both with and without path compression. In either case we combine two smaller sets to form a larger in each **union** operation. Observe that the collection of sets at time t is the same with or without path compression, and the trees have the same roots, although the trees will in general be shorter and bushier with path compression. Observe also that u becomes a descendant of v at time t with path compression if and only if u becomes a descendant of v at time t without path compression. However, without path compression, once u becomes a descendant of v, it remains a descendant of v forever, but with path compression, it might later become a non-descendant of v.

10.1 Ackermann's Function

The two heuristics will allow a sequence of **union** and **find** operations to be performed in $O((m+n)\alpha(n))$ time, where $\alpha(n)$ is the inverse of *Ackermann's function*. Ackermann's function is a famous function that is known for its extremely rapid growth. Its inverse $\alpha(n)$ grows extremely slowly. The texts [3, 100] give inequivalent definitions of Ackermann's function, and in fact there does not seem to be any general agreement on the definition of "the" Ackermann's function; but all these functions grow at roughly the same rate. Here is yet another definition that grows at roughly the same rate:

$$
\begin{aligned}
A_0(x) &= x + 1 \\
A_{k+1}(x) &= A_k^x(x)
\end{aligned}
$$

where A_k^i is the i-fold composition of A_k with itself:

$$
A_k^i = \underbrace{A_k \circ \cdots \circ A_k}_{i}
$$

or more accurately,

$$
A_k^0 = \text{the identity function}
$$

$$A_k^{i+1} = A_k \circ A_k^i .$$

In other words, to compute $A_{k+1}(x)$, start with x and apply A_k x times. It is not hard to show by induction that A_k is monotone in the sense that

$$x \le y \quad \rightarrow \quad A_k(x) \le A_k(y)$$

and that for all x, $x \le A_k(x)$.

As k grows, these functions get extremely huge extremely fast. For $x = 0$ or 1, the numbers $A_k(x)$ are small. For $x \ge 2$,

$$
\begin{aligned}
A_0(x) &= x + 1 \\
A_1(x) &= A_0^x(x) = 2x \\
A_2(x) &= A_1^x(x) = x2^x \ge 2^x \\
A_3(x) &= A_2^x(x) \ge \underbrace{2^{2^{2^{.^{.^{.^2}}}}}}_{x} = 2 \uparrow x \\
A_4(x) &= A_3^x(x) \ge \underbrace{2 \uparrow (2 \uparrow \cdots \uparrow (2 \uparrow 2) \cdots)}_{x} = 2 \uparrow\uparrow x
\end{aligned}
$$

$$\vdots$$

For $x = 2$, the growth of $A_k(2)$ as a function of k is beyond comprehension. Already for $k = 4$, the value of $A_4(2)$ is larger than the number of atomic particles in the known universe or the number of nanoseconds since the Big Bang.

$$
\begin{aligned}
A_0(2) &= 3 \\
A_1(2) &= 4 \\
A_2(2) &= 8 \\
A_3(2) &= 2^{11} = 2048 \\
A_4(2) &\ge 2 \uparrow 2048 = \underbrace{2^{2^{2^{.^{.^{.^2}}}}}}_{2048}
\end{aligned}
$$

We define a unary function that majorizes all the A_k (*i.e.*, grows asymptotically faster than all of them):

$$A(k) = A_k(2)$$

and call it Ackermann's function. This function grows asymptotically faster than any primitive recursive function, since it can be shown that all primitive recursive functions are bounded almost everywhere by one of the functions A_k. The primitive recursive functions are those computed by a simple PASCAL-like programming language over the natural numbers with **for** loops but no **while** loops. The level k corresponds roughly to the depth of nesting of the **for** loops [79].

The inverse of Ackermann's function is

$$\alpha(n) \;=\; \text{the least } k \text{ such that } A(k) \geq n$$

which for all practical purposes is 4. We will show next time that with our heuristics, any sequence of m **union** and **find** operations take at most $O((m+n)\alpha(n))$ time, which is not quite linear but might as well be for all practical purposes. This result is due to Tarjan (see [100]). A corresponding lower bound for pointer machines with no random access has also been established [99, 87].

Lecture 11   Analysis of Union-Find

Recall from last time the heuristics:

> - In a **union**, always merge the smaller tree into the larger.
> - In a **find**, use path compression.

We made several elementary observations about these heuristics:

- the contents of the trees are the same with or without path compression;

- the roots of the trees are the same with or without path compression;

- a vertex u becomes a descendant of v at time t with path compression if and only if it does so without path compression. With path compression, however, u may at some later point become a non-descendant of v.

Recall also the definitions of the functions A_k and α:

$$
\begin{aligned}
A_0(x) &= x + 1 \\
A_{k+1}(x) &= A_k^x(x) \\
\alpha(n) &= \text{least } k \text{ such that } A_k(2) \geq n
\end{aligned}
\tag{15}
$$

and that $\alpha(n) \leq 4$ for all practical values of n.

11.1   Rank of a Node

As in the last lecture, let σ be a sequence of m **union** and **find** instructions starting with n singleton sets. Let $T_t(u)$ denote the subtree rooted at u at time t in the execution of σ *without* path compression, and define the *rank* of u to be

$$\text{rank}\,(u) \;=\; 2 + \text{height}\,(T_m(u))\,, \tag{16}$$

where height (T) is the *height* of T or length of the longest path in T. In other words, we execute σ without path compression, then find the longest path in the resulting tree below u. The rank of u is defined to be two more than the length of this path. (Beware that our rank is two more than the rank as defined in [3, 100]. This is for technical reasons; the 2's in (15) and (16) are related.)

As long as u has no parent, the height of $T_t(u)$ can still increase, since other trees can be merged into it; but once u becomes a child of another vertex, then the tree rooted at u becomes fixed, since no trees will ever again be merged into it. Also, without path compression, the height of a tree can never decrease. It follows that if u ever becomes a descendant of v (with or without path compression), say at time t, then for all $s > t$ the height of $T_s(u)$ is less than the height of $T_s(v)$, therefore

$$\text{rank}\,(u) \;<\; \text{rank}\,(v)\,. \tag{17}$$

The following lemma captures the intuition that if we always merge smaller trees into larger, the trees will be relatively balanced.

Lemma 11.1

$$|T_t(u)| \;\geq\; 2^{\text{height}\,(T_t(u))}\,. \tag{18}$$

Proof. The proof is by induction on t, using the fact that we always merge smaller trees into larger. For the basis, we have $T_0(u) = \{u\}$, thus height $(T_0(u)) = 0$ and $|T_0(u)| = 1$, so (18) holds at time 0. If (18) holds at time t and the height of the tree does not increase in the next step, *i.e.* if height $(T_{t+1}(u)) = $ height $(T_t(u))$, then (18) still holds at time $t + 1$, since $|T_{t+1}(u)| \geq |T_t(u)|$. Finally, if height $(T_{t+1}(u)) > $ height $(T_t(u))$, then the instruction executed at time t must be a **union** instruction that merges a tree $T_t(v)$ into $T_t(u)$, making v a child of u in $T_{t+1}(u)$. Then

$$\text{height}\,(T_t(v)) \;=\; \text{height}\,(T_{t+1}(v)) \;=\; \text{height}\,(T_{t+1}(u)) - 1\,.$$

By the induction hypothesis,

$$|T_t(v)| \;\geq\; 2^{\text{height}\,(T_t(v))}\,.$$

Since we always merge smaller trees into larger,

$$|T_t(u)| \geq |T_t(v)| .$$

Therefore

$$
\begin{aligned}
|T_{t+1}(u)| &= |T_t(u)| + |T_t(v)| \\
&\geq 2^{\text{height } (T_t(v))} + 2^{\text{height } (T_t(v))} \\
&= 2^{\text{height } (T_t(v))+1} \\
&= 2^{\text{height } (T_{t+1}(u))} .
\end{aligned}
$$

$\square$

Lemma 11.2 *The maximum rank after executing σ is at most $\lfloor \log n \rfloor + 2$.*

Proof. By Lemma 11.1,

$$n \geq |T_m(u)| \geq 2^{\text{height } (T_m(u))} \geq 2^{\text{rank } (u)-2} ,$$

so

$$\lfloor \log n \rfloor \geq \text{rank } (u) - 2 .$$

$\square$

Lemma 11.3

$$|\{u \mid \text{rank } (u) = r\}| \leq \frac{n}{2^{r-2}} .$$

Proof. If rank $(u) = $ rank (v), then by (17) $T_m(u)$ and $T_m(v)$ are disjoint. Thus

$$
\begin{aligned}
n &\geq |\bigcup_{\text{rank } (u)=r} T_m(u)| \\
&= \sum_{\text{rank } (u)=r} |T_m(u)| \\
&\geq \sum_{\text{rank } (u)=r} 2^{r-2} \quad \text{by Lemma 11.1} \\
&= |\{u \mid \text{rank } (u) = r\}| \cdot 2^{r-2} .
\end{aligned}
$$

$\square$

Now consider the execution of σ with path compression. We will focus on the distance between u and parent (u) as measured by the difference in their ranks, and how this distance increases due to path compression. Recall that rank (u) is fixed and independent of time; however, rank (parent (u)) can change with time because the parent of u can change due to path compression. By (17), this value can only increase.

Specifically, we consider the following conditions, one for each k:

$$\text{rank} \, (\text{parent} \, (u)) \; \geq \; A_k(\text{rank} \, (u)) \, . \tag{19}$$

Define

$$\delta(u) \;\; = \;\; \text{the greatest } k \text{ for which (19) holds.}$$

The value of $\delta(u)$ is time-dependent and can increase with time due to path compression. Note that $\delta(u)$ exists if u has a parent, since by (17),

$$\text{rank} \, (\text{parent} \, (u)) \;\; \geq \;\; \text{rank} \, (u) + 1 \;\; = \;\; A_0(\text{rank} \, (u))$$

at the very least.

For $n \geq 5$, the maximum value $\delta(u)$ can take on is $\alpha(n) - 1$, since if $\delta(u) = k$,

$$\begin{aligned}
n \; &> \; \lfloor \log n \rfloor + 2 \\
&\geq \; \text{rank} \, (\text{parent} \, (u)) \quad \text{by Lemma 11.2} \\
&\geq \; A_k(\text{rank} \, (u)) \\
&\geq \; A_k(2) \, ,
\end{aligned}$$

therefore

$$\alpha(n) \;\; > \;\; k \, .$$

11.2   Analysis

Each **union** operation requires constant time, thus the time for all **union** instructions is $O(m)$.

Each instruction **find**(u) takes time proportional to the length of the path from u to v, where v is the root of the tree containing u. The path is traversed twice, once to find v and then once again to change all the parent pointers along the path to point to v. This amounts to constant time (say one time unit) per vertex along the path. We charge the time unit associated such a vertex x as follows:

- If x has an ancestor y on the path such that $\delta(y) = \delta(x)$, then charge x's time unit to x itself.

- If x has no such ancestor, then charge x's time unit to the **find** instruction.

Let us now tally separately the total number of time units apportioned to the vertices and to the **find** instructions and show that in each case the total is $O((m + n)\alpha(n))$.

There are at most $\alpha(n)$ time units charged to each **find** instruction, at most one for each of the $\alpha(n)$ possible values of δ, since for each such value k only the last vertex x on the path with $\delta(x) = k$ gets its time unit charged to the **find** instruction. Since there are at most m **find** instructions in all, the total time charged to **find** instructions is $O(m\alpha(n))$.

Let us now count all the charges to a particular vertex x over the course of the entire computation. For such a charge occurring at time t, x must have an ancestor y such that $\delta(y) = \delta(x) = k$ for some k. Then at time t,

$$\text{rank}\,(\text{parent}\,(x)) \;\geq\; A_k(\text{rank}\,(x))$$
$$\text{rank}\,(\text{parent}\,(y)) \;\geq\; A_k(\text{rank}\,(y))\;.$$

Suppose that in fact

$$\text{rank}\,(\text{parent}\,(x)) \;\geq\; A_k^i(\text{rank}\,(x))\;,\quad i \geq 1\;.$$

Let v be the last vertex on the path. Then at time t,

$$
\begin{aligned}
\text{rank}\,(v) \;&\geq\; \text{rank}\,(\text{parent}\,(y))\\
&\geq\; A_k(\text{rank}\,(y))\\
&\geq\; A_k(\text{rank}\,(\text{parent}\,(x)))\\
&\geq\; A_k(A_k^i(\text{rank}\,(x)))\\
&\geq\; A_k^{i+1}(\text{rank}\,(x))\;,
\end{aligned}
$$

and since v is the new parent of x at time $t + 1$, we have at time $t + 1$ that

$$\text{rank}\,(\text{parent}\,(x)) \;\geq\; A_k^{i+1}(\text{rank}\,(x))\;.$$

Thus at most rank (x) such charges can be made against x before

$$
\begin{aligned}
\text{rank}\,(\text{parent}\,(x)) \;&\geq\; A_k^{\text{rank}\,(x)}(\text{rank}\,(x))\\
&=\; A_{k+1}(\text{rank}\,(x))\;,
\end{aligned}
$$

and at that point

$$\delta(x) \;\geq\; k + 1\;.$$

Thus after at most rank (x) such charges against x, $\delta(x)$ increases by at least one. Since $\delta(x)$ can increase only $\alpha(n) - 1$ times, there can be at most rank $(x)\alpha(n)$ such charges against x in all. By Lemma 11.3, there are at most

$$r\alpha(n)\frac{n}{2^{r-2}} \;=\; n\alpha(n)\frac{r}{2^{r-2}}$$

charges against vertices of rank r. Summing over all values of r, we obtain the following bound on all charges to all vertices:

$$\sum_{r=0}^{\infty} n\alpha(n)\frac{r}{2^{r-2}} = n\alpha(n) \cdot \sum_{r=0}^{\infty} \frac{r}{2^{r-2}}$$
$$= 8n\alpha(n) \ .$$

We have shown

Theorem 11.4 *A sequence of m **union** and **find** operations starting with n singleton sets takes time at most $O((m+n)\alpha(n))$.*

Lecture 12   Splay Trees

A *splay tree* is a data structure invented by Sleator and Tarjan [94, 100] for maintaining a set of elements drawn from a totally ordered set and allowing membership testing, insertions, and deletions (among other operations) at an amortized cost of $O(\log n)$ per operation. The most interesting aspect of the structure is that, unlike balanced tree schemes such as 2-3 trees or AVL trees, it is not necessary to rebalance the tree explicitly after every operation—it happens automatically.

Splay trees are binary trees, but they need not be balanced. The height of a splay tree of n elements can be greater than $\log n$; indeed, it can be as great as $n-1$. Thus individual operations can take as much as linear time. However, as operations are performed on the tree, it tends to rebalance itself, and in the long run the amortized complexity works out to $O(\log n)$ per operation.

Data is represented at all nodes of a splay tree. The data values are distinct and drawn from a totally ordered set. The data items will always be maintained in inorder; that is, for any node x, the elements occupying the left subtree of x are all less than x, and those occupying the right subtree of x are all greater than x.

Splay trees support the following operations:

- **member**(i, S): determine whether element i is in splay tree S

- **insert**(i, S): insert i into S if it is not already there

- **delete**(i, S): delete i from S if it is there

- **join**(S, S'): join S and S' into a single splay tree, assuming that $x < y$ for all $x \in S$ and $y \in S'$

- **split**(i, S): split the splay tree S into two new splay trees S' and S'' such that $x \leq i \leq y$ for all $x \in S'$ and $y \in S''$.

All these operations are implemented in terms of a single basic operation, called a **splay**:

- **splay**(i, S): reorganize the splay tree S so that element i is at the root if $i \in S$, and otherwise the new root is either

$$\max\{k \in S \mid k < i\} \quad \text{or} \quad \min\{k \in S \mid k > i\} .$$

All of the operations mentioned above can be performed with a constant number of **splay**s in addition to a constant number of other low-level operations such as pointer manipulations and comparisons. For example, to do **join**(S, S'), first call **splay**$(+\infty, S)$ to reorganize S so that its largest element is at the root and all other elements are contained in the left subtree of the root; then make S' the right subtree. To do **delete**(i, S), call **splay**(i, S) to bring i to the root if it is there; then remove i and call **join** to merge the left and right subtrees.

12.1 Implementation of Splay

The **splay** operation can be implemented in terms of the even more elementary **rotate** operation. Given a binary tree S and a node x with parent y, the operation **rotate**(x) moves x up and y down and changes a few pointers, according to the following picture:

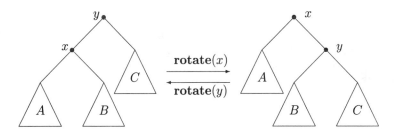

A very simple but important observation to make at this point is that the **rotate** operation preserves inorder numbering.

To implement **splay**(x, S), we might rotate x up until it becomes the root. However, in order to achieve the desired amortized complexity bounds, we need to be a little more careful. Depending on the relationship of x to its parent and grandparent, we distinguish three different cases:

(i) if x has a parent but no grandparent, we just **rotate**(x);

(ii) if x has a parent y and a grandparent, and if x and y are either both left children or both right children, we first **rotate**(y), then **rotate**(x);

(iii) if x has a parent y and a grandparent, and if one of x, y is a left child and the other is a right child, we first **rotate**(x) and then **rotate**(x) again.

Example 12.1 Apply **splay**$(1, S)$ to the following tree S:

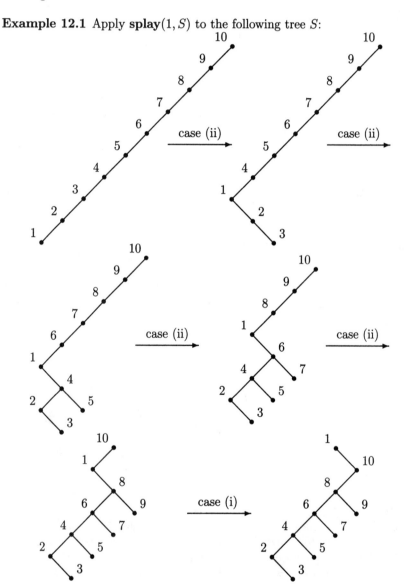

Applying **splay** to node 2 of the resulting tree yields:

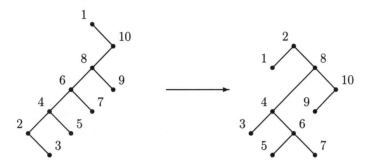

Note that the tree appears to become more balanced with each **splay**. □

12.2 Analysis

We will now show that the time required to perform m operations on a set of n elements is $O(m \log n)$. To do this, we use a credit accounting scheme similar to the one used in our analysis of Fibonacci heaps. Each node x of the splay tree has a savings account containing a certain number of *credits*. When x is created, some number of credits are charged to the **insert** operation that created x, and these credits are deposited to x's account. These credits can be used later to pay for restructuring operations.

For x a node of a splay tree, let $S(x)$ denote the subtree rooted at x. Let $|S|$ denote the number of nodes in tree S. Define

$$\mu(S) = \lfloor (\log |S|) \rfloor$$
$$\mu(x) = \mu(S(x)) .$$

We maintain the following *credit invariant*:

> Node x always has at least $\mu(x)$ credits on deposit.

Lemma 12.2 *Each operation* **splay**(x, S) *requires no more than*

$$3(\mu(S) - \mu(x)) + 1$$

credits to perform the operation and maintain the credit invariant.

Proof. Let y be the parent of x and z be the parent of y, if it exists. Let μ and μ' be the values of μ before and after the **splay** operation, respectively. We consider three cases:

(i) *Node z does not exist.* This is the last rotation in the **splay**; we perform
a single **rotate**(x). We are willing to pay no more than

$$3(\mu'(x) - \mu(x)) + 1$$

credits for this rotation. Note that

$$\mu'(x) = \mu(y)$$
$$\mu'(y) \leq \mu'(x) \ .$$

In order to maintain the invariant, we need to spend

$$\begin{aligned}
\mu'(x) + \mu'(y) - \mu(x) - \mu(y) &= \mu'(y) - \mu(x) \\
&\leq \mu'(x) - \mu(x) \\
&\leq 3(\mu'(x) - \mu(x))
\end{aligned}$$

credits. We are left with at least one credit left over to pay for the
constant number of low-level operations such as pointer manipulations
and comparisons.

(ii) *Node x is the left child of y and y is the left child of z (or both x and
y are right children).* In this case we perform a **rotate**(y) followed by
a **rotate**(x). We will show that it costs no more than $3(\mu'(x) - \mu(x))$
credits to perform these two **rotate** operations and maintain the credit
invariant. Thus if a sequence of these are done to move x up the tree as
in the example above, we will get a telescoping sum, so that the total
amount spent will be no more than $3(\mu(S) - \mu(x)) + 1$ (the $+1$ comes
from the last rotation as discussed in case (i)).
In order to maintain the invariant, we need

$$\mu'(x) + \mu'(y) + \mu'(z) - \mu(x) - \mu(y) - \mu(z) \tag{20}$$

extra credits. Since $\mu'(x) = \mu(z)$, we have

$$\begin{aligned}
\mu'(x) &+ \mu'(y) + \mu'(z) - \mu(x) - \mu(y) - \mu(z) \\
&= \mu'(y) + \mu'(z) - \mu(x) - \mu(y) \\
&= (\mu'(y) - \mu(x)) + (\mu'(z) - \mu(y)) \\
&\leq (\mu'(x) - \mu(x)) + (\mu'(x) - \mu(x)) \\
&= 2(\mu'(x) - \mu(x)) \ .
\end{aligned}$$

We can afford to pay for this and have $\mu'(x) - \mu(x)$ credits left over to
pay for the constant number of low-level operations needed to perform
these two rotations. Unfortunately, it may turn out that $\mu'(x) = \mu(x)$,
in which case we have nothing left over. We show that in this case the
quantity (20) is in fact strictly negative, thus the invariant is maintained

for free and we can even afford to spend one of our saved credits to pay for the low-level operations.

All we need to do is to show that the two assumptions

$$\mu'(x) = \mu(x)$$
$$\mu'(x) + \mu'(y) + \mu'(z) \geq \mu(x) + \mu(y) + \mu(z)$$

lead to a contradiction. Since $\mu(z) = \mu'(x) = \mu(x)$ and μ is monotone in the subterm ordering, we have

$$\mu(x) = \mu(y) = \mu(z) \, ,$$

therefore

$$\mu'(x) + \mu'(y) + \mu'(z) \geq 3\mu(z)$$
$$= 3\mu'(x)$$
$$\mu'(y) + \mu'(z) \geq 2\mu'(x) \, .$$

Because μ' is monotone in the subterm ordering,

$$\mu'(y) \leq \mu'(x)$$
$$\mu'(z) \leq \mu'(x) \, .$$

It follows that

$$\mu'(x) = \mu'(y) = \mu'(z) \, ,$$

and since $\mu(z) = \mu'(x)$, we have

$$\mu(x) = \mu(y) = \mu(z) = \mu'(x) = \mu'(y) = \mu'(z) \, . \tag{21}$$

Substituting in for the definition of μ and μ' will quickly show that this situation is untenable. If a is the size of the subtree rooted at x before the operation and b is the size of the subtree rooted at z after the operation, then (21) implies

$$\lfloor \log a \rfloor = \lfloor \log(a + b + 1) \rfloor = \lfloor \log b \rfloor \, . \tag{22}$$

Assuming without loss of generality that $a \leq b$,

$$\lfloor \log(a + b + 1) \rfloor \geq \lfloor \log 2a \rfloor$$
$$= 1 + \lfloor \log a \rfloor$$
$$> \lfloor \log a \rfloor \, .$$

This contradicts (22).

(iii) *Node x is a left child of y and y is a right child of z, or vice versa.* Here we do **rotate**(x) followed by **rotate**(x) again, and we are willing to pay no more than $3(\mu'(x) - \mu(x))$ credits for these two rotations. As in the previous case, we need

$$\mu'(x) + \mu'(y) + \mu'(z) - \mu(x) - \mu(y) - \mu(z)$$

credits to maintain the invariant, and this quantity is at most $2(\mu'(x) - \mu(x))$. This leaves at least $\mu'(x) - \mu(x)$ left over to pay for the low-level operations, which suffices unless $\mu'(x) = \mu(x)$. As in case (ii), we prove by contradiction that in this case

$$\mu'(x) + \mu'(y) + \mu'(z) \quad < \quad \mu(x) + \mu(y) + \mu(z) \ ,$$

thus the credit invariant is maintained for free and we have at least one extra credit to spend on the low-level operations.

$\square$

Theorem 12.3 *A sequence of m operations involving n **insert**s takes time $O(m \log n)$.*

Proof. First we note that the maximum value of $\mu(x)$ is $\lfloor \log n \rfloor$. It follows from Lemma 12.2 that at most $3\lfloor \log n \rfloor + 1$ credits are needed for each **splay** operation. Since each of the operations **member**, **insert**, **delete**, **split**, and **join** can be performed using a constant number of **splay**s and a constant number of low-level operations, each of these operations costs $O(\log n)$. Inserting a new item requires at most $O(\log n)$ credits to be deposited to its account for future use; we charge these credits to the **insert** operation. Hence each operation requires at most $O(\log n)$ credits. It follows that the total time required for a sequence of m such operations is $O(m \log n)$. $\square$

Lecture 13   Random Search Trees

In this lecture we will describe a very simple probabilistic data structure that allows inserts, deletes, and membership tests (among other operations) in expected logarithmic time.

These results were first obtained by Pugh in 1988 (see [88]), who called his probabilistic data structure *skip lists*. We will follow the presentation of Aragon and Seidel [7], whose data structure is somewhat different and more closely related to the self-adjusting trees presented in the last lecture, and whose probabilistic analysis is particularly elegant.

13.1   Treaps

Consider a binary tree, not necessarily balanced, with nodes drawn from a totally ordered set, ordered in inorder; that is, if i is in the left subtree of k and j is in the right subtree of k, then $i < k < j$. Recall that the **rotate** operation discussed in the previous lecture preserves this order.

Now suppose that each element k has a unique *priority* $p(k)$ drawn from some other totally ordered set, and that the elements are ordered in heap order according to priority; that is, an element of maximum priority in any subtree is found at the root of that subtree.

A tree in which the data values k are ordered in inorder and the priorities $p(k)$ are ordered in heap order is called a *treap* (for *tree-heap*, one supposes).

It may not be obvious at first that treaps always exist for every priority assignment. They do! Moreover, if the priorities are distinct, then the treap is unique.

Lemma 13.1 *Let X and Y be totally ordered sets, and let p be a function assigning a distinct priority in Y to each element of X. Then there exists a unique treap with nodes X and priorities p.*

Proof. Let k be the unique element of X of maximum priority; this must be the root. Partition the remaining elements into two sets

$$\{i \in X \mid i < k\}, \qquad \{i \in X \mid i > k\} \ .$$

Inductively build the unique treaps out of these two sets and make them the left and right subtrees of k, respectively. □

13.2   Random Treaps

A *random treap* is a treap in which the priorities have been assigned randomly. This is best done in practice by calling a random number generator each time a new element m is presented for insertion into the treap to assign a random priority to m. Under some highly idealized but reasonable assumptions about the random number generator[3], two elements receive the same priority with probability zero, and if all elements in the treap are sorted by priority, then every permutation is equally likely.

When a new element m is presented for insertion or to test membership, we start at the root and work our way down some path in the treap, comparing m to elements along the path to see which way to go to find m's appropriate inorder position. If we see m on the path on the way down, we can answer the membership query affirmatively. If we make it all the way down without seeing m, we can answer the membership query negatively.

If m is to be inserted, we attach m as a new leaf in its appropriate inorder position. At that point we call the random number generator to assign a random priority $p(m)$, which by Lemma 13.1 specifies a unique position in the treap. We then rotate m upward as long as its priority is greater than that of its parent, or until m becomes the root. At that point the tree is in heap order with respect to the priorities and in inorder with respect to the data values.

To delete m, we first find m by searching down from the root as described above, then rotate m down until it is a leaf, taking care to choose the direction

---

[3]A call to the random number generator gives a uniformly distributed random real number in the interval $[0, 1)$, and successive calls are statistically independent; *i.e.* if $x_1, \ldots, x_n$ are the results of n successive calls, then

$$\Pr(\bigwedge_{1 \le i \le n} x_i \in A_i) \quad = \quad \prod_{1 \le i \le n} \Pr(x_i \in A_i) \ .$$

of rotation so as to maintain heap order. For example, if the children of m are j and k and $p(j) > p(k)$, then we rotate m down in the direction of j, since the rotate operation will make j an ancestor of k. When m becomes a leaf, we prune it off.

The beauty of this approach is that the position of any element in the treap is determined once and for all at the time it is inserted, and it stays put at that level until it is deleted; there is not a lot of restructuring going on as with splay trees. Moreover, as we will show below, the expected number of rotations for an insertion or deletion is at most two.

13.3   Analysis

We now show that, averaged over all random priority assignments, the expected time for any insert, membership test, or delete is $O(\log n)$.

We will do the analysis for deletes only; it is not hard to see that the time bound for membership tests and inserts is proportionally no worse than for deletes. Suppose that at the moment, the treap contains n data items (without loss of generality, say $\{1, 2, \ldots, n\}$), and we wish to delete m. The priorities have been chosen randomly, so that if the set $\{1, 2, \ldots, n\}$ is sorted in decreasing order by priority to obtain a permutation σ of $\{1, 2, \ldots, n\}$, every σ is equally likely.

In order to locate m in the treap, we follow the path from the root down to m. The amount of time to do this is proportional to the length of the path. Let us calculate the expected length of this path, averaged over all possible random permutations σ.

Let

$$m_\leq = \{1, 2, \ldots, m\}$$
$$m_\geq = \{m, m+1, \ldots, n\} \ .$$

Let A be the set of ancestors of m, including m itself. The definitions of $m_\leq$ and $m_\geq$ do not depend on σ, but the definition of A does. Let X be the random variable

$$X = \text{length of the path from the root down to } m$$
$$= |m_\leq \cap A| + |m_\geq \cap A| - 2 \ .$$

The 2 is subtracted because m is counted in both $m_\leq$ and $m_\geq$.

We are interested in $\mathcal{E}X$, the expected value of X; by linearity of expectation, we have

$$\mathcal{E}X = \mathcal{E}|m_\leq \cap A| + \mathcal{E}|m_\geq \cap A| - 2 \ .$$

By symmetry, it will suffice to calculate $\mathcal{E}|m_\leq \cap A|$.

Note that if the elements of $m_\leq$ are sorted in descending order by priority, then

- every permutation of $m_\le$ is equally likely;

- an element of $m_\le$ is in A if and only if it is larger than all previous elements of $m_\le$ in sorted order.

In other words, permute $m_\le$ randomly, then scan the resulting list from left to right, checking off those elements k that are larger than anything to the left of k; the quantity $\mathcal{E}|m_\le \cap A|$ is the expected number of checks.

Example 13.2 Let $n = 10$ and $m = 8$. Suppose that when priorities are assigned randomly to $\{1, 2, \ldots, 10\}$ and these elements are sorted in decreasing order by priority, we get the permutation

$$\sigma \;=\; (4, 5, 9, 2, 1, 7, 3, 10, 8, 6) .$$

This results in the following treap:

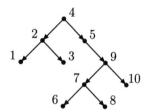

Then $m_\le = \{1, 2, 3, 4, 5, 6, 7, 8\}$. If we restrict the random permutation σ to this set, we obtain the permutation $(4, 5, 2, 1, 7, 3, 8, 6)$. Scanning from left to right and checking only those elements k that are greater than all elements to the left of k, we get the sequence $(4, 5, 7, 8)$. This is exactly the sequence of elements in $m_\le$ appearing on the path from the root down to m in the treap.

A symmetric argument using $m_\ge$ gives the sequence $(9, 8)$, which is the sequence of elements in $m_\ge$ appearing on the path from the root down to m. The length of the path is then the sum of the two lengths of these sequences less 2. $\qquad\square$

We are thus left with the problem of determining the expected value of the random variable H_m, the number of checks obtained when scanning a random permutation of $\{1, 2, \ldots, m\}$ from left to right and checking every element that is greater than anything to its left.

We claim that this number is exactly

$$\mathcal{E}H_m \;=\; \sum_{k=1}^{m} \frac{1}{k} . \tag{23}$$

We will obtain this by solving a simple recurrence, using the linearity of expectation.

Suppose we permute $\{1, \ldots, m\}$ randomly to get the random permutation σ. Deleting 1 from σ, we get a random permutation σ' of $\{2, 3, \ldots, m\}$. Note that an element other than 1 is checked when scanning σ if and only if it is checked when scanning σ'; thus the presence or absence of 1 does not affect whether 2 is checked (however, the presence or absence of 2 might very well affect whether 1 is checked). Thus the expected number of checks on elements other than 1 is the same in σ as in σ', or $\mathcal{E} H_{m-1}$. The element 1 is checked if and only if it occurs first in σ, and this occurs with probability $\frac{1}{m}$. Thus the expected number of checks on the element 1, averaged over all permutations, is $\frac{1}{m}$. By linearity of expectation,

$$\mathcal{E} H_m \;=\; \mathcal{E} H_{m-1} + \frac{1}{m} \,.$$

The unique solution to this recurrence with $\mathcal{E} H_1 = 1$ is (23).

The quantity (23) is $O(\log m)$. This can be verified by approximating the sum above and below with definite integrals involving the functions $\frac{1}{x}$ and $\frac{1}{x+1}$, and recalling from calculus that

$$\int_1^m \frac{dx}{x} \;=\; \ln m \;=\; \ln 2 \cdot \log_2 m \,.$$

13.4 Expected time for deletion

A similar analysis allows us to calculate the expected number of rotations necessary to delete m from its position in the treap. The number of rotations needed is the sum of the length of the rightmost path in the left subtree of m and the length of the leftmost path in the right subtree of m. To see this, try rotating m down; if you rotate to the left (right), the length of the rightmost (leftmost) path in the left (right) subtree decreases by one and the length of the leftmost (rightmost) path in the right (left) subtree stays the same.

Let us calculate the expected value of G_m, the length of the rightmost path of the left subtree of m. By symmetry, the expected length of the leftmost path of the right subtree of m is $\mathcal{E} G_{n-m+1}$, and by the linearity of expectation, the expected number of rotations to remove m is $\mathcal{E} G_m + \mathcal{E} G_{n-m+1}$. We will show below that this number is less than 2!

An analysis similar to the analysis for $\mathcal{E} H_m$ above reveals that $\mathcal{E} G_m$ is the expected number of checks obtained when scanning a random permutation of the set $\{1, 2, \ldots, m\}$ from left to right, where we check an element k provided that

- k occurs strictly to the right of m;

- k is greater than all elements of $\{1, 2, \ldots, m - 1\}$ occurring to the left of k and either to the left or to the right of m.

This is the same as the expected number of checks obtained when scanning a random permutation of the set $\{1, 2, \ldots, m-1\}$ from left to right, where we check element k if it is greater than all elements to its left, then place m randomly in the list and erase those checks occurring to the left of m.

Example 13.3 For $m = 3$, we have the following six situations, all occurring with equal probability:

$$
\begin{array}{ccc}
3 \ \overset{\checkmark}{1} \ \overset{\checkmark}{2} & \quad & 3 \ \overset{\checkmark}{2} \ 1 \\
1 \ 3 \ \overset{\checkmark}{2} & \quad & 2 \ 3 \ 1 \\
1 \ 2 \ 3 & \quad & 2 \ 1 \ 3
\end{array}
$$

The expected number of checks is $\frac{1}{6} \cdot 2 + \frac{1}{3} \cdot 1 = \frac{2}{3}$.   □

It is easy to see that the expected value of G_m is at most that of H_{m-1}, which we would get if the checks to the left of m were not erased; thus $\mathcal{E}G_m \leq \mathcal{E}H_{m-1} = O(\log m)$, and this suffices for our complexity bound.

In fact, it turns out that $\mathcal{E}G_m < 1$. As above, the expected number of checks on elements other than 1 is $\mathcal{E}G_{m-1}$, and the probability that 1 is checked is $\frac{1}{m(m-1)}$, since 1 is checked if and only if m occurs leftmost, followed immediately by 1. Again, by linearity of expectation, $\mathcal{E}G_m$ is the expected number of checks on elements other than 1 plus the expected number of checks on 1:

$$
\mathcal{E}G_m \ = \ \mathcal{E}G_{m-1} + \frac{1}{m(m-1)}
$$

and $\mathcal{E}G_1 = 0$. The solution to this recurrence is

$$
\mathcal{E}G_m \ = \ \frac{m-1}{m} .
$$

Lecture 14   Planar and Plane Graphs

Planar graphs have many important applications in computer science, for example in VLSI layout. Many problems that are hard or even *NP*-complete for arbitrary graphs are much easier for planar graphs. In the next lecture we will prove a nice result due to Lipton and Tarjan in 1977 [73] which opens up planar graphs to divide-and-conquer.

In this lecture, we will define planar and plane graphs and develop some of their basic properties. Our treatment will have a more combinatorial flavor than the classical treatment [48, 14]. Edmonds, the same one who showed the greedy algorithm only works for matroids, was the first to give a combinatorial definition of graph embeddings [31].

For the purposes of this lecture and the next, we will allow graphs to have multiple edges and self-loops, but we will prohibit isolated vertices (vertices with no adjacent edges). This assumption is for technical reasons that will become clear.

14.1   Planar and Plane Graphs—Traditional Version

According to the traditional definition, a graph is *planar* if it can be embedded on the plane or sphere in such a way that no two edges cross. A *plane graph* G is a planar graph together with such an embedding.

The complete graph on five vertices K_5 and the complete bipartite graph on two sets of three vertices $K_{3,3}$ are not planar:

$K_{3,3}$ K_5

An amazing result of Kuratowski states that *any* nonplanar graph must contain a subgraph that is topologically equivalent to one of these two graphs.

Theorem 14.1 (Kuratowski) *An undirected graph is nonplanar if and only if it contains a subgraph homeomorphic to K_5 or $K_{3,3}$.*

Here "homeomorphic to" means the edges can be paths. For more on Kuratowski's Theorem, see [48, 14].

14.2   The Plane Dual—Traditional Version

The *plane dual* of a plane graph G is a graph G^* whose vertices are the *faces* of G and whose edges are in one-to-one correspondence with the edges of G. Traditionally, a *face* is defined to be a maximal connected region of $\mathcal{R}^2 - G$, the plane with all vertices and edges of the embedded G removed. The plane dual of G is obtained by placing a vertex in each face and connecting two faces adjacent to a common edge e of G with an edge of G^* that crosses e once and crosses no other edges.

Example 14.2 The following picture shows K_4 and its plane dual K_4^*, which happens to be isomorphic to K_4:

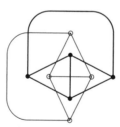

Note that any G^* is connected, and if G is connected, then G^{**} is isomorphic to G.   □

14.3   Plane Graphs—Combinatorial Version

An embedding of a planar graph G on the sphere determines an orientation function θ giving a counterclockwise ordering of edges about each vertex. The map θ determines the embedding uniquely (up to rearrangement of the connected components). While we will continue to use the traditional definitions of plane graph and plane dual as intuitive aids, in computational practice it is more convenient to forget the actual embedding and work only with θ.

We will therefore start afresh and give a purely combinatorial definition of plane graphs and duals in terms of θ. This is nice because we can deal with plane graphs purely combinatorially and escape the savage world of real analysis and topology. In addition, this approach works out more nicely when G is not connected. Keep in mind that the two approaches coincide when G is connected, but diverge when G is not.

In our combinatorial formalism, an undirected graph is a tuple

$$G = (E, \theta, \bar{\ })$$

where E is a set of even cardinality, $\bar{\ }$ is an involution on E (permutation of order 2) with no fixpoints, and θ is a permutation on E. The elements of E are thought of as *directed* edges; each undirected edge is represented as a pair $e, \bar{e} \in E$ of directed edges, one in each direction. The map $\bar{\ }$ reverses direction.

The map θ is supposed to give an orientation of the edges around each vertex. But, you may well ask, where are the vertices? They are *defined* to be the cycles of θ. A *cycle* of the permutation θ is a minimal nonempty subset of E closed under θ. It is not to be confused with a cycle of the graph G. An edge e is considered directed out of vertex u if u is the unique cycle of θ containing e. Correspondingly, e is considered directed into vertex v if v is the unique cycle of θ containing $\bar{e}$. Thus θ cyclically permutes the edges out of any vertex. From this definition it becomes clear why isolated vertices were disallowed: you cannot have empty cycles. The tail and head functions $\mathbf{t} : E \to V$ and $\mathbf{h} : E \to V$ giving the source and sink, respectively, of each edge are defined by

$$\mathbf{t}(e) = \{\text{the unique cycle of } \theta \text{ containing } e\}$$
$$\mathbf{h}(e) = \{\text{the unique cycle of } \theta \text{ containing } \bar{e}\}$$
$$= \mathbf{t}(\bar{e}) .$$

With these definitions the tuple

$$(V, E, \mathbf{h}, \mathbf{t}, \theta, \bar{\ })$$

gives a more conventional representation of the graph G.

Definition 14.3 Define the function $\theta^* : E \to E$ by:

$$\theta^*(e) = \theta(\bar{e}) .$$

A *face* of G is a cycle of the permutation θ^*. The set of faces of G is denoted V^*. □

Note that this definition makes sense even for nonplanar graphs.

According to Definition 14.3, to compute $\theta^*(e)$, we first reverse the direction of e to get $\bar{e}$, then rotate about the tail of $\bar{e}$. Intuitively, for plane graphs, the operation θ^* moves an edge *clockwise* around the face to its right:

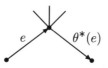

Definition 14.4 A *connected component* of G is an orbit of E under the permutation group generated by θ and $^-$. That is, it is a minimal nonempty subset of E closed under θ and $^-$.   □

Definition 14.5 Let $m = \frac{1}{2}|E|$, the number of *undirected* edges of G; $n = |V|$; $n^* = |V^*|$; and c the number of connected components of G. The *characteristic* of G is the quantity

$$\chi(G) \;=\; 2c + m - n - n^* \,.$$

The graph G is said to be *plane* if $\chi(G) = 0$.   □

Theorem 14.6 *A graph G is plane according to Definition 14.5 iff it is plane according to the traditional definition (i.e., if θ corresponds to the counterclockwise ordering induced by an embedding of G in the plane with no edges crossing).*

    Proof. Miscellaneous Exercise 11.   □

    Definition 14.5 is similar to the traditional definition of the *Euler characteristic*

$$c + 1 + m - n - n^* \,.$$

Euler's Theorem states that plane graphs have Euler characteristic 0. Our Definition 14.5 and Theorem 14.6 agree with the traditional version when $c = 1$, *i.e.* when G is connected. The difference comes from the definition of the dual—in our version, disconnected graphs have more faces than in the traditional version.

14.4   The Plane Dual—Combinatorial Version

Definition 14.7 Let G be the graph

$$G \;=\; (E,\, \theta,\, {}^-)\,.$$

The *dual* of G is the graph

$$G^* \;=\; (E,\, \theta^*,\, {}^-)\,.$$

     □

Note that this definition makes sense for graphs that are not plane.

The following theorem is immediate.

Theorem 14.8

(i) *If G is plane, then so is G^{*}.*

(ii) *G^{**} and G are isomorphic (in fact they are equal).*

This theorem is where our combinatorial definition wins out: (ii) is false for disconnected plane graphs under the traditional definition.

For computational purposes, a convenient representation of the undirected graph

$$G \;=\; (V,\; E,\; \mathbf{h},\; \mathbf{t},\; \theta,\; ^{-})$$

consists of a set of list elements, one for each vertex and one for each directed edge (element of E). The vertices are arranged in a linked list. The vertex v points to a circular list of edges e such that $\mathbf{t}(e) = v$ arranged in the order θ. The edge e points to $\mathbf{t}(e)$ and $\bar{e}$. This representation can be produced in linear time from a conventional adjacency list representation (Miscellaneous Homework 8).

14.5   Triangulation

Definition 14.9 A graph G is *triangulated* if every face of G is a triangle, *i.e.* has degree exactly three. A *triangulation* of G is a triangulated graph of which G is a subgraph.   □

Theorem 14.10 *Let G be a graph such that all faces have degree at least three. A triangulation $\widehat{G}$ of G can be produced in linear time such that $\chi(\widehat{G}) = \chi(G)$; in particular, if G is plane then so is its triangulation. If G is plane, then*

$$m \;\leq\; 3n - 6\,,$$

with equality holding when G is triangulated.

Proof. We triangulate G as follows. First find all connected components and connect them in a treelike fashion by adding edges between components. Two components can be connected by adding an edge between any vertex u in one component and any vertex v in the other, and the edge can go anywhere in the ordered edge lists of u and v without changing the characteristic or the property that each face is of degree at least three. This takes linear time using DFS, and at most $c - 1 = O(m)$ new edges are added. Then traverse each face, adding chords as necessary to break up faces of degree greater than three into triangles (don't worry about multiple edges). At most $O(m)$ time is needed since each edge is traversed at most once in each direction.

Now it will suffice to prove that

$$m = 3n - 6$$

for triangulated plane graphs. Since the graph is connected, $c = 1$. Since every edge is adjacent to exactly two faces and every face is adjacent to exactly three edges, the number of adjacent face-edge pairs is $3n^* = 2m$. The result now follows from Euler's Theorem.   □

Lecture 15   The Planar Separator Theorem

The Planar Separator Theorem of Lipton and Tarjan [73] says that in any undirected planar graph G there exists a small *separator* $S \subseteq V$ whose removal leaves two disjoint sets of vertices $A, B \subseteq V$ with no edge between them; moreover, each of A and B is at most a constant fraction of the size of V.

This theorem opens up planar graphs to divide-and-conquer. One can often solve a problem on a planar graph G recursively by splitting the graph into two subgraphs of size at most $\frac{2}{3}$ the size of G, recursively solving the problem on these two subgraphs, and then combining the two solutions into a solution for G. Because the sizes of the subproblems diminish geometrically, the depth of the recursion will be $O(\log n)$.

Theorem 15.1 (Planar Separator Theorem) *Let G be an undirected planar graph. There exists a partition of V into disjoint sets A, B and S such that:*

1. $|A|, |B| \leq \frac{2n}{3}$
2. $|S| \leq 4\sqrt{|V|}$
3. $(A \times B) \cap E = \emptyset$ *(S is a separator).*

Moreover, such a partition can be found in linear time.

Proof. Assume the graph is connected. (If not, perform the algorithm on the connected components and recombine the partitions into a solution for the whole graph; details omitted.)

First find a plane embedding in linear time using the algorithm of Hopcroft and Tarjan [52].

Choose an arbitrary vertex s and perform a breadth-first search (BFS) starting from s. Assign a level to each vertex, so that s is at level 0, any vertices adjacent to s are at level 1, any vertices adjacent to them that have not already been assigned a level are at level 2, and so forth. For technical reasons, we include an empty level $\ell + 1$, where ℓ is the level of the last vertex encountered. Let $L(t)$ denote the set of vertices at level t.

A property of BFS traversal is that no edge ever crosses two or more levels—all edges must connect vertices in the same or consecutive levels. This means that any $L(t)$, $0 < t < \ell$, is a separator.

Let t_1 be the middle level, *i.e.* the one such that $L(t_1)$ contains vertex $n/2$ in the breadth-first numbering. The set $L(t_1)$ has some of the properties of the separator we are looking for:

$$\left| \bigcup_{t < t_1} L(t) \right| < n/2$$

$$\left| \bigcup_{t > t_1} L(t) \right| < n/2 .$$

So if $|L(t_1)| \leq 4\sqrt{n}$, we are done. The trouble is that $L(t_1)$ may be too large. However, there exist levels with $\sqrt{n}$ or fewer vertices on either side of t_1 and not too far away:

Lemma 15.2 *There exist levels $t_0 \leq t_1$ and $t_2 > t_1$ such that $|L(t_0)| \leq \sqrt{n}$, $|L(t_2)| \leq \sqrt{n}$, and $t_2 - t_0 \leq \sqrt{n}$.*

Proof. Let t_0 be the largest number such that $t_0 \leq t_1$ and $|L(t_0)| \leq \sqrt{n}$. Such a t_0 exists since $|L(0)| = 1$. Let t_2 be the smallest number such that $t_2 > t_1$ and $|L(t_2)| \leq \sqrt{n}$. Such a t_2 exists since $|L(\ell + 1)| = 0$. Every level strictly between t_0 and t_2 contains more than $\sqrt{n}$ elements, so there must be fewer than $\sqrt{n}$ of them, otherwise there would be more than n vertices. □

Now let

$$C = \bigcup_{t < t_0} L(t)$$

$$D = \bigcup_{t_0 < t < t_2} L(t)$$

$$E = \bigcup_{t_2 < t} L(t) .$$

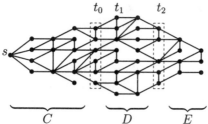

If $|D| \leq \frac{2}{3}n$ then we are done: take $S = L(t_0) \cup L(t_2)$, A the largest of C, D, E, and B the union of the other two.

We should be so lucky. If $|D| > \frac{2}{3}n$, then we at least have $|D|$ in a better shape, and this will make it easier to cut D up. The sets C and E are small: $|C|, |E| \leq \frac{n}{2}$. If we can find a $\frac{1}{3}$-$\frac{2}{3}$ separator for D with $2\sqrt{n}$ vertices or fewer, we will combine this with $L(t_0)$ and $L(t_2)$ to get a separator S of size at most $4\sqrt{n}$, combine the larger of C and E with the smaller of the two pieces of D to get A, and combine the smaller of C and E with the larger piece from D to get B. Both A and B will have no more than $\frac{2}{3}n$ vertices.

To construct a separator for D of size at most $2\sqrt{n}$, we will remove the rest of the graph, but add back the starting vertex s and connect it to everything on level $t_0 + 1$. We can do this maintaining the planarity of the graph because there were non-crossing paths back from each of those vertices to s in the original graph. Some paths may have joined on the way back to s, but they can be separated without violating planarity.

The main property of the new graph D that we will exploit is that *it has a spanning tree T of diameter at most $2\sqrt{n}$.* This is because every vertex is reachable from s by a path of length at most $\sqrt{n}$. We can construct T as follows: start with the vertices at the last level; for each such vertex, choose one edge back to the next-to-last level; repeat for the vertices on the next-to-last level, and so on all the way back to s. The $\frac{1}{3}$-$\frac{2}{3}$ separator for D will turn out to be a path in T.

We will need a useful property of plane duals. (Here we revert to the traditional definition since we need isolated vertices.)

Lemma 15.3 *Let $G = (V, E)$ be a connected plane graph with dual G^*. For any $E' \subseteq E$, the subgraph (V, E') of G has a cycle iff the subgraph $(V^*, E - E')$ of G^* is disconnected.*

Proof. ($\rightarrow$) Suppose there is a cycle in (V, E'). Choose any edge e of the cycle, and let $f, g \in V^*$ be the endpoints of e in G^*. One of f, g is inside the cycle and the other is outside. Then there is no path from f to g in $E - E'$, since no such path can cross the boundary of the cycle.

($\leftarrow$) Suppose $(V^*, E - E')$ is disconnected. Let A, B be a partition of V^* such that no edge in $E - E'$ connects A and B in G^*. Since G^* is connected, there exists at least one edge in E connecting A and B, and all such edges are in E'. These edges form a cycle in G. $\square$

Lemma 15.4 *Let $G = (V, E)$ be a connected plane graph with dual $G^* = (V^*, E)$, and let $E' \subseteq E$. Then (V, E') is a spanning tree in G iff $(V^*, E - E')$ is a spanning tree in G^*.*

Proof. The subgraph (V, E') forms a spanning tree in G iff it is connected and has no cycles. By Lemma 15.3, this occurs iff the subgraph $(V^*, E - E')$ of G^* is connected and has no cycles, *i.e.* is a spanning tree.   □

Now back to the Planar Separator Theorem. We have a plane graph D with spanning tree $T = (V, E_T)$ of diameter at most $2\sqrt{n}$. We can assume without loss of generality that D is triangulated; if not, we can triangulate it in linear time as described in the last lecture. We then construct the plane dual D^* (Miscellaneous Homework 9). This can also be done in linear time. Call the edges in $E - E_T$ *fronds*; according to Lemma 15.4, the fronds form a spanning tree $T^\dagger$ in D^*. We arbitrarily pick one face of D for the root of $T^\dagger$, say the outside face, and orient all the edges of $T^\dagger$ away from the root.

Let $e = (u, v)$ be a frond. There exists a unique path from u to v in T, which along with e forms a cycle $c(e)$.

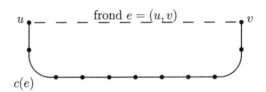

We now perform a DFS on $T^\dagger$, calculating the following information for each frond e inductively from leaves up:

- $I(e)$ = number of vertices strictly inside $c(e)$
- $|c(e)|$ = number of vertices on $c(e)$
- a list representation of $c(e)$.

There are four cases to consider, the first the base case in which e is a leaf of $T^\dagger$, and the remaining three cases induction steps:

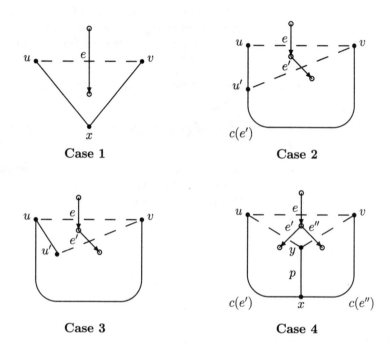

Case 1 In this case, we are at a leaf in $T^\dagger$ (this can be detected by counting adjacencies). Then

- $I(e) = 0$
- $|c(e)| = 3$ (T is triangulated)
- $c(e) = [u, x, v]$.

Case 2 We have calculated the information for the frond $e' = (u', v)$, e is a frond in the same triangle as e', and u' is on the cycle $c(e)$; this can be detected by checking that u is not on the list $c(e')$. Then

- $I(e) = I(e')$
- $|c(e)| = |c(e')| + 1$
- $c(e) = [u] \cdot c(e')$.

Case 3 We have calculated the information for the frond $e' = (u', v)$, e is a frond in the same triangle as e', and u' is not on the cycle $c(e)$; this can be detected by checking that u is on the list $c(e')$. Then

- $I(e) = I(e') + 1$
- $|c(e)| = |c(e')| - 1$
- $c(e)$ is $c(e')$ with u' cut off the front, i.e. $c(e') = [u'] \cdot c(e)$.

Case 4 We have calculated the information for the fronds $e' = (u, y)$ and $e'' = (y, v)$, and e is a frond in the same triangle as both e', e''. Let p be the path common to $c(e')$ and $c(e'')$ and let x be the other endpoint of p besides y.

- $I(e) = I(e') + I(e'') + |p| - 1$ (all vertices of p except x are inside $c(e)$)
- $|c(e)| = |c(e')| + |c(e'')| - 2|p| + 1$
- $c(e) = c' \cdot [x] \cdot c''$, where c' is $c(e')$ with p removed and c'' is $c(e'')$ with p removed.

We can compute $|p|$ and construct a list representation of $c(e)$ by scanning $c(e')$ and $c(e'')$ starting at y until we encounter the last common vertex, which is x. This does not destroy the linear time complexity, since we do this for the edges on p only once.

It remains to prove that there exists a frond e such that

$$I(e) \leq \frac{2n}{3}$$
$$n - (I(e) + |c(e)|) \leq \frac{2n}{3}.$$

Then we can just take $c(e)$ as the separator, the vertices inside $c(e)$ as A, and the vertices outside $c(e)$ as B.

Take the first frond e encountered on the way out from the leaves of $T^\dagger$ to the root such that $I(e) + |c(e)| \geq \frac{n}{3}$. Then the set of vertices outside of $c(e)$ is of cardinality $n - (I(e) + |c(e)|) \leq \frac{2n}{3}$, so it remains to show that $I(e) \leq \frac{2n}{3}$. The argument depends on the case 1 through 4 above in which e fell:

1. $I(e) = 0 \leq \frac{2n}{3}$.
2. $I(e) + |c(e)| = I(e') + |c(e')| + 1$ and $I(e') + |c(e')| < \frac{n}{3}$, so $I(e) + |c(e)| \leq \frac{2n}{3}$ (for $n \geq 3$).
3. $I(e) + |c(e)| = I(e') + |c(e')|$, so e could not have been the first frond encountered such that $I(e) + |c(e)| \geq \frac{n}{3}$.
4. Both $I(e') + |c(e')| \leq \frac{n}{3}$ and $I(e'') + |c(e'')| \leq \frac{n}{3}$, so

$$
\begin{aligned}
& I(e) + |c(e)| \\
={} & I(e') + I(e'') + |p| - 1 + |c(e')| + |c(e'')| - 2|p| + 1 \\
={} & I(e') + I(e'') + |c(e')| + |c(e'')| - |p| \\
\leq{} & \frac{2n}{3} - |p| \\
\leq{} & \frac{2n}{3}.
\end{aligned}
$$

This completes the proof of the Planar Separator Theorem. $\square$

Here is the entire algorithm:

Algorithm 15.5

1. Embed G in the plane using Hopcroft/Tarjan.

2. Do BFS on G, assigning level numbers.

3. Find t_0 and t_2 such that $|L(t_0)| \leq \sqrt{n}$, $|L(t_2)| \leq \sqrt{n}$, and $t_2 - t_0 \leq \sqrt{n}$. Divide the graph into C, D, E. If $|D| \leq \frac{2n}{3}$, we are done.

4. Otherwise, construct the spanning tree T of D of diameter at most $2\sqrt{n}$.

5. Triangulate if necessary.

6. Construct the plane dual D^* and spanning tree $T^\dagger$.

7. Do DFS on $T^\dagger$ to compute $I, |c|, c$.

8. Find the frond e such that $c(e)$ gives a $\frac{2}{3}$-$\frac{1}{3}$ separator. Let X and Y be the two sets into which D is separated.

9. Let A be the union of the larger of X, Y and the smaller of C, E, let B be the union of the smaller of X, Y and the larger of C, E, and let the separator be the union of $c(e)$, $L(t_0)$, and $L(t_2)$.

Lecture 16   Max Flow

Suppose we are given a tuple $G = (V, c, s, t)$, where V is a set of *vertices*, $s, t \in V$ are distinguished vertices called the *source* and *sink* respectively, and c is a function $c : V^2 \to \mathcal{R}_+$ assigning a nonnegative real *capacity* to each pair of vertices. We make G into a directed graph by defining the set of directed edges

$$ E = \{(u, v) \mid c(u, v) > 0\} \ . $$

Intuitively, we can think of the edges as wires or pipes along which electric current or fluid can flow; the capacity $c(e)$ represents the carrying capacity of the wire or pipe, say in amps or gallons per minute. The *max flow problem* is to determine the maximum possible flow that can be pushed from s to t, and to find a routing that achieves this maximum. The following definition is intended to capture the intuitive idea of a *flow*.

Definition 16.1 A function $f : V^2 \to R$ is called a *flow* if the following three conditions are satisfied:

(a) *skew symmetry*: for all $u, v \in V$,

$$ f(u, v) = -f(v, u) \ ; $$

(b) *conservation of flow at interior vertices*: for all vertices u not in $\{s, t\}$,

$$ \sum_{v \in V} f(u, v) = 0 \ ; $$

84

(c) *capacity constraints*: $f \leq c$ pointwise; *i.e.*, for all u, v,

$$f(u, v) \leq c(u, v) .$$

We say that (u, v) is *saturated* if $f(u, v) = c(u, v)$. □

If we think of edges (u, v) for which $f(u, v) > 0$ as carrying flow *out of* u, and edges (u, v) for which $f(u, v) < 0$ (or equivalently by (a), $f(v, u) > 0$) as carrying flow *into* u, then condition (b) says that the total flow out of any interior vertex is equal to the total flow into that vertex, or in other words, the *net flow* (total flow out minus total flow in) at any interior vertex is 0.

It follows from (a) that $f(u, u) = 0$ for any vertex u.

Figure 1 illustrates a graph with capacities c (ordinary typeface) and a flow f on that graph (italic). Edges not shown have a capacity of 0 and a flow that is the negative of the flow in the opposite direction; *e.g.*, $c(u, s) = 0$ and $f(u, s) = -4$. If neither an edge nor its opposite is shown (*e.g.* (s, t)), then the capacities and flows in both directions are 0.

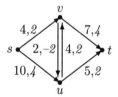

Figure 1

Definition 16.2 An s, t-*cut* (or just *cut*, when s, t are understood) is a pair A, B of disjoint subsets of V whose union is V such that $s \in A$, $t \in B$. The *capacity* of the cut A, B, denoted $c(A, B)$, is

$$c(A, B) \;=\; \sum_{u \in A, \; v \in B} c(u, v) ,$$

i.e., the total capacity of the edges from A to B. If f is a flow, we define the *flow across the cut* A, B to be

$$f(A, B) \;=\; \sum_{u \in A, \; v \in B} f(u, v) .$$

□

Note that by condition (a) of Definition 16.1, $f(A, B)$ gives the *net flow* across the cut from A to B; that is, the sum of the positive flow values on edges from A to B minus the sum of the positive flow values on edges from B to A.

Definition 16.3 The *value* of a flow f, denoted $|f|$, is defined to be

$$\begin{aligned} |f| &= f(\{s\}, V - \{s\}) \\ &= \sum_{v \in V} f(s, v) \,, \end{aligned}$$

or in other words the net flow out of s.   □

In the example of Figure 1, $|f| = 6$.

Although Definition 16.3 defines the value of the flow f with respect to the cut $\{s\}, V - \{s\}$, the flow value will be the same no matter where it is measured:

Lemma 16.4 *For any s,t-cut A, B and flow f,*

$$|f| = f(A, B) \,.$$

Proof. Induction on the cardinality of A, using condition (b) of Definition 16.1.   □

In particular,

$$f(\{s\}, V - \{s\}) = f(V - \{t\}, \{t\}) \,,$$

which says that the net flow out of s equals the net flow into t.

The flow across any cut surely cannot exceed the capacity of the cut. This is expressed in the following lemma:

Lemma 16.5 *For any s,t-cut A, B and flow f,*

$$|f| \leq c(A, B) \,.$$

Proof. Lemma 16.4 and condition (c).   □

The main result of this lecture will be the *Max Flow-Min Cut Theorem*, which states that the minimum cut capacity is achieved by some flow; *i.e.*, the inequality in Lemma 16.5 is an equality for some cut A, B and some flow f^*. The flow f^* necessarily has maximum value among all flows on G by Lemma 16.5, and is called a *max flow*. The flow f^* is not unique, but its value is.

16.1 Residual Capacity

Definition 16.6 Given a flow f on G with capacities c, we define the *residual capacity function* $r : V^2 \to R$ to be the pointwise difference

$$r = c - f \,.$$

The *residual graph* associated with $G = (V, E, c)$ and flow f is the graph $G_f = (V, E_f, r)$, where

$$E_f = \{(u, v) \mid r(u, v) > 0\} \,.$$

                                                                               □

The residual capacity $r(u, v)$ represents the amount of additional flow that could be pushed along the edge (u, v) without violating the capacity constraint (c) of Definition 16.1. In case the flow $f(u, v)$ is negative, this "additional flow" could involve backing off the positive flow from v to u. For example, if $c(u, v) = 8$ and $f(u, v) = 6$, and $(v, u) \notin G$ so that $c(v, u) = 0$, then $r(u, v) = 2$ and $r(v, u) = c(v, u) - f(v, u) = 0 - (-6) = 6$. The residual graph for the flow in Figure 1 is given in Figure 2 below.

Note that the residual graph G_f can have an edge where there was none in G. However, G_f has no edges (u, v) where neither (u, v) nor (v, u) were present in G, so $|E_f| \leq 2 \cdot |E|$.

Intuitively, the formation of the residual graph translates the problem by making f the new origin (zero flow). Solving the residual flow problem is tantamount to solving the original flow problem; a solution to the residual flow problem can be added to f to obtain a solution to the original problem. This observation is formalized in the following lemma.

Lemma 16.7 *Let f be a flow in G, and let G_f be its residual graph.*

(a) *The function f' is a flow in G_f iff $f + f'$ is a flow in G.*

(b) *The function f' is a max flow in G_f if $f + f'$ is a max flow in G.*

(c) *The value function is additive; i.e., $|f + f'| = |f| + |f'|$ and $|f - f'| = |f| - |f'|$.*

(d) *If f is any flow and f^* a max flow in G, then the value of a max flow in G_f is $|f^*| - |f|$.*

Proof.

(a) Since f is a flow, it satisfies skew symmetry $(f(u, v) = -f(v, u))$ and conservation at interior vertices $(\sum_v f(u, v) = 0)$. Thus f' satisfies these properties iff $f + f'$ does. To show that the capacity constraints are satisfied, recall that the capacities of G_f are given by $r = c - f$, where c is the capacity function of G. Then

$$f' \leq r \quad \text{iff} \quad f' \leq c - f$$
$$\text{iff} \quad f + f' \leq c .$$

(b) This follows directly from (a).

(c) By the definition of flow value,

$$|f \pm f'| = \sum_v (f(s, v) \pm f'(s, v))$$
$$= \sum_v f(s, v) \pm \sum_v f'(s, v)$$
$$= |f| \pm |f'| .$$

(d) This follows directly from (b) and (c).

$\square$

16.2   Augmenting Paths

Definition 16.8 Given G and flow f on G, An *augmenting path* is a directed path from s to t in the residual graph G_f.   □

An augmenting path represents a sequence of edges on which the capacity exceeds the flow, *i.e.*, on which the flow can be increased. As observed above, on some edges this "increase" may actually involve decreasing a positive flow in the opposite direction.

Figure 2 illustrates the residual graph associated with the flow in the example of Figure 1 and an augmenting path. The minimum capacity of any edge in this path is 2, so the flow can be increased on these edges by 2, resulting in a new flow in the original graph with value 2 greater than that of $|f|$. Note that the "increase" on (u, v) is essentially a decrease of a positive flow on (v, u).

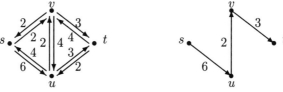

Figure 2

We are now ready to state and prove the main theorem of this lecture:

Theorem 16.9 (Max Flow-Min Cut Theorem [34])   *The following three statements are equivalent:*

(a) f is a max flow in $G = (V, E, c)$;

(b) there is an s, t-cut A, B with $c(A, B) = |f|$;

(c) there does not exist an augmenting path.

   Proof.
   (b) → (a) This is immediate from Lemma 16.5.
   (a) → (c) Suppose there is an augmenting path $u_0, u_1, \ldots, u_n$ with $s = u_0$ and $t = u_n$. Let

$$d \;=\; \min\{r(u_i, u_{i+1}) \mid 0 \le i < n\} \;>\; 0 \,.$$

The quantity d is the smallest residual capacity along the augmenting path and is called the *bottleneck capacity*. An edge along the augmenting path with that capacity is called a *bottleneck edge*. Define the following flow g in the residual graph G_f:

$$
\begin{aligned}
g(u_i, u_{i+1}) &= d, \quad 0 \le i < n \\
g(u_{i+1}, u_i) &= -d, \quad 0 \le i < n \\
g(u, v) &= 0, \quad \text{for all other pairs } (u, v).
\end{aligned}
$$

Then g is a flow in G_f with value d. By Lemma 16.7, $f + g$ is a flow in G and $|f + g| = |f| + |g| = |f| + d$.

(c) $\rightarrow$ (b) Assume there is no augmenting path. Let A consist of all vertices reachable from s by paths in the residual graph. Let $B = V - A$. There are no edges in the residual graph from A to B; thus in G, all edges from A to B are saturated, $i.e.$ $f(u, v) = c(u, v)$. It follows from Lemma 16.4 that $c(A, B) = |f|$. $\qquad\qquad\square$

Lecture 17   More on Max Flow

The Max Flow-Min Cut Theorem gives an algorithm for finding a flow with maximum value in a given network as long as the capacities are rational numbers. This algorithm was first published in 1956 by Ford and Fulkerson [34].

The algorithm works as follows. We begin with the zero flow, then repeatedly find an augmenting path p and push d additional units of flow along p from s to t, where $d > 0$ is the bottleneck capacity of p (minimum edge capacity along p). We continue until it is no longer possible to find an augmenting path, *i.e.* until the residual graph has no path from s to t. We know at that point by the Max Flow-Min Cut Theorem that we have a max flow.

If the edge capacities are integers, this algorithm increases the flow value by at least 1 with each augmentation, hence achieves a maximum flow after at most $|f^*|$ augmentations. Moreover, each augmentation increases the flow by an integral amount, so $|f^*|$ is an integer. Unfortunately, $|f^*|$ can be exponential in the representation of the problem, and the algorithm can run for this long if the augmenting paths are not chosen with some care.

Example 17.1 The following diagram illustrates the first few augmentations in a flow problem with large capacities. The residual graphs are shown on the left-hand side and the augmenting paths on the right. This sequence of augmentations will take 2^{101} steps to converge to a max flow, which has value 2^{101}.

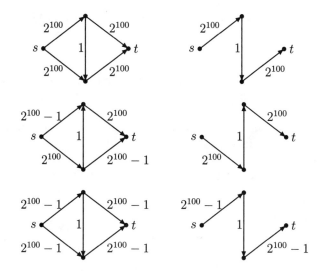

In fact, if the capacities are irrational, the process of repeated augmentation along indiscriminately chosen augmenting paths may not produce a max flow after a finite time, as the following example shows.

Example 17.2 Let r be the positive root of the quadratic $x^2 + x - 1$:

$$r = \frac{-1 + \sqrt{5}}{2} \approx .618\ldots$$

Then $r^2 = 1 - r$, and more generally, $r^{n+2} = r^n - r^{n+1}$ for any $n \geq 0$. Also, since $0 < r < 1$,

$$1 > r > r^2 > r^3 > \cdots > 0 .$$

Note

$$r + 2 = \frac{1}{1 - r} = \sum_{n=0}^{\infty} r^n .$$

Consider the following flow network:

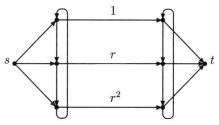

The three horizontal interior edges (call them the *flumes*) have the capacities shown, and all other edges have capacity $r + 2$. The max flow value is $1 + r + r^2 = 2$, since this is the minimum cut capacity obtained by cutting the flumes; any other cut has capacity at least $r + 2 > 2$.

Suppose that in the first augmenting step, we push one unit of flow directly from s to t along the top flume. This leaves residual capacities of $0, r$, and r^2 on the flumes.

Now we perform the following loop, which after n iterations will result in the flumes having residual capacities 0, r^{n+1}, and r^{n+2} in some order: choose the flume with minimum nonzero residual capacity, say d, and push d units of flow from s forward along that flume, back through the saturated flume, and then forward through the remaining flume to t. Suppose that we start with residual capacities $0, r^n$, and r^{n+1} on the flumes. The minimum nonzero residual capacity is r^{n+1}, and the new residual capacities will be r^{n+1}, $r^n - r^{n+1} = r^{n+2}$, and 0, respectively. The situation is the same as before, only rotated.

The loop can be repeated indefinitely, leaving ever higher powers of r on the flumes. We always have sufficient residual capacity on the non-flumes. The residual capacities tend to 0, so the flow value tends to the maximum flow value 2.

With irrational capacities, the sequence of augmentations need not even converge to the maximum flow value. An example of this behavior can be obtained from the graph above by adding an edge (s, t) of weight 1. The same infinite sequence of augmentations converges to a flow of value 2, but the maximum flow value is 3. $\qquad\square$

17.1   Edmonds and Karp's First Heuristic

Edmonds and Karp [30] suggested two heuristics to improve this situation. The first is the following:

> Always augment by a path of maximum bottleneck capacity.

Definition 17.3 A *path flow* in G is a flow f that takes nonzero values only on some simple path from s to t. In other words, there exist a number d and a simple path $u_0, u_1, \ldots, u_k$ with $s = u_0$, $t = u_k$, and such that

$$
\begin{aligned}
f(u_i, u_{i+1}) &= d, & 0 \le i \le k - 1 \\
f(u_{i+1}, u_i) &= -d, & 0 \le i \le k - 1 \\
f(u, v) &= 0, & \text{for all other } (u, v).
\end{aligned}
$$

$\qquad\square$

Lemma 17.4 *Any flow in G can be expressed as a sum of at most m path flows in G and a flow in G of value 0, where m is the number of edges of G.*

Proof. Let f be a flow in G. If $|f| = 0$, we are done. Otherwise, assume $|f| > 0$ (the argument for $|f| < 0$ is symmetric, interchanging the roles of s and t). Define a new capacity function $c'(e) = \max\{f(e), 0\}$ and let G' be the graph with these capacities. Then f is still a flow in G', and since $c' \leq c$, any flow in G' is also a flow in G. By the Max Flow-Min Cut Theorem, the null flow in G' must have an augmenting path, which is a path from s to t with positive capacities; by construction of G', every edge on this path is saturated by f. Take p to be the path flow on that path whose value is the bottleneck capacity. Then the two flows p and $f - p$ are both flows in G', and at least one edge on the path (the bottleneck edge) is saturated by p.

Now we repeat the process with $f - p$ to get $c'' \leq c'$ and G'', and so on. Note that G'' has strictly fewer edges than G', since at least the bottleneck edge of p has disappeared. This process can therefore be repeated at most m times before the flow value vanishes. The original f is then the sum of the remaining flow of value 0 and the path flows found in each step. □

We now consider the complexity of maximum-capacity augmentation.

Theorem 17.5 *If the edge capacities are integers, then the heuristic of augmentation by augmenting paths of maximum bottleneck capacity results in a maximum flow f^* in at most $O(m \log |f^*|)$ augmenting steps.*

Proof. By Lemma 17.4, f^* is a sum of at most m path flows and a flow of value 0, therefore one of the path flows must be of value $|f^*|/m$ or greater. An augmenting path of maximum bottleneck capacity must have at least this capacity. Augmenting by such a path therefore increases the flow value by at least $|f^*|/m$, so by Lemma 16.7(d) of the previous lecture, the max flow in the residual graph has value at most $|f^*| - |f^*|/m = |f^*|(\frac{m-1}{m})$. Thus after k augmenting steps, the max flow in the residual graph has value at most $|f^*|(\frac{m-1}{m})^k$. Hence the number of augmenting steps required to achieve a max flow is no more than the least number k such that

$$|f^*|(\frac{m-1}{m})^k < 1.$$

Using the estimate

$$\log m - \log(m-1) = \Theta(\frac{1}{m}), \tag{24}$$

we obtain $k = \Theta(m \log |f^*|)$. The estimate (24) follows from the limit

$$\lim_{n \to \infty} (1 - \frac{1}{n})^n = \frac{1}{e}.$$

□

Finding a maximum capacity augmenting path can be done efficiently using a modification of Dijkstra's algorithm (Homework 5).

17.2   Edmonds and Karp's Second Heuristic

The method described above is still less than completely satisfactory, since the complexity depends on the capacities. It would be nice to have an algorithm whose asymptotic worst-case complexity is a small polynomial in m and n alone.

The following algorithm produces a max flow in time independent of the edge capacities. This algorithm is also due to Edmonds and Karp [30]. It uses the following heuristic to achieve an $O(m^2n)$ running time:

> Always choose an augmenting path of minimum length.

Definition 17.6 The *level graph* L_G of G is the directed breadth-first search graph of G with root s with sideways and back edges deleted. The *level* of a vertex u is the length of a shortest path from s to u in G. □

Note that the level graph has no edges from level i to level j for $j \geq i+2$. This says that any shortest path from s to any other vertex is a path in the level graph. Any path with either a back or sideways edge of the breadth-first search graph would be strictly longer, since it must contain at least one edge per level anyway.

Lemma 17.7   *(a) Let p be an augmenting path of minimum length in G, let G' be the residual graph obtained by augmenting along p, and let q be an augmenting path of minimum length in G'. Then $|q| \geq |p|$. Thus the length of shortest augmenting paths cannot decrease by applying the above heuristic.*

   (b) We can augment along shortest paths of the same length at most $m = |E|$ times before the length of the shortest augmenting path must increase strictly.

Proof. Choose any path p from s to t in the level graph and augment along p by the bottleneck capacity. After this augmentation, at least one edge of p will be saturated (the bottleneck edge) and will disappear in the residual graph, and at most $|p|$ new edges will appear in the residual graph. All these new edges are back edges and cannot contribute to a shortest path from s to t as long as t is still reachable from s in the level graph. We continue finding paths in the level graph and augmenting by them as long as t is reachable from s. This can occur at most m times, since each time an edge in the level graph disappears. When t is no longer reachable from s in the level graph, then any augmenting path must use a back or side edge, hence must be strictly longer. □

This gives rise to the following algorithm:

Algorithm 17.8 (Edmonds and Karp [30]) Find the level graph L_G. Repeatedly augment along paths in L_G, updating residual capacities and deleting edges with zero capacity until t is no longer reachable from s. Then calculate a new level graph from the residual graph at that point and repeat. Continue as long as t is reachable from s.

With each level graph calculation, the distance from s to t increases by at least 1 by Lemma 17.7(a), so there are at most n level graph calculations. For each level graph calculation, there are at most m augmentations by Lemma 17.7(b). Thus there are at most mn augmentations in all. Each augmentation requires time $O(m)$ by DFS or BFS, or $O(m^2n)$ in all. It takes time $O(m)$ to calculate the level graphs by BFS, or $O(mn)$ time in all. Therefore the running time of the entire algorithm is $O(m^2n)$.

Lecture 18   Still More on Max Flow

18.1   Dinic's Algorithm

We follow Tarjan's presentation [100]. In the Edmonds-Karp algorithm, we continue to augment by path flows along paths in the level graph L_G until every path from s to t in L_G contains at least one saturated edge. The flow at that point is called a *blocking flow*. The following modification, which improves the running time to $O(mn^2)$, was given by Dinic in 1970 [29]. Rather than constructing a blocking flow path by path, the algorithm constructs a blocking flow all at once by finding a maximal set of minimum-length augmenting paths. Each such construction is called a *phase*.

The following algorithm describes one phase. As in Edmonds-Karp, there are at most n phases, because with each phase the minimum distance from s to t in the residual graph increases by at least one. We traverse the level graph from source to sink in a depth-first fashion, advancing whenever possible and keeping track of the path from s to the current vertex. If we get all the way to t, we have found an augmenting path, and we augment by that path. If we get to a vertex with no outgoing edges, we delete that vertex (there is no path to t through it) and retreat.

In the following, u denotes the vertex currently being visited and p is a path from s to u.

Algorithm 18.1 (Dinic [29])

Initialize. Construct a new level graph L_G. Set $u := s$ and $p := [s]$. Go to **Advance**.

Advance. If there is no edge out of u, go to **Retreat**. Otherwise, let (u, v) be such an edge. Set $p := p \cdot [v]$ and $u := v$. If $v \neq t$ then go to **Advance**. If $v = t$ then go to **Augment**.

Retreat. If $u = s$ then halt. Otherwise, delete u and all adjacent edges from L_G and remove u from the end of p. Set $u :=$ the last vertex on p. Go to **Advance**.

Augment. Let Δ be the bottleneck capacity along p. Augment by the path flow along p of value Δ, adjusting residual capacities along p. Delete newly saturated edges. Set $u :=$ the last vertex on the path p reachable from s along unsaturated edges of p; that is, the start vertex of the first newly saturated edge on p. Set $p :=$ the portion of p up to and including u. Go to **Advance**.

We now discuss the complexity of these operations.

Initialize. This is executed only once per phase and takes $O(m)$ time using BFS.

Advance. There are at most $2mn$ advances in each phase, because there can be at most n advances before an augment or retreat, and there are at most m augments and m retreats. Each advance takes constant time, so the total time for all advances is $O(mn)$.

Retreat. There are at most n retreats in each phase, because at least one vertex is deleted in each retreat. Each retreat takes $O(1)$ time plus the time to delete edges, which in all is $O(m)$; thus the time taken by all retreats in a phase is $O(m + n)$.

Augment. There are at most m augments in each phase, because at least one edge is deleted each time. Each augment takes $O(n)$ time, or $O(mn)$ time in all.

Each phase then requires $O(mn)$ time. Because there are at most n phases, the total running time is $O(mn^2)$.

18.2 The MPM Algorithm

The following algorithm given by Malhotra, Pramodh-Kumar, and Maheshwari in 1978 [77] produces a max flow in $O(n^3)$ time. The overall structure is similar to the Edmonds-Karp or Dinic algorithms. Blocking flows are found for level graphs of increasing depth. The algorithm's superior time bound is due a faster $(O(n^2))$ method for producing a blocking flow.

For this algorithm, we need to consider the capacity of a vertex as opposed to the capacity of an edge. Intuitively, the capacity of a vertex is the maximum amount of commodity that can be pushed through that vertex.

Definition 18.2 The *capacity* $c(v)$ of a vertex v is the minimum of the total capacity of its incoming edges and the total capacity of its outgoing edges:

$$c(v) \;=\; \min\{\sum_{u\in V} c(u,v), \; \sum_{u\in V} c(v,u)\} \;.$$

□

This definition applies as well to residual capacities obtained by subtracting a nonzero flow.

The MPM algorithm proceeds in phases. In each phase, the residual graph is computed for the current flow, and the level graph L is computed. If t does not appear in L, we are done. Otherwise, all vertices not on a path from s to t in the level graph are deleted.

Now we repeat the following steps until a blocking flow is achieved:

1. Find a vertex v of minimum capacity d according to Definition 18.2. If $d = 0$, do step 2. If $d \neq 0$, do step 3.

2. Delete v and all incident edges and update the capacities of the neighboring vertices. Go to 1.

3. Push d units of flow from v to the sink and pull d units of flow from the source to v to increase the flow through v by d. This is done as follows:

   Push to sink. The outgoing edges of v are saturated in order, leaving at most one partially saturated edge. All edges that become saturated during this process are deleted. This process is then repeated on each vertex that received flow during the saturation of the edges out of v, and so on all the way to t. It is always possible to push all d units of flow all the way to t, since every vertex has capacity at least d.

   Pull from source. The incoming edges of v are saturated in order, leaving at most one partially saturated edge. All edges that become saturated by this process are deleted. This process is then repeated on each vertex from which flow was taken during the saturation of the edges into v, and so on all the way back to s. It is always possible to pull all d units of flow all the way back to s, since every vertex has capacity at least d.

   Either all incoming edges of v or all outgoing edges of v are saturated and hence deleted, so v and all its remaining incident edges can be deleted from the level graph, and the capacities of the neighbors updated. Go to 1.

It takes $O(m)$ time to compute the residual graph for the current flow and level graph using BFS. Using Fibonacci heaps, it takes $O(n \log n)$ time amortized over all iterations of the loop to find and delete a vertex of minimum capacity. It takes $O(m)$ time over all iterations of the loop to delete all the fully saturated edges, since we spend $O(1)$ time for each such edge. It takes $O(n^2)$ time over all iterations of the loop to do the partial saturations, because it is done at most once in step 3 at each vertex for each choice of v in step 1.

Note that when we delete edges, we must decrement the capacities of neighboring vertices; this is done using the decrement facility of Fibonacci heaps.

The loop thus achieves a blocking flow in $O(n^2)$ time. As before, at most n blocking flows have to be computed, because the distance from s to t in the level graph increases by at least one each time. This gives an overall worst-case time bound of $O(n^3)$.

The max flow problem is still an active topic of research. Although $O(n^3)$

remains the best known time bound for general graphs, new approaches to the max flow problem and better time bounds for sparse graphs have appeared more recently [38, 98, 4, 41, 95, 37].

18.3 Applications of Max Flow

Bipartite Matching

Definition 18.3 A *matching M* of a graph G is a subset of edges such that no two edges in M share a vertex. We denote the size of M by $|M|$. A *maximum matching* is one of maximum size.   □

We can use any max flow algorithm to produce a maximum matching in a bipartite graph $G = (U, V, E)$ as follows. Add a new source vertex s and a new sink vertex t, connect s to every vertex in U, and connect every vertex in V to t. Assign every edge capacity 1. The edges from U to V used by a maximum integral flow give a maximum matching.

Minimum Connectivity

Let $G = (V, E)$ be a connected undirected graph. What is the least number of edges we need to remove in order to disconnect G? This is known as the *minimum connectivity problem*.

The minimum connectivity problem can be solved by solving $n - 1$ max flow problems. Replace each undirected edge with two directed edges, one in each direction. Assign capacity 1 to each edge. Let s be a fixed vertex in V and let t range over all other vertices. Find the max flow for each value of t, and take the minimum over all choices of t. This also gives a minimum cut, which gives a solution to the minimum connectivity problem.

Lecture 19   Matching

Matching refers to a class of problems with many important applications. Assigning instructors to courses or students to seminars with limited enrollment are two examples of matching problems.

Formally, matching problems are expressed as problems on graphs. We will consider four different versions, depending on whether the graph is bipartite or not and whether the graph is weighted or unweighted. The bipartite case is considerably easier, so we will concentrate on that case.

Definition 19.1 Given an undirected graph $G = (V, E)$ with edge weights w, a *matching* is a subset $M \subseteq E$ such that no two edges in M share a vertex. The *maximum-weight matching problem* is to find a matching M such that the sum of the weights of the edges in M is maximum over all possible matchings. If all the weights are 1, then we get the *unweighted matching problem*, which just asks for a matching of maximum cardinality.   □

Definition 19.2 Given a matching M in $G = (V, E)$, an edge $e \in E$ is *matched* if $e \in M$ and *free* if $e \in E - M$. A vertex v is *matched* if v has an incident matched edge, *free* otherwise.   □

Definition 19.3 A *perfect matching* is a matching in which every vertex is matched.   □

Definition 19.4 Given a matching M in $G = (V, E)$, a path (cycle) in G is an *alternating path (cycle)* with respect to the matching M if it is simple (*i.e.,*

has no repeated vertices) and consists of alternating matched and free edges.
The length of a path or cycle p is the number of edges in p and is denoted $|p|$.
An alternating path is an *augmenting path* (with respect to M) if its endpoints
are free.   □

For example, consider the following graph.

The solid edges form a maximum matching that is also a perfect matching.
The dashed edges form a maximal matching that is not maximum (it is maximal because it is not a proper subset of any other matching). With respect to
the dashed matching, the edges (1,4) and (2,5) are matched, the edges (1,5),
(2,6), and (3,4) are free, the vertices 1,2,4, and 5 are matched, and the vertices
3 and 6 are free. With respect to the dashed matching, the alternating path
3,4,1,5,2,6 is an augmenting path.

Let $\oplus$ be the symmetric difference operator on sets:

$$
\begin{aligned}
A \oplus B &= (A \cup B) - (A \cap B) \\
&= (A - B) \cup (B - A) .
\end{aligned}
$$

In other words, $A \oplus B$ is the set of elements that are in one of A or B, but not
both. If M is a matching and p an augmenting path with respect to M, then
considering p as its set of edges, the set $M \oplus p$ is a matching of cardinality
$|M| + 1$. Note that $M \oplus p$ agrees with M on edges outside of p, and every
edge in p that is matched in M is unmatched in $M \oplus p$ and vice-versa.

The following early theorem of Berge [10] gives the foundation for an efficient matching algorithm.

Theorem 19.5 (Berge [10]) *A matching M in a graph G is a maximum
matching if and only if there is no augmenting path in M.*

This theorem follows immediately from the following enhanced version due
to Hopcroft and Karp [51].

Theorem 19.6 (Hopcroft and Karp [51]) *If M is a matching in G, M^*
is a maximum matching in G, and $k = |M^*| - |M|$, then with respect to M
there is a set of k vertex-disjoint augmenting paths. Moreover, at least one of
them has length at most $\frac{n}{k} - 1$, where n is the number of vertices in G.*

Proof. Consider $M \oplus M^*$. No vertex can have more than one incident edge from M or more than one incident edge from M^*, so no vertex can have more than two incident edges from $M \oplus M^*$. The set $M \oplus M^*$ therefore consists of a collection of vertex-disjoint alternating paths and cycles, as illustrated. Here the solid lines indicate edges of M and the dashed lines indicate edges of M^*.

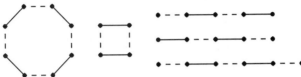

Each odd-length path p has either one more M edge than M^* edge or one more M^* edge than M edge. However, the former is impossible, since then p would be an augmenting path with respect to M^*, thus M^* would not be maximum.

Using the assumption that $|M^*| = |M| + k$,

$$
\begin{aligned}
|M^* - M| &= |M^*| - |M^* \cap M| \\
&= |M| - |M^* \cap M| + k \\
&= |M - M^*| + k \ .
\end{aligned}
$$

In other words there are exactly k more M^* edges in $M^* \oplus M$ than M edges. The extra k M^* edges must come from paths of odd length with one more M^* edge than M edge. Cycles and paths of even length have the same number of M as M^* edges, and as we have observed, there are no odd-length paths with one more M than M^* edge. These k odd-length paths with one more M^* than M edge have endpoints that are free with respect to M, therefore are augmenting paths in M.

It is impossible for all of these paths to have length greater than $\frac{n}{k} - 1$, because then we would have more than n vertices. Therefore at least one of the paths has length less than or equal to $\frac{n}{k} - 1$. $\square$

19.1 Weighted Matchings

Definition 19.7 Let M be a matching in a graph G with edge weights w. For any set A of edges, define

$$
w(A) \;=\; \sum_{e \in A} w(e) \ .
$$

Define the *incremental weight* $\Delta(p)$ of a set B of edges to be the total weight of the unmatched edges in B minus the total weight of the matched edges in B:

$$
\Delta(B) \;=\; w(B - M) - w(B \cap M) \ .
$$

$\square$

If p is an augmenting path with respect to M, then $\Delta(p)$ is the net change in the weight of the matching after augmenting by p:

$$w(M \oplus p) \;=\; w(M) + \Delta(p) \;. \tag{25}$$

Here is a good heuristic to use when selecting augmenting paths for maximum weight matching:

> Always use an augmenting path of maximum incremental weight.

Lemma 19.8 *If M is a matching of size k that is of maximum weight among all matchings of size k, and if p is an augmenting path with respect to M of maximum incremental weight, then $M \oplus p$ is a matching of size $k+1$ that is of maximum weight among all matchings of size $k+1$.*

Proof. By (25), it suffices to show that if M' is a matching of maximum weight among all matchings of size $k+1$, then there exists an augmenting path p with respect to M such that

$$
\begin{aligned}
w(M') &= w(M \oplus p) \\
&= w(M) + \Delta(p) \;.
\end{aligned}
$$

Consider $M \oplus M'$. As before, this is a set of vertex-disjoint cycles, even-length paths, and odd-length paths. The incremental weight of each cycle must be 0, because otherwise it would be possible to exchange the M and M' edges on this cycle to increase the weight of either M or M', which by assumption is impossible. The even-length paths must have incremental weight 0 for the same reason. Thus only the odd-length paths in $M \oplus M'$ can have nonzero weight.

Each odd-length path has either an extra M edge or an extra M' edge. Since there is one more edge in M' than in M, there must be exactly one more path with an extra M' edge than there are paths with an extra M edge.

Pair each path with an extra M edge with a path with an extra M' edge. This will leave all paths paired except for one path p which has an extra M' edge. The incremental weight of each pair must be 0, because otherwise it would be possible to increase the weight of either M or M' by switching M and M' edges in this pair. Therefore

$$
\begin{aligned}
\Delta(p) &= \Delta(M \oplus M') \\
&= w(M') - w(M) \;.
\end{aligned}
$$

The path p is an augmenting path with respect to M, and the matching $M \oplus p$ has $k+1$ edges and weight equal to the weight of M', therefore it too is of maximum weight among all matchings of size $k+1$. $\square$

In the next lecture we will show

Lemma 19.9 *Let M^* be a matching of maximum weight among all matchings and let M be a matching of size k of maximum weight over all matchings of size at most k. If $w(M^*) > w(M)$, then M has an augmenting path with respect to M of positive incremental weight.*

Theorem 19.10 *If one always augments by an augmenting path of maximum incremental weight, then one arrives at a matching of maximum weight after at most $\frac{n}{2}$ steps.*

Lecture 20   More on Matching

Let G be an undirected graph with weight function w. Recall from last lecture that the weight of a matching M in G, denoted $w(M)$, is the sum of the weights of the edges in M, and the incremental weight of a set A of edges, denoted $\Delta(A)$, is the sum of the weights of the unmatched edges in A less the sum of the weights of the matched edges in A. For an augmenting path p, $\Delta(p)$ gives the net change in weight that would be obtained by augmenting by p.

We ended the last lecture by proving the following lemma:

Lemma 20.1 *Let M be a matching of size k of maximum weight among all matchings of size k. If we augment M by an augmenting path of maximum incremental weight, then we obtain a matching of size $k+1$ of maximum weight among all matchings of size $k + 1$.*

We also need to know that an augmenting path of positive incremental weight exists. This is established in the following lemma.

Lemma 20.2 *Let M be a matching of size k of maximum weight among all matchings of size at most k and let M^* be a matching of maximum weight among all matchings in G. If $w(M^*) > w(M)$, then M has an augmenting path of positive incremental weight.*

Proof. Again, consider the symmetric difference $M^* \oplus M$. As argued in the last lecture, this is a set of vertex-disjoint cycles and paths of alternating edges from M and M^*. We pair the odd-length paths as we did in the last lecture, with each pair consisting of one path with one more M than M^* edge and the other with one more M^* than M edge. We are left with a number of odd-length paths.

Each cycle and path of even length has incremental weight 0, otherwise the M and M^* edges could be switched to increase the weight of either M or M^*, contradicting the maximality of M or M^*. By the same argument, the incremental weights of the pairs of odd-length paths are 0. Thus we are left with a set of unpaired odd-length paths. Either all these paths have one more M^* edge than M edge or they all have one more M edge than M^* edge (otherwise there would be another pair). The latter is impossible, because then M^* would be a matching of greater weight and smaller cardinality than M, contradicting our assumptions. Thus all these unpaired paths are augmenting paths with respect to M. If we augment by all of them simultaneously, we achieve a maximum matching of weight $w(M^*) > w(M)$; therefore, at least one of them must have positive incremental weight.   □

Thus we can construct a maximum-weight matching by beginning with the empty matching and repeatedly performing augmentations using augmenting paths of maximum incremental weight until a maximum matching is achieved. This takes at most $\frac{n}{2}$ augmentations, since the number of matched vertices increases by two each time. We will show below how to obtain augmenting paths efficiently in bipartite graphs.

20.1   Unweighted Bipartite Matching

Now we will see an $O(m\sqrt{n})$ algorithm of Hopcroft and Karp [51] for unweighted matching in bipartite graphs. Micali and Vazirani [80, 105] have given an algorithm of similar complexity for general graphs.

The idea underlying the algorithm of Hopcroft and Karp is similar to Dinic's idea for maximum flow. The algorithm proceeds in phases. In each phase, we find a maximal set of vertex-disjoint minimum-length augmenting paths, and augment by them simultaneously. In other words, we find a set S of augmenting paths with the following properties:

(i) if the minimum-length augmenting path is of length k, then all paths in S are of length k;

(ii) no two paths in S share a vertex;

(iii) if p is any augmenting path of length k not in S, then p shares a vertex with some path in S; *i.e.*, S is a setwise maximal set with the properties (i) and (ii).

We will need the following three lemmas:

Lemma 20.3 *A maximal set S of vertex-disjoint minimum-length augmenting paths can be found in time $O(m)$.*

Lemma 20.4 *After each phase, the length of a minimum-length augmenting path increases by at least two.*

Lemma 20.5 *There are at most $\sqrt{n}$ phases.*

Proof of Lemma 20.3. Let $G = (U, V, E)$ be the undirected bipartite graph we are working in, and let M be a matching in G. We will grow a "Hungarian tree" from G and M. Calling it a tree is somewhat misleading, since the Hungarian tree is really a dag. It is obtained in linear time by a procedure similar to breadth-first search. We start with the free (unmatched) vertices in U at level 0. Starting from an even level $2k$, the vertices at level $2k + 1$ are obtained by following *free (unmatched)* edges from vertices at level $2k$. Starting from an odd level $2k + 1$, the vertices at level $2k + 2$ are obtained by following *matched* edges from vertices at level $2k + 1$. Since the graph is bipartite, the even levels contain only vertices in U and the odd levels contain only vertices in V. We do not expand a vertex that has been seen at an earlier level.

We continue building the Hungarian tree and adding more levels until all vertices have been seen at least once before or until we encounter a free vertex at an odd level (say t). In the latter case, every free vertex at level t is in V and is the terminus of an augmenting path of minimum length. Note that free vertices in U can be encountered only at level 0, since vertices at even levels greater than 0 are matched.

Example 20.6 The following figure illustrates a bipartite graph with a partial matching and its Hungarian tree. The solid lines indicate matched edges and the dashed lines free edges.

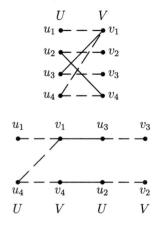

$\square$

Now we find a maximal set S of vertex-disjoint paths in the Hungarian tree. We will use a technique called *topological erase*, called so because it is reminiscent of the topological sort algorithm we saw in Lecture 1. With each vertex x except those at level 0 we associate an integer counter initially containing the number of edges entering x from the previous level. Starting at a free vertex v at the last level t, we trace a path back until arriving at a free vertex u at level 0. This path is an augmenting path, and we include it in S. We then place all vertices along this path on a deletion queue. As long as the deletion queue is nonempty, we remove a vertex from the queue and delete it and all incident edges from the Hungarian tree. Whenever an edge is deleted, the counter associated with its right endpoint is decremented. If the counter becomes 0, the vertex is placed on the deletion queue (there can be no augmenting path in the Hungarian tree through this vertex, since all incoming edges have been deleted). After the queue becomes empty, if there is still a free vertex v at level t, then there must be a path from v backwards through the Hungarian tree to a free vertex on the first level, so we can repeat the process. We continue as long as there exist free vertices at level t. The entire process takes linear time, since the amount of work is proportional to the number of edges deleted.   □

In order to prove Lemma 20.4 we will use the following lemma:

Lemma 20.7 *Let p be an augmenting path of minimum length with respect to some matching M, let M' be the matching obtained by augmenting M by p, and let q be an augmenting path in M'. Then*

$$|q| \geq |p| + 2|p \cap q| , \tag{26}$$

where $|q|$ and $|p|$ denote the number of edges of q and p, respectively, and $p \cap q$ denotes the set of edges common to p and q.

Proof of Lemma 20.7. If q and p are vertex-disjoint, then q is also an augmenting path with respect to M. Then $|q| \geq |p|$, since p is of minimum length, and (26) holds since the intersection is empty.

Otherwise, consider the symmetric difference $p \oplus q$ of the two paths. We observe the following facts.

(i) All edges in $q - p$ are in M if and only if they are in M'. This is because augmenting M by p only changes the status of edges on p.

(ii) Each time q joins (leaves) p it is immediately after (before) a free edge. This is because each vertex in p already has one adjacent edge in $p \cap M'$.

(iii) The endpoints of q are not contained in p, since they are free in M'.

It follows from property (iii) that $p \oplus q$ contains exactly four free vertices with respect to the original matching M, namely the endpoints of p and the endpoints of q. Thus $p \oplus q$, considered with respect to M, consists of exactly two augmenting paths and possibly some disjoint cycles as well. Each of the two paths must be at least as long as p, since p was of minimum length; thus $|p \oplus q| \geq 2|p|$. But

$$|q| + |p| = |p \oplus q| + 2|p \cap q| \geq 2|p| + 2|p \cap q|,$$

from which (26) follows. □

Example 20.8 Lemma 20.7 is illustrated in the following picture.

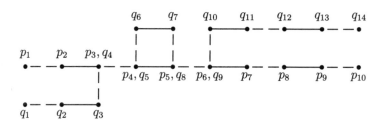

In this example, the solid lines represent edges in M and the dashed lines represent edges not in M. The path $p_1, \ldots, p_{10}$ is an augmenting path with respect to the matching M, and $q_1, \ldots, q_{14}$ is an augmenting path after augmenting M by $p_1, \ldots, p_{10}$. The paths $p_1, p_2, p_3, q_3, q_2, q_1$ and $q_{14}, \ldots, q_9, p_7, \ldots, p_{10}$ are also augmenting paths with respect to M. The path $q_5, \ldots, q_8$ forms an alternating cycle with respect to M. □

Proof of Lemma 20.4. Suppose that at some phase we augmented M by a maximal set S of vertex-disjoint paths of minimum length k to obtain a new matching M'. Consider any augmenting path q with respect to M'. If q is vertex-disjoint from every path in S, then its length must be greater than k, otherwise S was not maximal. If on the other hand q shares a vertex with $p \in S$, then $p \cap q$ contains at least one edge in M', since every vertex in p is matched in M'. By Lemma 20.7, $|q|$ exceeds $|p|$ by at least two. □

Proof of Lemma 20.5. Let M^* be a maximum matching and let M be the matching obtained after $\frac{1}{2}\sqrt{n}$ phases. The length of any augmenting path with respect to M is at least $\sqrt{n}$. By a lemma from the last lecture, $M^* \oplus M$ contains a set T of exactly $|M^*| - |M|$ vertex-disjoint augmenting paths, and augmenting by all of them gives a maximum matching. But there can be at most $\sqrt{n}$ elements of T, otherwise they would account for more than n vertices. Thus $|M^*| - |M| \leq \sqrt{n}$. Since each phase increases the size of the matching by at least one, at most $\sqrt{n}$ more phases are needed. □

Since each phase requires $O(m)$ time and there are at most $O(\sqrt{n})$ phases, the total running time of the algorithm is $O(m\sqrt{n})$.

Lecture 21   Reductions and
NP-Completeness

We have seen several problems such as maximum flow and matching that at first glance appear intractible, but upon closer study admit very efficient algorithms. Unfortunately, this is the exception rather than the rule. For every interesting problem with a polynomial-time algorithm, there are dozens for which all known solutions require exponential time in the worst case. These problems occur in various fields, to wit:

Logic:

- *CNF satisfiability (CNFSat):* given a Boolean formula $\mathcal{B}$ in conjunctive normal form (CNF), is there a truth assignment that satisfies $\mathcal{B}$?

Graph Theory:

- *Clique:* given a graph $G = (V, E)$ and an integer m, does G contain K_m (the complete graph on m vertices) as a subgraph?

- *k-Colorability:* given a graph $G = (V, E)$ and an integer k, is there a coloring of G with k or fewer colors? A *coloring* is a map $\chi : V \to C$ such that no two adjacent vertices have the same color; *i.e.*, if $(u, v) \in E$ then $\chi(u) \neq \chi(v)$.

Operations Research:

- Any of a number of generalizations of the one-processor scheduling problem of Miscellaneous Exercise 4.

- *Integer Programming*: given a set of linear constraints A and a linear function f, find an integer point maximizing f subject to the constraints A.

- The *Traveling Salesman Problem (TSP)*: given a set of cities and distances between them, find a tour of minimum total distance visiting all cities at least once.

None of these problems are known to have a polynomial time solution. For example, the best known solutions to the Boolean satisfiability problem are not much better than essentially evaluating the given formula on all 2^n truth assignments. On the other hand, no one has been able to prove that no substantially better algorithm exists, either.

However, we can show that all these problems are computationally equivalent in the sense that if one of them is solvable by an efficient algorithm, then they all are. This involves the concept of *reduction*. Intuitively, a problem A is said to be *reducible* to a problem B if there is a way to encode instances x of problem A as instances $\sigma(x)$ of problem B. The encoding function σ is called a *reduction*. If σ is suitably efficient, then any efficient algorithm for B will yield an efficient algorithm for A by composing it with σ.

The theory has even deeper implications than this. There is a very general class of decision problems called *NP*, which roughly speaking consists of problems that can be solved efficiently by a nondeterministic guess-and-verify algorithm. A problem is said to be *NP-complete* if it is in this class and every other problem in *NP* reduces to it. Essentially, it is a hardest problem in the class *NP*. If an *NP*-complete problem has an efficient deterministic solution, then so do all problems in *NP*. All of the problems named above are known to be *NP*-complete.

The theory of efficient reductions and *NP*-completeness was initiated in the early 1970s. The two principal papers that first demonstrated the importance of these concepts were by Cook [22], who showed that Boolean satisfiability was *NP*-complete, and Karp [57, 58] who showed that many interesting combinatorial problems were interreducible and hence *NP*-complete. Garey and Johnson's text [39] provides an excellent introduction to the theory of *NP*-completeness and contains an extensive list of *NP*-complete problems. By now the problems known to be *NP*-complete number in the thousands.

21.1   Some Efficient Reductions

We have seen examples of reductions in previous lectures. For example, Boolean matrix multiplication and transitive closure were shown to be reducible to each other. To illustrate the concept further, we show that CNFSat, the satisfiability problem for Boolean formulas in conjunctive normal form, is reducible to the clique problem.

Definition 21.1 Let B be a Boolean formula. A *literal* is either a variable or the negation of a variable (we write $\neg x$ and $\overline{x}$ interchangeably). A *clause* is a disjunction of literals, *e.g.* $C = (x_1 \vee \neg x_2 \vee x_3)$. The formula B is said to be in *conjunctive normal form (CNF)* if it is a conjunction of clauses $C_1 \wedge C_2 \wedge \cdots \wedge C_m$. □

Note that to satisfy a formula in CNF, a truth assignment must assign the value *true* to at least one literal in each clause, and different occurrences of the same literal in different clauses must receive the same truth value.

Given a Boolean formula B in CNF, we show how to construct a graph G and an integer k such that G has a clique of size k iff B is satisfiable. We take k to be the number of clauses in B. The vertices of G are all the *occurrences* of literals in B. There is an edge of G between two such occurrences if they are in different clauses and the two literals are not complementary. For example, the formula

$$\begin{array}{ccccc} C_1 & & C_2 & & C_3 \\ (x_1 \vee x_2) & \wedge & (\overline{x}_1 \vee \overline{x}_2) & \wedge & (x_1 \vee \overline{x}_2) \end{array}$$

would yield the graph

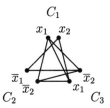

The graph G is k-partite and has a k-clique iff B is satisfiable. Essentially, an edge between two occurrences of literals represents the ability to assign them both *true* without a local conflict; a k-clique thus represents the ability to assign *true* to at least one literal from each clause without global conflict. In the example above, $k = 3$ and there are two 3-cliques (triangles) corresponding to two ways to satisfy the formula.

Let us prove formally that G has a k-clique iff B is satisfiable. First assume that B is satisfiable. Let $\tau : \{x_1, \ldots, x_n\} \rightarrow \{true, false\}$ be a truth assignment satisfying B. At least one literal in each clause must be assigned *true* under τ. Choose one such literal from each clause. The vertices of G corresponding to these true literals are all connected to each other because no pair is complementary, so they form a k-clique. Conversely, suppose G has a k-clique. Since G is k-partite and the partition elements correspond to the clauses, the k-clique must have exactly one vertex in each clause. Assign *true* to the literals corresponding to the vertices in the clique. This can be done without conflict, since no pair of complementary literals appears in the clique. Assign truth values to the remaining variables arbitrarily. The resulting truth assignment assigns *true* to at least one literal in each clause, thus satisfies $\mathcal{B}$.

We have just shown how to encode a given instance of the CNFSat problem in an instance of the clique problem, or in the accepted parlance, *reduced* the CNFSat problem to the clique problem.

An important caveat: a reduction reduces the problem being encoded to the problem encoding it. Sometimes you hear it said backwards; for example, that the construction above reduces Clique to CNFSat. This is incorrect.

Although we do not know how to solve Clique or CNFSat in any less than exponential time, we do know by the above reduction that if tomorrow someone were to come up with a polynomial-time algorithm for Clique, we would immediately be able to derive a polynomial-time algorithm for CNFSat: given $\mathcal{B}$, just produce the graph G and k as above, and apply the polynomial-time algorithm for Clique. For the same reason, if tomorrow someone were to show an exponential lower bound for CNFSat, we would automatically have an exponential lower bound for Clique.

We show for purposes of illustration that there is a simple reduction in the other direction as well. To reduce Clique to CNFSat, we must show how to construct from a given undirected graph $G = (V, E)$ and a number k a Boolean formula $\mathcal{B}$ in CNF such that G has a clique of size k if and only if $\mathcal{B}$ is satisfiable.

Given $G = (V, E)$ and k, take as Boolean variables x_i^u for $u \in V$ and $1 \leq i \leq k$. Intuitively, x_i^u says, "u is the ith element of the clique." The formula $\mathcal{B}$ is the conjunction of three subformulas $\mathcal{C}$, $\mathcal{D}$ and $\mathcal{E}$, with the following intuitive meanings and formal definitions:

- $\mathcal{C}$ = "For every i, $1 \leq i \leq k$, there is at least one $u \in V$ such that u is the ith element of the clique."

$$\mathcal{C} = \bigwedge_{i=1}^{k} (\bigvee_{u \in V} x_i^u) .$$

- $\mathcal{D}$ = "For every i, $1 \leq i \leq k$, no two distinct vertices are both the ith element of the clique."

$$\mathcal{D} = \bigwedge_{i=1}^{k} \bigwedge_{\substack{u, v \in V \\ u \neq v}} (\neg x_i^u \vee \neg x_i^v) .$$

- $\mathcal{E}$ = "If u and v are in the clique, then (u, v) is an edge of G. Equivalently, if (u, v) is not an edge, then either u is not in the clique or v is not in the clique."

$$\mathcal{E} \;=\; \bigwedge_{(u,v)\notin E} \bigwedge_{1\le i,j\le k} (\neg x_i^u \lor \neg x_j^v) \,.$$

We take $\mathcal{B} = \mathcal{C} \land \mathcal{D} \land \mathcal{E}$. Any satisfying assignment τ for $\mathcal{C} \land \mathcal{D}$ picks out a set of k vertices, namely those u such that $\tau(x_i^u) = true$ for some i, $1 \le i \le k$. If τ also satisfies $\mathcal{E}$, then those k vertices form a clique. Conversely, if $u_1, \ldots, u_k$ is a k-clique in G, set $\tau(x_i^{u_i}) = true$, $1 \le i \le k$, and set $\tau(y) = false$ for all other variables y; this truth assignment satisfies $\mathcal{B}$.

It is perhaps surprising that two problems so apparently different as CN-FSat and Clique should be computationally equivalent. However, this turns out to be a widespread phenomenon.

Lecture 22   More on Reductions and
NP-Completeness

Before we give a formal definition of reduction, let us clarify the notion of a
decision problem. Informally, a decision problem is a yes-or-no question. A
decision problem is given by a description of the *problem domain, i.e.* the set
of all possible instances of the problem, along with a description of the set of
"yes" instances.

For example, consider the problem of determining whether a given undirected graph G has a k-clique. An instance of the problem is a pair (G, k),
and the problem domain is the set of all such pairs. The "yes" instances are
the pairs (G, k) for which G has a clique of size k.

There are many interesting discrete problems that are not decision problems. For example, many optimization problems like the traveling salesman
problem or the integer programming problem ask for the calculation of an
object that maximizes some objective function. However, many of these problems have closely related decision problems that are no simpler to solve than
the optimization problem. For the purposes of this discussion of reductions
and *NP*-completeness, we will restrict our attention to decision problems.

Definition 22.1 Let $A \subseteq \Sigma$ and $B \subseteq \Gamma$ be decision problems. (Here Σ and
Γ are the problem domains, and A and B are the "yes" instances.) We write
$A \leq^{\mathrm{p}}_{\mathrm{m}} B$ and say that A *reduces to* B *in polynomial time* if there is a function
$\sigma : \Sigma \to \Gamma$ such that

- σ is computable by a deterministic Turing machine in polynomial time;

- for all problem instances $x \in \Sigma$,

$$x \in A \quad \text{iff} \quad \sigma(x) \in B .$$

We write $A \equiv_{\mathrm{m}}^{\mathrm{P}} B$ if both $A \leq_{\mathrm{m}}^{\mathrm{P}} B$ and $B \leq_{\mathrm{m}}^{\mathrm{P}} A$.   □

The reducibility relation $\leq_{\mathrm{m}}^{\mathrm{P}}$ is often called *polynomial-time many-one* or *Karp* reducibility. The superscript p stands for *polynomial-time*. The subscript m stands for *many-one* and describes the function σ, and is included to distinguish $\leq_{\mathrm{m}}^{\mathrm{P}}$ from another popular polynomial-time reducibility relation $\leq_{\mathrm{T}}^{\mathrm{P}}$, often called *polynomial-time Turing* or *Cook* reducibility. The relation $\leq_{\mathrm{m}}^{\mathrm{P}}$ is stronger than $\leq_{\mathrm{T}}^{\mathrm{P}}$ in the sense that

$$A \leq_{\mathrm{m}}^{\mathrm{P}} B \quad \to \quad A \leq_{\mathrm{T}}^{\mathrm{P}} B .$$

The formal definition of $\leq_{\mathrm{T}}^{\mathrm{P}}$ involves oracle Turing machines and can be found in [39, pp. 111ff.].

Intuitively, if $A \leq_{\mathrm{m}}^{\mathrm{P}} B$ then A is no harder than B. In particular,

Theorem 22.2 *If $A \leq_{\mathrm{m}}^{\mathrm{P}} B$ and B has a polynomial-time algorithm, then so does A.*

Proof. Given an instance x of the problem A, compute $\sigma(x)$ and ask whether $\sigma(x) \in B$. Note that the algorithm for B runs in polynomial time in the size of its input $\sigma(x)$, which might be bigger than x; but since σ is computable in polynomial time on a Turing machine, the size of $\sigma(x)$ is at most polynomial in the size of x, and the composition of two polynomials is still a polynomial, so the overall algorithm is polynomial in the size of x.   □

In the last lecture we showed that CNFSat $\equiv_{\mathrm{m}}^{\mathrm{P}}$ Clique. Below we give some more examples of polynomial-time reductions between problems.

Definition 22.3 (Independent Set) An *independent set* in an undirected graph $G = (V, E)$ is a subset U of V such that $U^2 \cap E = \emptyset$, *i.e.* no two vertices in U are connected by an edge in E. The *independent set problem* is to determine, given $G = (V, E)$ and $k \geq 0$, whether G has an independent set U of cardinality at least k.   □

Note that the use of "independent" here is *not* in the sense of matroids.

There exist easy polynomial reductions from/to the clique problem. Consider the complementary graph $\overline{G} = (V, \overline{E})$, where

$$\overline{E} \;=\; \{(u, v) \mid u \neq v, \; (u, v) \notin E\} .$$

Then G has a clique of size k iff $\overline{G}$ has an independent set of size k. This simple one-to-one correspondence gives reductions in both directions, therefore Independent Set $\equiv_{\mathrm{m}}^{\mathrm{P}}$ Clique.

Definition 22.4 (Vertex Cover) A *vertex cover* in an undirected graph $G = (V, E)$ is a set of vertices $U \subseteq V$ such that every edge in E is adjacent to some vertex in U. The *vertex cover problem* is to determine, given $G = (V, E)$ and $k \geq 0$, whether there exists a vertex cover U in G of cardinality at most k. □

Again, there exist easy polynomial reductions from/to Independent Set: $U \subseteq V$ is a vertex cover iff $V - U$ is an independent set. Therefore Vertex Cover $\equiv_m^P$ Independent Set.

Definition 22.5 (k-CNFSat) A Boolean formula is in *k-conjunctive normal form (k-CNF)* if it is in conjuctive normal form and has at most k literals per clause. The problem k-CNFSat is just CNFSat with input instances restricted to formulas in k-CNF. In other words, given a Boolean formula in k-CNF, does it have a satisfying assignment? □

In the general CNFSat problem, the number of literals per clause is not restricted and can grow as much as linearly with the size of the formula. In the k-CNFSat problem, the number of literals per clause is restricted to k, independent of the size of the formula. The k-CNFSat problem is therefore a restriction of the CNFSat problem, and could conceivably be easier to solve than CNFSat. It turns out that 2CNFSat (and hence 1CNFSat also) is solvable in linear time, whereas k-CNFSat is as hard as CNFSat for any $k \geq 3$. We prove the latter statement by exhibiting a reduction CNFSat $\leq_m^P$ 3CNFSat.

Let $\mathcal{B}$ be an arbitrary Boolean formula in CNF. For each clause of the form

$$(\ell_1 \vee \ell_2 \vee \cdots \vee \ell_{m-1} \vee \ell_m) \tag{27}$$

with $m \geq 4$, let $x_1, x_2, \ldots, x_{m-3}$ be new variables and replace the clause (27) in $\mathcal{B}$ with the formula

$$(\ell_1 \vee \ell_2 \vee x_1) \wedge (\neg x_1 \vee \ell_3 \vee x_2) \wedge (\neg x_2 \vee \ell_4 \vee x_3) \wedge \cdots$$
$$\wedge (\neg x_{m-4} \vee \ell_{m-2} \vee x_{m-3}) \wedge (\neg x_{m-3} \vee \ell_{m-1} \vee \ell_m) .$$

Let $\mathcal{B}'$ be the resulting formula. Then $\mathcal{B}'$ is in 3CNF, and $\mathcal{B}'$ is satisfiable iff $\mathcal{B}$ is. This follows from several applications of the following lemma:

Lemma 22.6 *For any Boolean formulas $\mathcal{C}, \mathcal{D}, \mathcal{E}$ and variable x not appearing in $\mathcal{C}, \mathcal{D},$ or $\mathcal{E}$, the formula*

$$(x \vee \mathcal{C}) \wedge (\neg x \vee \mathcal{D}) \wedge \mathcal{E} \tag{28}$$

is satisfiable if and only if the formula

$$(\mathcal{C} \vee \mathcal{D}) \wedge \mathcal{E} \tag{29}$$

is satisfiable.

Proof. This is just the *resolution rule* of propositional logic. Any satisfying truth assignment for (28) gives a satisfying truth assignment for (29), since one of x, $\neg x$ is false, so either $\mathcal{C}$ or $\mathcal{D}$ is true. Conversely, in any satisfying truth assignment for (29), one of $\mathcal{C}, \mathcal{D}$ is true. If $\mathcal{C}$, assign $x := \textit{false}$. If $\mathcal{D}$, assign $x := \textit{true}$. We can assign x freely since it does not appear in $\mathcal{C}, \mathcal{D}$ or $\mathcal{E}$. In either case (28) is satisfied. $\square$

The formula $\mathcal{B}'$ is easily constructed from $\mathcal{B}$ in polynomial time. This constitutes a polynomial-time reduction from CNFSat to 3CNFSat. Furthermore, 3CNFSat is trivially reducible to k-CNFSat for any $k \geq 3$, which in turn is trivially reducible to CNFSat. Since $\leq^{\mathrm{p}}_{\mathrm{m}}$ is transitive, k-CNFSat $\equiv^{\mathrm{p}}_{\mathrm{m}}$ CNFSat for $k \geq 3$.

The problem 2CNFSat is solvable in linear time. In this case the clauses in $\mathcal{B}$ contain at most two literals, and we can assume exactly two without loss of generality by replacing any clause of the form (ℓ) with $(\ell \vee \ell)$. Now we think of every two-literal clause $(\ell \vee \ell')$ as a pair of implications

$$(\neg \ell \rightarrow \ell') \quad \text{and} \quad (\neg \ell' \rightarrow \ell) . \tag{30}$$

Construct a directed graph $G = (V, E)$ with a vertex for every literal and directed edges corresponding to the implications (30).

We claim that $\mathcal{B}$ is satisfiable iff no pair of complementary literals both appear in the same strongly connected component of G. Under any satisfying truth assignment, all literals in a strong component of G must have the same truth value. Therefore, if any variable x appears both positively and negatively in the same strong component of G, $\mathcal{B}$ is not satisfiable.

Conversely, suppose that no pair of complementary literals both appear in the same strong component of G. Consider the quotient graph G' obtained by collapsing the strong components of G as described in Lecture 4. As proved in that lecture, the graph G' is acyclic, therefore induces a partial order on its vertices. This partial order extends to a total order. We assign $x := \textit{false}$ if the strong component of x occurs before the strong component of $\neg x$ in this total order, and $x := \textit{true}$ if the strong component of $\neg x$ occurs before the strong component of x. It can be shown that this gives a satisfying assignment.

We know how to find the strong components of G in linear time. This gives a linear-time algorithm test for 2CNF satisfiability. We can also produce a satisfying assignment in linear time, if one exists, using topological sort to totally order the strong components.

Definition 22.7 (*k*-Colorability) Let C a finite set of *colors* and $G = (V, E)$ an undirected graph. A *coloring* is a map $\chi : V \rightarrow C$ such that $\chi(u) \neq \chi(v)$ for $(u, v) \in E$. Given G and k, the *k-colorability problem* is to determine whether there exists a coloring using no more than k colors. $\square$

For $k = 2$, the problem is easy: a graph is 2-colorable iff it is bipartite iff it has no odd cycles. This can be checked by BFS or DFS in linear time. We show that for $k = 3$, the problem is as hard as CNFSat by giving a reduction CNFSat $\leq_m^P$ 3-colorability.

Let $\mathcal{B}$ be a Boolean formula in CNF. We will construct a graph G that is 3-colorable iff $\mathcal{B}$ is satisfiable.

There will be three special vertices called **R**, **B**, and **G**, which will be connected in a triangle. In any 3-coloring, they will have to be colored with different colors, so we assume without loss of generality that they are colored red, blue, and green, respectively.

We include a vertex for each literal, and connect each literal to its complement and to the vertex **B** as shown.

In any 3-coloring, the vertices corresponding to the literals x and $\bar{x}$ will have to be colored either red or green, and not both red or both green. Intuitively, a legal 3-coloring will represent a satisfying truth assignment in which the green literals are true and the red literals are false.

To complete the graph, we add a subgraph like the one shown below for each clause in $\mathcal{B}$. The one shown below would be added for the clause $(x \vee y \vee \bar{z} \vee u \vee \bar{v} \vee w)$. The vertices in the picture labeled **G** are all the same vertex, namely the vertex **G**.

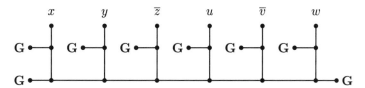

This subgraph has the property that a coloring of the vertices on the top row with either red or green can be extended to a 3-coloring of the whole subgraph iff at least one of them is colored green. If all vertices on the top row are colored red, then all the vertices on the middle row adjacent to vertices on the top row must be colored blue. Starting from the left, the vertices along the bottom row must be colored alternately red and green. This will lead to a conflict with the last vertex in the bottom row. (If the number of literals in the clause is odd instead of even as pictured, then the rightmost vertex in the bottom row is **R** instead of **G**.)

Conversely, suppose one of the vertices on the top row is colored green. Pick one such vertex. Color the vertex directly below it in the middle row red and the vertex directly below that on the bottom row blue. Color all other vertices on the middle row blue. Starting from the left and right ends, color the vertices along the bottom row as forced, either red or green. The coloring can always be completed.

Thus if there is a legal 3-coloring, then the subgraph corresponding to each clause must have at least one green literal, and truth values can be assigned so that the green literals are true. This gives a satisfying assignment. Conversely, if there is a satisfying assignment, color the true variables green and the false ones red. Then there is a green literal in each clause, so the coloring can be extended to a 3-coloring of the whole graph.

From this it follows that $\mathcal{B}$ is satisfiable iff G is 3-colorable, and the graph G can be constructed in polynomial time. Therefore CNFSat $\leq_m^P$ 3-colorability.

One can trivially reduce 3-colorability to k-colorability for $k > 3$ by appending a $k - 3$ clique and edges from every vertex of the $k - 3$ clique to every other vertex.

One may be tempted to conclude that in problems like k-CNFSat and k-colorability, larger values of k always make the problem harder. On the contrary, we shall see in the next lecture that the k-colorability problem for planar graphs is easy for $k \leq 2$ and $k \geq 4$, but as hard as CNFSat for $k = 3$.

Lecture 23   More *NP*-Complete Problems

23.1   Planar Graph Colorability

Often in problems with a parameter k like k-CNFSat and k-colorability, larger values of k make the problem harder. This is not always the case. Consider the problem of determining whether a *planar* graph has a k-coloring. The problem is trivial for $k = 1$, easy for $k = 2$ (check by DFS or BFS whether the graph is bipartite, *i.e.* has no odd cycles), and trivial for $k = 4$ or greater by the Four Color Theorem, which says that every planar graph is 4-colorable. This leaves $k = 3$. We show below that 3-colorability of planar graphs is no easier than 3-colorability of arbitrary graphs. This result is due to Garey, Johnson, and Stockmeyer [40]; see also Lichtenstein [72] for some other *NP*-completeness results involving planar graphs.

We will reduce 3-colorability of an arbitrary graph to the planar case. Given an undirected graph $G = (V, E)$, possibly nonplanar, embed the graph in the plane arbitrarily, letting edges cross if necessary. We will replace each

122

edge crossing with the planar widget W shown below.

$W \quad = \quad$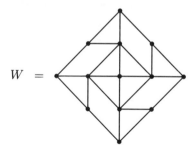

The widget W is a planar graph with the following interesting properties:

(i) in any legal 3-coloring of W, the opposite corners are forced to have the same color;

(ii) any assignment of colors to the corners such that opposite corners have the same color extends to a 3-coloring of all of W.

To see this, color the center of W red; then the vertices adjacent to the center must be colored blue or green alternately around the center, say

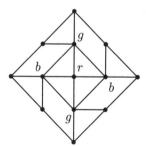

Now the northeast vertex can be colored either red or green. In either case, the colors of all the remaining vertices are forced (proceed counterclockwise to obtain the left hand coloring and clockwise to obtain the right hand coloring):

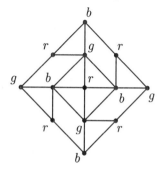
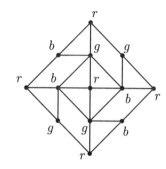

All other colorings are obtained from these by permuting the colors.

For each edge (u, v) in E, replace each point at which another edge crosses (u, v) in the embedding with a copy of W. Identify the adjacent corners of these copies of W and identify the outer corners of the extremal copies with u and v, all except for one pair, which are connected by an edge. The following diagram illustrates an edge (u, v) with four crossings before and after this operation. In this diagram, the copy of W closest to v is connected to v by an edge, and all other adjacent corners of copies of W are identified.

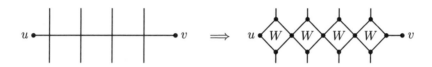

The resulting graph $G' = (V', E')$ is planar. If

$$\chi : V' \rightarrow \{\text{red, blue, green}\}$$

is a 3-coloring of G', then property (i) of W implies that χ restricted to V is a 3-coloring of G. Conversely, if $\chi : V \rightarrow \{\text{red, blue, green}\}$ is a 3-coloring of G, then property (ii) of W allows χ to be extended to a 3-coloring of G'.

We have given a reduction of the 3-colorability problem for an arbitrary graph to the same problem restricted to planar graphs. Thus the latter problem is as hard as the former.

23.2   *NP*-Completeness

The following definitions lay the foundations of the theory of *NP*-completeness. More detail can be found in [3, 39].

We fix once and for all a finite alphabet Σ consisting of at least two symbols. From now on, we take Σ to be the problem domain, and assume that instances of decision problems are encoded as strings in Σ^* in some reasonable way.

Definition 23.1 The complexity class *NP* consists of all decision problems $A \subseteq \Sigma^*$ such that A is the set of input strings accepted by some polynomial-time-bounded nondeterministic Turing machine. The complexity class P consists of all decision problems $A \subseteq \Sigma^*$ such that A is the set of input strings accepted by some polynomial-time-bounded deterministic Turing machine. □

Note that $P \subseteq NP$ since every deterministic machine is a nondeterministic one that does not happen to make any choices. It is not known whether $P = NP$; this is arguably the most important outstanding open problem in computer science.

Definition 23.2 The set A is *NP-hard (with respect to the reducibility relation $\leq_m^P$)* if $B \leq_m^P A$ for all $B \in NP$. □

Theorem 23.3 *If A is NP-hard and $A \in P$, then $P = NP$.*

Proof. For any $B \in NP$, compose the polynomial-time algorithm for A with the polynomial-time function reducing B to A to get a polynomial time algorithm for B. □

Definition 23.4 The set A is *NP-complete* if A is *NP*-hard and $A \in NP$. □

Theorem 23.5 *If A is NP-complete, then*

$$A \in P \quad \leftrightarrow \quad P = NP .$$

Definition 23.6 The complexity class *coNP* is the class of sets $A \subseteq \Sigma^*$ whose complements $\overline{A} = \Sigma^* - A$ are in *NP*. A set B is *coNP-hard* if every problem in *coNP* reduces in polynomial time to B. It is *coNP-complete* if in addition it is in *coNP*. □

The following theorem is immediate from the definitions.

Theorem 23.7

1. $A \leq_m^P B$ iff $\overline{A} \leq_m^P \overline{B}$.
2. A is *NP*-hard iff $\overline{A}$ is *coNP*-hard.
3. A is *NP*-complete iff $\overline{A}$ is *coNP*-complete.
4. If A is *NP*-complete then $A \in coNP$ iff $NP = coNP$.

It is unknown whether $NP = coNP$.

We will show later that the problems CNFSat, 3CNFSat, Clique, Vertex Cover, and Independent Set, which we have shown to be $\equiv_m^P$-equivalent, are all in fact *NP*-complete.

23.3   More *NP*-complete problems

Before we prove the *NP*-completeness of the problems we have been considering, let us consider some more problems in this class. Some of these problems, such as Traveling Salesman, Bin Packing, and Integer Programming, are very natural and important in operations research and industrial engineering. We start with the *exact cover problem*.

Definition 23.8 (Exact Cover) Given a finite set X and a family of subsets S of X, is there a subset $S' \subseteq S$ such that every element of X lies in exactly one element of S'? □

We show that the problem Exact Cover is *NP*-hard by reduction from the problem of 3-colorability of undirected graphs. See [39] for a different approach involving the 3-dimensional matching problem.

Lemma 23.9 *3-Colorability $\leq_m^P$ Exact Cover.*

Proof. Suppose we are given an undirected graph $G = (V, E)$. We show how to produce an instance (X, S) of the exact cover problem for which an exact cover exists iff G has a 3-coloring.

Let $C = \{$red, blue, green$\}$. For each $u \in V$, let $N(u)$ be the set of neighbors of u in G. Since G is undirected, $u \in N(v)$ iff $v \in N(u)$.

For each $u \in V$, we include u in X along with $3(|N(u)| + 1)$ additional elements of X. These $3(|N(u)| + 1)$ additional elements are arranged in three disjoint sets of $|N(u)| + 1$ elements each, one set corresponding to each color. Call these three sets S_u^{red}, S_u^{blue}, S_u^{green}. For each color $c \in C$, pick a special element p_u^c from S_u^c and associate the remaining $|N(u)|$ elements of S_u^c with the elements of $N(u)$ in a one-to-one fashion. Let q_{uv}^c denote the element of S_u^c associated with $v \in N(u)$.

The set S will contain all two element sets of the form

$$\{u, p_u^c\} \tag{31}$$

for $u \in V$ and $c \in C$, as well as all the sets S_u^c for $u \in V$ and $c \in C$. Here is a picture of what we have so far for a vertex u of degree 5 with $v \in N(u)$. The ovals represent the three sets S_u^c and the lines represent the three two-element sets (31).

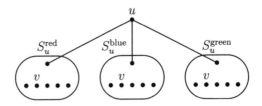

To complete S, we include all two element sets of the form

$$\{q_{uv}^c, q_{vu}^{c'}\} \tag{32}$$

for all $(u, v) \in E$ and $c, c' \in C$ with $c \neq c'$. Here is a picture showing a part of the construction for two vertices u and v of degrees 5 and 3 respectively, where (u, v) in E. The six lines in the center represent the two-element sets (32).

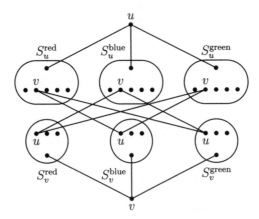

We now argue that the instance (X, S) of Exact Cover just constructed is a "yes" instance, *i.e.* an exact cover $S' \subseteq S$ of X exists, iff the graph G has a 3-coloring. Suppose first that G has a 3-coloring $\chi : V \to C$. We construct an exact cover $S' \subseteq S$ as follows. For each vertex u, let S' contain the sets $\{u, p_u^{\chi(u)}\}$ and S_u^c for $c \neq \chi(u)$. This covers everything except points of the form $q_{uv}^{\chi(u)}$, where $(u, v) \in E$. For each edge (u, v), let S' also contain the set $\{q_{uv}^{\chi(u)}, q_{vu}^{\chi(v)}\}$. This set is in S since $\chi(u) \neq \chi(v)$. This covers all the remaining points, and each point is covered by exactly one set in S'.

Conversely, suppose S' is an exact cover. Each u is covered by exactly one set in S', and it must be of the form $\{u, p_u^c\}$ for some c. Let $\chi(u)$ be that c; we claim that χ is a valid coloring, *i.e.* that if $(u, v) \in E$ then $\chi(u) \neq \chi(v)$. For each u, since $\{u, p_u^{\chi(u)}\} \in S'$, we cannot cover p_u^c for $c \neq \chi(u)$ by any set of the form (31), since u is already covered; therefore they must be covered by the sets S_u^c, which are the only other sets containing the points p_u^c. The sets $\{u, p_u^{\chi(u)}\}$ and S_u^c, $c \neq \chi(u)$ cover all points except those of the form $q_{uv}^{\chi(u)}$, $(u, v) \in E$. The only way S' can cover these remaining points is by the sets (32). By construction of S, these sets are of the form $\{q_{uv}^{\chi(u)}, q_{vu}^{\chi(v)}\}$ for $(u, v) \in E$ and $\chi(u) \neq \chi(v)$. □

Lecture 24 Still More *NP*-Complete Problems

In this lecture we use the basic *NP*-complete problems given in previous lectures, which may have appeared contrived, to show that several very natural and important decision problems are *NP*-complete.

We first consider a collection of problems with many applications in operations research and industrial engineering.

Definition 24.1 (Knapsack) Given a finite set S, integer weight function $w : S \to \mathcal{N}$, benefit function $b : S \to \mathcal{N}$, weight limit $W \in \mathcal{N}$, and desired benefit $B \in \mathcal{N}$, determine whether there exists a subset $S' \subseteq S$ such that

$$\sum_{a \in S'} w(a) \leq W$$
$$\sum_{a \in S'} b(a) \geq B .$$

□

The name is derived from the problem of trying to decide what you really need to take with you on your camping trip. For another example: you are the coach of a crew team, and you wish to select a starting squad of rowers with a combined weight not exceeding W and combined strength at least B.

Definition 24.2 (Subset Sum) Given a finite set S, integer weight function $w : S \to \mathcal{N}$, and target integer B, does there exist a subset $S' \subseteq S$ such that

$$\sum_{a \in S'} w(a) = B ?$$

$\square$

Definition 24.3 (Partition) Given a finite set S and integer weight function $w : S \to \mathcal{N}$, does there exist a subset $S' \subseteq S$ such that

$$\sum_{a \in S'} w(a) = \sum_{a \in S - S'} w(a) ?$$

$\square$

Trivially, Partition reduces to Subset Sum by taking

$$B = \frac{1}{2} \sum_{a \in S} w(a) .$$

Also, Subset Sum reduces to Partition by introducing two new elements of weight $N - B$ and $N - (\Sigma - B)$, respectively, where

$$\Sigma = \sum_{a \in S} w(a)$$

and N is a sufficiently large number (actually $N > \Sigma$ will do). The number N is chosen large enough so that both new elements cannot go in the same partition element, because together they outweigh all the other elements. Now we ask whether this new set of elements can be partitioned into two sets of equal weight (which must be N). By leaving out the new elements, this gives a partition of the original set into two sets of weight B and $\Sigma - B$.

Both Subset Sum and Partition reduce to Knapsack. To reduce Partition to Knapsack, take $b = w$ and $W = B = \frac{1}{2}\Sigma$.

We show that these three problems are as hard as Exact Cover by reducing Exact Cover to Subset Sum. Assume that $X = \{0, 1, \ldots, m - 1\}$ in the given instance (X, S) of Exact Cover. For $x \in X$, define

$$\#x = |\{A \in S \mid x \in A\}| ,$$

the number of elements of S containing x. Let p be a number exceeding all $\#x$, $0 \le x \le m - 1$. Encode $A \in S$ as the number

$$w(A) = \sum_{x \in A} p^x$$

and take

$$B = \sum_{x=0}^{m-1} p^x = \frac{p^m - 1}{p - 1} .$$

In p-ary notation, $w(A)$ looks like a string of 0's and 1's with a 1 in position x for each $x \in A$ and 0 elsewhere. The number B in p-ary notation looks like a string of 1's of length m. Adding the numbers $w(A)$ simulates the union of the sets A. The number p was chosen big enough so that we do not get into trouble with carries. Asking whether there is a subset sum that gives B is the same as asking for an exact cover of X.

The *bin packing problem* is an important problem that comes up in industrial engineering and computer memory management.

Definition 24.4 (Bin Packing) Given a finite set S, volumes $w : S \to \mathcal{N}$, and bin size $B \in \mathcal{N}$, what is the minimum number of bins needed to contain all the elements of S? Expressed as a decision problem, given the above data and a natural number k, does there exist a packing into k or fewer bins? □

We can easily reduce Partition to Bin Packing by taking B to be half the total weight of all elements of S and $k = 2$.

An extremely important and general problem in operations research is the integer programming problem.

Definition 24.5 (Integer Programming) Given rational numbers a_{ij}, c_j, and b_i, $1 \le i \le m$, $1 \le j \le n$, find integers $x_1, x_2, \ldots, x_n$ that maximize the linear function

$$\sum_{j=1}^{n} c_j x_j$$

subject to the linear constraints

$$\sum_{j=1}^{n} a_{ij} x_j \; \le \; b_i \; , \;\; 1 \le i \le m \; . \tag{33}$$

The corresponding decision problem is to test whether there exists a point with integer coordinates in a region defined by the intersection of half-spaces: given a_{ij} and b_i, $1 \le i \le m$, $1 \le j \le n$, test whether there exists an integer point $x_1, \ldots, x_n$ in the region (33). □

In *linear programming*, the x_i's are not constrained to be integers, but may be real. The linear programming problem was shown to be solvable in polynomial time in 1980 by Khachian [60] using a method that has become known as the *ellipsoid method*. In 1984, a more efficient polynomial time algorithm was given by Karmarkar [56]; his method has become known as the *interior point method*. Since that time, several refinements have appeared [90, 102]. The older *simplex method*, originally due to Dantzig (see [19]), is used successfully in practice but is known to be exponential in the worse case.

The integer programming problem is *NP*-hard, as the following reduction from Subset Sum shows: the instance of Subset Sum consisting of a set S with weights $w : S \rightarrow \mathcal{N}$ and threshold B has a positive solution iff the Integer Programming instance

$$0 \leq x_a \leq 1 , \quad a \in S$$

$$\sum_{a \in S} w(a)x_a = B$$

has an integer solution. It is also possible to show that Integer Programming is in *NP* by showing that if there exists an integer solution, then there exists one with only polynomially many bits as a function of the size of the input (n, m, and number of bits in the a_{ij}, b_i, and c_j) [16]. The integer solution can then be guessed and verified in polynomial time.

Definition 24.6 (Hamiltonian Circuit) A *Hamiltonian circuit* in a directed or undirected graph $G = (V, E)$ is a circuit that visits each vertex in the graph exactly once. It is like an Euler circuit, except the constraint is on vertices rather than edges. The *Hamiltonian circuit problem* is to determine for a given graph G whether a Hamiltonian circuit exists.   □

We reduce Vertex Cover to Hamiltonian Circuit. Recall that a *vertex cover* in an undirected graph $G = (V, E)$ is a set of vertices $U \subseteq V$ such that every edge in E is adjacent to some vertex in U. The *vertex cover problem* is to determine, given $G = (V, E)$ and $k \geq 0$, whether there exists a vertex cover U in G of cardinality at most k.

We will build a graph H which will have a Hamiltonian circuit iff G has a vertex cover of size k. The main building block of H for the directed Hamiltonian circuit problem is a widget consisting of four vertices connected as shown.

For the undirected version, we use an undirected widget with twelve vertices:

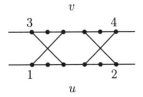

There is one widget corresponding to each edge $(u,v) \in E$. In the widget corresponding to the edge (u,v), one side corresponds to the vertex u and the other to the vertex v.

These widgets have the following interesting property: any Hamiltonian circuit that enters at vertex 1 must leave at vertex 2, and there are only two ways to pass through, either straight through or in a zigzag pattern that crosses to the other side and back. If it goes straight through, then all the vertices on the u side and none of the vertices on the v side are visited. If it crosses to the other side and back, then all the vertices on both sides are visited. Any other path through the widget leaves some vertex stranded, so the path could not be a part of a Hamiltonian circuit. Thus any Hamiltonian circuit that enters at 1 either picks up the vertices in the widget all at once using the zigzag path, or goes straight through and picks up only the vertices on one side, then re-enters at 3 later on to pick up the vertices on the other side.

The graph H is formed as follows. For each vertex u, we string together end-to-end all the u sides of all the widgets corresponding to edges in E incident to u. Call this the u *loop*. In addition, H has a set K of k extra vertices, where k is the parameter of the given instance of Vertex Cover denoting the size of the vertex cover we are looking for. There is an edge from each vertex in K to the first vertex in the u loop, and an edge from the last vertex in the u loop to each vertex in K.

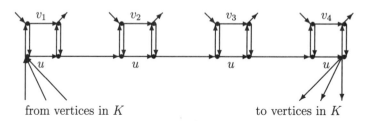

from vertices in K to vertices in K

We now show that there is a vertex cover of size k in G iff H has a Hamiltonian circuit. Suppose there is a vertex cover $\{u_1, \ldots, u_k\}$ of G of size k. Then H has a Hamiltonian circuit: starting from the first vertex of K, go through the u_1 loop. When passing through the widget corresponding to an edge (u_1, v) of G, take the straight path if v is in the vertex cover, *i.e.* if $v = u_j$ for some j (the other side of the widget will be picked up later when we traverse the u_j loop), and take the zigzag path if v is not in the vertex cover. When leaving the u_1 loop, go to the second vertex of K, then through the u_2 loop, and so on, all the way around and back to the first vertex of K.

Conversely, if H has a Hamiltonian circuit, the number of u loops traversed must be exactly k, and that set of vertices u forms a vertex cover of G.

This argument holds for both the directed and undirected case. Thus, determining the existence of a Hamiltonian circuit in a directed or undirected graph is *NP*-hard. It is also in *NP*, since a Hamiltonian circuit can be guessed and verified in polynomial time.

Finally, we consider the *Traveling Salesman Problem (TSP)*. The optimization version of this problem asks for a tour through a set of cities minimizing the total distance. There are several versions of TSP, depending on the properties of the graph and distance function and the type of tour desired. We consider here a quite general formulation.

Definition 24.7 (Traveling Salesman (TSP)) Given a number $k \geq 0$ and a directed graph $G = (V, E)$ with nonnegative edge weights $w : E \rightarrow \mathcal{N}$, does there exist a tour of total weight at most k visiting every vertex at least once and returning home?   □

Garey and Johnson [39] use a slightly more restricted version which asks for a tour visiting each vertex exactly once. We prefer the more general version above, since to get anywhere from Ithaca and back usually involves at least two stops in Pittsburgh.

TSP is in *NP* provided we can argue that optimal tours are short enough that they can be guessed and verified in polynomial time. Each vertex can be visited at most n times in an optimal tour, because otherwise we could cut out a loop and still visit all vertices. We can thus guess a tour of length at most n^2 and verify that its total weight is at most k.

TSP is *NP*-hard, since there is a straightforward reduction from Hamiltonian Circuit: give all edges unit weight and ask for a TSP tour of weight n.

Combining arguments from the last several lectures, we have:

Theorem 24.8 *The CNF Satisfiability problem reduces via $\leq_m^P$ to all the following problems: Knapsack, Partition, Subset Sum, Exact Cover, Bin Packing, Integer Programming, directed and undirected Hamiltonian Circuit, and Traveling Salesman.*

Lecture 25   Cook's Theorem

In this lecture we will prove the *NP*-hardness of CNFSat by exhibiting a reduction from an arbitrary problem in *NP* to CNFSat. We use the standard definition of one-tape deterministic and nondeterministic Turing machines; see for example [3, pp. 25ff.]. This landmark result was proved by S. Cook in 1971 [22]. A similar result was proved independently by L. Levin in the Soviet Union in 1973 [71].

Theorem 25.1 *If $A \in NP$ then $A \leq_m^P$ CNFSat.*

Proof. Let $A \subseteq \Sigma^*$ be an arbitrary but fixed language in *NP*. Then A is accepted by some nondeterministic Turing machine M. We will describe a function σ that from a given $x \in \Sigma^*$ computes a Boolean formula $\mathcal{B} = \sigma(x)$ that is satisfiable iff M accepts x. The function σ must be computable in polynomial time deterministically, and its description may depend on M.

Here is the main idea. The possible executions of M on input $x \in \Sigma^*$ form a branching tree of *configurations*, where each configuration gives a snapshot of the current instantaneous state of the computation and includes all relevant information that can affect the computation, such as tape contents, head position, and current state of the finite control. Since M is polynomially time bounded, we can assume that the depth of this tree is at most $N = |x|^k$ for some fixed k. The exponent k may depend on M but does not depend on x. A valid computation sequence of length N can use no more than N tape cells, since at the very worst the machine moves right one tape cell in each step. Thus there are at most N time units and N tape cells we need to consider.

134

We will encode computations of M on input x as truth assignments to various arrays of Boolean variables, which describe things like where the read head is at time i, which symbol is occupying cell j at time i, and so forth. We will write down clauses involving these variables that will describe legal moves of the machine and legal starting and accepting configurations of M on x. A truth assignment will simultaneously satisfy all these clauses iff it describes a valid computation sequence of M on input x. We will then take $\mathcal{B} = \sigma(x)$ to be the conjuction of all these clauses. Then the satisfying truth assignments to $\mathcal{B}$ correspond in a one-to-one fashion to the accepting computations of M on x, therefore $\mathcal{B}$ will be satisfiable iff M has an accepting computation on input x, i.e. iff $x \in A$.

Here are the Boolean variables, along with their intuitive interpretations. Let Q denote the set of states of the finite control of M, and let Σ denote the tape alphabet of M.

- Q_i^q, $0 \leq i \leq N$, $q \in Q$; intuitively,

$$Q_i^q \quad = \quad \text{"At time } i \text{, the machine is in state } q \text{."}$$

- H_{ij}, $0 \leq i, j \leq N$; intuitively,

$$H_{ij} \quad = \quad \text{"At time } i \text{, the machine's read/write head is} \\ \text{scanning tape cell } j \text{."}$$

- S_{ij}^a, $0 \leq i, j \leq N$, $a \in \Sigma$; intuitively,

$$S_{ij}^a \quad = \quad \text{"At time } i \text{, tape cell } j \text{ contains symbol } a \text{."}$$

The machine starts in its start state s scanning the left endmarker $\vdash$ with the input x filling the first $|x|$ spaces on the tape followed by blank characters $\natural$. This situation is captured by the following formula:

$$Q_0^s \wedge H_{00} \wedge S_{00}^{\vdash} \wedge \bigwedge_{1 \leq j \leq |x|} S_{0j}^{x_j} \wedge \bigwedge_{|x|+1 \leq j \leq N} S_{0j}^{\natural} \ .$$

Assume that M never prints its left endmarker $\vdash$ anyplace except in the leftmost cell of the tape, and that upon seeing $\vdash$ in any state, it never moves left. Assume further that if M wants to accept, it first erases its tape and moves its head all the way to the left before entering the accept state t, and subsequently does not move its head or change state. These assumptions are without loss of generality, since if A is accepted by a nondeterministic polynomial time machine at all, then it is accepted by another machine that satisfies these conditions.

The acceptance condition can then be represented by the formula

$$Q_N^t \wedge H_{N,0} \wedge S_{N,0}^{\vdash} \wedge \bigwedge_{1 \leq j \leq N} S_{0,j}^{\natural} \ .$$

The computation of the machine obeys certain constraints, which are represented by various formulas:

- "At any time, the machine is in exactly one state."

$$\bigwedge_{0 \leq i \leq N} (\bigvee_{q \in Q} Q_i^q) \quad \wedge \quad \bigwedge_{0 \leq i \leq N} \bigwedge_{\substack{p,q \in Q \\ p \neq q}} (\neg Q_i^p \vee \neg Q_i^q)$$

- "At any time, each tape cell contains exactly one symbol."

$$\bigwedge_{0 \leq i,j \leq N} (\bigvee_{a \in \Sigma} S_{i,j}^a) \quad \wedge \quad \bigwedge_{0 \leq i,j \leq N} \bigwedge_{\substack{a,b \in \Sigma \\ a \neq b}} (\neg S_{ij}^a \vee \neg S_{ij}^b)$$

- "At any time, the machine is scanning exactly one cell."

$$\bigwedge_{0 \leq i \leq N} (\bigvee_{0 \leq j \leq N} H_{ij}) \quad \wedge \quad \bigwedge_{0 \leq i \leq N} \bigwedge_{0 \leq j < k \leq N} (\neg H_{ij} \vee \neg H_{ik})$$

The last set of conditions we need to write down are the most crucial to this construction. They say that computation follows the transition relation of M. There are clauses that specify, based on the state, head position, and contents of the tape at time i, the possible state, head position, and contents of the tape at time $i + 1$.

The transition relation of M is the part of the specification of M that tells which actions M can take in a given situation. Formally, it is a finite set δ of tuples of the form $((p, a), (q, b, d))$, where

- p and q are states of the finite control,
- a and b are tape symbols, and
- d is a direction, either -1 (left), 0 (stationary), or $+1$ (right).

If the tuple $((p, a), (q, b, d))$ is in δ, this says that whenever the machine is in state p scanning symbol a, it can take the following actions: print b on that tape cell, move the head in direction d, and enter state q. Since δ is a relation and not a function, there may be several such actions (q, b, d) possible for a given (p, a), but it is important to note that the number of such (q, b, d) depends only on M and is independent of the size of the input x.

The following two formulas express that the configuration at time $i + 1$ follows from that at time i according to the transition relation δ. Formula (34) says that for a given $p \in Q$, $a \in \Sigma$, and $0 \leq i, j \leq N$, if M at time i is in state p scanning cell j on which is written the symbol a, then for some tuple $((p, a), (q, b, d)) \in \delta$, at time $i+1$ there will be a b occupying cell j and M will be in state q scanning cell $j + d$. Formula (35) says that any cell not being scanned at time i contains the same symbol at time $i + 1$ as at time i.

$$Q_i^p \wedge H_{ij} \wedge S_{ij}^a \quad \rightarrow \quad \bigvee_{((p,a),(q,b,d)) \in \delta} (Q_{i+1}^q \wedge H_{i+1,j+d} \wedge S_{i+1,j}^b) \qquad (34)$$

$$S_{ij}^a \wedge \neg H_{ij} \quad \rightarrow \quad S_{i+1,j}^a . \qquad (35)$$

These formulas are not in CNF as they stand, but can be transformed into equivalent CNF formulas using the distributive and DeMorgan laws of propositional logic. Do not worry about (34) and (35) getting too big in this process—their lengths depend only on M and not on the size of the input x, hence are $O(1)$. We take the conjunction of (34) and (35) over all i and j in the range 0 to N.

The formula $\mathcal{B}$ is the conjuction of all these formulas. It is in conjunctive normal form, and its length is polynomial in $|x|$. Moreover, it can be constructed from x in polynomial time. Every satisfying truth assignment to $\mathcal{B}$ gives rise to an accepting computation of the machine, and vice-versa.   □

Lecture 26   Counting Problems and #P

In this lecture we discuss the complexity of counting problems. Instead of just determining whether a solution to a given problem exists, we will be interested in counting the number of different solutions to a given problem. Counting problems are naturally associated with many of the decision problems we have already discussed. The notion of a *witness function* formalizes this association.

Definition 26.1 Let $w : \Sigma^* \to \mathcal{P}(\Gamma^*)$, where $\mathcal{P}(\Gamma^*)$ denotes the power set of Γ^*, and let $x \in \Sigma^*$. We refer to the elements of $w(x)$ as *witnesses* for x. We associate a decision problem $A_w \subseteq \Sigma^*$ with w:

$$A_w \;=\; \{x \in \Sigma^* \mid w(x) \neq \emptyset\} \;.$$

In other words, A_w is the set of strings that have witnesses.   □

Example 26.2 Let $x \in \Sigma^*$ be an encoding of a Boolean formula and $y \in \Gamma^*$ an encoding of a truth assignment. If

$$w(x) \;=\; \{\text{truth assignments satisfying } x\} \;,$$

then

$$A_w \;=\; \{\text{satisfiable Boolean formulas}\} \;.$$

□

138

It is possible for a counting problem to be harder than the associated decision problem. In order to characterize the additional difficulty of these problems, Valiant [103] proposed a new class of problems called #*P*. His definition is essentially equivalent to the following.

Definition 26.3 The class #*P* is the class of witness functions w such that:

(i) there is a polynomial-time algorithm to determine, for a given x and y, whether $y \in w(x)$;

(ii) there exists a constant $k \in \mathcal{N}$ such that for all $y \in w(x)$, $|y| \leq |x|^k$. (The constant k can depend on w).

$\square$

The following theorem relates counting problems in this new class to their associated decision problems.

Theorem 26.4 *The following relationships hold between witness functions in #P and decision problems in NP:*

(i) if $w \in$ #P then $A_w \in$ NP;

(ii) if $A \in$ NP, then there exists a $w \in$ #P such that $A = A_w$.

Proof.

(i) Guess a witness $y \in \Gamma^*$ in polynomial time using Definition 26.3(ii) and verify in polynomial time that y is indeed a witness using Definition 26.3(i).

(ii) Let M be a nondeterministic Turing machine accepting A. Take $w(x)$ to be the set of accepting computation paths of M on input x.

$\square$

It is interesting to observe how counting problems v and w are related under the process of reduction. For this purpose, we introduce the notion of *counting reductions* and *parsimonious reductions*.

Definition 26.5 Let

$$w : \Sigma^* \rightarrow \mathcal{P}(\Gamma^*)$$
$$v : \Pi^* \rightarrow \mathcal{P}(\Delta^*)$$

be counting problems. A *polynomial-time many-one counting reduction* from w to v consists of a pair of polynomial-time computable functions

$$\sigma : \Sigma^* \rightarrow \Pi^*$$
$$\tau : \mathcal{N} \rightarrow \mathcal{N}$$

such that

$$|w(x)| \; = \; \tau(|v(\sigma(x))|) \; .$$

When such a reduction exists we say that w *reduces to* v.   □

Intuitively, if one can easily count the number of witnesses of $v(y)$, then one can easily count the number of witnesses of $w(x)$.

Some reductions preserve the number of solutions to a problem exactly. We call such reductions *parsimonious*. Formally,

Definition 26.6 A counting reduction σ, τ is *parsimonious* if τ is the identity function.   □

Example 26.7 Here are a number of examples of parsimonious and non-parsimonious reductions.

- Cook's Theorem is parsimonious in the sense that the number of satisfying assignments to the Boolean formula constructed in the proof of the theorem corresponds exactly to the number of accepting computations of the nondeterministic Turing machine being simulated.

- The reduction Clique $\leq_m^P$ Vertex Cover as presented in a previous lecture is parsimonious: the number of cliques of $G = (V, E)$ of size k is the same as the number of vertex covers of $\overline{G} = (V, \overline{E})$ of size $n - k$.

- The reduction CNFSat $\leq_m^P$ 3CNFSat as presented in a previous lecture is not parsimonious, but it can easily be made so.

- The reduction 3CNFSat $\leq_m^P$ Clique as presented in a previous lecture is not parsimonious, but again can easily be made so.

                    □

Example 26.8 We show how the reduction 3CNFSat $\leq_m^P$ Clique can be made parsimonious. Recall that we constructed from a given CNF formula $\mathcal{B}$ a graph G with a vertex for each occurrence of a literal in $\mathcal{B}$ and edges between occurrences of literals in different clauses if the literals were not complementary. The problem with this construction is that one truth assignment might correspond to several cliques. For example, the formula

$$(x \vee y) \wedge (x \vee \overline{y})$$

has two satisfying assignments but three 2-cliques.

We can remedy this by first replacing each clause

$$\cdots \wedge (x \vee y \vee z) \wedge \cdots$$

in $\mathcal{B}$ by the equivalent subformula

$$\cdots \wedge \left(x\,y\,z \vee x\,y\,\overline{z} \vee x\,\overline{y}\,z \vee x\,\overline{y}\,\overline{z} \vee \overline{x}\,y\,z \vee \overline{x}\,y\,\overline{z} \vee \overline{x}\,\overline{y}\,z \right) \wedge \cdots$$

with seven terms. The number of satisfying assignments is the same, since the formulas are equivalent. Now we construct G with one vertex for each of the seven terms in each of these subformulas and edges connecting terms xyz and uvw in different clauses if the two terms contain no complementary literals. One can show that there is exactly one clique of size k (the number of clauses) for each satisfying assignment.   □

As with the NP-complete problems, we can define the class of $\#P$-*complete problems* that represent the hardest problems in the class $\#P$. All the counting problems we have mentioned so far are $\#P$-complete.

One $\#P$-complete problem is that of computing the *permanent* of a matrix. Intuitively, the permanent of an $n \times n$ 0-1 matrix is the number of ways to place n rooks on the matrix so that every rook sits on a 1 and no rook can capture another. Officially,

Definition 26.9 Given an $n \times n$ matrix A (not necessarily 0-1), the *permanent* of A is the quantity

$$\operatorname{perm} A \;=\; \sum_{\sigma \in S_n} \prod_{i=1}^{n} A_{i,\sigma(i)}$$

where the σ are permutations of the set $\{1, 2, \ldots, n\}$ and S_n is the set of all such permutations.   □

The definition of the permanent of a matrix is very similar to the definition of determinant:

$$\det A \;=\; \sum_{\sigma \in S_n} (-1)^{\operatorname{sign} \sigma} \prod_{i=1}^{n} A_{i,\sigma(i)} \;.$$

The only difference is that the sign[4] of the permutation (even or odd) is included in the determinant. It is thus quite surprising that the permanent should be $\#P$-complete, since the determinant is computable in polynomial time by Gaussian elimination.

That the permanent is $\#P$-complete is even more surprising in light of its relationship to the bipartite matching problem. Given a bipartite graph $G = (U, V, E)$ with $|U| = |V| = n$, the permanent of the $n \times n$ bipartite adjacency matrix of G gives the number of perfect matchings. Thus, despite the fact that a perfect matching can be found in polynomial time, counting the number of them is as hard as counting the number of satisfying assignments to a Boolean formula.

---

[4]The *sign* of a permutation of $\{1, 2, \ldots, n\}$ is the number (mod 2) of pairs that are out of order.

Theorem 26.10 (Valiant [103]) *The problem of counting the number of perfect matchings in a bipartite graph is #P-complete.*

Actually, this problem is #P-complete with respect to a slightly more general reducibility than the one defined in Definition 26.5. We will discuss this later on.

Example 26.11 Consider the following bipartite graph and its associated bipartite adjacency matrix.

	a	b	c
1	1	1	0
2	1	1	1
3	1	0	1

This graph has exactly three perfect matchings corresponding to the three possible legal rook placements.

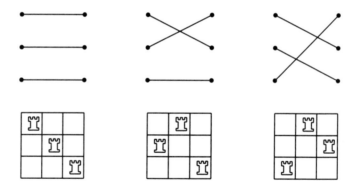

For non-bipartite directed graphs, we might ask what the permanent of the adjacency matrix represents. Here, a legal rook placement corresponds to a *cycle cover*, or a collection of vertex-disjoint cycles containing all vertices. The permanent thus computes the number of cycle covers. The picture below illustrates the relationship between cycle covers and permutations corresponding to nonzero terms in the definition of the permanent.

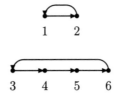

Lecture 27   Counting Bipartite Matchings

In this lecture we prove that computing the number of perfect matchings in a bipartite graph is #P complete, making it at least as difficult as computing the number of satisfying truth assignments for a Boolean expression.

We noted last time that the number of perfect matchings in a bipartite graph with the same number of vertices on each side is equal to the *permanent* of its 0-1 adjacency matrix, given by

$$\operatorname{perm} A \;\; = \;\; \sum_{\sigma \in S_n} \prod_{i=1}^{n} A_{i,\sigma(i)}$$

where S_n is the set of permutations of the set $\{1, 2, \ldots, n\}$. For a general directed graph with n vertices and its $n \times n$ (nonbipartite) adjacency matrix, the permanent gives the number of cycle covers.

Our proof begins using the same construction that we used to reduce Vertex Cover to Hamiltonian Circuit. Recall that we constructed a graph H from G built from a set of widgets, one for each edge in G.

For each vertex u in G, the sides of the widgets corresponding to u are connected end-to-end to form a u *loop*. The ends of each u loop are connected to each element of a set K of k new vertices as shown; here k is the size of the vertex cover in G we are looking for.

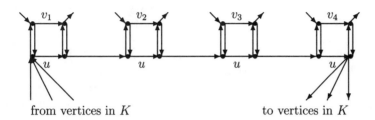

from vertices in K to vertices in K

We showed in Lecture 24 that H contains a Hamiltonian circuit if and only if G contains a vertex cover of size k. However, although every Hamiltonian circuit in H determines a unique vertex cover in G, there are in general many different Hamiltonian circuits giving the same vertex cover. How many? For each vertex cover C, each Hamiltonian circuit corresponding to C is determined by the connections between K and the loops corresponding to C, thus we are essentially looking at the number of Hamiltonian circuits in a complete bipartite graph on two sets of k vertices. This number is $k!(k-1)!$, since for each of the $(k-1)!$ cyclic orderings of the vertices in one of the sets of the bipartition, there are $k!$ ways to insert the vertices in the other set so that the two sets alternate.

Similar thinking leads to the conclusion that there are exactly $(k!)^2$ cycle covers in H corresponding to a given vertex cover C in G. This is the number of ways to select two perfect matchings in a complete bipartite graph on two sets of k vertices independently, one to model the edges from K to C and the other to model the edges from C to K.

It would be nice if these cycle covers corresponding to vertex covers included all possible cycle covers in H. We could immediately conclude that by computing the permanent of the adjacency matrix for H and dividing by $(k!)^2$ we could obtain the number of vertex covers in G. Alas, life is not quite this simple; in fact, we are just warming up to the real task.

The problem is that the widgets contain cycles of length two that are included in cycle covers counted by the permanent. Such cycle covers do not correspond to any vertex cover. Let us define a cycle cover to be *bad* if it contains a cycle of length two, *good* otherwise. Good cycle covers must traverse widgets properly, therefore correspond to vertex covers as described above. We can conclude

Theorem 27.1 *The number of good cycle covers in H is $(k!)^2$ times the number of vertex covers of G of size k.*

Thus we would like to count only the good cycle covers of H. Unfortunately, the permanent counts all cycle covers, good and bad. We need to figure out how to prevent bad covers from contributing to the value of the permanent of the adjacency matrix. This leads us to Valiant's Excellent Idea #1: try to assign weights, possibly negative, to the interior edges of widgets so that the product of the edge weights in each good cycle cover is 1, but the product of edge weights in each bad cycle cover is 0. The permanent will then count the number of good cycle covers.

Unfortunately, the task of trying to assign edge weights by trial and error quickly leads nowhere. Even if we throw in more edges—in fact, we might as well consider the complete graph with self-loops—the problem of assigning weights appears hopeless. This brings us to Valiant's Excellent Idea #2: forget the widget itself and look at its adjacency matrix instead, and try to write down the essential properties of the matrix that will give us the desired behavior.

Consider the 4×4 submatrix of the adjacency matrix of H corresponding to one copy W of the widget. There are columns of H corresponding to the "input" vertices 1 and 3 of W and rows of H corresponding to the "output" vertices 2 and 4. In a bad cycle cover involving the two cycles of length two in W, no edge coming into 1 or 3 or leaving 2 or 4 is part of the cycle cover. In terms of the associated legal rook placement, this says that the rooks in columns 1 and 3 and rows 2 and 4 must lie in the submatrix corresponding to W. Moreover, since there are no edges from vertices 1 or 3 to vertices outside of W, i.e. all entries in rows 1 and 3 outside of the submatrix W are zero, the rooks in these rows must lie in the submatrix W. This says that there are exactly 4 rooks on the submatrix W, and they form a legal rook placement on W.

When this happens, the remaining rooks must lie in the complementary subgraph W^* of W, i.e. that subgraph of H obtained by deleting the rows and columns of W. The sum of all terms in the permanent corresponding to cycle covers containing these two cycles is then given by

$$\operatorname{perm} W \cdot \operatorname{perm} W^* .$$

If we could pick weights so that $\operatorname{perm} W = 0$, then the net contribution of all these cycles to the calculation of the permanent would be 0.

With this insight, we proceed to write down all the conditions on the adjacency matrix that guarantee the desired behavior. The intra-widget connections will be as a complete graph with self-loops, and the edges will be weighted. The inter-widget connections will be the same as in H, with all edge weights 1.

Let A denote the 4×4 adjacency matrix of this weighted widget (the weights have yet to be determined). Let $A(i; j)$ denote the submatrix of A obtained by deleting row(s) i and column(s) j.

The desired behavior can be summarized as follows:

$$\text{perm } A(4; 3) = \text{perm } A(2; 1) = \text{perm } A(2, 4; 1, 3) = 1$$
$$\text{perm } A(4; 1) = \text{perm } A(2; 3) = \text{perm } A = 0 .$$

The first line insures that the net contribution to the permanent of all legal rook placements corresponding to a good cycle cover in H is 1. The three permanents correspond to the three acceptable ways of traversing the widget in a good cycle cover: two zigzag paths and a pair of straight paths. The second line insures that the net contribution of all legal rook placements corresponding to a bad cycle cover is 0. For example, the equation

$$\text{perm } A(4; 1) = 0$$

says that the net contribution to the permanent of all cycle covers that have an edge entering the widget at 1 and leaving 4, and no other connections to the outside, is 0.

We do not need to write down any conditions to rule out different numbers of entering and leaving edges; these cases are already taken care of by the rules of rook placement. Essentially, in any cycle cover, the number of edges leaving a subgraph must equal the number of edges entering it.

One can now look for a 4×4 matrix satisfying these constraints. There are many possibilities. One such is

$$A = \begin{bmatrix} 1 & 1 & -1 & 0 \\ \frac{1}{2} & \frac{1}{2} & \frac{1}{2} & 0 \\ 0 & 0 & 0 & 1 \\ 1 & -1 & 0 & 0 \end{bmatrix}$$

For instance,

$$\text{perm } A(4; 3) = \text{perm } \begin{bmatrix} 1 & 1 & 0 \\ \frac{1}{2} & \frac{1}{2} & 0 \\ 0 & 0 & 1 \end{bmatrix}$$
$$= 1 \cdot \frac{1}{2} \cdot 1 + 1 \cdot \frac{1}{2} \cdot 1$$
$$= 1$$

and

$$\text{perm } A(4;1) = \text{perm } \begin{bmatrix} 1 & -1 & 0 \\ \frac{1}{2} & \frac{1}{2} & 0 \\ 0 & 0 & 1 \end{bmatrix}$$
$$= 1 \cdot \frac{1}{2} \cdot 1 - 1 \cdot \frac{1}{2} \cdot 1$$
$$= 0 .$$

The full adjacency matrix B with submatrices A corresponding to these four-node widgets counts 1 for each good cycle cover in H and 0 for each bad cycle cover, thus its permanent is equal to $(k!)^2$ times the number of vertex covers in G.

We have argued that computing the permanent of a matrix containing elements in $\{-1, 0, \frac{1}{2}, 1\}$ is $\#P$-hard, but there is still a ways to go. The next step is to note that

$$\text{perm } 2B = 2^n \cdot \text{perm } B ,$$

and this implies that computing the permanent of a matrix with elements in $\{-2, 0, 1, 2\}$ is hard for $\#P$. We now show that this problem reduces to computing the permanents of polynomially many matrices over $\{0, 1\}$. The reduction we use here is somewhat weaker than the one we have been using in that it will require several instances of the $\{0, 1\}$ permanent problem to encode a given instance of the $\{-2, 0, 1, 2\}$ permanent problem, but the reduction still has the property that any fast algorithm for the $\{0, 1\}$ problem would give a fast algorithm for the $\{-2, 0, 1, 2\}$ problem.

Let B be an $n \times n$ matrix over $\{-2, 0, 1, 2\}$. A bound on the absolute value of perm B is given by the case in which each entry of B is 2; then

$$|\text{perm } B| \leq 2^n n! .$$

It thus suffices to compute perm B modulo any $N > 2^{n+1} n!$, and from this we will be able to recover the value of perm B.

Let $p_1, p_2, \ldots, p_k$ be the first k primes, where k is the least number such that

$$N = \prod_{i=1}^{k} p_i > 2^{n+1} n! .$$

It is not hard to show that $k \leq n + 1$. Moreover, since p_m is $\Theta(m \log m)$ (see [49, p. 10]), we can generate the first k primes in polynomial time using the sieve of Eratosthenes. Before proceeding further, we need the following theorem.

Theorem 27.2 (Chinese Remainder Theorem)   *Let $m_1, m_2, \ldots, m_k$ be pairwise relatively prime positive integers, and let $m = \prod_{i=1}^{k} m_i$. Let $\mathcal{Z}_n$*

denote the ring of integers modulo n. The ring $\mathcal{Z}_m$ and the direct product of rings

$$\mathcal{Z}_{m_1} \times \mathcal{Z}_{m_2} \times \cdots \times \mathcal{Z}_{m_k}$$

are isomorphic under the function

$$f : \mathcal{Z}_m \quad \to \quad \mathcal{Z}_{m_1} \times \mathcal{Z}_{m_2} \times \cdots \times \mathcal{Z}_{m_k}$$

given by

$$f(x) \;=\; (x \bmod m_1, x \bmod m_2, \ldots, x \bmod m_k) \ .$$

This just says that the numbers mod m and the k-tuples of numbers mod m_i, $1 \le i \le k$, are in one-to-one correspondence, and that arithmetic is preserved under the map f. For example, in the following table, we have compared $\mathcal{Z}_{15}$ to $\mathcal{Z}_3 \times \mathcal{Z}_5$.

x	0	1	2	3	4	5	6	7	8	9	10	11	12	13	14
$x \bmod 3$	0	1	2	0	1	2	0	1	2	0	1	2	0	1	2
$x \bmod 5$	0	1	2	3	4	0	1	2	3	4	0	1	2	3	4

Note that each pair in $\mathcal{Z}_3 \times \mathcal{Z}_5$ occurs exactly once. This is because 3 and 5 are relatively prime. Arithmetic is preserved as well: for example, 4 and 7 correspond to the pairs $(1, 4)$ and $(1, 2)$, respectively; multiplying these pairwise gives the pair $(1, 3)$ (mod 3 and 5, respectively), which occurs under 13; and $4 \times 7 = 28 = 13$ (mod 15).

Also, f and f^{-1} are computable in polynomial time. To compute $f(x)$, we just reduce x modulo $m_1, \ldots, m_k$. To compute $f^{-1}(x_1, \ldots, x_k)$, we first compute, for each $1 \le i \le k$, integers s and t such that

$$sm_i + t \prod_{\substack{1 \le j \le k \\ j \ne i}} m_j \;=\; 1$$

and take

$$u_i \;=\; t \prod_{\substack{1 \le j \le k \\ j \ne i}} m_j \ .$$

The numbers s and t are available as a byproduct of the Euclidean algorithm. For each $1 \le i, j \le k$, $u_i \equiv 1 \bmod m_i$ and $u_i \equiv 0 \bmod m_j$, $i \ne j$. Take

$$f^{-1}(x_1, \ldots, x_k) \;=\; x_1 u_1 + \cdots + x_k u_k \bmod m \ .$$

For further details and a proof of the Chinese Remainder Theorem see [3, pp. 289ff.].

Using the Chinese Remainder Theorem, we can compute perm B by computing perm $B \bmod p_i$, $1 \leq i \leq k$. For each i, $1 \leq i \leq k$, we replace all -2 entries in B by $p_i - 2$; modulo p_i, they are the same. We then compute the permanent of this matrix and reduce modulo p_i to get perm $B \bmod p_i$. The advantage of this is that we have now reduced the problem to that of computing the permanents of matrices with small nonnegative entries only.

All that remains is to show how to reduce the computation of the permanent of a matrix over $\{0, 1, 2, p-2\}$ to the problem of computing the permanent of a matrix over $\{0, 1\}$.

Recall the equivalence between the permanent of a matrix and the cycle covers of a directed graph. We must reduce the problem of computing the number of cycle covers of a weighted directed graph with positive integral weights to the problem of computing the number of cycle covers of an unweighted directed graph. This is accomplished by replacing every weighted edge with a subgraph consisting of several new vertices and edges.

The following figure shows this construction for an edge of weight 3.

The above process is repeated for each edge in G. The resulting graph G' is unweighted. Each cycle cover in G involving edges (u_i, v_i) with weights m_i, $1 \leq i \leq n$, is simulated by $m_1 m_2 \cdots m_n$ cycle covers in G', each of weight 1, thus the permanents are the same. Also, G' can be constructed in polynomial time.

This completes the proof that the problem of counting the number of perfect matchings in a bipartite graph (equivalently, counting the number of cycle covers in a directed graph) is $\#P$-complete.

Lecture 28   Parallel Algorithms and *NC*

Parallel computing is a popular current research topic. The successful design of parallel algorithms requires identifying sources of data independence in a problem that allow it to be decomposed into independent subproblems, which can then be solved in parallel. This process often involves looking deeply into the mathematical structure of the problem.

Aside from specific architectures such as the hypercube, there are many different general models of parallel computation in use. Among the most popular are:

- *Parallel Random Access Machines (PRAMs)*. A PRAM consists of a set of processors that have access to a common shared memory. Each processor may have registers and local memory of its own. We charge one time unit for a memory access (which many consider an unreasonable assumption). PRAMs can be exclusive or concurrent read and exclusive or concurrent write, giving four versions, denoted CRCW, CREW, ERCW, EREW. An EREW PRAM does not allow processors to read and write simultaneously to the same memory location, and requires the programmer to insure that this does not happen. A CRCW PRAM does allow this, and resolves conflicts arbitrarily.

- *Vector machines*. This model can be *SIMD (Single Instruction Multiple Data)* or *MIMD (Multiple Instruction Multiple Data)*. The processors are arranged in an array and all execute synchronously. The SIMD machines all execute the same instruction, but execute it on different data. Processors communicate by message passing.

- *Boolean and arithmetic circuits.* These are essentially dags with input nodes, output nodes, and basic bit operations or arithmetic operations associated with internal nodes. This model is quite common, especially in the theory of *NC*. The size of the circuit (number of nodes) corresponds roughly to the number of processors in a PRAM, and the depth of the circuit (length of the longest path from an input to an output) corresponds to time. Since each circuit has only a fixed number of input nodes, there must be a different circuit for each input length.

Many object to these models on the grounds that they do not adequately capture the "communication bottleneck", since communication complexity is not usually counted. These arguments do have merit, and one should not immediately take a parallel complexity bound obtained in one of these models as an accurate indication of the performance one would expect of a parallel implementation under current technology. However, independent of whether or not the complexity bounds are realistic, the important matter is to identify the fundamental sources of independence in a computational problem that allow efficient parallelization. These are mathematical properties that transcend technology; they will be there to exploit in any parallel machine or machine model now or in the future.

28.1   The Class *NC*

The complexity class *NC* plays the same role in parallel computation that *P* plays in sequential computation. A problem is considered to be "efficiently parallelizable" (at least in theory) if it can be shown to be in *NC*. The name *NC* stands for *Nick's Class*, after Nick Pippenger, who invented it.

Like *P*, the definition of *NC* is quite robust in the sense that it is impervious to minor perturbations of the machine model. It is the class of problems that can be solved on a PRAM in $(\log n)^{O(1)}$ or polylogarithmic time using $n^{O(1)}$ or polynomially many processors. It can also be defined as the class of problems accepted by a *uniform* family of Boolean circuits, one for each input length, of polylogarithmic depth and polynomial size. The uniformity condition says essentially that the nth circuit in this family is easily constructed, and is a technical condition that allows circuits and PRAMs to simulate each other efficiently. See the survey paper [23] for details.

The question $NC \stackrel{?}{=} P$ is analogous to the $P \stackrel{?}{=} NP$ question. There is an *NC* reducibility relation and a notion of *P*-completeness with respect to that reducibility relation. There is a set of problems known to be *P*-complete, among them the circuit value problem [67] and max flow [42]. The classes *P* and *NC* are equal if any of these problems turn out to be in *NC*.

28.2   Parallel Matrix Multiplication

To illustrate, we give a simple parallel algorithm to compute the product of two $n \times n$ matrices in time $1 + \log n$ with n^3 processors. We use the arithmetic circuit model.

Let A and B be two $n \times n$ matrices. We assume that the entries A_{ij} of A and B_{ij} of B are available at the n^2 input nodes of the circuit. Recall that

$$(AB)_{ij} \;=\; \sum_{k=1}^{n} A_{ik} B_{kj} \;. \tag{36}$$

In parallel, compute the n^3 products $A_{ik}B_{kj}$ for each triple i, j, k. This can be done in one step, since we have n^3 processors. Then allocate n processors to each pair i, j and compute the sums (36) from the data computed in the first step. This sum can be obtained in $\log n$ time in parallel by placing each of the n summands at the leaves of a complete binary tree, and summing adjacent pairs. This requires $\log n$ stages, since at each stage the number of data items is halved. The value at the root of the binary tree is the sum of the elements at the leaves.

28.3   Parallel Prefix

This circuit is a very useful subroutine in many parallel algorithms. Suppose we have n elements $x_0, x_1, \ldots, x_{n-1}$ and a binary operation $\cdot$ that is associative but not necessarily commutative. We wish to compute the *prefix products* y_i, $0 \le i \le n - 1$, where

$$y_i \;=\; x_0 \cdot x_1 \cdot x_2 \cdots x_i \;.$$

Consider the following circuit with n input gates and n output gates. The ith input gate receives x_i and the ith output gate gives y_i. In the first step, every processor i passes its data to processor $i + 1$, and the two data items are multiplied. In the next stage, data is passed from each i to $i + 2$; in the next stage, from i to $i + 4$; and so on for $\log n$ stages. The following illustration gives the circuit for $n = 16$.

$$x_0 \quad x_1 \quad x_2 \quad x_3 \quad x_4 \quad x_5 \quad x_6 \quad x_7 \quad x_8 \quad x_9 \quad x_{10} \, x_{11} \, x_{12} \, x_{13} \, x_{14} \, x_{15}$$

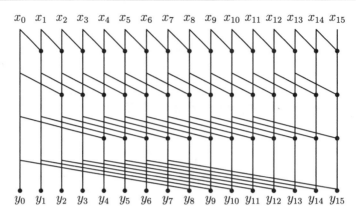

$$y_0 \quad y_1 \quad y_2 \quad y_3 \quad y_4 \quad y_5 \quad y_6 \quad y_7 \quad y_8 \quad y_9 \quad y_{10} \, y_{11} \, y_{12} \, y_{13} \, y_{14} \, y_{15}$$

This construction works even if n is not a power of 2. See [68] for an alternative construction.

This parallel algorithm has a particularly nice implementation on a hypercube. We can embed the circuit of 2^n processors on a hypercube of dimension n in such a way that all message routing can be done with no collisions and no message travels more than a distance of 2 on the cube.

This embedding will be defined in terms of the *Gray representation* of the numbers in the set $\{0, 1, 2, \ldots, 2^n - 1\}$, as opposed to the usual binary representation. Both representations pair elements of this set with the n-bit binary strings in a one-to-one fashion. In the natural order

$$0 < 1 < 2 < \cdots < 2^n - 1 \,,$$

the corresponding sequence of strings in the binary representation is obtained by starting from $0 \ldots 0$ and successively adding 1 in binary. For example, for $n = 4$ we get the sequence

0000, 0001, 0010, 0011, 0100, 0101, 0110, 0111, 1000, ..., 1111 .

In the Gray representation, the sequence is

0000, 0001, 0011, 0010, 0110, 0111, 0101, 0100, 1100, ..., 1000 .

Each element is obtained from the last by flipping one bit. If we graph the sequence of bits that are flipped, the picture looks similar to an English ruler with demarcations for inches, half inches, quarter inches, and so forth.

Now consider the unit cube in n-dimensional Euclidean space. Its vertices are points with Euclidean coordinates $(a_0, \ldots, a_{n-1})$ where each $a_i \in \{0, 1\}$. We map the processor that is i^{th} from the left in the parallel prefix circuit to the point of the cube whose Euclidean coordinates give i in the Gray representation. For $n = 3$, the Gray ordering is

$$000, \ 001, \ 011, \ 010, \ 110, \ 111, \ 101, \ 100$$

and this corresponds to the following Hamiltonian circuit in the cube:

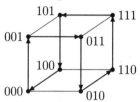

It is easy to convert back and forth between the binary and Gray representations. Let b_i and g_i denote the binary and Gray representations of i respectively. Then the jth bit of g_i (counting from the left and starting at 0) is the exclusive-or of the jth and $j - 1^{\text{st}}$ bits of b_i, and the jth bit of b_i is obtained from g_i by taking the exclusive-or of the jth bit of g_i and all bits to its left. Converting b_i to g_i takes time $O(1)$ with n processors and converting g_i to b_i takes time $O(\log n)$ with n processors using parallel prefix.

In the next lecture we will see how to characterize these operations algebraically. This will give a convenient means for proving properties of binary and Gray representations and of routing on the hypercube. We will then use these tools to analyze our hypercube implementation of parallel prefix.

Lecture 29   Hypercubes and the Gray Representation

In this lecture we will take an algebraic approach to routing on the hypercube. We will develop some algebraic tools, which we will then use to analyze the hypercube implementation of parallel prefix described in the last lecture.

Let $\mathcal{Z}_2$ be the field of integers mod 2. The field $\mathcal{Z}_2$ has 2 elements $\{0, 1\}$. Its multiplication operation is the same as Boolean $\wedge$, and its addition operation is the same as Boolean exclusive-or.

Let $\mathcal{Z}_2[x]$ denote the ring of univariate polynomials with coefficients in $\mathcal{Z}_2$. A typical element of this ring is $1 + x + x^2 + x^5 + x^8 + x^9$. Note that all coefficients are either 0 or 1, and $+$ and $-$ are the same thing, since $1 = -1$ in $\mathcal{Z}_2$.

Now we take the elements of $\mathcal{Z}_2[x]$ modulo the polynomial x^n to get the quotient ring $\mathcal{Z}_2[x]/x^n$. This is just like asserting that $x^n = 0$. It implies that $x^m = 0$ for all $m \geq n$, since $x^m = x^n \cdot x^{m-n} = 0 \cdot x^{m-n} = 0$. Elements of $\mathcal{Z}_2[x]/x^n$ are thus polynomials of degree $n - 1$ or less, and there are exactly 2^n such polynomials, the same number as bit strings of length n. We therefore identify bit strings of length n and elements of $\mathcal{Z}_2[x]/x^n$ under the one-to-one correspondence

$$a_0 a_1 \cdots a_{n-1} \;\mapsto\; \sum_{i=0}^{n-1} a_i x^i \;.$$

For example, for $n = 5$, the bit string 10011 corresponds to the polynomial $1 + x^3 + x^4$. (*Warning*: the *least* significant bit in the binary representation

156

of a number is the coefficient of the *highest* degree term in the corresponding polynomial.)

Under this correspondence, shifting right one bit corresponds to multiplication by x in $\mathcal{Z}_2[x]/x^n$, and componentwise exclusive-or corresponds to addition in $\mathcal{Z}_2[x]/x^n$. Thus the procedure for converting from binary to Gray (shift right and exclusive-or with the original) corresponds to multiplying by $1 + x$. In other words, if b_i and g_i are the polynomials in $\mathcal{Z}_2[x]/x^n$ corresponding to the binary and Gray representations of i respectively, then

$$\begin{aligned} g_i &= b_i + xb_i \\ &= (1+x)b_i \ . \end{aligned}$$

As we mentioned in the last lecture, this operation is invertible. Recall that to convert Gray to binary, we calculate the kth bit of the binary representation by taking the mod 2 sum of the kth bit of the Gray representation and all bits to its left. Algebraically, this corresponds to the fact that the polynomial $1+x$ has a multiplicative inverse in $\mathcal{Z}_2[x]/x^n$, namely $1 + x + x^2 + \cdots + x^{n-1}$:

$$\begin{aligned} (1+x) &\cdot (1 + x + x^2 + \cdots + x^{n-1}) \\ &= (1 + x + \cdots + x^{n-1}) + (x + x^2 + \cdots + x^n) \\ &= 1 + (x + x) + (x^2 + x^2) + \cdots + (x^{n-1} + x^{n-1}) + x^n \\ &= 1 + x^n \quad \text{since } q + q = 0 \\ &= 1 \quad \text{since } x^n = 0. \end{aligned}$$

The procedure for converting from Gray to binary then corresponds to multiplication by $1 + x + x^2 + \cdots + x^{n-1}$. (In fact, an element of $\mathcal{Z}_2[x]/x^n$ is invertible iff its constant coefficient is 1. The inverse of $1 + xp$ is $\sum_{i=0}^{n-1} x^i p^i$.)

In the kth stage of the parallel prefix circuit, we pass messages from node i to node $i + 2^k$. The distance between these nodes on the hypercube is the number of bits on which g_i and g_{i+2^k} differ. This is often called the *Hamming distance*. We now show that the Hamming distance between the Gray representations of i and $i + 2^k$ is 2 if $k \geq 1$ and 1 if $k = 0$.

Let e_{ik} be the degree of the highest power of x that divides $b_i + b_{i+2^k}$. The significance of e_{ik} is that it measures the distance that the carry propagates when adding 2^k to i in binary. Specifically, the binary representation of 2^k has a 1 in bit position $n - k - 1$ and 0 elsewhere. A carry is propagated to the left of the $n - k - 1^{\text{st}}$ bit position as long as we see a 1 in b_i. The carry stops at the first bit position to the left of $n - k$ at which b_i contains a 0, and e_{ik} is that bit position (counting from the left and starting at 0), or 0 if no such position exists. The exclusive-or of the bit strings b_i and b_{i+2^k} is of the form $\cdots 00011111000 \cdots$, with 1 in bit positions e_{ik} through $n - k - 1$ inclusive and 0 elsewhere.

In terms of the polynomial representation,

$$b_i + b_{i+2^k} = \sum_{j=e_{ik}}^{n-k-1} x^j .$$

Converting to Gray, we have

$$
\begin{aligned}
g_i + g_{i+2^k} &= (1+x)b_i + (1+x)b_{i+2^k} \\
&= (1+x) \cdot (b_i + b_{i+2^k}) \\
&= (1+x) \sum_{j=e_{ik}}^{n-k-1} x^j \\
&= x^{e_{ik}} + x^{n-k} .
\end{aligned}
$$

This says that the Gray representations of i and $i + 2^k$ differ only in bits e_{ik} and $n - k$. In the case $k = 0$, they differ only in bit e_{ik}, since $x^n = 0$. For example,

$$
\begin{aligned}
b_i &= 1001011101111111100010100111 \\
b_{2^k} &= 0000000000000001000000000000 \\
b_{i+2^k} &= 1001011110000000100010100111 \\
b_i + b_{i+2^k} &= 0000000011111111000000000000 \\
g_i + g_{i+2^k} &= 0000000010000000100000000000 \\
&\qquad\quad\uparrow\qquad\quad\uparrow \\
&\qquad\quad e_{ik}\qquad n - k
\end{aligned}
$$

We have shown that the Hamming distance between g_i and g_{i+2^k}, and hence the routing distance on the hypercube between processor i and $i + 2^k$, is at most 2. Thus in each stage of our parallel prefix circuit, messages must be passed a distance of at most 2. However, we still need to show how to route the messages so as to avoid collisions.

Let us use the following protocol. At stage 0, processor i passes its value to processor $i + 1$. Processor i can compute the Gray representation of the destination processor by flipping bit e_{i0} of its own Gray representation. There are no collisions, since $i \mapsto i + 1$ is a Hamiltonian circuit.

Subsequently, in stage k, messages are passed from i to $i + 2^k$ in two rounds. In the first round, each processor i of even parity flips bit $n - k$ of its Gray representation and sends its message to the processor with that Gray representation. (The *parity* of i is the low order bit of b_i, *i.e.* the coefficient of x^{n-1}, or the mod 2 sum of the bits of g_i.) Each processor i of odd parity flips bit e_{ik} of its Gray representation and sends its message to the processor with that Gray representation. In the second round, those processors receiving the messages flip the remaining bit and forward the messages to their final destinations.

There is no collision along wires, *i.e.* no messages are sent from i to j and simultaneously from j to i, because any two nodes with a direct connection in the hypercube have different parity, and if i and j are of different parity then they are flipping different bits in each of the two rounds, so the two messages cannot be traveling along the same wire at the same time.

However, it is still conceivable that messages might collide at a vertex, *i.e.* i and j might both pass to ℓ in the first round. We show that this cannot happen either. If i and j are of different parity, then the messages are going to processors of different parity. If i and j are of the same parity, then either in round 1 or round 2 the $n - k^{th}$ bit is being flipped in both transmissions, and this is a one-to-one map.

Hypercube embeddings and message routing are an active topic of research. For more information and references, see [54, 55, 104].

Lecture 30   Integer Arithmetic in NC

30.1   Integer Addition

Addition of two n-bit binary numbers can be performed in $\log n$ depth with n processors. We will use parallel prefix to calculate the carry string. Once the carry is computed, the sum is easily computed in constant time with n processors by taking the exclusive-or of the two summands and the carry string.

The carry string is defined as follows:

- The lowest order carry bit is always 0.

- If the ith bits of the two summands (counting from the right) are both 0, then the $i + 1^{\text{st}}$ bit of the carry will be 0, irrespective of the ith bit of the carry.

- If the ith bits of the two summands are both 1, then the $i + 1^{\text{st}}$ bit of the carry will be 1, irrespective of the ith bit of the carry.

- If the ith bits of the two summands are 0 and 1, then the $i + 1^{\text{st}}$ bit of the carry will be the same as the ith bit of the carry. In this case we say that the carry is *propagated* from i to $i + 1$.

To compute the carry using parallel prefix, we will use a three element algebra $\{0, 1, p\}$ with associative binary operation $\cdot$ defined below. Intuitively, the

160

element 0 means, "carry 0", the element 1 means "carry 1", and the element p means, "propagate the carry from the previous bit position".

The binary operation $\cdot$ is defined by the following table:

$\cdot$	0	1	p
0	0	0	0
1	1	1	1
p	0	1	p

In other words, for any $x \in \{0, 1, p\}$,

$$
\begin{aligned}
0 \cdot x &= 0 \\
1 \cdot x &= 1 \\
p \cdot x &= x .
\end{aligned}
$$

Note that $\cdot$ is associative but not commutative: $0 \cdot 1 = 0$ but $1 \cdot 0 = 1$.

Let u be a string over $\{0, 1, p\}$ with a 0 in position 0, a 0 in position $i+1$ if the ith bits of the two summands are both 0, a 1 in position $i+1$ if the ith bits of the two summands are both 1, and a p in position $i+1$ if one of the ith bits of the two summands is 0 and the other is 1. The string u can be computed in constant time from a and b with n processors. The carry string is obtained by computing the suffix products of u.

Example 30.1 Let $a = 100101011101011$ and $b = 110101001010001$. The string u over $\{0, 1, p\}$ for these two numbers, the carry string obtained as the suffixes of u, and the binary sum are as illustrated.

$$
\begin{aligned}
u &= 1p01010p1ppp0p10 \\
carry &= 1001010110000110 \\
a &= 100101011101011 \\
b &= 110101001010001 \\
\hline
sum &= 1011010100111100
\end{aligned}
$$

□

30.2 Integer Multiplication

Consider a multiplication problem involving two n-bit binary numbers. The grade school algorithm for multiplication gives n partial sums, which then can be added to get the product. For example,

$$
\begin{array}{r}
101101 \\
\times\ 101011 \\
\hline
101101 \\
101101 \\
000000 \\
101101 \\
000000 \\
+\ 101101 \\
\hline
11110001111
\end{array}
\tag{37}
$$

This can be done in time $O((\log n)^2)$ with $O(n^2)$ processors in a straightforward way. First compute all the bits of the partial sums, then add the partial sums in pairs in a tree-like fashion. It takes constant time to compute the partial sums with $O(n^2)$ processors, and $O((\log n)^2)$ to do the additions.

By being slightly more clever, we can reduce the time to $O(\log n)$ by reducing the problem of adding three n-bit binary numbers to adding two $n+1$-bit binary numbers. Look at the partial sums obtained by adding each 3-bit column individually:

$$
\begin{array}{r}
101100111 \\
101011100 \\
+\ 101111101 \\
\hline
10 \\
01 \\
11 \\
10 \\
10 \\
10 \\
11 \\
00 \\
+\ 11 \\
\hline
\end{array}
$$

Rearranging, we get

$$
\begin{array}{r}
10 \\
01 \\
11 \\
10 \\
10 \\
10 \\
11 \\
00 \\
+\ 11 \\
\hline
\end{array}
\qquad \longrightarrow \qquad
\begin{array}{r}
101111101 \\
+\ 101000110 \\
\hline
\end{array}
$$

Thus, in constant time we have reduced the problem of adding three binary numbers to adding two binary numbers. To apply this to the multiplication problem (37), we partition the partial sums into sets of three and perform this step in parallel for all the sets. This reduces the problem of adding n numbers to the problem of adding $\frac{2n}{3}$ numbers. We repeat this step until we have only two numbers, then we just add them using the $O(\log n)$ time addition algorithm described above. After the first stage, we have $\frac{2}{3}n$ numbers; after the second stage, $(\frac{2}{3})^2 n$, and so on. The number of numbers decreases geometrically, thus there are only $O(\log n)$ stages. Each stage takes $O(1)$ time and $O(n^2)$ processors.

30.3 Integer Division

We wish to do integer division with remainder in *NC*. That is, given binary numbers s and t, compute the unique quotient q and remainder r such that $s = qt + r$ and $0 \leq r < t$.

Our algorithm is based on *Newton's method*, a useful technique for approximating roots of differentiable functions. Newton's method works as follows. Starting from an initial guess x_0, compute a sequence of approximations

$$x_{i+1} = x_i - \frac{f(x_i)}{f'(x_i)} , \tag{38}$$

where $f' = df/dx$. For real-valued functions of a real variable, this is equivalent to finding the line tangent to the curve $y = f(x)$ at x_i and taking x_{i+1} to be the point where that line intersects the x axis.

In general, Newton's method is not guaranteed to converge to a root. However, if the function is well-behaved and the initial guess x_0 is close enough to a root, then the method converges very quickly: the number of bits of accuracy roughly doubles with each iteration. In this application, although we are using an approximation technique, we will be using only exact binary arithmetic (no floating point), and will obtain an exact solution.

We first show how to approximate the reciprocal $\frac{1}{t}$ of a given number t in binary. We will do this by approximating the root of the function

$$f(x) = t - \frac{1}{x}$$

using Newton's method.

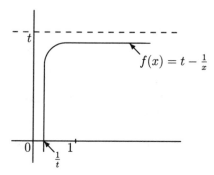

In this case, $f'(x) = x^{-2}$, and (38) becomes

$$x_{i+1} = 2x_i - tx_i^2 \ .$$

We take as our first approximation x_0 the unique fractional power of 2 in the interval $(\frac{1}{2t}, \frac{1}{t}]$. This can be found in $O(\log n)$ time by finding the unique power of 2 in the interval $[t, 2t)$ and taking its reciprocal by reversing the order of the binary digits and placing a binary point after the first 0. We then iterate Newton's method to get the sequence of approximations $x_0, x_1, x_2, \dots$. These approximations blast in toward $\frac{1}{t}$ quickly: we start with an error of at most $\frac{1}{2t}$, and at each step we roughly square the error, thus doubling the number of bits of accuracy. This is called *quadratic convergence*.

Lemma 30.2 *The sequence* $x_0, x_1, \dots$ *obtained from Newton's method is non-decreasing and converges quadratically to* $\frac{1}{t}$.

Proof. By definition,

$$\frac{1}{2t} \ < \ x_0 \ \le \ \frac{1}{t} \ ,$$

or in other words,

$$0 \ \le \ 1 - tx_0 \ < \ \frac{1}{2} \ .$$

For $i \ge 0$,

$$
\begin{aligned}
1 - tx_{i+1} &= 1 - t(2x_i - tx_i^2) \\
&= (1 - tx_i)^2 \ .
\end{aligned}
$$

It follows by induction that

$$
\begin{aligned}
1 - tx_i &= (1 - tx_0)^{2^i} \\
&< 2^{-2^i} \ ,
\end{aligned}
$$

thus

$$\frac{1}{t} - x_i \ < \ \frac{1}{2^{2^i} t} \ .$$

From these facts we can conclude that

$$\frac{1}{2t} < x_0 \le x_1 \le x_2 \le \cdots \le \frac{1}{t} \ .$$

$\square$

After $k = \lceil \log \log \frac{s}{t} \rceil$ iterations we have

$$1 - t x_k \ < \ \frac{t}{s} \ .$$

From this and the fact that $x_k \le \frac{1}{t}$ we have that

$$0 \ \le \ \frac{s}{t} - s x_k \ < \ 1 \ .$$

Therefore the desired integer part of $\frac{s}{t}$ is either $\lfloor s x_k \rfloor$ or $\lceil s x_k \rceil$, and the remainder can be found by subtracting.

Each Newton iteration took $O(\log n)$ time (we did not do enough iterations to let the numbers get too big) and we needed $\log \log \frac{s}{t} = O(\log n)$ iterations.

For some interesting ramifications of the division problem, including an $O(\log n)$-depth circuit for integer division under a slightly weaker uniformity condition, see [9].

Lecture 31   Csanky's Algorithm

In 1976, Csanky gave a parallel algorithm to invert matrices [26]. This was one of the very first NC algorithms. It set the stage for a large body of research in parallel linear algebra that culminated with Mulmuley's 1986 result that the rank of a matrix over an arbitrary field can be computed in NC [82].

In this lecture we will develop Csanky's algorithm. Along the way, we give some NC algorithms for problems of independent interest, including the calculation of the characteristic polynomial and determinant of a matrix and the solution of linear recurrences. First we recall some basic NC algorithms:

Inner product   The inner product of two vectors $a = (a_1, \ldots, a_n)$ and $b = (b_1, \ldots, b_n)$ can be computed in $O(\log n)$ parallel arithmetic steps by n processors. First, produce in parallel the products $a_i b_i$, $1 \leq i \leq n$; then add the products in a treelike fashion.

Matrix multiplication   If A is an $m \times n$ matrix and B is an $n \times p$ matrix, their product AB can be computed by $O(mpn)$ processors in $O(\log n)$ time. AB has mp entries, each obtained as the inner product of a row of A and a column of B.

Powers of A   The powers $A^1, A^2, \ldots, A^n$ of an $n \times n$ matrix A can be obtained as the products of prefixes of the n-component sequence $(A, A, \ldots, A)$. This can be accomplished in $O(\log^2 n)$ time by $O(n^4)$ processors arranged in a parallel prefix circuit of width n in which the associative operation is $n \times n$ matrix multiplication.

31.1 Inversion of Lower Triangular Matrices

Given an $n \times n$ lower triangular matrix A, break it up into submatrices

$$A = \left[\begin{array}{c|c} B & 0 \\ \hline C & D \end{array} \right]$$

where B is $\lfloor \frac{n}{2} \rfloor \times \lfloor \frac{n}{2} \rfloor$, C is $\lceil \frac{n}{2} \rceil \times \lfloor \frac{n}{2} \rfloor$, and D is $\lceil \frac{n}{2} \rceil \times \lceil \frac{n}{2} \rceil$. Recursively compute B^{-1} and D^{-1} in parallel. Then

$$A^{-1} = \left[\begin{array}{c|c} B^{-1} & 0 \\ \hline -D^{-1}CB^{-1} & D^{-1} \end{array} \right].$$

The parallel computation time of this algorithm satisfies the relation

$$T(n) = T\left(\frac{n}{2}\right) + 2M\left(\frac{n}{2}\right)$$

where $T(\frac{n}{2})$ is the time needed to invert B and D in parallel and $2M(\frac{n}{2})$ is the time needed to form the matrix product $-D^{-1}CB^{-1}$. With $O(n^3)$ processors, we have $M(n) = O(\log n)$, whence $T(n) = O(\log^2 n)$.

31.2 Solution of Linear Recurrences

It may seem surprising that the nth term of a linear recurrence such as the Fibonacci sequence $F_0 = 1$, $F_1 = 1$, $F_{n+2} = F_{n+1} + F_n$ should be computable without first computing the first $n - 1$ terms. In fact, the nth term of any linear recurrence can be computed in parallel polylog time.

A general linear recurrence is a system of the form

$$\begin{array}{rcl}
x_1 & = & c_1 \\
x_2 & = & a_{21}x_1 + c_2 \\
x_3 & = & a_{31}x_1 + a_{32}x_2 + c_3 \\
& \vdots & \\
x_n & = & a_{n1}x_1 + \cdots + a_{n,n-1}x_{n-1} + c_n
\end{array}$$

where the a_{ij} and c_i are given, and we wish to solve for the x_i. For example, the Fibonacci sequence is given by the system $c_1 = c_2 = 1$ and $c_i = 0$ for $i \geq 3$, $a_{i,i-1} = a_{i,i-2} = 1$ for $i \geq 3$, and all other $a_{ij} = 0$.

Let $a_{ij} = 0$ for $j \geq i$, let A be the $n \times n$ matrix (a_{ij}), let x be the vector (x_i), and let c be the vector (c_i). The system above is then equivalent to the matrix-vector equation

$$Ax + c = x,$$

or equivalently,

$$c = (I - A)x .$$

The matrix $I - A$ is lower triangular with 1's on the diagonal, and thus can be inverted in NC by the method described in the previous section. This allows us to solve for x:

$$x = (I - A)^{-1}c .$$

31.3   The Characteristic Polynomial of a Matrix

We give a linear recurrence for the coefficients of the characteristic polynomial of a given matrix A, which can then be solved by the method of the previous section. This linear recurrence was known to Sir Isaac Newton.

The characteristic polynomial of a matrix A is defined to be

$$\begin{aligned}
\det (xI - A) &= x^n - s_1 x^{n-1} + s_2 x^{n-2} - \cdots \pm s_n \\
&= \prod_{i=1}^{n} (x - \lambda_i)
\end{aligned}$$

where x is an indeterminate, $\lambda_1, \ldots, \lambda_n$ are the eigenvalues of A (multiplicities counted), and $\det B$ is the determinant of B. The coefficient s_1 is called the *trace* of A and is denoted $\operatorname{tr} A$. It is both the sum of the eigenvalues and the sum of the diagonal elements of A:

$$\begin{aligned}
s_1 &= \operatorname{tr} A \\
&= \sum_{i=1}^{n} \lambda_i \\
&= \sum_{i=1}^{n} a_{ii} ,
\end{aligned}$$

so it can be easily computed in NC. It can also be shown that λ_i^m is an eigenvalue of A^m of the same multiplicity as λ_i of A, therefore

$$\operatorname{tr} A^m = \sum_{i=1}^{n} \lambda_i^m .$$

The constant coefficient s_n is the determinant of A and is the product of the eigenvalues:

$$\begin{aligned}
s_n &= \det A \\
&= \prod_{i=1}^{n} \lambda_i .
\end{aligned}$$

The intermediate coefficients are called the *elementary symmetric polynomials* in $\lambda_1, \ldots, \lambda_n$ and are given by

$$s_k = \sum_{1 \le i_1 < \cdots < i_k \le n} \lambda_{i_1} \lambda_{i_2} \cdots \lambda_{i_k} \; ;$$

in other words, the sum of all products of k-element submultisets of the multiset of eigenvalues of A.

Define

$$f_k^m = \sum_{\substack{1 \le i_1 < \cdots < i_k \le n \\ j \notin \{i_1, \ldots, i_k\}}} \lambda_{i_1} \lambda_{i_2} \cdots \lambda_{i_k} \lambda_j^m \; .$$

At the extremes,

$$f_k^0 = (n-k)s_k$$
$$f_0^m = \operatorname{tr} A^m \; .$$

Then

$$s_k \cdot \operatorname{tr} A^m$$
$$= \Big(\sum_{1 \le i_1 < \cdots < i_k \le n} \lambda_{i_1} \lambda_{i_2} \cdots \lambda_{i_k} \Big) \cdot \Big(\sum_{j=1}^{n} \lambda_j^m \Big)$$
$$= \sum_{\substack{1 \le i_1 < \cdots < i_k \le n \\ j \notin \{i_1, \ldots, i_k\}}} \lambda_{i_1} \lambda_{i_2} \cdots \lambda_{i_k} \lambda_j^m + \sum_{\substack{1 \le i_1 < \cdots < i_k \le n \\ j \in \{i_1, \ldots, i_k\}}} \lambda_{i_1} \lambda_{i_2} \cdots \lambda_{i_k} \lambda_j^m$$
$$= f_k^m + f_{k-1}^{m+1} \; .$$

It follows that

$$s_k \cdot \operatorname{tr} A^0 - s_{k-1} \cdot \operatorname{tr} A^1 + s_{k-2} \cdot \operatorname{tr} A^2 - \cdots \pm s_1 \cdot \operatorname{tr} A^{k-1} \mp \operatorname{tr} A^k$$
$$= (f_k^0 + fk - 1^1) - (f_{k-1}^1 + f_{k-2}^2) + \cdots \pm (f_1^{k-1} + f_0^k) \mp f_0^k$$
$$= f_k^0$$
$$= (n-k)s_k \; .$$

This gives a recurrence for s_k in terms of $s_1, \ldots, s_{k-1}$:

$$s_k = \frac{1}{k}(s_{k-1} \cdot \operatorname{tr} A - s_{k-2} \cdot \operatorname{tr} A^2 + \cdots \pm \operatorname{tr} A^k) \; . \tag{39}$$

The $\operatorname{tr} A^m$ can be computed in NC by computing the powers of A using parallel prefix and summing the diagonal elements. The recurrence (39) can then be solved using the method of the previous section.

31.4   Inversion of Arbitrary Nonsingular Matrices

We use the *Cayley-Hamilton Theorem*, which says that every matrix satisfies its characteristic equation:

$$A^n - s_1 A^{n-1} + s_2 A^{n-2} - \cdots \mp s_{n-1} A \pm s_n I \; = \; 0 \,.$$

Multiplying by A^{-1} and rearranging terms, we get

$$A^{-1} \; = \; \frac{1}{s_n}(s_{n-1}I - s_{n-2}A + \cdots \pm s_1 A^{n-2} \mp A^{n-1}) \,. \tag{40}$$

The coefficients s_k of the characteristic polynomial and powers of A are computed by the method of the previous section. The matrix polynomial (40) can be computed in time $O(\log n)$ using $O(n^3)$ processors. The complete algorithm to compute A^{-1} from A runs in $O(\log^2 n)$ parallel arithmetic steps on $O(n^4)$ processors.

Lecture 32   Chistov's Algorithm

Many important computational problems in algebra (such as the solution of polynomial equations) depend strongly on basic algorithms in linear algebra. In turn, many problems in linear algebra reduce to the computation of the rank of a matrix. This problem thus occupies a central position in computational algebra. NC algorithms for matrix rank were given by Ibarra, Moran, and Rosier in 1980 for matrices over the complex numbers [53] and over general fields in 1986 by Mulmuley [82]. We will devote a future lecture to this topic, but for now we lay the groundwork by showing how to calculate the characteristic polynomial of a matrix over an arbitrary field in NC.

The major limitation of Csanky's algorithm for computing the characteristic polynomial of a matrix is that it does not work in all fields, since it involves a division by k in (39). This won't be possible for example if the field is $\mathcal{Z}_p$ and k is a multiple of p. Berkowitz [11] and Chistov [18] gave the first deterministic NC algorithms for computing characteristic polynomials over arbitrary fields. Here we present Chistov's method [18].

Recall that the characteristic polynomial of A, denoted $\chi_A(x)$, is defined by:

$$\begin{aligned} \chi_A(x) &= \det(xI - A) \\ &= x^n - s_1 x^{n-1} + s_2 x^{n-2} - \cdots \pm s_n . \end{aligned}$$

We will compute the polynomial that has the same coefficients, but in reverse order:

$$x^n \chi_A\left(\frac{1}{x}\right) = 1 - s_1 x + s_2 x^2 + \cdots \pm s_n x^n$$
$$= \det(I - xA).$$

Define $B = I - xA$ and let B_m denote the $m \times m$ submatrix in the lower right corner of B:

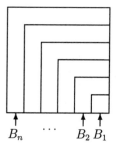

$$B_n \quad \cdots \quad B_2 \ B_1$$

Let A_m be defined in the same way from A. Then $B_m = I_m - xA_m$. Define $\Delta_m = \det B_m$.

Cramer's rule gives a useful formula for the inverse of a matrix C in terms of determinants of its submatrices:

$$C_{ij}^{-1} = (-1)^{i+j} \frac{\det \overline{C}_{ji}}{\det C}$$

where $\overline{C}_{ji}$ denotes the submatrix obtained from C by removing the jth row and i^{th} column. Applying Cramer's rule, we get

$$(B_m^{-1})_{11} = \frac{\Delta_{m-1}}{\Delta_m}.$$

But wait, this is all a bit suspicious, since B_m and Δ_m contain the indeterminate x. How can we invert a matrix with indeterminates? To make sense of this, we have to work in the field of *rational functions* over the base field k. This will let us divide by polynomials. The rational functions over k are the formal fractions

$$k(x) = \left\{ \frac{p}{q} \ \middle| \ p, q \in k[x], \ q \neq 0 \right\},$$

or more accurately, the equivalence classes of such fractions obtained by identifying p_1/q_1 and p_2/q_2 if $p_1 q_2 = p_2 q_1$. This construction is 100% analogous to the construction of the rational numbers from the integers.

Using the formal power series expansion of rational functions, the inverse of B_m can be expressed as an infinite formal sum

$$B_m^{-1} = \sum_{i=0}^{\infty} x^i A_m^i. \tag{41}$$

To convince yourself that this works, multiply (41) by $B_m = I_m - xA_m$. The expression (41) denotes a matrix of rational functions, because B_m is invertible as a linear map over the field $k(x)$: its determinant is $\Delta_m \neq 0$, as can be seen by evaluating at $x = 0$.

We can express $1/\Delta_n$, the determinant of B_n^{-1}, as a telescoping product like this:

$$
\begin{aligned}
\frac{1}{\Delta_n} &= \frac{\Delta_{n-1}}{\Delta_n} \cdot \frac{\Delta_{n-2}}{\Delta_{n-1}} \cdots \frac{\Delta_0}{\Delta_1} \\
&= (B_n^{-1})_{11} \cdot (B_{n-1}^{-1})_{11} \cdots (B_1^{-1})_{11} \\
&= (\sum_{i=0}^{\infty} x^i A_n^i)_{11} \cdot (\sum_{i=0}^{\infty} x^i A_{n-1}^i)_{11} \cdots (\sum_{i=0}^{\infty} x^i A_1^i)_{11} \qquad (42) \\
&= 1 - xH(x) , \qquad (43)
\end{aligned}
$$

where H is a humongous power series. The last step is justified by observing that the constant coefficients of all the factors in (42) are 1, therefore the constant coefficient of (43) is 1. Now recall that the polynomial we were originally looking for was Δ_n, which is the inverse of (43). We can therefore express Δ_n as a power series in terms of $H(x)$:

$$
\begin{aligned}
\Delta_n &= \sum_{i=0}^{\infty} x^i H(x)^i \\
&= 1 - s_1 x + s_2 x^2 + \cdots \pm s_n x^n
\end{aligned}
$$

and we know that the power series is a polynomial, so that all coefficients are zero after a certain point. Thus, despite all the infinite power series we have been using, all the terms after x^n vanish in the result. Therefore if we do all the calculations mod x^{n+1}, and take only the first $n + 1$ terms of each series, we will still get the same answer.

This can be turned into a fast parallel algorithm, and since it involves no divisions, it will work in arbitrary fields.

32.1   The Characteristic Polynomial and Matrix Rank

The significance of the characteristic polynomial in matrix rank calculations is summed up in the following key lemma.

Lemma 32.1 *Let B be a square matrix over a field. If* rank B = rank B^2, *then* rank $B = n - k$, *where x^k is the highest power of x that divides the characteristic polynomial $\chi_B(x)$.*

This lemma allows us to calculate the rank of a matrix by calculating its characteristic polynomial, provided its square has the same rank. A proper proof of this lemma would span a good portion of a first course in linear algebra, including Jordan canonical form and the Cayley-Hamilton Theorem, so it is a bit beyond our scope. Nevertheless, here it is in a nutshell.

When an $n \times n$ matrix B acts as a linear map on the vector space k^n, some vectors may be annihilated. These form a linear subspace called the kernel of B and denoted ker B. The dimension of this subspace is $n -$ rank B. Vectors that are not annihilated by B get mapped around, and some may be mapped into the kernel, so that if the space is hit with B a second time, those vectors will be wiped out. The proviso rank $B^2 =$ rank B in Lemma 32.1 says that this does not happen. In other words, if a vector is ever going to be wiped out by some power of B, then it is already wiped out by B. For any B, the degree of the highest power of x that divides the characteristic polynomial of B is the dimension of the subspace of all vectors that ever get wiped out by some power of B. Thus if rank $B^2 =$ rank B, then this subspace is just the kernel of B, and its dimension is $n -$ rank B.

The key property here is that the degree of the highest power of x that divides χ_B is the dimension of the subspace of all vectors that ever get wiped out by some power of B. Let's give this subspace a name:

$$E_0 = \bigcup_{i=0}^{\infty} \ker B^i$$
$$= \ker B^n .$$

The last equation follows from the fact that the subspaces ker B^i are ordered by inclusion, ker $B^i = n - \dim \operatorname{im} B^i$ (im B^i denotes the image of the whole space under the map B^i), and the image can only shrink in dimension n times before it disappears completely.

Another way of stating our key property is that $\dim E_0$ is the multiplicity of 0 as an eigenvalue of B. More generally, for each eigenvalue λ of B, we can define

$$E_\lambda = \bigcup_{i=0}^{\infty} \ker (\lambda I - B)^i$$
$$= \ker (\lambda I - B)^n .$$

The subspace E_λ is called the *generalized eigenspace* of λ, and consists of all vectors of k^n that are annihilated by some power of the matrix $\lambda I - B$. The kernel of $\lambda I - B$ is called the *eigenspace* of λ.

Two nice things about the subspaces E_λ are that

(i) they are setwise invariant under the action of any matrix of the form $\mu I - B$; and

(ii) every vector can be represented *uniquely* as a sum of vectors, one from each generalized eigenspace.

Property (i) says that hitting the subspace E_λ repeatedly with the matrix $\lambda I - B$ does not move any vector outside of E_λ, but keeps shrinking it until it finally disappears; and if $\mu \neq \lambda$, then $\mu I - B$ is a bijection on E_λ. Property (ii) says that k^n is the *direct sum* of the subspaces E_λ; in symbols,

$$k^n \cong \bigoplus_\lambda E_\lambda$$

where $\cong$ denotes isomorphism of vector spaces and $\bigoplus$ denotes direct sum.

Now pick a new basis consisting of vectors in the subspaces E_λ. Under the change of basis, because of property (i), B becomes block diagonal with a block for each eigenvalue λ. (Judicious choice of these basis elements will even give us *Jordan canonical form*, with eigenvalues on the diagonal, 1's and 0's on the off-diagonal just above, and 0's elsewhere). The size of the block corresponding to λ is the dimension of E_λ. The change of basis is effected by a similarity transformation $B \mapsto U^{-1}BU$, which does not change the characteristic polynomial:

$$
\begin{aligned}
\det\left(xI - U^{-1}BU\right) &= \det U^{-1}(xI - B)U \\
&= \det U^{-1} \cdot \det\left(xI - B\right) \cdot \det U \\
&= \det\left(xI - B\right).
\end{aligned}
$$

But the characteristic polynomial of a block diagonal matrix is the product of the characteristic polynomials of the blocks, which are $(x - \lambda)^{\dim E_\lambda}$. Thus

$$\chi_B(x) = \prod_\lambda (x - \lambda)^{\dim E_\lambda}. \tag{44}$$

If one of the eigenvalues is 0 (*i.e.*, if B has a nontrivial kernel), then $x^{\dim E_0}$ and no higher power of x will divide χ_B. This is what we wanted to show.

This conclusion also leads to an understanding of the *Cayley-Hamilton Theorem*: every matrix satisfies its characteristic equation. From (44) we get

$$
\begin{aligned}
\chi_B(B) &= \prod_\lambda (B - \lambda I)^{\dim E_\lambda} \\
&= \pm \prod_\lambda (\lambda I - B)^{\dim E_\lambda}.
\end{aligned}
$$

Applied to the whole space k^n, the factor

$$(\lambda I - B)^{\dim E_\lambda}$$

wipes out E_λ and fixes the other generalized eigenspaces setwise. Applying $\chi_B(B)$ to k^n applies these factors for each eigenvalue λ in succession, which successively wipe out all the E_λ, leaving nothing. Thus $\chi_B(B)$ is the zero matrix.

Lecture 33 Matrix Rank

Recall that the *rank* of an $m \times n$ matrix A over a field k is the maximum number of linearly independent rows (or columns) of A. It is the dimension of the image of the linear map $k^n \to k^m$ defined by A; equivalently, it is n minus the dimension of the kernel (the set of vectors in k^n annihilated by the map).

Once we have an *NC* algorithm to calculate the rank of a matrix, the door is opened for a wide variety of other *NC* algorithms in linear algebra. For example, to compute a basis for the vector space spanned by the columns of some matrix, we can compute the ranks of all sets of columns $\{c_1, \ldots, c_i\}$, $1 \leq i \leq n$, and add c_i to the basis only if the rank of $\{c_1, \ldots, c_i\}$ is one greater than the rank of $\{c_1, \ldots, c_{i-1}\}$.

We will start with the algorithm of Ibarra, Moran, and Rosier [53], which computes the rank of a matrix over the complex numbers $\mathcal{C}$.

Recall the following lemma from the last lecture:

Lemma 33.1 *Let C be an $n \times n$ matrix over any field. If* $\operatorname{rank} C^2 = \operatorname{rank} C$, *then we can compute* $\operatorname{rank} C$ *in NC by computing the characteristic polynomial* $\det(xI - C)$ *and finding the highest power of x that divides it, say x^d. Then* $\operatorname{rank} C = n - d$.

Let A be a matrix over $\mathcal{C}$, not necessarily square. The *conjugate transpose* of A, denoted $\overline{A}^T$, is the transpose of A with every entry replaced by its complex conjugate. Recall that the conjugate $\overline{z}$ of a complex number z is obtained by reflecting in the real axis: if $z = a + ib$, where a and b are real, then $\bar{z} = a - ib$. Note that the product $z\bar{z}$ is always a nonnegative real number:

$$(a + ib) \cdot (a - ib) \;=\; a^2 + b^2 \,.$$

Let $B = \overline{A}^T A$. We will prove that A and B have the same rank; moreover, rank $B^2 =$ rank B and B is square, so Lemma 33.1 applies.

The matrix B is of a particularly nice form: it is *Hermitian*, which means that $B = \overline{B}^T$. A Hermitian matrix is the complex analog of a symmetric matrix.

Lemma 33.2 *For any complex vector* $y \in C^n$, $\bar{y}^T y = 0$ *iff* $y = 0$.

Proof. If $y = (a_1, a_2, \ldots, a_n)$ then

$$\begin{aligned}
\bar{y}^T y \;&=\; (\bar{a}_1, \bar{a}_2, \ldots, \bar{a}_n) \cdot (a_1, a_2, \ldots, a_n) \\
&=\; \sum_{i=1}^{n} \bar{a}_i \cdot a_i \,.
\end{aligned}$$

Now $\bar{a}_i \cdot a_i$ is always a nonnegative real number, and it can only be zero if $a_i = 0$. The sum of nonnegative reals can only be zero if each term, and hence each a_i, is zero. □

Recall that the *kernel* of a linear map is the set of vectors that are mapped to the origin. Thus if the linear map is represented by the matrix A, then

$$\ker A \;=\; \{x \in C^n \mid Ax = 0\} \,.$$

The rank of A is the dimension of the image of A, which is the same as $n - \dim \ker A$. The following lemma shows that it is sufficient to find the dimension of the kernel of $\overline{A}^T A$.

Lemma 33.3 $\ker A = \ker \overline{A}^T A$.

Proof.
($\subseteq$) If $x \in \ker A$ then $Ax = 0$, which implies that $\overline{A}^T A x = 0$.
($\supseteq$) Suppose $x \in \ker \overline{A}^T A$. Then

$$\begin{aligned}
\overline{A}^T A x = 0 \;\;&\to\;\; \bar{x}^T \overline{A}^T A x = 0 \\
&\to\;\; \overline{(Ax)}^T A x = 0 \\
&\to\;\; Ax = 0 \qquad \text{by Lemma 33.2.}
\end{aligned}$$

□

Lemma 33.4 *If B is Hermitian, then* rank $B =$ rank B^2.

Proof. It suffices to show that the kernels of B and B^2 coincide. Surely $\ker B \subseteq \ker B^2$. Now suppose $x \in \ker B^2$. Then

$$
\begin{aligned}
B^2 x = 0 \quad &\rightarrow \quad \overline{x}^T BB x = 0 \\
&\rightarrow \quad \overline{x}^T \overline{B}^T B x = 0 \quad \text{because } B \text{ is Hermitian, so } B = \overline{B}^T \\
&\rightarrow \quad \overline{(Bx)}^T B x = 0 \\
&\rightarrow \quad Bx = 0 \qquad \text{by Lemma 33.2.}
\end{aligned}
$$

Therefore $x \in \ker B$. $\qquad\qquad\qquad\qquad\qquad\qquad\qquad\qquad\qquad\qquad\square$

Putting all this together, here is the algorithm for computing the rank of A: compute the square matrix $B = \overline{A}^T A$, compute the characteristic polynomial using Csanky or Chistov, and find the highest power x^d of x that divides it. The rank of A is $n - d$. As we have seen, all these steps can be performed in NC.

33.1   Mulmuley's Algorithm

For a complex matrix A, we showed that A, $\overline{A}^T A$, and $(\overline{A}^T A)^2$ all have the same rank, thus we can apply Lemma 33.1 to the square Hermitian matrix $\overline{A}^T A$. In the special case of real matrices, this says that A, $A^T A$, and $(A^T A)^2$ all have the same rank, and we can apply Lemma 33.1 to the symmetric matrix $A^T A$.

Unfortunately, this does not work for fields of finite characteristic. For example, over the field $\mathcal{Z}_5$, $(1, 2) \cdot (1, 2) = 0$; moreover, the matrix

$$
A = \begin{bmatrix} 1 & 2 \\ 2 & 4 \end{bmatrix}
\tag{45}
$$

is symmetric and of rank 1, but $A^T A = A^2 = 0$.

This pathological state of affairs was partially resolved by Borodin, von zur Gathen, and Hopcroft [15], who gave a probabilistic NC algorithm, and Chistov [18] who gave a nonuniform deterministic algorithm. Mulmuley [82] gave the first deterministic NC algorithm, which we describe here.

Mulmuley keeps inner products from vanishing by throwing in indeterminates. The idea being exploited here is that even over fields of finite characteristic, a polynomial expression in the indeterminate x vanishes if and only if all its coefficients vanish; in other words, the indeterminate x is *transcendental* over the field k (it is not the root of any polynomial with coefficients in k). If not too many indeterminates are used and the degrees of the polynomials involved are not too big, then the computations can still be done efficiently in parallel, except that now we work *symbolically*, using polynomial arithmetic. This may require another factor of n more processors, but can still be done in NC.

Officially, we will be working in the transcendental extension $k(x)$ of k. This is isomorphic to the field of rational functions over k described in Lecture 32. It is the smallest field that contains k and the single indeterminate x, and is unique up to isomorphism. The rational function p/q can be represented as the pair of polynomials (p, q), and the operations $+$ and $\cdot$ in $k(x)$ can be done using polynomial arithmetic on the numerators and denominators:

$$\frac{p_1}{q_1} + \frac{p_2}{q_2} = \frac{p_1 q_2 + p_2 q_1}{q_1 q_2}$$

$$\frac{p_1}{q_1} \cdot \frac{p_2}{q_2} = \frac{p_1 p_2}{q_1 q_2}.$$

To test equality, we need to reduce these fractions to lowest terms by factoring out the gcd of the numerator and denominator, but this can be done in NC, as will be shown in the next lecture.

To illustrate the technique, consider the matrix A of (45) over $\mathcal{Z}_5$. Instead of working with A, we can work instead with the matrix XA, where x is an indeterminate and

$$X = \begin{bmatrix} 1 & 0 \\ 0 & x \end{bmatrix}.$$

Then

$$XA = \begin{bmatrix} 1 & 0 \\ 0 & x \end{bmatrix} \cdot \begin{bmatrix} 1 & 2 \\ 2 & 4 \end{bmatrix} = \begin{bmatrix} 1 & 2 \\ 2x & 4x \end{bmatrix}.$$

The matrix X has entries in $k(x)$ and is nonsingular, therefore XA has the same rank as A. Moreover, the matrix

$$(XA)^2 = \begin{bmatrix} 1 & 2 \\ 2x & 4x \end{bmatrix}^2 = \begin{bmatrix} 1 + 4x & 2 + 3x \\ 2x + 3x^2 & 4x + x^2 \end{bmatrix}$$

also has rank 1 (the second row is $2x$ times the first). Since $(XA)^2$, XA, and A all have the same rank, we can apply Lemma 33.1 to XA and the problem is solved.

This works in general. Let A be an $m \times n$ matrix, $m \geq n$, over an arbitrary field k. We note that going from k to $k(x)$ does not affect the rank of A, since the rank of A is r iff A has a nonzero $r \times r$ minor (determinant of an $r \times r$ submatrix), and this computation does not care whether we are over k or $k(x)$.

We can assume without loss of generality that A is square and symmetric; if not, we consider instead the square symmetric matrix

$$\begin{bmatrix} 0 & A \\ A^T & 0 \end{bmatrix}$$

of size $(m + n) \times (m + n)$, whose rank is exactly twice that of A.

Now assume A is $n \times n$ and symmetric. Let X be the $n \times n$ diagonal matrix with $1, x, x^2, \ldots, x^{n-1}$ on the diagonal.

Lemma 33.5 (Mulmuley [82]) *The matrices A, XA and $(XA)^2$ all have the same rank.*

Proof. Certainly

$$\text{rank } XAXA \;\leq\; \text{rank } XA \;\leq\; \text{rank } A \,.$$

Since X is nonsingular, rank $XAXA =$ rank AXA, therefore in order to show that rank $A \leq$ rank $XAXA$ it suffices to show that rank $A \leq$ rank AXA. Assume for a contradiction that there is a vector $u \in k(x)^n$ such that $Au \neq 0$ but $AXAu = 0$. By multiplying through by the denominators of the elements of u, we can assume without loss of generality that $u = u(x) \in k[x]$. Let $v = Au$ and let $u(y)$ be $u(x)$ with x replaced by a new indeterminate y. Then $v(y) = Au(y)$ and

$$v(y)^T X v(x) \;=\; u(y)^T A X A u(x) \;=\; 0 \,. \tag{46}$$

But if d is the maximum degree of any element of v and t is the maximum index for which v_t is of degree d, then the coefficient of $y^d x^{t-1} x^d$ is nonzero. This can be seen by writing out $v(y)^T X v(x)$ as a sum

$$v(y)^T X v(x) \;=\; \sum_{i=1}^{n} v(y)_i x^{i-1} v(x)_i$$

and noting that there is exactly one nonzero term in this expression with the monomial $y^d x^{t-1} x^d$, which cannot be canceled. This contradicts (46). $\square$

Lecture 34   Linear Equations and Polynomial GCDs

It is still open whether one can find the greatest common divisor (gcd) of two integers in NC. In this lecture we will show how to compute the gcd of two polynomials in NC. We essentially reduce the problem to linear algebra. First we show how to solve systems of linear equations in NC; then we reduce the polynomial gcd problem to such a linear system.

34.1   Systems of Linear Equations

We are given a system of m linear equations in n unknowns

$$
\begin{aligned}
a_{11}x_1 + a_{12}x_2 + \cdots + a_{1n}x_n &= b_1 \\
a_{21}x_1 + a_{22}x_2 + \cdots + a_{2n}x_n &= b_2 \\
&\vdots \\
a_{m1}x_1 + a_{m2}x_2 + \cdots + a_{mn}x_n &= b_m
\end{aligned} \tag{47}
$$

and wish to find a solution vector $x_1, \ldots, x_n$ if one exists. This is equivalent to solving the matrix-vector equation

$$
Ax = b \tag{48}
$$

where A is an $m \times n$ matrix whose ij^{th} element is a_{ij}, x is a column vector of n unknowns, and b is an m-vector whose i^{th} element is b_i.

We have already seen how to solve the following problems in NC:

- compute the rank of a matrix;

- find a maximal linearly independent set of columns of a matrix;

- invert a nonsingular square matrix.

The last allows us to solve the system (47) if A is square and nonsingular. What about cases where the system is not square, or where it is square but A is singular?

If we just wish to determine whether the system (48) has a solution at all, we can append b to A as a new column and ask whether this matrix has the same rank as A. If so, then b can be expressed as a linear combination of the columns of A; the coefficients of this linear combination provide a solution x to (48). If not, then b lies outside the subspace spanned by the columns of A and no such solution exists.

The following NC algorithm will produce a solution to (48) if one exists. First we can assume without loss of generality that A is of full column rank; that is, the columns are linearly independent. If not, we can find a maximal linearly independent set A' of columns of A; if b can be expressed as a linear combination of columns of A, then it can be expressed as a linear combination of the columns of A', and any solution to $A'x = b$ gives a solution to (48) by extending the solution vector with zeros.

Assume now that A is of full column rank. Using the same technique, we can find a maximal linearly independent set of rows. Since the row rank and column rank of a matrix are equal, the resulting matrix A'' is square and nonsingular, so the system $A''x = b''$ has a unique solution, where b'' is obtained from b by dropping the same rows as were dropped from A to get A''. Either x is also a solution to (48), or no solution exists.

34.2   Resultants and Polynomial GCDs

Suppose we are given two polynomials

$$
\begin{aligned}
f(x) &= a_m x^m + a_{m-1} x^{m-1} + \cdots + a_0 \\
g(x) &= b_n x^n + b_{n-1} x^{n-1} + \cdots + b_0
\end{aligned}
$$

and wish to find their gcd. The usual sequential method is the *Euclidean algorithm*, which generates a sequence of polynomials

$$
f_0, f_1, \ldots, f_n \ ,
$$

where $f_0 = f$, $f_1 = g$, and f_{i+1} is the remainder obtained when dividing f_{i-1} by f_i. In other words, f_{i+1} is the unique polynomial of degree less than the degree of f_i for which there exists a quotient q_i such that

$$
f_{i-1} = q_i f_i + f_{i+1} \ . \tag{49}
$$

This sequence is called the *Euclidean remainder sequence*. It must end, since the degrees of the f_i decrease strictly. The last nonzero polynomial f_n in the list is the gcd of f and g. This is proved by showing that a polynomial divides f_{i-1} and f_i iff it divides f_i and f_{i+1}, which is immediate from (49). It follows that all adjacent pairs f_i, f_{i+1} in the sequence have the same gcd. Since $f_{n+1} = 0$, f_n divides f_{n-1}, therefore gcd $(f_n, f_{n-1}) = f_n$ and gcd $(f, g) = f_n$ as well.

One can obtain an *NC* algorithm using the classical *Sylvester resultant* [17, 15]. This technique is based on the following relationship:

Lemma 34.1

(i) *There exist polynomials s and t with $\deg s < \deg g$ and $\deg t < \deg f$ such that* gcd $(f, g) = sf + tg$.

(ii) *For any polynomials s and t,* gcd (f, g) *divides $sf + tg$.*

Proof.

(i) The proof is by backwards induction on n. For the basis, take $s = 0$ and $t = 1$. Then $\deg s = -1 < \deg f_n$ ($\deg 0 = -1$ by convention), $\deg t = 0 < \deg f_{n-1}$, and $sf_{n-1} + tf_n = f_n$. For the induction step, assume there exist s and t with $\deg s < \deg f_{i+1}$, $\deg t < \deg f_i$, and $sf_i + tf_{i+1} = f_n$. Using (49), we have

$$\begin{aligned} f_n &= sf_i + tf_{i+1} \\ &= sf_i + t(f_{i-1} - q_i f_i) \\ &= tf_{i-1} + (s - q_i)f_i \ . \end{aligned}$$

Moreover, since $\deg q_i = \deg f_{i-1} - \deg f_i$, we have that $\deg t < \deg f_i$ and $\deg(s - q_i) < \deg f_{i-1}$.

(ii) Certainly gcd (f, g) divides f and g. It therefore divides any $sf + tg$.

$\square$

Using Lemma 34.1, we can express the polynomial gcd problem as a problem in linear algebra. Arrange the coefficients of f and g in staggered columns to form a square matrix S as in the following figure, with $n = \deg g$ columns of coefficients of f and $m = \deg f$ columns of coefficients of g. The figure illustrates the case $m = 5$ and $n = 4$.

$$S \; = \; \begin{bmatrix} a_5 & 0 & 0 & 0 & b_4 & 0 & 0 & 0 & 0 \\ a_4 & a_5 & 0 & 0 & b_3 & b_4 & 0 & 0 & 0 \\ a_3 & a_4 & a_5 & 0 & b_2 & b_3 & b_4 & 0 & 0 \\ a_2 & a_3 & a_4 & a_5 & b_1 & b_2 & b_3 & b_4 & 0 \\ a_1 & a_2 & a_3 & a_4 & b_0 & b_1 & b_2 & b_3 & b_4 \\ a_0 & a_1 & a_2 & a_3 & 0 & b_0 & b_1 & b_2 & b_3 \\ 0 & a_0 & a_1 & a_2 & 0 & 0 & b_0 & b_1 & b_2 \\ 0 & 0 & a_0 & a_1 & 0 & 0 & 0 & b_0 & b_1 \\ 0 & 0 & 0 & a_0 & 0 & 0 & 0 & 0 & b_0 \end{bmatrix} \qquad (50)$$

$$\underbrace{\hphantom{aaaaaaaaaa}}_{n} \quad \underbrace{\hphantom{aaaaaaaaaaaa}}_{m}$$

The matrix S is called the *Sylvester matrix* of f and g. If we multiply S on the right by a column vector

$$x \; = \; (s_{n-1}, s_{n-2}, \ldots, s_0, t_{m-1}, t_{m-2}, \ldots, t_0)^T$$

containing the coefficients of polynomials s and t of degree at most $n - 1$ and $m-1$, respectively, then the product Sx gives the coefficients of the polynomial $sf + tg$, which is of degree at most $m + n - 1$.

Theorem 34.2 *The matrix S is nonsingular if and only if the gcd of f and g is 1.*

Proof.
($\rightarrow$) Suppose $\gcd (f, g) \neq 1$. Then $\deg \gcd (f, g) > 0$. By Lemma 34.1(ii), there exist no s and t with $sf + tg = 1$, therefore the system $Sx = (0, \ldots, 0, 1)^T$ has no solution.
($\leftarrow$) Suppose S is singular. Then there exists some nonzero vector x such that $Sx = 0$. This says there exists some pair of polynomials s, t such that $sf + tg = 0$, $\deg s < \deg g$, and $\deg t < \deg f$. Then $sf = -tg$ and $\deg sf = \deg tg < \deg fg$. Since f and g both divide $sf = -tg$, so does their least common multiple (lcm), thus $\deg \operatorname{lcm} (f, g) < \deg fg$. Since $\gcd (f, g) \cdot \operatorname{lcm} (f, g) = fg$,

$$\deg \gcd (f, g) \; = \; \deg fg - \deg \operatorname{lcm} (f, g) \; > \; 0,$$

therefore $\gcd (f, g) \neq 1$. $\qquad\qquad \square$

By Theorem 34.2, we can determine whether the polynomials f and g have a nontrivial gcd by computing the determinant of S. This quantity is called the *resultant* of f and g.

Let us now show how to compute the gcd. Suppose

$$\gcd (f, g) \; = \; x^d + c_{d-1} x^{d-1} + c_{d-2} x^{d-2} + \cdots + c_1 x + c_0,$$

assuming without loss of generality that the leading coefficient is 1. Let c be the column vector

$$c = (0, 0, \ldots, 0, 1, c_{d-1}, c_{d-2}, \ldots, c_1, c_0)^T .$$

By Lemma 34.1(i), $Sx = c$ for some x. For any e, let $S^{(e)}$ be the matrix obtained by dropping the last e rows of S, and let $c^{(e)}$ be the vector obtained by dropping the last e elements of c. Let $u^{(e)}$ be the vector of the form $(0, 0, \ldots, 0, 1)^T$ of length $m + n - e$. Note that $c^{(d)} = u^{(d)}$, where d is the degree of gcd (f, g). Since $Sx = c$, we have

$$S^{(d)}x = u^{(d)} = c^{(d)} . \tag{51}$$

Moreover, for no $e < d$ does

$$S^{(e)}x = u^{(e)} \tag{52}$$

have a solution; if it did, then Sx would give a polynomial $sf + tg$ of degree strictly less than the degree of gcd (f, g), contradicting Lemma 34.1(ii). We can thus find the degree d of gcd (f, g) by trying all e in parallel and taking d to be the least e such that (52) has a solution. Once we have found d and a solution x for (51), we are done: the solution vector x is also a solution to $Sx = c$, thereby giving coefficients of polynomials s and t such that

$$\gcd (f, g) = sf + tg = Sx .$$

It is interesting to note that the traditional Euclidean algorithm for polynomial gcd amounts to triangulation of the Sylvester matrix (50) by Gaussian elimination.

Lecture 35   The Fast Fourier Transform (FFT)

Consider two polynomials

$$f(x) = a_0 + a_1 x + a_2 x^2 + \ldots + a_n x^n$$
$$g(x) = b_0 + b_1 x + b_2 x^2 + \ldots + b_m x^m .$$

We can represent these two polynomials as vectors of some length $N \geq n + m + 1$. The ith element of the vector is the coefficient of x^i.

$$f = (a_0, a_1, a_2, \ldots, a_n, 0, 0, \ldots, 0)$$
$$g = (b_0, b_1, b_2, \ldots, b_m, 0, 0, \ldots, 0) . \tag{53}$$

The product of f and g will then be represented by the vector

$$(a_0 b_0, a_1 b_0 + a_0 b_1, a_2 b_0 + a_1 b_1 + a_0 b_2, \ldots) .$$

This vector is called the *convolution* of the vectors (53).

The obvious way to compute the convolution of two vectors takes N^2 processors and $\log N$ time. We would like to reduce the processor bound to N. To do this, we will use a different representation of polynomials. Recall that a polynomial of degree $N - 1$ is uniquely determined by its values on N data points. Thus if we have N distinct data points $\xi_0, \xi_1, \ldots, \xi_{N-1}$, we can represent the polynomial f by the vector

$$(f(\xi_0), f(\xi_1), f(\xi_2), \ldots, f(\xi_{N-1})) . \tag{54}$$

186

The nice thing about this representation is that since

$$fg(\xi_i) \;=\; f(\xi_i)g(\xi_i)\,,$$

we can calculate the product of two polynomials by doing a componentwise product of the two vectors in constant time with N processors, provided the degree of the product is at most $N - 1$.

The problem now is to find a way to convert from one representation to the other. For any choice of ξ_i, we can convert from (53) to (54) by evaluating the polynomials on the ξ_i; this amounts to multiplying (53) by the matrix

$$\begin{bmatrix} 1 & \xi_0 & \xi_0^2 & \cdots & \xi_0^{N-1} \\ 1 & \xi_1 & \xi_1^2 & \cdots & \xi_1^{N-1} \\ 1 & \xi_2 & \xi_2^2 & \cdots & \xi_2^{N-1} \\ \vdots & \vdots & \vdots & \ddots & \vdots \\ 1 & \xi_{N-1} & \xi_{N-1}^2 & \cdots & \xi_{N-1}^{N-1} \end{bmatrix} \tag{55}$$

called a *Vandermonde matrix*. We can convert back by interpolation, which amounts to multiplying (54) by the inverse of the matrix (55).

Judicious choice of the ξ_i can make this conversion very efficient. If we are working in a field containing N^{th} roots of unity (roots of the polynomial $x^N - 1$) and a multiplicative inverse of N (*i.e.*, the characteristic of the field does not divide N), then we can get very efficient conversion algorithms by taking the ξ_i to be the Nth roots of unity. For example, in the complex numbers $\mathcal{C}$, let $\omega = e^{\frac{2\pi i}{N}}$ and take $\xi_i = \omega^i$. These points lie uniformly spaced on the complex unit circle (recall that to multiply two complex numbers, you add their angles and multiply their lengths).

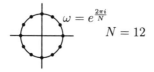

The Nth roots of unity form a cyclic group under multiplication. An Nth root of unity ξ is called *primitive* ([3] uses the term *principal*) if it is a generator of this group, *i.e.* if every N^{th} root of unity is some power of ξ. Not all N^{th} roots of unity are primitive; for $N = 12$ in $\mathcal{C}$, the primitive roots are ω, ω^5, ω^7, and ω^{11}. The root ω^2 is not primitive, because its powers are all of the form ω^{2k}, so it is impossible to obtain odd powers of ω. In general, if ξ is a primitive root, then ξ^k is a primitive root if and only if k and N are relatively prime.

Over any field containing all N^{th} roots of unity, the polynomial $x^N - 1$ factors into linear factors

$$x^N - 1 \;=\; \prod_{i=0}^{N-1} (x - \omega^i)\,,$$

where ω is a primitive N^{th} root of unity. This is because each of the Nth roots of unity is a root of $x^N - 1$, and there can be at most N of them. Since

$$x^N - 1 \;=\; (x-1)(x^{N-1} + x^{N-2} + \cdots + x + 1)\,,$$

every N^{th} root of unity except $\omega^0 = 1$ is a root of the polynomial

$$\sum_{j=0}^{N-1} x^j \,.$$

This gives the following technical property, which we will find useful:

$$\sum_{j=0}^{N-1} \omega^{ij} \;=\; \begin{cases} 0\,, & \text{if } i \not\equiv 0 \bmod N \\ N\,, & \text{otherwise.} \end{cases} \tag{56}$$

The $N \times N$ Vandermonde matrix (55) for these data points has as its ij^{th} element ω^{ij}, $0 \le i, j \le N - 1$. We denote this matrix F_N. When applied to a vector containing the coefficients of a polynomial

$$f(x) \;=\; a_0 + a_1 x + \cdots + a_{N-1} x^{N-1}\,,$$

F_N gives the vector of values of f at the N roots of unity.

$$\begin{bmatrix} 1 & 1 & 1 & \cdots & 1 \\ 1 & \omega^1 & \omega^2 & \cdots & \omega^{N-1} \\ 1 & \omega^2 & \omega^4 & \cdots & \omega^{2N-2} \\ \vdots & \vdots & \vdots & \ddots & \vdots \\ 1 & \omega^{N-1} & \omega^{2N-2} & \cdots & \omega^{(N-1)^2} \end{bmatrix} \begin{bmatrix} a_0 \\ a_1 \\ a_2 \\ \vdots \\ a_{N-1} \end{bmatrix} = \begin{bmatrix} f(1) \\ f(\omega) \\ f(\omega^2) \\ \vdots \\ f(\omega^{N-1}) \end{bmatrix}$$

The linear map represented by the matrix F_N is called the *discrete Fourier transform*.

The inverse of F_N is particularly easy to describe: its ij^{th} element is

$$(F_N^{-1})_{ij} \;=\; \frac{\omega^{-ij}}{N}\,.$$

Thus F_N^{-1} is $\frac{1}{N}$ times the Fourier transform matrix of a different primitive N^{th} root of unity, namely $\omega^{-1} = \omega^{N-1}$. To show that F_N and F_N^{-1} are indeed inverses, we just calculate their product, using property (56) at the critical step:

$$\begin{aligned} (F_N \cdot F_N^{-1})_{ij} &= \sum_{k=0}^{N-1} \omega^{ik} \cdot \frac{\omega^{-kj}}{N} \\ &= \frac{1}{N} \sum_{k=0}^{N-1} \omega^{k(i-j)} \\ &= \begin{cases} 1\,, & \text{if } i = j \\ 0\,, & \text{otherwise,} \end{cases} \end{aligned}$$

thus $F_N F_N^{-1}$ is the identity matrix.

Now we want to find a way to compute $F_N f$ quickly, where

$$f = (a_0, a_1, \ldots, a_{N-1})$$

is the vector of coefficients of the polynomial $f(x)$. We use a divide-and-conquer approach in which we split f into two polynomials each of size $\frac{N}{2}$ (assume for simplicity that N is a power of 2), apply $F_{\frac{N}{2}}$ to each of them in parallel, then combine the two results to form $F_N f$.

Given

$$f(x) = a_0 + a_1 x + a_2 x^2 + \ldots + a_{N-1} x^{N-1} \, ,$$

define

$$
\begin{aligned}
f_0(x) &= a_0 + a_2 x^2 + a_4 x^4 + \ldots + a_{N-2} x^{N-2} \\
\widehat{f_0}(x) &= a_0 + a_2 x + a_4 x^2 + \ldots + a_{N-2} x^{\frac{N}{2}-1} \\
f_1(x) &= a_1 + a_3 x^2 + a_5 x^4 + \ldots + a_{N-1} x^{N-2} \\
\widehat{f_1}(x) &= a_1 + a_3 x + a_5 x^2 + \ldots + a_{N-1} x^{\frac{N}{2}-1} \, .
\end{aligned}
$$

Then

$$
\begin{aligned}
f(x) &= f_0(x) + x f_1(x) \\
f_0(x) &= \widehat{f_0}(x) \circ x^2 \\
f_1(x) &= \widehat{f_1}(x) \circ x^2
\end{aligned}
$$

where $\circ$ represents functional composition (substitute the right polynomial for the variable in the left polynomial). Both $\widehat{f_0}$ and $\widehat{f_1}$ have degree at most $\frac{N}{2} - 1$. We recursively apply $F_{\frac{N}{2}}$ to the vectors $\widehat{f_0} = (a_0, a_2, \ldots, a_{N-2})$ and $\widehat{f_1} = (a_1, a_3, \ldots, a_{N-1})$ to get $F_{\frac{N}{2}} \widehat{f_0}$ and $F_{\frac{N}{2}} \widehat{f_1}$. The primitive $\frac{N}{2}^{\text{th}}$ root of unity used in the formation of $F_{\frac{N}{2}}$ is ω^2.

Now we show that the N-vector $F_N f_0$ is obtained by concatenating two copies of the $\frac{N}{2}$-vector $F_{\frac{N}{2}} \widehat{f_0}$, and similarly for f_1. The ith element of $F_N f_0$ is

$$
\begin{aligned}
f_0(\omega^i) &= (\widehat{f_0} \circ x^2)(\omega^i) \\
&= \widehat{f_0}(\omega^{2i}) \, ,
\end{aligned}
$$

which is the $i^{\text{th}} \bmod \frac{N}{2}$ element of $F_{\frac{N}{2}} \widehat{f_0}$. The argument is similar for f_1.

Finally

$$
\begin{aligned}
F_N f &= F_N (f_0 + x f_1) \\
&= F_N f_0 + F_N (x f_1) \\
&= F_N f_0 + F_N x \cdot F_N f_1 \, ,
\end{aligned}
$$

where · represents componentwise multiplication. We have already computed $F_N f_0$ and $F_N f_1$ by recursively computing the Fourier transform of two vectors of size $\frac{N}{2}$; and

$$F_N x = (1, \omega, \omega^2, \dots, \omega^{N-1}) \, ,$$

so we have all we need to compute $F_N f$.

With N processors, it takes us constant time to split f into $\hat{f}_0$ and $\hat{f}_1$. We then do two recursive calls in parallel to calculate $F_N f_0$ and $F_N f_1$, each using $\frac{N}{2}$ processors. Finally, it takes constant time to recombine the results to get $F_N f$. Therefore, the algorithm uses $O(\log N)$ time and N processors.

This gives a very efficient parallel algorithm for multiplying two polynomials: compute their Fourier transforms, multiply the resulting vectors componentwise, then take the inverse Fourier transform. The entire algorithm takes $O(\log N)$ time and N processors.

It is interesting to ask what happens when the degrees of the polynomials are so large that the degree of their product exceeds $N - 1$. The answer is that terms that fall off the right side of the vector wrap around; in other words, the coefficient of the term x^{N+i} in the product is added to the coefficient of x^i. Mathematically, what is going on is that the product of the two polynomials is being computed modulo the polynomial $x^N - 1$:

$$F_N^{-1}(F_N f \cdot F_N g) = fg \bmod x^N - 1 \, .$$

A fancy way of saying this is that the Fourier transform gives an isomorphism

$$F_N : k[x]/(x^N - 1) \;\; \to \;\; k^N$$

between two N-dimensional algebras over the field k, namely the algebra of polynomials mod $x^N - 1$ with ordinary polynomial multiplication and the direct product k^N with componentwise multiplication.

The parallel algorithm for the FFT given here is essentially implicit in the 1965 paper of Cooley and Tukey [24], although that was well before anyone had ever heard of NC.

Lecture 36   Luby's Algorithm

In this lecture and the next we develop a probabilistic NC algorithm of Luby for finding a maximal independent set in an undirected graph. Recall that a set of vertices of a graph is *independent* if the induced subgraph on those vertices has no edges. A *maximal* independent set is one contained in no larger independent set. A maximal independent set need not be of maximum cardinality among all independent sets in the graph.

There is a simple deterministic polynomial-time algorithm for finding a maximal independent set in a graph: just start with an arbitrary vertex and keep adding vertices until all remaining vertices are connected to at least one vertex already taken. Luby [76] and independently Alon, Babai, and Itai [6] showed that the problem is in random NC (RNC), which means that there is a parallel algorithm using polynomially many processors that can make calls on a random number generator such that the *expected* running time is polylogarithmic in the size of the input.

The problem is also in (deterministic) NC. This was first shown by Karp and Wigderson [59]. Luby [76] also gives a deterministic NC algorithm, but his approach has a decidedly different flavor: he gives a probabilistic algorithm first, then develops a general technique for converting probabilistic algorithms to deterministic ones under certain conditions. We will see how to do this in the next lecture.

Luby's algorithm is a good vehicle for discussing probabilistic algorithms, since it illustrates several of the most common concepts used in the analysis of such algorithms:

Law of Sum. The *law of sum* says that if $\mathcal{A}$ is a collection of pairwise disjoint events, *i.e.* if $A \cap B = \emptyset$ for all $A, B \in \mathcal{A}$, $A \neq B$, then the probability that at least one of the events in $\mathcal{A}$ occurs is the sum of the probabilities:

$$\Pr(\bigcup \mathcal{A}) \;=\; \sum_{A \in \mathcal{A}} Pr(A) \;.$$

Expectation. The *expected value* $\mathcal{E}X$ of a discrete random variable X is the weighted sum of its possible values, each weighted by the probability that X takes on that value:

$$\mathcal{E}X \;=\; \sum_{n} n \cdot \Pr(X = n) \;.$$

For example, consider the toss of a coin. Let

$$X \;=\; \begin{cases} 1 \,, & \text{if the coin turns up heads} \\ 0 \,, & \text{otherwise.} \end{cases} \tag{57}$$

Then $\mathcal{E}X = \frac{1}{2}$ if the coin is unbiased. This is the expected number of heads in one flip. Any function $f(X)$ of a discrete random variable X is a random variable with expectation

$$\begin{aligned} \mathcal{E}f(X) \;&=\; \sum_{n} n \cdot \Pr(f(X) = n) \\ &=\; \sum_{m} f(m) \cdot \Pr(X = m) \;. \end{aligned}$$

It follows immediately from the definition that the expectation function $\mathcal{E}$ is linear. For example, if X_i are the random variables (57) associated with n coin flips, then

$$\mathcal{E}(X_1 + X_2 + \cdots + X_n) \;=\; \mathcal{E}X_1 + \mathcal{E}X_2 + \cdots + \mathcal{E}X_n \;,$$

and this gives the expected number of heads in n flips. The X_i need not be independent; in fact, they might all be the same flip.

Conditional Probability and Conditional Expectation. The *conditional probability* $\Pr(A \mid B)$ is the probability that event A occurs given that event B occurs. Formally,

$$\Pr(A \mid B) \;=\; \frac{\Pr(A \cap B)}{Pr(B)} \;.$$

The conditional probability is undefined if $\Pr(B) = 0$.

The *conditional expectation* $\mathcal{E}(X \mid B)$ is the expected value of the random variable X given that event B occurs. Formally,

$$\mathcal{E}(X \mid B) \;=\; \sum_{n} n \cdot Pr(X = n \mid B) \;.$$

If the event B is that another random variable Y takes on a particular value m, then we get a real-valued function $\mathcal{E}(X \mid Y = m)$ of m. Composing this function with the random variable Y itself, we get a new random variable, denoted $\mathcal{E}(X \mid Y)$, which is a function of the random variable Y. The random variable $\mathcal{E}(X \mid Y)$ takes on value n with probability

$$\sum_{\mathcal{E}(X|Y=m)=n} \Pr(Y = m) \ ,$$

where the sum is over all m such that $\mathcal{E}(X \mid Y = m) = n$. The expected value of $\mathcal{E}(X \mid Y)$ is just $\mathcal{E}X$:

$$\begin{aligned}
\mathcal{E}(\mathcal{E}(X \mid Y)) &= \sum_m \mathcal{E}(X \mid Y = m) \cdot \Pr(Y = m) \\
&= \sum_m \sum_n n \cdot \Pr(X = n \mid Y = m) \cdot \Pr(Y = m) \\
&= \sum_n n \cdot \sum_m \Pr(X = n \wedge Y = m) \qquad (58) \\
&= \sum_n n \cdot \Pr(X = n) \\
&= \mathcal{E}X
\end{aligned}$$

(see [33, p. 223]).

Independence and Pairwise Independence. A set of events $\mathcal{A}$ are *independent* if for any subset $\mathcal{B} \subseteq \mathcal{A}$,

$$\Pr(\bigcap \mathcal{B}) \ = \ \prod_{A \in \mathcal{B}} \Pr(A) \ .$$

They are *pairwise independent* if for every $A, B \in \mathcal{A}$, $A \neq B$,

$$\Pr(A \cap B) \ = \ \Pr(A) \cdot \Pr(B) \ .$$

For example, the probability that two successive flips of a fair coin both come up heads is $\frac{1}{4}$. Pairwise independent events need not be independent: consider the three events

- the first flip gives heads

- the second flip gives heads

- of the two flips, one is heads and one is tails.

The probability of each pair is $\frac{1}{4}$, but the three cannot happen simultaneously. If A and B are independent, then $\Pr(A \mid B) = \Pr(A)$.

Inclusion-Exclusion Principle. It follows from the law of sum that for any events A and B, disjoint or not,

$$\Pr(A \cup B) = \Pr(A) + \Pr(B) - \Pr(A \cap B) .$$

More generally, for any collection $\mathcal{A}$ of events,

$$\Pr(\bigcup \mathcal{A})$$
$$= \sum_{A \in \mathcal{A}} Pr(A) - \sum_{\substack{\mathcal{B} \subseteq \mathcal{A} \\ |\mathcal{B}| = 2}} \Pr(\bigcap \mathcal{B}) + \sum_{\substack{\mathcal{B} \subseteq \mathcal{A} \\ |\mathcal{B}| = 3}} \Pr(\bigcap \mathcal{B}) - \cdots \pm \Pr(\bigcap \mathcal{A}) .$$

This equation is often used to estimate the probability of a join of several events. The first term alone gives an upper bound and the first two terms give a lower bound:

$$\Pr(\bigcup \mathcal{A}) \leq \sum_{A \in \mathcal{A}} Pr(A)$$
$$\Pr(\bigcup \mathcal{A}) \geq \sum_{A \in \mathcal{A}} Pr(A) - \sum_{\substack{A, B \in \mathcal{A} \\ A \neq B}} \Pr(A \cap B) .$$

36.1   Luby's Maximal Independent Set Algorithm

Luby's algorithm is executed in stages. Each stage finds an independent set I in parallel, using calls on a random number generator. The set I, the set $N(I)$ of neighbors of I, and all edges incident to $I \cup N(I)$ are deleted from the graph. The process is repeated until the graph is empty. The final maximal independent set is the union of all the independent sets I found in each stage. We will show that the expected number of edges deleted in each stage is at least a constant fraction of the edges remaining; this will imply that the expected number of stages is $O(\log n)$ (Homework 10, Exercise 1).

If v is a vertex and A a set of vertices, define

$$N(v) = \{u \mid (u, v) \in E\} = \{neighbors\ of\ v\}$$
$$N(A) = \bigcup_{u \in A} N(u) = \{neighbors\ of\ A\}$$
$$d(v) = the\ degree\ of\ v = |N(v)| .$$

Here is the algorithm to find I in each stage.

Algorithm 36.1

1. Create a set S of candidates for I as follows. For each vertex v in parallel, include $v \in S$ with probability $\frac{1}{2d(v)}$.

2. For each edge in E, if both its endpoints are in S, discard the one of lower degree; ties are resolved arbitrarily (say by vertex number). The resulting set is I.

Note that in step 1 we favor vertices with low degree and in step 2 we favor vertices of high degree.

Define a vertex to be *good* if

$$\sum_{u \in N(v)} \frac{1}{2d(u)} \geq \frac{1}{6} .$$

Intuitively, a vertex is good if it has lots of neighbors of low degree. This will give it a decent chance of making it into $N(I)$. Define an edge to be *good* if at least one of its endpoints is good. A vertex or edge is *bad* if it is not good. We will show that at least half of the edges are good, and each stands a decent chance of being deleted, so we will expect to delete a reasonable fraction of the good edges in each stage.

Lemma 36.2 *For all v, $\Pr(v \in I) \geq \frac{1}{4d(v)}$.*

Proof. Let $L(v) = \{u \in N(v) \mid d(u) \geq d(v)\}$. If $v \in S$, then v does not make it into I only if some element of $L(v)$ is also in S. Then

$$\begin{aligned}
\Pr(v \notin I \mid v \in S) &\leq \Pr(\exists u \in L(v) \cap S \mid v \in S) \\
&\leq \sum_{u \in L(v)} \Pr(u \in S \mid v \in S) \\
&= \sum_{u \in L(v)} \Pr(u \in S) \quad \text{(by pairwise independence)} \\
&\leq \sum_{u \in L(v)} \frac{1}{2d(u)} \\
&\leq \sum_{u \in L(v)} \frac{1}{2d(v)} \quad \text{(since } d(u) \geq d(v)) \\
&\leq \frac{d(v)}{2d(v)} = \frac{1}{2} .
\end{aligned}$$

Now

$$\begin{aligned}
\Pr(v \in I) &= \Pr(v \in I \mid v \in S) \cdot \Pr(v \in S) \\
&\geq \frac{1}{2} \cdot \frac{1}{2d(v)} = \frac{1}{4d(v)} .
\end{aligned}$$

$\square$

Lemma 36.3 *If v is good, then $\Pr(v \in N(I)) \geq \frac{1}{36}$.*

Proof. If v has a neighbor u of degree 2 or less, then

$$\begin{aligned}
\Pr(v \in N(I)) &\geq \Pr(u \in I) \\
&\geq \frac{1}{4d(u)} \quad \text{(by Lemma 36.2)} \\
&\geq \frac{1}{8} .
\end{aligned}$$

Otherwise $d(u) \geq 3$ for all $u \in N(v)$. Then for all $u \in N(v)$, $\frac{1}{2d(u)} \leq \frac{1}{6}$, and since v is good,

$$\sum_{u \in N(v)} \frac{1}{2d(u)} \geq \frac{1}{6} \; .$$

There must exist a subset $M(v) \subseteq N(v)$ such that

$$\frac{1}{6} \leq \sum_{u \in M(v)} \frac{1}{2d(u)} \leq \frac{1}{3} \; . \tag{59}$$

Then

$$
\begin{aligned}
\Pr(v \in N(I)) \;\geq\;& \Pr(\exists u \in M(v) \cap I) \\
\geq\;& \sum_{u \in M(v)} \Pr(u \in I) - \sum_{\substack{u,w \in M(v) \\ u \neq w}} \Pr(u \in I \wedge w \in I) \\
& \text{(by inclusion-exclusion)} \\
\geq\;& \sum_{u \in M(v)} \frac{1}{4d(u)} - \sum_{\substack{u,w \in M(v) \\ u \neq w}} \Pr(u \in S \wedge w \in S) \\
\geq\;& \sum_{u \in M(v)} \frac{1}{4d(u)} - \sum_{\substack{u,w \in M(v) \\ u \neq w}} \Pr(u \in S) \cdot \Pr(w \in S) \\
& \text{(by pairwise independence)} \\
=\;& \sum_{u \in M(v)} \frac{1}{4d(u)} - \sum_{u \in M(v)} \sum_{w \in M(v)} \frac{1}{2d(u)} \cdot \frac{1}{2d(w)} \\
=\;& \Big(\sum_{u \in M(v)} \frac{1}{2d(u)} \Big) \cdot \Big(\frac{1}{2} - \sum_{w \in M(v)} \frac{1}{2d(w)} \Big) \\
\geq\;& \frac{1}{6} \cdot \frac{1}{6} \;=\; \frac{1}{36} \quad \text{by (59)}.
\end{aligned}
$$

$\square$

We will continue the analysis of Luby's algorithm in the next lecture.

Lecture 37 Analysis of Luby's Algorithm

In the previous lecture we proved that for each good vertex v, the probability that v is deleted in the current stage is at least $\frac{1}{36}$. Recall that a vertex v is *good* if

$$\sum_{u \in N(v)} \frac{1}{2d(u)} \geq \frac{1}{6} \tag{60}$$

(intuitively, if it has lots of neighbors of low degree), and that an edge is *good* if it is incident to at least one good vertex. Since the probability that a good edge is deleted is at least as great as the probability that its good endpoint is deleted (if both its endpoints are good, so much the better), a good edge is deleted with probability at least $\frac{1}{36}$.

Lemma 37.1 *At least half the edges in the graph are good.*

Proof. Direct each edge toward its endpoint of higher degree, breaking ties arbitrarily. Then each bad vertex has at least twice as many edges going out as coming in, since if not then at least a third of the vertices adjacent to v would have degree $d(v)$ or lower, and this would imply (60).

Using this fact, we can assign to each bad edge e directed into a bad vertex v a pair of edges (bad or good) directed out of v so that each bad edge is assigned a unique pair. This implies that there are at least twice as many edges in all as bad edges. Equivalently, at least half the edges are good. $\square$

We can now argue that the expected number of edges removed at a given stage is at least a constant fraction of the number of edges present.

Theorem 37.2 *Let the random variable X represent the number of edges deleted in the current stage. Then*

$$\mathcal{E}X \;\geq\; \frac{|E|}{72}\;.$$

Proof. Let G denote the set of good edges. For $e \in E$, define the random variable

$$X_e \;=\; \begin{cases} 1\,, & \text{if } e \text{ is deleted} \\ 0\,, & \text{otherwise.} \end{cases}$$

Then $X = \sum_{e \in E} X_e$, and by linearity of expectation,

$$
\begin{aligned}
\mathcal{E}X \;&=\; \sum_{e \in E} \mathcal{E}X_e \\
&\geq\; \sum_{e \in G} \mathcal{E}X_e \\
&\geq\; \sum_{e \in G} \frac{1}{36} \quad \text{(by Lemma 36.3)} \\
&=\; \frac{|G|}{36} \\
&\geq\; \frac{|E|}{72} \quad \text{(by Lemma 37.1).}
\end{aligned}
$$

$\square$

We have shown that we can expect to delete at least a fixed fraction of the remaining edges at each stage. This implies that the expected number of stages required until all m edges are deleted is $O(\log m)$. We leave this argument as a homework exercise (Homework 10, Exercise 1).

37.1   Making Luby's Algorithm Deterministic

As described in the last lecture, each stage of Luby's algorithm makes n independent calls on a random number generator, one for each vertex. We can think of the call for vertex u as a flip of a biased coin with $\Pr(\text{heads}) = \frac{1}{2d(u)}$ and $\Pr(\text{tails}) = 1 - \frac{1}{2d(u)}$. It can be shown that $\Omega(n)$ truly random bits (independent flips of a fair coin) are necessary to generate these n independent biased coin flips.

However, a quick check reveals that the analysis of Luby's algorithm never used the independence of the biased coin flips, but only the weaker condition of *pairwise independence*. Recall from the last lecture that a collection of events $\mathcal{A}$ are *independent* if for all subsets $\mathcal{B} \subseteq \mathcal{A}$,

$$\Pr(\bigcap \mathcal{B}) = \prod_{A \in \mathcal{B}} \Pr(A) ;$$

for *pairwise independence*, this only has to hold for subsets $\mathcal{B}$ of size two.

After observing that only pairwise independence was necessary for the analysis, Luby made the beautiful observation that only $O(\log n)$ truly random bits are needed to generate the n pairwise independent biased coin flips. This leads to a deterministic NC algorithm: in parallel, consider all possible bit strings of length $O(\log n)$ representing all possible outcomes of $O(\log n)$ flips of a fair coin (there are only $2^{O(\log n)} = n^{O(1)}$ of them). Use each such bit string to generate the n pairwise independent biased coin flips as if that string were obtained from a random number generator, and carry on with the algorithm. Since we expect to delete at least a constant fraction of the edges, one of the deterministic simulations must delete at least that many edges. Pick the one that discards the most edges and throw the other parallel computations out, then repeat the whole process. Everything is deterministic and at least a constant fraction of the edges are removed at each stage.

Here is how to simulate the n pairwise independent biased coin flips with $O(\log n)$ independent fair coin flips. Let p be a prime number in the range n to $2n$ (such a prime exists by *Bertrand's postulate*; see [49, p. 343]). Assume the vertices of the graph are elements of the finite field $\mathcal{Z}_p$. For each vertex u, let a_u be an integer in the range $0 \leq a_u < p$ such that the fraction $\frac{a_u}{p}$ is as close as possible to the desired bias $\frac{1}{2d(u)}$. (We will not get the exact bias $\frac{1}{2d(u)}$, but only the approximation $\frac{a_u}{p}$. This will be close enough for our analysis.)

Let A_u be any subset of $\mathcal{Z}_p$ of size a_u. To simulate the biased coin flips, choose elements x and y uniformly at random from $\mathcal{Z}_p$ and calculate $x + uy$ in $\mathcal{Z}_p$ for each vertex u. Declare the flip for vertex u to be heads if $x + uy \in A_u$, tails otherwise.

Note that the random selection of x and y, since they are chosen with uniform probability from a set of size p, requires $2 \log p = O(\log n)$ truly random bits.

For each $z, y \in \mathcal{Z}_p$, there is exactly one $x \in \mathcal{Z}_p$ such that $x + uy = z$, namely $x = z - uy$. Using this fact at the critical step, we calculate the probability of heads for the vertex u:

$$\Pr(x + uy \in A_u) = \frac{1}{p^2} |\{(x, y) \mid x + uy \in A_u\}|$$

$$= \frac{1}{p^2} \sum_{z \in A_u} |\{(x, y) \mid x + uy = z\}|$$

$$= \frac{1}{p^2} \sum_{z \in A_u} p$$

$$= \frac{a_u}{p} \; .$$

Finally, we show pairwise independence. For any $u, v, z, w \in \mathcal{Z}_p$, $u \neq v$, there is exactly one solution x, y to the linear system

$$\begin{bmatrix} 1 & u \\ 1 & v \end{bmatrix} \cdot \begin{bmatrix} x \\ y \end{bmatrix} = \begin{bmatrix} z \\ w \end{bmatrix}$$

over $\mathcal{Z}_p$, since the matrix is nonsingular. Thus

$$
\begin{aligned}
&\Pr(x + uy \in A_u \wedge x + vy \in A_v) \\
&= \frac{1}{p^2} \, |\{(x,y) \mid x + uy \in A_u \wedge x + vy \in A_v\}| \\
&= \frac{1}{p^2} \sum_{z \in A_u} \sum_{w \in A_v} |\{(x,y) \mid x + uy = z \wedge x + vy = w\}| \\
&= \frac{1}{p^2} \sum_{z \in A_u} \sum_{w \in A_v} 1 \\
&= \frac{a_u a_v}{p^2} \\
&= \Pr(x + uy \in A_u) \cdot \Pr(x + vy \in A_v) \; .
\end{aligned}
$$

We have seen how to generate up to p pairwise independent events with only $2 \log p$ truly random bits. A generalization of this technique allows us to generate up to p d-wise independent events with only $d \log p$ truly random bits: pick $x_0, \ldots, x_{d-1} \in \mathcal{Z}_p$ uniformly at random; the uth event is

$$x_0 + x_1 u + x_2 u^2 + \cdots + x_{d-1} u^{d-1} \;\; \in \;\; A_u \; .$$

The analysis of this generalization is left as an exercise (Homework 10, Exercise 2).

Lecture 38   Miller's Primality Test

Factoring integers into their prime factors is one of the oldest and most important computational problems. It is a problem that goes back to Euclid and is still thriving today. It is generally assumed that factoring is computationally intractible, and many modern cryptographic protocols are based on this assumption. If someone discovered an efficient factoring algorithm tomorrow, there would be a lot of unhappy CIA and KGB agents around.

A simpler related problem is testing whether a given number n is prime. Primality tests have been given by Miller [81], Schönhage and Strassen [96], Rabin [89], and Bach [8] to mention a few. We will develop Miller's primality test in this and the next lecture. It is a polynomial-time probabilistic test with the following probabilistic behavior:

- If n is prime, the algorithm answers "prime" with probability 1.

- If n is composite, the algorithm answers "composite" with probability at least $\frac{1}{2}$.

Thus, if we run Miller's algorithm on input n and it responds "composite", then we are sure that n is composite, and we can stop. If on the other hand the algorithm answers "prime", then we are not sure, but we can run the algorithm again. Assuming our source of randomness provides truly independent trials, if we run the algorithm 25 times and it answers "prime" each time, then we can be 99.99999702% certain that n is indeed prime.

201

Adleman and Huang [1] have given a complementary probabilistic algorithm that recognizes composites with probability 1 and primes with probability at least $\frac{1}{2}$. It is still unknown whether primes can be recognized deterministically in polynomial time.

Miller's algorithm gives rise to a deterministic polynomial-time algorithm under the *Extended Riemann Hypothesis (ERH)*, a famous unverified conjecture of analytic number theory dealing with the distribution of zeros of certain analytic functions in the complex plane. The ERH is a stronger version of the *Riemann Hypothesis*, which states that the zeros of the *Riemann zeta function*

$$\zeta(s) \;=\; \sum_{n=1}^{\infty} n^{-s}$$

all lie on the line $\Re(s) = \frac{1}{2}$ ($\Re(\cdot) =$ "real part of"). We will not treat the deterministic version here.

Miller's algorithm is quite simple:

Algorithm 38.1 (Miller's Primality Test) Given $n \geq 1$:

1. Let $n - 1 = 2^e m$, m odd.

2. Choose a random number $a \in \{1, 2, \ldots, n - 1\}$.

3. Calculate $a^m \bmod n$. If $a^m \equiv 1(n)$, halt and output "prime".

4. Calculate $a^m, a^{2m}, a^{4m}, \ldots, a^{2^e m} = a^{n-1}$ modulo n by repeated squaring. If $a^{n-1} \not\equiv 1(n)$, halt and output "composite".

5. Find the largest k such that $a^{2^k m} \not\equiv 1(n)$. If $a^{2^k m} \equiv -1(n)$, output "prime", otherwise output "composite".

Theorem 38.2

(i) If n is prime, then Algorithm 38.1 always outputs "prime".

(ii) If n is composite, then Algorithm 38.1 outputs "composite" with probability at least $\frac{1}{2}$.

Proof of (i). Suppose n is prime. If the algorithm halts and outputs "prime" in step 3, then there is nothing to prove, so suppose the algorithm gets to step 4. Fermat's Theorem states that if n is prime and a is relatively prime to n, then $a^{n-1} \equiv 1(n)$ (read "a^{n-1} is congruent to 1 mod n"), thus the algorithm does not answer "composite" in step 4, so the algorithm proceeds to step 5. Now we use the fact that for n prime, the ring $\mathcal{Z}_n$ of integers modulo n is a field, so all nonzero elements have a multiplicative inverse. In any field, a polynomial of degree d has at most d roots; thus in $\mathcal{Z}_n$, the polynomial $x^2 - 1$ has roots 1 and -1 only (note $-1 \equiv n - 1(n)$). Therefore, if k is the largest number such that $a^{2^k m} \not\equiv 1(n)$, then $(a^{2^k m})^2 = a^{2^{k+1} m} \equiv 1(n)$, therefore $a^{2^k m} \equiv -1(n)$ and the algorithm answers "prime" in step 5. □

What happens if n is composite? In order to handle this case, we will need some elementary number-theoretic machinery. We will break the argument up into two cases, depending on whether or not n is a *Carmichael number*. A Carmichael number is a composite number that looks like a prime as far as Fermat's Theorem is concerned. We begin with a very basic but important lemma.

Lemma 38.3 *The following are equivalent:*

(i) *a and n are relatively prime; i.e., $(a, n) = 1$ (recall (a, n) stands for the gcd of a and n);*

(ii) *a is invertible modulo n; i.e., there exists an s such that $as \equiv 1(n)$.*

Proof.

$$
\begin{aligned}
(a, n) = 1 \quad &\leftrightarrow \quad \exists s, t \ as + nt = 1 \ \text{ by the Euclidean algorithm} \\
&\leftrightarrow \quad \exists s \ n \mid (1 - as) \\
&\leftrightarrow \quad \exists s \ as \equiv 1(n) \ .
\end{aligned}
$$

□

Let

$$
\mathcal{Z}_n^* \quad = \quad \{a \in \mathcal{Z}_n \mid (a, n) = 1\} \ .
$$

Under multiplication modulo n, this set forms a group: it is closed under multiplication, since if two numbers share no common factor with n, then neither does their product; and Lemma 38.3 implies that any element of $\mathcal{Z}_n^*$ has a multiplicative inverse in $\mathcal{Z}_n^*$.

The group $\mathcal{Z}_n^*$ is known as the *group of invertible elements modulo n*. Its order, the number of integers between 0 and n that are relatively prime to n, is denoted $\varphi(n)$. The function φ is often called the *Euler totient function*.

If n is prime, then $\varphi(n) = n - 1$ and $\mathcal{Z}_n^* = \{1, 2, \ldots, n - 1\}$, since every positive number less than n is relatively prime to n. If n is composite, then $\varphi(n) < n - 1$. It can be show without too much difficulty that if the prime factorization of n is $\prod_{i=1}^k p_i^{e_i}$, then

$$
\varphi(n) \quad = \quad \prod_{i=1}^k p_i^{e_i - 1}(p_i - 1) \ .
$$

For example, $\mathcal{Z}_{12}^* = \{1, 5, 7, 11\}$ and $\mathcal{Z}_{15}^* = \{1, 2, 4, 7, 8, 11, 13, 14\}$. The multiplication table for $\mathcal{Z}_{12}^*$ is

·	1	5	7	11
1	1	5	7	11
5	5	1	11	7
7	7	11	1	5
11	11	7	5	1

Lemma 38.4 *If m and n are relatively prime, then Z^*_{mn} and $Z^*_m \times Z^*_n$ are isomorphic as groups.*

Proof. By the Chinese Remainder Theorem, Z_{mn} and $Z_m \times Z_n$ are isomorphic as rings under the map

$$a \;\mapsto\; (a \bmod m, a \bmod n) \;.$$

This map specializes to a group isomorphism between Z^*_{mn} and its image when restricted to domain Z^*_{mn}. But

$$
\begin{aligned}
a \in Z^*_{mn} \;\; &\rightarrow \;\; (a, mn) = 1 \\
&\rightarrow \;\; (a, m) = 1 \\
&\rightarrow \;\; (a - mt, m) = 1 \;\; \text{for any } t \\
&\rightarrow \;\; a \bmod m \in Z^*_m \;,
\end{aligned}
$$

and similarly,

$$a \bmod n \in Z^*_n \;.$$

Thus the image of the map is $Z_m \times Z_n$. $\square$

Fermat's Theorem says that if n is prime and $a \in Z^*_n$, then $a^{n-1} \equiv 1(n)$. This is true because for n prime, Z^*_n is a group of order $n - 1$ under multiplication mod n, thus the order of every subgroup must divide $n - 1$, including the cyclic subgroup generated by a. Thus if m is the least number such that $a^m \equiv 1(n)$, then $m \mid n - 1$ and $a^{n-1} \equiv 1(n)$.

If n is composite and $a \in Z_n - Z^*_n$, then $a^{n-1} \not\equiv 1(n)$, since otherwise a would have an inverse mod n (namely a^{n-2}), which would contradict Lemma 38.3. If n is composite and $a \in Z^*_n$, then it may or may not be the case that $a^{n-1} \equiv 1(n)$.

Definition 38.5 A composite number n is called a *pseudoprime* with respect to $a \in Z^*_n$ if $a^{n-1} \equiv 1(n)$. A composite number n is called a *Carmichael number* if n is pseudoprime with respect to all $a \in Z^*_n$. $\square$

It is unknown whether infinitely many Carmichael numbers exist (see [49, p. 72]). For the purposes of Algorithm 38.1, Carmichael numbers are bad, because Fermat's test $a^{n-1} \equiv 1(n)$ is not going to help much in distinguishing them from primes.

For the remainder of this lecture, we will prove Theorem 38.2(ii) for the case n not a Carmichael number. We will show that if n is not a Carmichael number, *i.e.* if there exists an $a \in Z^*_n$ such that $a^{n-1} \not\equiv 1(n)$, then at least half the elements of Z^*_n satisfy this property, so the probability of the algorithm hitting one in step 2 and thus answering "composite" in step 4 is pretty good.

Definition 38.6 For fixed n, define

$$\mathcal{K}_d \;=\; \{a \in \mathcal{Z}_n \mid a^d \equiv 1(n)\} \;.$$

$\square$

Surely $\mathcal{K}_d \subseteq \mathcal{Z}_n^*$, since every element $a \in \mathcal{K}_d$ is invertible (its inverse is a^{d-1}). Moreover, $\mathcal{K}_d$ forms a subgroup of $\mathcal{Z}_n^*$, since it is the kernel of the group homomorphism $a \mapsto a^d$.

Proof of Theorem 38.2(ii) for n not a Carmichael number. If n is composite but not a Carmichael number, then $\mathcal{K}_{n-1} \neq \mathcal{Z}_n^*$. But since $\mathcal{K}_{n-1}$ is a subgroup of $\mathcal{Z}_n^*$, its order must divide that of $\mathcal{Z}_n^*$, thus

$$|\mathcal{K}_{n-1}| \;\leq\; \frac{|\mathcal{Z}_n^*|}{2} \;.$$

Thus with probability at least $\frac{1}{2}$, the random choice of a in step 2 gives an a in $\mathcal{Z}_n - \mathcal{K}_{n-1}$. In this case, the algorithm will answer "composite" in step 4.

$\square$

We treat the remaining case, n a Carmichael number, in the next lecture.

Lecture 39   Analysis of Miller's Primality Test

Last time we were engaged in proving the correctness of:

Algorithm 39.1 (Miller's Primality Test) Given $n \geq 1$:

1. Let $n - 1 = 2^e m$, m odd.

2. Choose a random number $a \in \{1, 2, \ldots, n - 1\}$.

3. Calculate $a^m \bmod n$. If $a^m \equiv 1(n)$, halt and output "prime".

4. Calculate $a^m, a^{2m}, a^{4m}, \ldots, a^{2^e m} = a^{n-1}$ modulo n by repeated squaring. If $a^{n-1} \not\equiv 1(n)$, halt and output "composite".

5. Find the largest k such that $a^{2^k m} \not\equiv 1(n)$. If $a^{2^k m} \equiv -1(n)$, output "prime", otherwise output "composite".

Theorem 39.2

   (i) If n is prime, then Algorithm 39.1 always outputs "prime".

   (ii) If n is composite, then Algorithm 39.1 outputs "composite" with probability at least $\frac{1}{2}$.

Recall from last time the definitions of the multiplicative groups

$$\begin{aligned} \mathcal{Z}_n^* &= \{a \in \mathcal{Z}_n \mid (a, n) = 1\} \\ \mathcal{K}_d &= \{a \in \mathcal{Z}_n^* \mid a^d \equiv 1(n)\} \end{aligned}$$

206

and that a composite number n is a *Carmichael number* if $\mathcal{K}_{n-1} = \mathcal{Z}_n^*$. Last time we proved Theorem 39.2(i) and (ii) for the case n not a Carmichael number. In this lecture we complete the proof of Theorem 39.2.

The idea behind this case is that if n is a Carmichael number, then it has at least two distinct prime factors, and if it has exactly k distinct prime factors all different from 2, then $\mathcal{Z}_n^*$ contains exactly 2^k square roots of unity. Moreover, the probability of seeing a weird square root of unity (one not equal to 1 or -1) in step 5 is at least as good as the probability of seeing 1 or -1.

Lemma 39.3 *Prime powers p^d, $d \geq 2$, cannot be Carmichael numbers.*

Proof. Consider $p^{d-1} + 1$. Surely $p^{d-1} + 1$ and p^d are relatively prime, and computing modulo p^d,

$$
\begin{aligned}
(p^{d-1} + 1)^{p^d - 1} &= \sum_{i=0}^{p^d - 1} \binom{p^d - 1}{i} p^{(d-1)i} \\
&\equiv 1 + (p^d - 1)p^{d-1} \\
&\equiv 1 - p^{d-1} \\
&\not\equiv 1 .
\end{aligned}
$$

□

By Lemma 39.3, if n is a Carmichael number, then it has at least two distinct prime factors. We now wish to show that if n has exactly k distinct prime factors all different from 2, then $\mathcal{Z}_n^*$ contains exactly 2^k distinct square roots of unity.

Example 39.4 Consider $n = 15$ with prime factors 3 and 5. By the Chinese Remainder Theorem, $\mathcal{Z}_{15}$ and $\mathcal{Z}_3 \times \mathcal{Z}_5$ are isomorphic under the map

$$
x \;\mapsto\; (x \bmod 3, x \bmod 5) . \tag{61}
$$

The correspondence between the elements of $\mathcal{Z}_{15}$ and the pairs (i, j) of $\mathcal{Z}_3 \times \mathcal{Z}_5$ is given in the table below. Note that every pair (i, j) occurs exactly once.

x	0	1	2	3	4	5	6	7	8	9	10	11	12	13	14
$x \bmod 3$	0	1	2	0	1	2	0	1	2	0	1	2	0	1	2
$x \bmod 5$	0	1	2	3	4	0	1	2	3	4	0	1	2	3	4

Certainly 1 and $-1 = 14$ are square roots of 1 mod 15. Under the isomorphism (61), these correspond to the pairs $(1, 1)$ and $(2, 4)$. But note that if we exchange second components, the pairs $(1, 4)$ and $(2, 1)$ square to give 1 as well (recall multiplication in a direct product is componentwise). Looking in the table above, we see that $(1, 4)$ and $(2, 1)$ correspond under the isomorphism (61) to 4 and 11 respectively, and $4^2 = 16 \equiv 1(15)$ and $11^2 = 121 \equiv 1(15)$.

□

In general, if $n = p_1^{d_1} p_2^{d_2} \cdots p_k^{d_k}$ is the prime factorization of n, then

$$\mathcal{Z}_n \;\cong\; \mathcal{Z}_{p_1^{d_1}} \times \cdots \times \mathcal{Z}_{p_k^{d_k}} \;, \tag{62}$$

and $(a_1, \ldots, a_k)$ is a square root of unity in $\mathcal{Z}_{p_1^{d_1}} \times \cdots \times \mathcal{Z}_{p_k^{d_k}}$ iff each a_i is a square root of unity in $\mathcal{Z}_{p_i^{d_i}}$. Since any $\mathcal{Z}_{p^d}$ has at least two square roots of unity 1 and -1 (provided $p^d \neq 2$; but if 2 divides n then we already know that n is composite), $\mathcal{Z}_n$ has at least 2^k square roots of unity, one corresponding to each vector of the form $(u_1, \ldots, u_k)$, where $u_i \in \{-1, 1\}$. In fact, it has exactly 2^k, because $\mathcal{Z}_{p^d}$ has exactly two, although we do not need to know this for the purposes of Theorem 39.2.

Fact 39.5 *If p is an odd prime, then the ring $\mathcal{Z}_{p^d}$ has exactly two square roots of 1, namely 1 and -1.*

Proof. If $a^2 \equiv 1(p^d)$, then $(a-1)(a+1) = a^2 - 1 \equiv 0(p^d)$, thus $p^d \mid (a-1)(a+1)$. Since $p \neq 2$, p cannot divide both $a-1$ and $a+1$. Thus $p^d \mid a-1$ or $p^d \mid a+1$, therefore either $a \equiv 1(p^d)$ or $a \equiv -1(p^d)$. □

Recall that $n - 1 = 2^e m$ where m is odd. We wish to show now that each element $b \in \mathcal{K}_{2^e}$ is equally likely to be hit by choosing a random element $a \in \mathcal{Z}_n^*$ and raising it to the mth power. The following lemma will be useful.

Lemma 39.6 *If c and d are relatively prime, then*

$$\mathcal{K}_{cd} \;\cong\; \mathcal{K}_c \times \mathcal{K}_d \;.$$

Proof. Consider the map

$$a \;\mapsto\; (a^d, a^c) \;.$$

It is easily shown that this is a group homomorphism $\mathcal{K}_{cd} \to \mathcal{K}_c \times \mathcal{K}_d$. It is one-to-one, since if s and t are integers such that $sc + td = 1$, then

$$(a^d, a^c) = (b^d, b^c) \;\;\rightarrow\;\; a^{sc+td} = b^{sc+td}$$
$$\rightarrow\;\; a = b \;.$$

It is onto, since for any $a \in \mathcal{K}_c$, $b \in \mathcal{K}_d$,

$$
\begin{aligned}
a^t b^s \;\mapsto\; & (a^{td} b^{sd}, a^{tc} b^{sc}) \\
= \; & (a^{td}, b^{sc}) \\
= \; & (a^{sc+td}, b^{sc+td}) \\
= \; & (a, b) \;.
\end{aligned}
$$

□

By Lemma 39.6,

$$\mathcal{K}_{n-1} = \mathcal{K}_{2^e m}$$
$$\cong \mathcal{K}_{2^e} \times \mathcal{K}_m ,$$

with the isomorphism given by $a \mapsto (a^m, a^{2^e})$. The image of $\mathcal{K}_{n-1}$ under the map $a \mapsto a^m$ is therefore $\mathcal{K}_{2^e}$, and the kernel of this map is $\mathcal{K}_m$. The inverse image of any $b \in \mathcal{K}_{2^e}$ is a coset of $\mathcal{K}_m$ and is the same size as $\mathcal{K}_m$. Therefore, by choosing an $a \in \mathcal{K}_{n-1}$ at random and raising it to the mth power, we are equally likely to hit any $b \in \mathcal{K}_{2^e}$.

Now arrange the elements of $\mathcal{K}_{2^e}$ in a tree with edges (a, a^2). The root of the tree is the element 1, and the elements at level d are all the elements of $\mathcal{K}_{2^d}$. The elements at level 1 are all the square roots of unity. If w is a square root of unity, $w \neq 1$, let T_w be the set of elements above w in this tree; these are the $b \in \mathcal{K}_{2^e}$ such that $b^{2^d} = w$ for some $d \geq 0$.

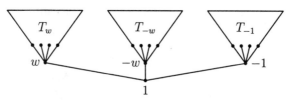

As shown, if a is a random element of $\mathcal{Z}_n^*$, then a^m is equally likely to be any element of this tree. In step 4, we repeatedly square the element, and this corresponds to moving down in the tree level by level. The algorithm responds "composite" correctly in step 5 iff this process eventually encounters a weird square root of unity w (one other than 1 or -1). Thus we will be done if we can show that the probability that a randomly chosen element of this tree is in T_w for some weird w is at least as great as the probability that it is in T_{-1} or 1. This follows immediately from the following lemma and the fact that there are at least two weird square roots of unity:

Lemma 39.7 *If $w^2 = 1$, then $|T_w| \geq |T_{-1}|$.*

Proof. We again make use of the Chinese Remainder Theorem. For any square root of unity $w \neq 1$, let $\ell(w)$ be the height of the tree T_w; thus $\ell(w)$ is the maximum number for which there exists an a such that $a^{2^{\ell(w)}} \equiv w(n)$. Then

$$\ell(w) \geq \ell(-1) , \qquad (63)$$

since if w, a, and b correspond under the isomorphism (62) to

$$w \mapsto (-1, -1, \ldots, -1, 1, 1, 1, \ldots, 1)$$

$$\underbrace{\qquad\qquad}_{j} \underbrace{\qquad}_{k-j}$$

$$a \mapsto (a_1, a_2, \ldots, a_j, a_{j+1}, \ldots, a_k)$$
$$b \mapsto (a_1, a_2, \ldots, a_j, a_{j+1}^2, \ldots, a_k^2)$$

respectively, and if $a^{2^d} \equiv -1(n)$, then $b^{2^d} \equiv w(n)$.

Now

$$
\begin{aligned}
|T_w| &= \left| \bigcup_{d=0}^{\ell(w)} \{ a \in \mathcal{Z}_n^* \mid a^{2^d} = w \} \right| \\
&= \sum_{d=0}^{\ell(w)} |\{ a \in \mathcal{Z}_n^* \mid a^{2^d} = w \}| \\
&= \sum_{d=0}^{\ell(w)} |\mathcal{K}_{2^d}| \ ;
\end{aligned}
$$

the last equation holds because the set

$$
\{ a \in \mathcal{Z}_n^* \mid a^{2^d} = w \}
$$

is a coset of the subgroup $\mathcal{K}_{2^d}$, therefore has the same cardinality: if $c^{2^d} = w$, then

$$
\begin{aligned}
\{ a \in \mathcal{Z}_n^* \mid a^{2^d} = w \} &= c\mathcal{K}_{2^d} \\
&= \{ ca \mid a \in \mathcal{K}_{2^d} \} \ ,
\end{aligned}
$$

and the map $a \mapsto ca$ gives a one-to-one correspondence.

It follows from (63) that

$$
|T_w| \ \geq \ |T_{-1}| \ .
$$

$\square$

By Lemma 39.7, given that the a selected in step 2 is in $\mathcal{Z}_n^*$, the probability is at least $\frac{1}{2}$ that the algorithm will encounter a weird square root of unity in step 4 and thus answer "composite" in step 5. If the a chosen in step 2 is not in $\mathcal{Z}_n^*$, then the algorithm will answer "composite" in step 4. This completes the proof of Theorem 39.2.

Lecture 40   Probabilistic Tests with Polynomials

In this lecture, we give a useful probabilistic technique for testing properties that are equivalent to the vanishing of some polynomial of low degree. This technique has many interesting applications, not only in algebraic algorithms, but also in graph theory and combinatorics. Several examples of its use will be given later.

Good deterministic algorithms sometimes require considerable effort to program, whereas "quick and dirty" methods involving random choices are often just as good in practice. For example, it is quite difficult to test deterministically whether a multivariate polynomial given by a straight-line program is identically zero; however, there is a fast probabilistic test: evaluate the polynomial on a randomly chosen input and check whether the result is 0. If not, the polynomial is certainly not identically 0; if so, chances are good that it is.

The technique is based on the following theorem due to Zippel [111] and independently to Schwartz [92]. It says essentially that the solutions of a multivariate polynomial equation of low degree are sparse. Intuitively, this theorem is true over the real numbers for any polynomial, regardless of degree: the set

$$\{(x_1, \ldots, x_n) \in \mathcal{R}^n \mid p(x_1, \ldots, x_n) = 0\}$$

is a surface of dimension $n - 1$. For example, a linear equation

$$\sum_{i=1}^{n} a_i x_i \;=\; a$$

describes a hyperplane; in three dimensions, the quadratic equation

$$x^2 + y^2 - z^2 \;=\; 0$$

describes the surface of a cone. A randomly chosen point with respect to almost any reasonable probability distribution will almost certainly not lie on that surface. Under the degree restriction, the theorem is also true over other fields besides the reals, including finite fields.

Theorem 40.1 *Let k be a field and let $S \subseteq k$ be an arbitrary subset of k. Let $p(\overline{x})$ be a polynomial of n variables $\overline{x} = x_1, \ldots, x_n$ and total degree[5] d with coefficients in k. Then the equation $p(\overline{x}) = 0$ has at most $d \cdot |S|^{n-1}$ solutions in S^n.*

Proof. The proof is by induction on n and d. For $n = 1$, the result follows from the fact that a univariate polynomial of degree d can have no more than d roots in k. For $d = 1$, we need to show that a hyperplane

$$a_1 x_1 + a_2 x_2 + \cdots + a_n x_n \;=\; a \tag{64}$$

in k^n can intersect S^n in at most $|S|^{n-1}$ points. Pick some $a_i \neq 0$, say without loss of generality $a_1 \neq 0$. Then for all solutions $\overline{x}$ of (64),

$$x_1 \;=\; \frac{1}{a_1}(a - \sum_{i=2}^{n} a_i x_i) \;,$$

therefore the value of x_1 is uniquely determined by the values of $x_2, \ldots, x_n$. There are exactly $|S|^{n-1}$ assignments to $x_2, \ldots, x_n$ from S, thus at most $|S|^{n-1}$ solutions to (64).

Now suppose we have a polynomial p of degree $d > 1$ with $n > 1$ variables. If p is not irreducible, *i.e.* if p has a nontrivial factorization $p = qr$ into two polynomials q and r of lower total degree, then by the induction hypothesis, q has no more than $\deg q \cdot |S|^{n-1}$ zeros in S^n and r has no more than $\deg r \cdot |S|^{n-1}$ zeros in S^n. But $p(\overline{a}) = 0$ iff $q(\overline{a})r(\overline{a}) = 0$ iff either $q(\overline{a}) = 0$ or $r(\overline{a}) = 0$, thus

$$\{\text{zeros of } p \text{ in } S^n\} \;=\; \{\text{zeros of } q \text{ in } S^n\} \cup \{\text{zeros of } r \text{ in } S^n\} \;.$$

It follows that

$$
\begin{aligned}
&|\{\text{zeros of } p \text{ in } S^n\}| \\
&= \; |\{\text{zeros of } q \text{ in } S^n\} \cup \{\text{zeros of } r \text{ in } S^n\}| \\
&\leq \; |\{\text{zeros of } q \text{ in } S^n\}| + |\{\text{zeros of } r \text{ in } S^n\}| \\
&\leq \; \deg q \cdot |S|^{n-1} + \deg r \cdot |S|^{n-1} \\
&= \; (\deg q + \deg r) \cdot |S|^{n-1} \\
&= \; d \cdot |S|^{n-1} \;.
\end{aligned}
$$

---

[5]Maximum degree of any term.

Finally, we are left with the case that p is irreducible of degree $d > 1$ with $n+1$ variables $x_1, \ldots, x_{n+1}$. Let $\overline{x} = x_1, \ldots, x_n$. Then $p = p(\overline{x}, x_{n+1})$. For each $s \in S$, consider the polynomial $p(\overline{x}, s) \in k[\overline{x}]$. By the induction hypothesis, $p(\overline{x}, s)$ has at most $d \cdot |S|^{n-1}$ zeros in S^n (unless $p(\overline{x}, s)$ is identically zero; but we show below that this cannot happen if p is irreducible). Since $p(\overline{x}, s)$ has at most $d \cdot |S|^{n-1}$ zeros in S^n, p has at most $|S| \cdot d \cdot |S|^{n-1} = d \cdot |S|^n$ zeros in S^{n+1}.

To show that $p(\overline{x}, s)$ is not identically zero, we show that if it were, then the polynomial $x_{n+1} - s$ would divide p, contradicting the irreducibility of p. Suppose then that $p(\overline{x}, s) = 0$. Collect terms of p with like powers of x_{n+1} so that p is expressed as a polynomial in x_{n+1} with coefficients in the polynomial ring $k[\overline{x}]$. Divide p by the polynomial $x_{n+1} - s$ using ordinary polynomial division with remainder. Then

$$p(\overline{x}, x_{n+1}) \;=\; q(\overline{x}, x_{n+1})(x_{n+1} - s) + r$$

where the degree of the remainder r is less than the degree of the divisor $x_{n+1} - s$, so r is a constant. Evaluating both sides of the equation at $x_{n+1} = s$, we get that $r = 0$. Thus

$$p(\overline{x}, x_{n+1}) \;=\; q(\overline{x}, x_{n+1})(x_{n+1} - s) ,$$

contradicting the irreducibility of p.   □

The following corollary is immediate.

Corollary 40.2 *Let $p(x_1, x_2, \ldots, x_n)$ be a nonzero polynomial of degree d with coefficients in a field k, and let $S \subseteq k$. If p is evaluated on a random element $(s_1, \ldots, s_n) \in S^n$, then*

$$\Pr(p(s_1, \ldots, s_n) = 0) \;\leq\; \frac{d}{|S|} .$$

40.1   Applications

We give three applications of Theorem 40.1 and Corollary 40.2: finding perfect matchings, testing isomorphism of labeled trees, and computing the rank of a matrix over a finite field.

Perfect Matchings

We know how to test for the existence of a perfect matching in a bipartite graph G and find one if it exists in polynomial time. It is unknown whether this problem is in NC. However, the following approach, based on an observation of Lovász [74], gives a random NC algorithm.

Assign to each edge (i, j) of G an indeterminate x_{ij} and consider the $n \times n$ bipartite adjacency matrix X with these indeterminates instead of 1's. For example,

$$X = \begin{bmatrix} x_{11} & x_{12} & 0 \\ 0 & x_{22} & x_{23} \\ x_{31} & x_{32} & 0 \end{bmatrix}$$

The determinant $\det X$ is a polynomial of degree n in the indeterminates x_{ij} with one term for each perfect matching, and none of these terms cancel. For example, the graph above has two perfect matchings

corresponding to the two terms of the determinant

$$\det X = x_{12}x_{23}x_{31} - x_{11}x_{23}x_{32} .$$

Thus G has a perfect matching iff $\det X$ is not identically 0. This is difficult to test deterministically, since $\det X$ may be quite large. Chistov's or Berkowitz' algorithm gives a polylog-depth circuit with inputs x_{ij} that computes the value of $\det X$ for any specialization of the indeterminates x_{ij}, but it is difficult to test deterministically whether all such specializations give 0.

However, we can test this in RNC by assigning randomly chosen elements of a large enough finite field (say $\mathcal{Z}_p$, where p is some prime greater than $2n$) to the x_{ij}, and then asking whether the determinant evaluated at those random elements is 0. This will happen with probability 1 if $\det X$ is indeed identically 0, and with probability at most $\frac{n}{2n} = \frac{1}{2}$ if not, by Corollary 40.2.

Given the ability to test for the existence of a perfect matching, we can then find one by deleting edges one by one and testing for the existence of a perfect matching without that edge.

Isomorphism of Unordered Directed Trees

Here is an efficient probabilistic test for deciding whether two unordered[6] directed trees of height h and size n are isomorphic. Associate with each vertex v a polynomial f_v in the variables $x_0, x_1, \ldots, x_h$ inductively, as follows. For each leaf v, set $f_v = x_0$. For each internal node v of height k with children $v_1, \ldots, v_m$, set

$$f_v = (x_k - f_{v_1})(x_k - f_{v_2}) \cdots (x_k - f_{v_m}) .$$

The degree of f_v is equal to the number of leaves in the subtree rooted at v. Using the fact that polynomial factorization is unique, it can be shown that two trees are isomorphic iff the polynomials associated with the roots of the trees are equal. This gives an efficient probabilistic test for unordered tree isomorphism: test whether the difference of these two polynomials is identically zero by evaluating it on a random input.

---

[6]A directed tree is *ordered* if the left-to-right order of each node's children is given.

Matrix Rank

Mulmuley's algorithm computes the rank of a matrix over an arbitrary field k. Recall that for a square matrix A, if rank $A = $ rank A^2, then rank A is given by the index of the last nonzero term in the characteristic polynomial of A. I.e., if

$$\chi_A(\lambda) \;=\; \lambda^n - s_1\lambda^{n-1} + s_2\lambda^{n-2} - \cdots \pm s_r\lambda^{n-r}$$

where $s_r \neq 0$, then rank $A = r$. If rank $A \neq$ rank A^2 and we are working in the complex numbers, then we can take $\overline{A}^T A$, where $\overline{A}^T$ is the conjugate transpose of A. As shown in Lecture 33, this matrix has the same rank as A and the same rank as its square. Over finite fields, however, this does not work. Mulmuley's algorithm closes this gap, but his construction introduces an extra indeterminate, and dealing with the resulting symbolic expressions requires more processors.

Here is a probabilistic approach suggested in [15] that saves a factor of n in the processor bound over Mulmuley's deterministic algorithm. Multiply A on the left by a random matrix R. The elements of R are chosen uniformly at random from a sufficiently large set. By Corollary 40.2, R is nonsingular with high probability: R is singular if and only if its determinant vanishes, and this is a polynomial equation of low degree. Therefore, with high probability, RA has the same rank as A, since the rank of RA is the dimension of the image of RA as a linear map.

We argue also that with high probability, RA and $(RA)^2$ have the same rank, allowing us to compute the rank from the characteristic polynomial of RA as in Lemma 32.1.

Let $r = $ rank A. The condition

$$\text{rank } (RA)^2 = \text{rank } RA = \text{rank } A \tag{65}$$

is equivalent to the condition that the subspaces im RA and ker A are of complementary dimension and intersect in the trivial subspace 0; in other words, that every vector in k^n can be represented uniquely as the sum of a vector in im RA and one in ker A. In symbols,

$$k^n \;\cong\; \text{im } RA \oplus \text{ker } A \tag{66}$$

where $\oplus$ denotes direct sum and $\cong$ denotes isomorphism of vector spaces.

Now select a basis for im A among the columns of A. These columns will comprise an $n \times r$ matrix B. Let C be an $n \times (n - r)$ matrix whose columns span ker A. Then condition (66) is equivalent to the condition that the $n \times n$ matrix $[RB|C]$ formed by juxtaposing the columns of RB and C is nonsingular; equivalently, $\det [RB|C] \neq 0$. By Corollary 40.2, this occurs with high probability.

The beauty of this approach is that we never need to compute B or C; we are happy enough just knowing that they exist.

II Homework Exercises

Homework 1

1. (a) Let $(S, \mathcal{I})$ be a matroid and let $A \subseteq S$. Prove that all maximal independent subsets of A have the same cardinality. (This number is called the *rank* of A. The rank of the matroid is the rank of the set S.)

   (b) Let I be a maximal independent set and let $x \notin I$. Prove that there is a unique cycle contained in $I \cup \{x\}$. (This is called the *fundamental cycle* of x and I.)

   (c) Let $G = (V, E)$ be an undirected graph, not necessarily connected. Consider the system $(E, \mathcal{I})$, where $\mathcal{I}$ consists of all subsets $E' \subseteq E$ such that the subgraph (V, E') has no cycles. Show that $(E, \mathcal{I})$ is a matroid. What is its rank? What are its maximal independent sets?

2. Let $G = (V, E)$ be a directed graph. A *transitive reduction* or *Hasse diagram* of G is a subgraph $G_H = (V, E_H)$ with minimum number of edges such that E and E_H have the same transitive closure.

   (a) Prove that if G is acyclic, then the transitive reduction of G is unique.

   (b) Give an efficient algorithm to find the transitive reduction of G in case G is acyclic. Your algorithm should have roughly the same complexity as transitive closure. (We will see later that the problem is *NP*-complete when G is cyclic.)

3. An Euler circuit in a connected undirected graph $G = (V, E)$ is a circuit that traverses all edges exactly once.

   (a) Prove that G has an Euler circuit iff G is connected and the degree of every vertex is even.

   (b) Give an $O(|E|)$ algorithm to find an Euler circuit if one exists. Give a proof of correctness and detailed complexity analysis.

Homework 2

1. Give a linear-time algorithm for topological sort based on depth-first search.

2. Let $G = (V, E)$ be an undirected graph, and let θ be a circular ordering of the edges adjacent to each vertex. The ordering θ is said to be *consistent* with an embedding of G in the plane if for each vertex v, the ordering of the edges adjacent to v given by θ agrees with their counterclockwise ordering around v in the embedding.

   (a) Give a linear-time algorithm that determines whether a given θ is consistent with some plane embedding.

   (b) Consider two embeddings to be the same if one can be transformed into the other by a smooth motion in the plane without tearing or cutting. Assume that G is connected. How many distinct plane embeddings are consistent with a given θ? (*Extra credit.* Remove the assumption of connectedness.)

3. A *scorpion* is an undirected graph G of the following form: there are three special vertices, called the *sting*, the *tail*, and the *body*, of degree 1, 2, and $n - 2$, respectively. The sting is connected only to the tail; the tail is connected only to the sting and the body; and the body is connected to all vertices except the sting. The other vertices of G may be connected to each other arbitrarily.

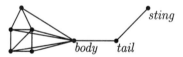

Give an algorithm that makes only $O(n)$ probes of the adjacency matrix of G and determines whether G is a scorpion. (This is a counterexample to an earlier version of the famous *Anderaa-Rosenberg conjecture*, which stated that any nontrivial graph property that is invariant under graph isomorphism requires $\Omega(n^2)$ probes of the adjacency matrix to test. Anderaa disproved this version in 1975 using a different counterexample (see [91]), but conjectured that it held for *monotone* properties (those that cannot change from false to true when edges are deleted). This was later verified by Rivest and Vuillemin [91].)

Homework 3

1. Verify that the family $\mathbf{Reg}_\Sigma$ of regular expressions over an alphabet Σ with the operations defined as in Lecture 6, Example 6.2 is a Kleene algebra.

2. Let R be the standard interpretation of regular expressions over $\mathbf{Reg}_\Sigma$. Prove that for regular expressions α, β, γ and interpretation I over a Kleene algebra $\mathcal{K}$,

$$I(\alpha\beta\gamma) \;\;=\;\; \sup_{x\in R(\beta)} I(\alpha x\gamma) \ .$$

   In other words, the supremum of the set

$$\{I(\alpha x\gamma) \mid x \in R(\beta)\}$$

   exists and is equal to $I(\alpha\beta\gamma)$. (*Hint.* Try induction on β, using the axioms of Kleene algebra.) Note that Lemma 7.1 of Lecture 7 is a special case with $\alpha = \gamma = 1$.

3. Modify Dijkstra's algorithm to produce the minimum-weight paths themselves, not just their weights.

Homework 4

1. The following algorithm, known as *Prim's algorithm*, produces a minimum spanning tree T in a connected undirected graph with edge weights. Initially, we choose an arbitrary vertex and let T be the tree consisting of that vertex and no edges. We then repeat the following step $n - 1$ times: find an edge of minimum weight with exactly one endpoint in T and include that edge in T.

   (a) Argue that Prim's algorithm is correct.

   (b) Give an implementation that runs in time $O(m + n \log n)$.

2. The Planar Separator Theorem gives $\frac{1}{3}$-$\frac{2}{3}$ separators of size $O(\sqrt{n})$ for arbitrary planar graphs. Show that this is the best you can do in general; *i.e.*, give a family of planar graphs whose smallest $\frac{1}{3}$-$\frac{2}{3}$ separators are of size $\Omega(\sqrt{n})$.

Homework 5

1. (a) Given a flow f on a directed graph G with positive edge capacities, show how to construct the residual graph G_f in $O(m)$ time.

   (b) Using (a), show how to calculate efficiently an augmenting path of maximum bottleneck capacity. (*Hint.* Modify Dijkstra's algorithm.)

2. Give an efficient algorithm for the s, t-*connectivity problem*: given a directed or undirected graph $G = (V, E)$ and elements $s, t \in V$, $s \neq t$, decide whether there exist k edge-disjoint paths from s to t, and find them if so. (The vertex-disjoint version of this problem is *NP*-complete; see Homework 7 Exercise 3.)

3. Give an efficient algorithm for the *min cut* problem: given an undirected graph $G = (V, E)$, elements $s, t \in V$, $s \neq t$, and edge weights $w : E \to \mathcal{R}^+$, find an s, t-cut of minimum weight; *i.e.*, find a partition A, B of V with $s \in A$, $t \in B$ minimizing

$$\sum_{(u,v)\in E\cap(A\times B)} w(u, v) \ .$$

(Several minor variants of this problem are *NP*-complete. For example, the *max cut* problem is *NP*-complete.)

Homework 6

1. (The *stable marriage problem.*) In a group of n boys and n girls, each girl ranks the n boys according to her preference, and each boy ranks the n girls according to his preference. A *marriage* is a perfect matching between the boys and the girls. A marriage is *unstable* if there is a pair who are not married to each other but who like each other more than they like their respective spouses, otherwise it is *stable*. Prove that a stable marriage always exists, and give an efficient algorithm to find one.

2. Prove the *König-Egerváry Theorem*: in a bipartite graph, the size of a maximum matching is equal to the size of a minimum vertex cover.

3. Let $G = (U, V, E)$ be a bipartite graph. For $S \subseteq U$, let $N(S)$ be the set of neighbors of S; *i.e.*,

$$N(S) \;=\; \{v \in V \mid \exists u \in S \; (u, v) \in E\} \,.$$

Prove *Hall's Theorem*: G has a matching in which every vertex of U is matched iff for every subset S of U,

$$|N(S)| \;\geq\; |S| \,.$$

(*Hint.* Use 2.)

4. An undirected graph is *regular* if all vertices have the same degree. Prove that any nontrivial regular bipartite graph has a perfect matching. (*Hint.* Use 2 or 3.)

Homework 7

1. Consider a restricted version of CNFSat in which formulas may contain at most k occurrences of any variable, either negated or unnegated, where k is fixed.

   (a) Show that the problem is *NP*-complete if $k \geq 3$.

   (b) Show that the problem is solvable in polynomial time if $k \leq 2$.

2. Suppose that TSP $\in P$; that is, suppose there is a polynomial-time algorithm which, given any directed graph G with integral edge weights and positive integer k, determines whether there exists a tour of weight at most k that visits every vertex at least once. Give a polynomial-time algorithm to find such a tour of minimum weight.

3. In Homework 5 Exercise 2 we gave an efficient algorithm for the s, t-connectivity problem. Formulate a version of this problem in which the requirement "edge-disjoint" is replaced by "vertex-disjoint" (this problem is called the *disjoint connecting paths problem* in [39, p. 217]), and show that it is *NP*-complete. (*Hint*. Use 3CNFSat. Let k be the number of clauses plus the number of variables.)

Homework 8

1. Let $\mathcal{Z}_p$ denote the field of integers modulo a fixed prime p. Consider the problem of determining whether a given expression involving $+, -, \cdot, 0, 1$, and variables ranging over $\mathcal{Z}_p$ vanishes for all possible values for the variables. Show that this problem is *coNP*-complete. (*Hint*. You may want to use *Fermat's Theorem*: $a^{p-1} = 1$ for all nonzero $a \in \mathcal{Z}_p$.)

2. Consider a restricted version of the TSP such that distances are symmetric and satisfy the triangle inequality:

$$
\begin{aligned}
d(u, v) &= d(v, u) \\
d(u, w) &\leq d(u, v) + d(v, w) .
\end{aligned}
$$

   (a) Argue that this restricted version is still *NP*-complete.

   (b) Give a polynomial-time algorithm that finds a tour visiting all cities exactly once whose total distance is at most twice optimal. (*Hint*. Start with a minimum spanning tree.)

3. Recall that a *transitive reduction* or *Hasse diagram* of a directed graph G is a subgraph with as few edges as possible having the same transitive closure as G. Show that the problem of determining whether a given G has a transitive reduction with k or fewer edges is *NP*-complete.

Homework 9

1. Give an NC algorithm for obtaining a topological sort of a given directed acyclic graph. (*Hint.* Use Miscellaneous Exercise 27.)

2. Show that the problem of determining whether a given undirected graph is bipartite, *i.e.* does not have an odd cycle, is in NC.

3. A linear recurrence is of *order k* if it is of the form

$$x_i = c_i, \quad 0 \le i \le k-1$$
$$x_n = a_1 x_{n-1} + a_2 x_{n-2} + \cdots + a_k x_{n-k} + c, \quad n \ge k$$

where the c_i, a_i, and c are constants. For example, the Fibonacci sequence is of order 2 with $c_0 = c_1 = a_1 = a_2 = 1$ and $c = 0$. Show that the nth term of a linear recurrence of order k can be computed in time

(a) $O(k^2 \log n)$ with a single processor. (*Hint.* Use Miscellaneous Exercise 22.)

(b) $O(\log k \log n)$ with $O(k^\alpha)$ processors, where $\alpha = 2.81\ldots$ is the constant in Strassen's matrix multiplication algorithm.

(c) $O(\log k + \log n)$ with $O(kn)$ processors, assuming that the ring we are working in supports an FFT. (*Hint.* Work with the generating function

$$x(y) = \sum_{i=0}^{\infty} x_i y^i$$

where y is an indeterminate and the coefficients x_i are the solution to the recurrence.)

Homework 10

1. In Luby's algorithm, we need to show that if we expect to delete at least a fixed fraction of the remaining edges in each stage, then the expected number of stages is logarithmic in the number of edges. We can formalize this as follows.

Proposition   *Let $m \geq 0$ and $0 < \epsilon < 1$. Let X_1, X_2,... and S_0, S_1, S_2,... be nonnegative integer-valued random variables such that*

$$S_n = X_1 + \cdots + X_n \leq m$$
$$\mathcal{E}(X_{n+1} \mid S_n) \geq \epsilon \cdot (m - S_n) .$$

Then the expected least n such that $S_n = m$ is $O(\log m)$.

In our application, m is the number of edges in the original graph, X_n is the number of edges deleted in stage n, S_n is the total number of edges deleted so far after stage n, and $\epsilon = \frac{1}{72}$.

(a) Show that

$$\mathcal{E} S_n \geq m(1 - (1 - \epsilon)^n) .$$

   (*Hint.* Using the fact $\mathcal{E}(\mathcal{E}(X_{n+1} \mid S_n)) = \mathcal{E} X_{n+1}$ shown in class, give a recurrence for $\mathcal{E} S_n$.)

(b) Using the definition of expectation, show also that

$$\mathcal{E} S_n \leq m - 1 + \Pr(S_n = m)$$

and therefore

$$\Pr(S_n = m) \geq 1 - m(1 - \epsilon)^n .$$

(c) Conclude that the expected least n such that $S_n = m$ is $O(\log m)$.
   (*Hint.* Define the function

$$f(x) = \begin{cases} 1, & \text{if } x < m \\ 0, & \text{otherwise} \end{cases}$$

and compute the expectation of the random variable

$$R = f(S_0) + f(S_1) + f(S_2) + \cdots$$

that counts the number of rounds.)

2. A collection $\mathcal{A}$ of events are *d-wise independent* if for any subset $\mathcal{B} \subseteq \mathcal{A}$ of size d or less, the probability that all events in $\mathcal{B}$ occur is the product of their probabilities. Consider the following generalization of Luby's scheme. For each $u \in \mathcal{Z}_p$, let A_u be any subset of $\mathcal{Z}_p$. Randomly select $x_0, \dots, x_{d-1} \in \mathcal{Z}_p$. Show that the p events

$$x_0 + x_1 u + x_2 u^2 + \cdots + x_{d-1} u^{d-1} \in A_u$$

for $u \in \mathcal{Z}_p$ are d-wise independent. (*Hint.* Consider $d \times d$ Vandermonde matrices over $\mathcal{Z}_p$ with rows

$$(1, \ u, \ u^2, \ \dots, \ u^{d-1})$$

shown in class to be nonsingular.)

3. Consider the following random NC algorithm for finding a maximal (not maximum) matching in an undirected graph $G = (V, E)$. The algorithm proceeds in stages. At each stage, a matching M is produced, and the matched vertices and all adjacent edges are deleted. Each stage proceeds as follows:

   (a) In parallel, each vertex u chooses a neighbor $t(u)$ at random. Set

   $$H := \{(u, t(u)) \mid u \in V\} \ .$$

   (b) If there are two or more edges $(u, t(u))$ in H with $t(u) = v$, then v chooses one of them arbitrarily and deletes the rest from H.

   (c) Let U be the set of vertices with at least one incident edge in H. Each vertex in the graph (U, H) has degree 1 or 2. If 2, it randomly selects one of its two incident edges as its favorite. If 1, it selects its one incident edge as its favorite.

   (d) For each edge $e \in H$, e is included in M if it is the favorite of both its endpoints.

Show that M is a matching, and the expected number of edges deleted is at least a constant fraction of the remaining edges. Conclude that the expected number of stages before achieving a maximal matching is $O(\log m)$.

Miscellaneous Exercises

1. Let $(S, \mathcal{I}, w)$ be a weighted matroid. Let M be the family of all maximal independent sets of minimum weight, and let $\mathcal{I}_{\max}$ be the family of all subsets of elements of M. Show that $(S, \mathcal{I}_{\max})$ is a matroid. (*Hint.* Use the blue rule to give a procedure for finding an $x \in J - I$ such that $I \cup \{x\} \in \mathcal{I}_{\max}$ whenever $I, J \in \mathcal{I}_{\max}$ and $|I| < |J|$.)

2. Let $T = (V, E)$ be a connected undirected tree such that each vertex has degree at most 3. Let $n = |V|$. Show that T has an edge whose removal disconnects T into two disjoint subtrees with no more than $\frac{2n+1}{3}$ vertices each. Give a linear-time algorithm to find such an edge.

3. Show how to solve the all-pairs shortest path problem on directed graphs when negative edge weights are allowed. (If there is no lower bound to the weights of paths from s to t, then we define the distance from s to t to be $-\infty$.)

4. Suppose that we wish to schedule n unit-time jobs on a single processor, starting at time 0. Associated with each job j is a deadline $d_j \geq 1$ and a penalty $p_j \geq 0$. Job j must be completed by time d_j or the penalty p_j is incurred.

   (a) Let S be the set of jobs. Call a subset $A \subseteq S$ *independent* if all the jobs in A can be scheduled without violating their deadlines, irrespective of the jobs not in A. Thus A is independent if, when the elements of A are sorted by deadline, the ith element in sorted order has deadline $d(i) \geq i$. Let $\mathcal{I}$ be the set of independent subsets of S. Show that $(S, \mathcal{I})$ is a matroid.

   (b) Give an efficient algorithm to produce a schedule that minimizes the total penalty.

5. A *pattern* is a finite-length string over the alphabet $\{0, 1, *\}$. A pattern σ *covers* a string x of 0's and 1's if x can be obtained from σ by replacing each occurrence of $*$ with either 0 or 1. For example, the pattern $0 * *1$ covers the four strings 0001, 0011, 0101, and 0111. A set A of patterns *covers* a set B of strings if every string in B is covered by some pattern in A. Show that the following problem is *coNP*-complete: given a set of patterns of length n, do they cover all strings of 0's and 1's of length n?

6. (The *Carpenter's Rule Problem*) Prove that the following problem is *NP*-complete: given a sequence of rigid rods of various integral lengths connected end-to-end by hinges, can it be folded so that its overall length is as most k?

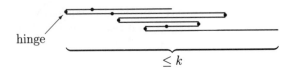

hinge

$$\leq k$$

7. Give a parsimonious reduction from CNFSat to 3CNFSat.

8. The standard adjacency list representation of an undirected graph G, as described for example in [3, p. 51], consists of a linked list of vertices in which the list element for vertex u contains a pointer to a linked list of pointers to all vertices adjacent to u. For plane graphs, the counterclockwise order of the vertices about u is given by the list order.

   For our purposes, this representation is inadequate for two reasons. First, in the representation of Lecture 14, the function $^-$ which reverses direction cannot be computed in constant time. In addition, the representation does not deal adequately with multiple edges; for example, it does not distinguish the following two nonisomorphic[1] plane graphs:

   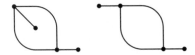

   Describe an enhanced adjacency list representation in which distinct undirected graphs with multiple edges and self-loops have distinct representations, each of the functions θ, $^-$, $\mathbf{h}$, and $\mathbf{t}$ can be computed in constant time, and single edges or vertices with all adjacent edges can be deleted in time proportional to the number of objects deleted. In the absence of multiple edges and self-loops, show how to obtain the new representation from the old one in linear time. All computations are to be done with pure pointer manipulation; no random access is allowed.

9. Let $G = (E, \theta, \,^-)$ be an undirected graph in the formalism described in Lecture 14. Assume that G is represented by the adjacency list representation constructed in Miscellaneous Exercise 8. Show how to construct the dual G^* of G in linear time.

10. Let $G = (E, \theta, \,^-)$ be an undirected graph in the formalism described in Lecture 14. Show that its characteristic $\chi(G)$ is always a nonnegative even number.

11. Prove Theorem 14.6 of Lecture 14: a graph $G = (E, \theta, \,^-)$ has characteristic $\chi(G) = 0$ iff θ corresponds to the counterclockwise ordering induced by some plane embedding of G. (*Hint.* Use Exercise 10.)

---

[1]They are isomorphic as graphs, but not as *plane* graphs.

12. The following problem arose recently in Keith Marzullo's META project. Given an undirected graph with black and red vertices, does there exist a maximal clique with no red vertices? Show that this problem is *NP*-complete.

13. Show that the partition problem can be solved in polynomial time if the weights are restricted to be integers and bounded in absolute value by a fixed polynomial in the number of items.

14. Given $n > 0$, prove that there exists a number k such that when the binary-to-Gray operation is applied k times in succession starting with any bit string of length n, we get back the original bit string. What is the smallest such k as a function of n?

15. (a) In the proof given in Lecture 27 of the #*P*-completeness of the permanent, show that the four-node widget can be replaced by a three-node widget.

   (b) Show that no two-node widget exists.

16. Consider the following scheduling problem. You are given positive integers m and t and an undirected graph $G = (V, E)$ whose vertices specify unit-time jobs and whose edges specify that the two jobs cannot be scheduled simultaneously. Can the jobs be scheduled on m identical processors so that all jobs complete within t time units?

   (a) Give a polynomial time algorithm for $t = 2$. (*Hint.* Use Miscellaneous Exercise 13.)

   (b) Show that the problem is *NP*-complete for $t \geq 3$.

17. Let G be a directed graph with positive and negative edge weights and let s and t be vertices of G. Recall that a path or cycle of G is *simple* if it has no repeated vertices.

   (a) Give a polynomial-time algorithm to determine whether G contains a simple cycle of negative weight.

   (b) Show that the problem of determining whether G contains a simple path from s to t of negative weight is *NP*-complete.

18. Show how matching can be used to give efficient algorithms for the following two problems.

   (a) Given an undirected graph with no isolated vertices, find an edge cover of minimum cardinality. (An *edge cover* is a subset of the edges such that every vertex is an endpoint of some edge in the subset.)

   (b) Find a vertex cover in a given undirected graph that is at most twice the cardinality of the smallest vertex cover.

19. Give a fast algorithm to determine whether a given directed graph has a cycle cover.

20. Given a bipartite graph $G = (U, V, E)$, say that $D \subseteq U$ is *deficient* if $|D| > |N(D)|$, where $N(D)$ denotes the set of neighbors of D; *i.e.*,

$$N(D) = \{v \in V \mid \exists u \in D\ (u, v) \in E\}\ .$$

Give a polynomial-time algorithm for finding a minimal deficient set if one exists. (*Hint.* Use Hall's Theorem; see Exercise 3, Homework 6. Grow a Hungarian tree.)

21. Let G be a connected undirected graph. We say G is *k-connected* if the deletion of any $k - 1$ vertices leaves G connected. Give a polynomial-time algorithm (ideally, $O(k^2 mn)$) for testing k-connectivity, and for finding a set of $k - 1$ disconnecting vertices if G is not k-connected. (*Hint.* Use *Menger's Theorem*, which states that G is k-connected if and only if any pair of vertices is connected by at least k vertex-disjoint paths, then use maximum flow. You need not prove Menger's Theorem.)

22. Let p be a monic univariate polynomial of degree k:

$$p(x) = x^k + a_{k-1}x^{k-1} + \cdots + a_1 x + a_0\ .$$

The *companion matrix* of p is the $k \times k$ matrix

$$C_p = \begin{bmatrix} 0 & 1 & 0 & 0 & 0 & 0 \\ 0 & 0 & 1 & 0 & 0 & 0 \\ 0 & 0 & 0 & 1 & 0 & 0 \\ 0 & 0 & 0 & 0 & 1 & 0 \\ 0 & 0 & 0 & 0 & 0 & 1 \\ -a_0 & -a_1 & -a_2 & -a_3 & -a_4 & -a_5 \end{bmatrix}$$

here illustrated for the case $k = 6$. The characteristic polynomial of C_p is p itself. Show how to compute the nth power of C_p in time $O(k^2 \log n)$.

23. Let k be a finite field with q elements. Let A be an $n \times n$ matrix over k of rank r. Prove that for an $n \times n$ matrix R with entries chosen independently and uniformly at random from k,

$$\Pr(\text{rank}\ (RA)^2 = \text{rank}\ RA = \text{rank}\ A) = \prod_{i=1}^{r}(1 - \frac{1}{q^i})\ .$$

24. The following problem arose recently in Tim Teitelbaum's synthesizer generator project. Let f be a binary function symbol, a and b constant symbols, and $X = \{x, y, \ldots\}$ a set of variables. A *term* is a well-formed expression over f, a, b, and X; for example, the following are terms:

$$a \hspace{10em} (1)$$

$$b \tag{2}$$
$$x \tag{3}$$
$$f(a,b) \tag{4}$$
$$f(a,x) \tag{5}$$
$$f(b,x) \tag{6}$$
$$f(f(x,y),z) \tag{7}$$

A term is a *ground term* if it contains no variables; for example, (1), (2) and (4) above are ground terms. A ground term t is a *substitution instance* of a term s if t can be obtained from s by substituting ground terms for the variables of s; for example, (4) is a substitution instance of (5) obtained by substituting b for x. A set of terms T is a *cover* if every ground term is a substitution instance of some term in T; for example, (1), (2), (5), (6), (7) form a cover.

(a) Show that determining whether a given set of terms is a cover is *coNP*-hard. (*Hint.* Encode the problem of Miscellaneous Exercise 5.)

(b) *Extra credit.* Show that the problem is *coNP*-complete.

25. Give an *NC* algorithm for finding the preorder numbering of a directed tree. That is, the algorithm should label each node of the tree with number of vertices visited before it in a preorder traversal.

26. An *outerplanar* is a graph that can be embedded in the plane so that every vertex is on the outer face. An *outerplane graph* is an outerplanar graph along with such an embedding.

An outerplane graph.

(a) Give a linear-time algorithm for testing whether a graph is outer-planar, and for finding an outerplane embedding if one exists. You may use for free the Hopcroft-Tarjan linear-time algorithm for finding a plane embedding of an arbitrary planar graph [52]. *Warning:* an arbitrary plane embedding of an outerplanar graph is not necessarily an outerplane embedding. Here are two embeddings of the same outerplanar graph, one outerplane and one not:

(b) Find the best $s(n)$ possible such that any outerplanar graph has a $\frac{1}{3}$-$\frac{2}{3}$ separator of size $s(n)$; *i.e.*, such that there exists a partition A, S, B of the vertices with $|A|, |B| \leq \frac{2n}{3}$, $|S| \leq s(n)$, and there are no edges between A and B. Give a linear time algorithm for finding the separator. (*Hint.* Use Miscellaneous Exercise 2.)

27. Assuming that comparisons between data elements take one unit of time on one processor, give parallel sorting algorithms that run on a CREW PRAM in

(a) time $O(\log n)$ with $O(n^2)$ processors

(b) time $O((\log n)^2)$ with $O(n)$ processors

where n is the number of inputs. Your algorithm should produce an array of length n containing the input data in sorted order.

28. An $n \times n$ matrix is called a *circulant matrix* if the ith row is obtained from the first row by a right rotation of i positions, $0 \leq i \leq n-1$. For example,

$$\begin{bmatrix} a & b & c & d \\ d & a & b & c \\ c & d & a & b \\ b & c & d & a \end{bmatrix}$$

is a 4×4 circulant matrix.

(a) Find an algorithm to multiply two $n \times n$ circulant matrices in time $O(\log n)$ with $O(n^2)$ processors.

(b) Assuming that the field contains all n^{th} roots of unity and a multiplicative inverse of n, show that the processor bound in part (a) can be reduced to $O(n)$. Represent circulant matrices by their first row. (*Hint.* See [3, pp. 256–257].)

(c) Under the assumptions of (b), find an algorithm to invert a nonsingular circulant matrix in $O(\log n)$ time with $O(n)$ processors.

29. In Lecture 40 we gave an *RNC* algorithm to test for the existence of a perfect matching in a given bipartite graph. In this exercise we extend this technique to arbitrary undirected graphs.

The *Tutte matrix* of an undirected graph $G = (V, E)$ is an $n \times n$ matrix T with rows and columns indexed by V such that

$$T_{uv} = \begin{cases} x_{uv}, & \text{if } (u, v) \in E \text{ and } u < v \\ -x_{vu}, & \text{if } (u, v) \in E \text{ and } u > v \\ 0, & \text{if } (u, v) \notin E \end{cases}$$

where the x_{uv}, $u < v$, are indeterminates.

(a) Show that $\det T \neq 0$ iff G has a perfect matching.

(b) Use this fact to give an RNC test for the existence of a perfect matching in G.

(c) If G has a perfect matching, show how to compute one in random polynomial time.

III   Homework Solutions

Homework 1 Solutions

1. (a) Suppose I and J are maximal independent subsets of A, but $|I| < |J|$. By property (ii) of matroids, we can find an $x \in J - I$ such that $I \cup \{x\} \in \mathcal{I}$. But then I was not a maximal independent subset of A; this is a contradiction.

   Incidentally, it can be shown that for systems $(S, \mathcal{I})$ satisfying axiom (i) of matroids that the property we have just proved is equivalent to axiom (ii) of matroids.

   (b) The set $I \cup \{x\}$ is dependent, since I is a maximal independent set. It therefore contains a minimal dependent set D. We show that D is unique. First, $x \in D$, since any subset of I is independent. Suppose there were two such cycles D and D'; assume without loss of generality that $y \in D - D'$. The set $(D \cup D') - \{x\}$ is a subset of I and is therefore independent. The set $D - \{y\}$ is also independent, since D is minimal, and its cardinality is no more than that of $(D \cup D') - \{x\}$. By property (ii) of matroids, elements of $(D \cup D') - \{x\}$ can be added to $D - \{y\}$ until the cardinality is the same as $(D \cup D') - \{x\}$, maintaining independence. Then y is not in the resulting set, since then D would be a subset, and D is dependent. Therefore the resulting set must be $(D \cup D') - \{y\}$. But this set contains D' as a subset, which is dependent; this is a contradiction.

   (c) Property (i) holds trivially, since removing an edge from a graph cannot add any cycles. To show (ii), let $E', E'' \subseteq E$ such that (V, E') and (V, E'') have no cycles. Let c' and c'' be the number of connected components of (V, E') and (V, E''), respectively, $m' = |E'|$, $m'' = |E''|$, and $n = |V|$. Suppose that $m' < m''$. By the equation $m + c = n$ proved in class, $c' > c''$. Then there must be an edge of E'' between two distinct connected components of (V, E'), otherwise all components of (V, E'') would be contained in components of (V, E'), implying that $c'' \geq c'$. Adding that edge to E' cannot give a cycle.

   The rank is $n - c$ and the maximal independent sets are the spanning forests.

   Two good references about matroids in optimization problems are [85, 70]. An excellent reference on matroid theory itself is [107].

2. (a) Since the graph is acyclic, all directed paths are of length at most $n - 1$. Define

$$E_{uv} = \{e \in E \mid e \text{ lies on some } E\text{-path from } u \text{ to } v \text{ of maximum length}\}$$

$$E_H = \bigcup_{u,v \in V} E_{uv}.$$

For any $(x, y) \in E_H$, the only E-path from x to y is the edge (x, y) itself; if there were a longer path, then (x, y) would never lie on any maximal length path and would not be in E_H. Thus

$$E_H = \{(u, v) \in E \mid \text{the length of the longest} \tag{1}$$
$$\text{path from } u \text{ to } v \text{ is } 1\} .$$

Let F be an arbitrary subset of E such that $F^* = E^*$. For $e \in E_H$, if $e \notin F$, then F^* would not contain e either, by (1); this contradicts $F^* = E^*$. Thus $E_H \subseteq F$. Moreover, $E_H^* = E^*$, since any two vertices connected by a path are connected by a path of maximum length. Since $E_H^* = E^*$ and E_H is contained in every subset of E whose transitive closure is E^*, it is the unique minimal such set.

(b) Our algorithm to find E_H simply removes all edges (u, v) of E for which there exists a path of length two or more from u to v. We use the adjacency matrix representation. Let E denote this matrix. Using Boolean matrix multiplication ($\vee$ instead of $+$, $\wedge$ instead of $\cdot$), the matrix E^k has a 1 in position (u, v) iff there is a path from u to v of length exactly k. Compute the transitive closure matrix

$$\begin{aligned} E^* &= I \vee E \vee E^2 \vee \cdots \vee E^{n-1} \vee E^n \vee \cdots \\ &= I \vee E \vee E^2 \vee \cdots \vee E^{n-1} \quad \text{(why?)} \\ &= (I \vee E)^{n-1} . \end{aligned}$$

This can be done by repeated squaring in time $O(M(n) \log n)$, where $M(n)$ is the time to multiply two $n \times n$ matrices. (We can actually compute E^* in time $O(M(n))$, as we will see later.) Then compute $E^2 \cdot E^*$. This matrix has a nonzero value in position (u, v) iff there is a path of length at least 2 from u to v. Finally, the adjacency matrix of E_H is given by $E \wedge \neg(E^2 \cdot E^*)$.

In this problem the goal was to minimize the running time. If the goal were to minimize the amount of extra space used, then an in-place algorithm would be better; see [46]. The original paper showing that transitive reduction is as easy as transitive closure is [2].

3. This solution is from [85].

(a) Suppose the graph is connected and each vertex is of even degree. Starting from an arbitrary vertex v, trace an arbitrary path, traversing edges at most once (mark each edge as traversed as we encounter it), until we return to v. This must happen eventually: because each vertex is of even degree, is impossible to get stuck. Now delete the cycle we have found. Deleting a cycle maintains the invariant that all vertices are of even degree, but the graph may no longer be connected.

However, we can repeat the process on the connected components, and so on until all edges have been deleted. Now we string the cycles together to form one long cycle. Two cycles that contain a vertex v can be combined into one cycle in a figure 8, with v at the intersection point. Since the graph is connected, it is possible to string all the cycles together in this way to get one long cycle, an Euler circuit.

Conversely, if there is an Euler circuit, then each vertex v is of even degree, since each occurrence of v on the circuit accounts for two incident edges.

(b) We assume an adjacency list representation of the graph. Starting at vertex v_0, trace an arbitrary path until we return to v_0 as in part (a), giving a cycle $c = v_0, v_1, \ldots, v_{n-1}, v_0$ (the v_i's need not be distinct). As we traverse c, we delete each edge from the graph and create a doubly-linked circular list of these edges in the order they are encountered. Now for each v_i in order, we recursively find an Euler circuit c_i beginning and ending with v_i in the connected component containing v_i. We link c_i into c at v_i and then go on to v_{i+1}. In the recursive call to get an Euler circuit in the connected component of v_i, any v_j, $j > i$, in that connected component will have all remaining edges deleted, so by the time the algorithm gets to v_j, the connected component of v_j will consist only of v_j and there will be no work to do.

The algorithm runs in $O(m)$ time, because there is only a constant amount of work done for each edge.

Homework 2 Solutions

1. As shown in Theorem 4.8, a directed graph is a dag iff the DFS tree has no
   back edges. It was also shown that if the DFS tree is numbered in postorder,
   then all edges go from higher numbered vertices to lower numbered vertices.
   Then this numbering gives a topological sort.

2. (a) The graph G has an embedding consistent with θ iff this is true for
   every connected component of G, so we can assume without loss of
   generality that G is connected.

   Assume the adjacency lists are ordered according to θ. Then a depth-
   first search corresponds to traversing the edges clockwise around each
   face. All back edges can be drawn going up the right side of the path
   from the root down to the source of the back edge. The very first back
   edge encountered can be taken to be on the outer face. We need only
   maintain a stack of back edges that we are "inside", and make sure
   that any new back edge does not go up higher than the destination
   vertex of the innermost back edge that we are inside. The back edges
   that we are inside form a chain.

   In Lecture 14, Theorem 14.6 and Miscellaneous Exercise 11 we will
   see another approach using Euler's Theorem, which states that $n +
   n^* - m = 2$ for a connected plane graph G, where n, n^*, m are the
   number of vertices, faces, and edges of G, respectively. We will use the
   theorem in the opposite direction: given θ, we calculate the number
   n^* of "faces". We will show that $n + n^* - m = 2$ iff θ does indeed
   correspond to a plane embedding with n^* faces.

   (b) If G is not planar then it has no planar embeddings. Otherwise, G
   has exactly one embedding on the sphere consistent with θ. We can
   choose the North Pole to be in any one of the faces of the embedding
   and then project the graph onto the plane from the North Pole. Each
   choice of face for the pole gives a different embedding in the plane.
   Thus there are as many different embeddings as faces of G.

   Suppose now that G is not connected. Number the connected components $0, 1, \ldots, c-1$ and let f_i be the number of faces of component
   i. There are f_i ways to choose the outer face of the component i, so
   there are $f_0 f_1 \cdots f_{c-1}$ ways to choose all the outer faces. To get the
   number of embeddings, we must multiply this by the number of ways
   to place the components inside the inner faces of other components.

   For example, when $c = 2$, there are $f_1 - 1$ ways to place component 0
   inside an inner face of component 1, $f_0 - 1$ ways to place component
   1 inside an inner face of component 0, and one way to place the
   components so that neither occurs inside the other. This gives

   $$(f_0 - 1) + (f_1 - 1) + 1 .$$

We claim that with c components this number is

$$(1 + \sum_{i=0}^{c-1}(f_i - 1))^{c-1} .$$

Each embedding determines a labeled forest whose vertices are the components. A component i is a child of another component j in this forest if it occurs inside an inner face of j with no intervening components. The component i can be placed inside any one of $f_j - 1$ inner faces of j; let us indicate this by labeling the edge (i,j) in the forest with the factor $f_j - 1$. Thus the number we are seeking is the sum over all labeled forests of the product of the edge labels on that forest.

We modify an argument of Prüfer that there are n^{n-2} labeled trees on n nodes (see [62]). We establish a one-to-one correspondence between labeled forests and sequences of length $c - 1$ from the set

$$\{\top, 0, 1, \ldots, c - 1\} \tag{2}$$

as follows. Given a labeled forest, start with the null sequence and repeat the following operation until there is only one vertex left. Prune off the lowest numbered leaf i and append j to the sequence, where j is the parent of i. If i has no parent, then append $\top$ to the sequence. Then each labeled forest determines a sequence of length $c - 1$, and it is not difficult to reconstruct the forest uniquely from the sequence.

For each sequence $a_0, a_1, \ldots, a_{c-2}$ of length $c - 1$ over the set (2), the product of the edge labels on the labeled forest corresponding to that sequence is

$$g(a_0)g(a_1)\cdots g(a_{c-2}) ,$$

where $g(i) = f_i - 1$ and $g(\top) = 1$. The number we are seeking is the sum of all such products. This number is

$$(g(\top) + g(0) + g(1) + \cdots + g(c - 1))^{c-1} = (1 + \sum_{i=0}^{c-1}(f_i - 1))^{c-1} .$$

The total number of embeddings is this number times the number of ways of choosing the outer faces of the components, or

$$(1 + \sum_{i=0}^{c-1}(f_i - 1))^{c-1} \prod_{i=0}^{c-1} f_i .$$

3. Here is an algorithm that takes $5n$ probes of the adjacency matrix. Let $d(v)$ be the degree of vertex v. The main difficulty is to locate one of the

interesting vertices (the body, tail, or sting); once we have done that, we can locate all the other interesting vertices with $3n$ probes and check that the graph is a scorpion. For example, if we have found a vertex v with $d(v) = n - 2$, then that vertex must be the body if the graph is a scorpion. By scanning the vth row of the matrix, we can check that $d(v) = n - 2$ and determine its unique non-neighbor u, which must be the sting if the graph is a scorpion. Then by scanning the uth row, we can verify that $d(u) = 1$ and find its unique neighbor w, which must be the tail; and with n more probes we can verify that $d(w) = 2$.

We start with an arbitrary vertex v, and scan the vth row. If $d(v) = 0$ or $n - 1$, the graph is not a scorpion. If $d(v) = 1$, 2, or $n - 2$, then either v is interesting itself or one of its 1 or 2 neighbors is, and we can determine all the interesting vertices as above and check whether the graph is a scorpion with at most $4n$ additional probes.

Otherwise, $3 \leq d(v) \leq n - 3$, and v is boring. Let B be the set of neighbors of v and let $S = V - (B \cup \{v\})$. The body must be in B and the sting and tail must be in S. Choose arbitrary $x \in B$ and $y \in S$ and repeat the following: if x and y are connected, then delete y from S (y cannot be the sting) and choose a new $y \in S$. If x and y are not connected, then delete x from B (x is not the body unless y is the sting) and choose a new $x \in B$. If the graph is indeed a scorpion, then when this process ends, B will be empty and y will be the sting. To see this, observe that B cannot be emptied without encountering the sting, because the body cannot be deleted from B by any vertex in S except the sting; and once the sting is encountered, all remaining elements of B will be deleted.

Whether or not the graph is a scorpion, the loop terminates after at most n probes of the adjacency matrix, since after each probe some vertex is discarded.

If a property is such that we have to look at *every* entry in the adjacency matrix, then that property is said to be *evasive*. Many monotone graph properties have been conjectured to be evasive. Yao [110] has shown that all monotone bipartite graph properties are evasive if we are given a bipartite adjacency matrix representation. The question for general graphs remains open. Bollobás discusses this issue in his book [13]. He gives a $6n$-probe solution to the scorpion problem there.

Homework 3 Solutions

1. The structure $(\mathbf{Reg_\Sigma}, \cup, \cdot, {}^*, \emptyset, \{\epsilon\})$ is a Kleene algebra if it satisfies the axioms of Kleene algebra. We therefore need to show, for any regular sets A, B and C,

$$
\begin{aligned}
A \cup (B \cup C) &= (A \cup B) \cup C \\
A \cup B &= B \cup A \\
A \cup A &= A \\
A \cup \emptyset &= \emptyset \cup A = A \\
A \cdot (B \cdot C) &= (A \cdot B) \cdot C \\
A \cdot \{\epsilon\} &= \{\epsilon\} \cdot A = A \\
\emptyset \cdot A &= A \cdot \emptyset = \emptyset \\
A \cdot (B \cup C) &= A \cdot B \cup A \cdot C \\
(B \cup C) \cdot A &= B \cdot A \cup C \cdot A \\
A \cdot B^* \cdot C &= \sup_{n \geq 0} A \cdot B^n \cdot C . \tag{3}
\end{aligned}
$$

Note that the natural order on $\mathbf{Reg_\Sigma}$ is set inclusion $\subseteq$, since

$$
A \subseteq B \quad \leftrightarrow \quad A \cup B = B .
$$

Most of the above properties are obvious. The only one we will verify explicitly is (3). Recall the definition of the * operator in $\mathbf{Reg_\Sigma}$:

$$
B^* = \{\epsilon\} \cup \{y_1 y_2 \cdots y_n \mid n \geq 1 \text{ and } y_i \in B, \ 1 \leq i \leq n\} .
$$

Recall also that, by definition,

$$
\begin{aligned}
B^0 &= \{\epsilon\} \\
B^{n+1} &= B \cdot B^n .
\end{aligned}
$$

It follows by induction on n that

$$
B^n = \{y_1 y_2 \cdots y_n \mid y_i \in B, \ 1 \leq i \leq n\} .
$$

To be in the regular set on the left side of equation (3), a string must be of the form $x y_1 y_2 \cdots y_n z$ for some $n \geq 0$, where $x \in A$, $z \in C$, and $y_i \in B$, $1 \leq i \leq n$. Here we allow the possibility $n = 0$, in which case the string would be of the form xz. Thus the left side of (3) is equal to the set

$$
\bigcup_{n \geq 0} A \cdot B^n \cdot C .
$$

This is the least upper bound of the sets $A \cdot B^n \cdot C$, $n \geq 0$, with respect to set inclusion $\subseteq$: it is an upper bound, since it includes all the $A \cdot B^n \cdot C$ as subsets; and it is the least upper bound, since any set that includes all the $A \cdot B^n \cdot C$ must include their union.

2. Let $\mathbf{RExp}_\Sigma = \{$regular expressions over $\Sigma\}$, let $\mathcal{K}$ be an arbitrary Kleene algebra, and let I be an interpretation

$$I : \mathbf{RExp}_\Sigma \;\to\; \mathcal{K} \;.$$

The proof will proceed by induction on the structure of β. There are three base cases, corresponding to the regular expressions $b \in \Sigma$, 1, and 0. For $b \in \Sigma$, we have $R(b) = \{b\}$ and

$$\sup_{x \in R(b)} I(\alpha x \gamma) \;=\; I(\alpha b \gamma) \;.$$

The case of 1 is similar, since $R(1) = \{\epsilon\}$. Finally, since $R(0) = \emptyset$ and since the element $0_\mathcal{K}$ is the least element in $\mathcal{K}$ and therefore the supremum of the empty set,

$$\begin{aligned}
\sup_{x \in R(0)} I(\alpha x \gamma) \;&=\; \sup \emptyset \\
&=\; 0_\mathcal{K} \\
&=\; I(0) \\
&=\; I(\alpha 0 \gamma) \;.
\end{aligned}$$

There are three cases to the inductive step, one for each of the operators $+$, $\cdot$, *. We give a step-by-step argument for the case $+$, followed by a justification of each step.

$$\begin{aligned}
I(\alpha(\beta_1 + \beta_2)\gamma) \;&=\; I(\alpha) \cdot (I(\beta_1) + I(\beta_2)) \cdot I(\gamma) & (4) \\
&=\; (I(\alpha) \cdot I(\beta_1) \cdot I(\gamma)) + (I(\alpha) \cdot I(\beta_2) \cdot I(\gamma)) & (5) \\
&=\; I(\alpha\beta_1\gamma) + I(\alpha\beta_2\gamma) & (6) \\
&=\; \sup_{x \in R(\beta_1)} I(\alpha x \gamma) + \sup_{y \in R(\beta_2)} I(\alpha y \gamma) & (7) \\
&=\; \sup_{z \in R(\beta_1) \cup R(\beta_2)} I(\alpha z \gamma) & (8) \\
&=\; \sup_{z \in R(\beta_1 + \beta_2)} I(\alpha z \gamma) \;. & (9)
\end{aligned}$$

Equation (4) follows from the properties of the map I; (5) follows from the distributive laws of Kleene algebra satisfied by $\mathcal{K}$; (6) again follows from the properties of the map I; (7) follows from the induction hypothesis on β_1 and β_2; (8) follows from the general property of Kleene algebras that if A and B are two sets whose suprema $\sup A$ and $\sup B$ exist, then the supremum of $A \cup B$ exists and is equal to $\sup A + \sup B$ (this requires proof—see below); finally, equation (9) follows from the definition of the map R interpreting regular expressions as regular sets.

The general property used in equation (8) states that if A and B are two subsets of a Kleene algebra whose suprema $\sup A$ and $\sup B$ exist, then the supremum $\sup A \cup B$ of $A \cup B$ exists and

$$\sup A \cup B \;=\; \sup A + \sup B \;.$$

To prove this, we must show two things:

(i) $\sup A + \sup B$ is an upper bound for $A \cup B$; that is, for any $x \in A \cup B$, $x \leq \sup A + \sup B$; and

(ii) $\sup A + \sup B$ is the least such upper bound; that is, for any other upper bound y of the set $A \cup B$, $\sup A + \sup B \leq y$.

To show (i),

$$
\begin{aligned}
x \in A \cup B \quad &\rightarrow \quad x \in A \text{ or } x \in B \\
&\rightarrow \quad x \leq \sup A \text{ or } x \leq \sup B \\
&\rightarrow \quad x \leq \sup A + \sup B \ .
\end{aligned}
$$

To show (ii), let y be any other upper bound for $A \cup B$. Then

$$
\begin{aligned}
\forall x \in A \cup B \ x \leq y \quad &\rightarrow \quad \forall x \in A \ x \leq y \text{ and } \forall x \in B \ x \leq y \\
&\rightarrow \quad \sup A \leq y \text{ and } \sup B \leq y \\
&\rightarrow \quad \sup A + \sup B \leq y + y \ = \ y \ .
\end{aligned}
$$

We give a similar chain of equalities for the case of the operator $\cdot$, but omit the justifications.

$$
\begin{aligned}
I(\alpha(\beta_1\beta_2)\gamma) &= I(\alpha) \cdot I(\beta_1) \cdot I(\beta_2) \cdot I(\gamma) \\
&= I(\alpha\beta_1(\beta_2\gamma)) \\
&= \sup_{x \in R(\beta_1)} I(\alpha x(\beta_2\gamma)) \\
&= \sup_{x \in R(\beta_1)} I((\alpha x)\beta_2\gamma) \\
&= \sup_{x \in R(\beta_1)} \sup_{y \in R(\beta_2)} I(\alpha xy\gamma) \\
&= \sup_{x \in R(\beta_1), \ y \in R(\beta_2)} I(\alpha xy\gamma) \\
&= \sup_{z \in R(\beta_1\beta_2)} I(\alpha z\gamma) \ .
\end{aligned}
$$

Finally, for the case $*$, we have

$$
\begin{aligned}
I(\alpha\beta^*\gamma) &= I(\alpha) \cdot I(\beta)^* \cdot I(\gamma) \\
&= \sup_{n \geq 0} I(\alpha) \cdot I(\beta)^n \cdot I(\gamma) \\
&= \sup_{n \geq 0} I(\alpha\beta^n\gamma) \\
&= \sup_{n \geq 0} \sup_{x \in R(\beta^n)} I(\alpha x\gamma) \\
&= \sup_{n \geq 0, \ x \in R(\beta^n)} I(\alpha x\gamma)
\end{aligned}
$$

$$= \sup_{x \in \bigcup_{n \geq 0} R(\beta^n)} I(\alpha x \gamma)$$

$$= \sup_{x \in R(\beta^*)} I(\alpha x \gamma) .$$

3. Suppose we are given a directed graph $G = (V, E, \ell)$ with nonnegative edge weights ℓ. The quantity $\ell(e)$ is called the *length* of $e \in E$. Define the *length* $\ell(p)$ of a directed path p to be the sum of the edge lengths along p; thus

$$\ell(e_1 e_2 \cdots e_n) = \sum_{i=1}^{n} \ell(e_i) .$$

In the version of Dijkstra's algorithm of Lecture 5, we use the loop invariant that the variable X contains the set of vertices whose minimal distance from s has already been determined, and $D(y)$ gives the minimum distance from s to y through only elements of X. Here we have to keep track of the paths themselves. To do this we will use pointers $P(\cdot)$. The new invariants are:

- for $v \in V$, the path $p(v) = v, P(v), P(P(v)), \ldots$ is a shortest path from v back to s such that all vertices except possibly v lie in X, or $\perp$ if no such path exists;

- $D(v) = \ell(p(v))$;

- for any $u \in X$, $v \notin X$, $D(u) \leq D(v)$.

Here is the algorithm:

```
X := {s};
P(s) := nil;
for each v ∈ V − {s} do
        if (s, v) ∈ E then
                P(v) := s;
                D(v) := ℓ(s, v)
        else
                P(v) := ⊥;
                D(v) := ∞
        end if
end for;
while X ≠ V do
        let u ∈ V − X such that D(u) is a minimum;
        X := X ∪ {u};
        for each edge (u, v) with v ∈ V − X do
                if D(u) + ℓ(u, v) < D(v) then
                        P(v) := u;
                        D(v) := D(u) + ℓ(u, v)
                end if
        end for
end while
```

Homework 4 Solutions

1. (a) The algorithm is correct because each step is an instance of the blue rule in the spanning tree matroid.

   (b) Prim's algorithm is a variant of Dijkstra's shortest-path algorithm. The implementation is very similar to the solution to Exercise 3 of Homework 3. We maintain a Fibonacci heap containing the set $V - T$, where V is the set of all vertices and T is the set of vertices in the portion of the spanning tree chosen up to that point. The value $D(v)$ for the purposes of **findmin**, **deletemin** and **decrement** is the weight of the minimum-weight edge connecting v to a vertex in T, or ∞ if no such edge exists. In addition, we maintain with each vertex v in the heap a pointer $P(v)$ to a vertex in T closest to v; *i.e.*, a $u \in T$ such that $d(u, v) = D(v)$.

   We initialize the values $D(v)$ and $P(v)$ after the first vertex u is chosen by setting $D(v) := d(u, v)$ and $P(v) := u$ for each vertex v adjacent to u and $D(v) := \infty$ and $P(v) := $ **nil** for each vertex v not adjacent to u.

   At each step, we find the element w of the heap such that $D(w)$ is minimum, delete it from the heap, and add it to T. We also add the edge $(w, P(w))$ to the spanning tree. Then we update distances as follows: for each edge (w, v), $v \notin T$, if $d(w, v)$ is less than $D(v)$, we set $D(v) := d(w, v)$ and $P(v) := w$.

   It takes constant time for each edge or $O(m)$ time in all to do the updates. Using the Fibonacci heap, it takes $O(n \log n)$ time amortized over the entire sequence of operations to maintain the heap, find the minima and delete them, and decrement the values $D(v)$ when necessary.

2. Let C_k be the $k \times k$ checkerboard graph:

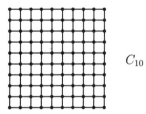

C_{10}

   The number of vertices is $n = k^2$. We show that the smallest $\frac{1}{3}$-$\frac{2}{3}$ separators of C_k are of size at least $\frac{k}{\sqrt{3}} - \frac{1}{2} = \Omega(\sqrt{n})$.

   Consider an arbitrary partition of the vertices of C_k into A, B, and S such that $|A|, |B| \leq 2n/3$ and there are no edges between A and B. If there is an element of S in every row or an element of S in every column, we are done. Otherwise, there must be some row r and some column c with no S vertices. The row r must contain all A vertices or all B vertices, since if it contained some of each, it would have to have an S vertex to separate them. Without loss of generality assume it contains only A vertices. Similarly, c contains only A vertices or only B vertices, and they must be A vertices, since c intersects r. Thus there is an A vertex in every column and every row, since every row intersects c and every column intersects r. If a column or row has a B vertex, then it must also have an S vertex to separate it from the A vertices. So any column or row containing a B vertex must also contain an S vertex. Thus there are at most $|S|$ columns containing a B vertex and at most $|S|$ rows containing a B vertex; hence at the very most,

$$|B| \;\leq\; |S|^2 \;.$$

However, since $|A| \leq 2n/3$,

$$
\begin{aligned}
|B| \;&=\; n - (|A| + |S|) \\
&\geq\; \frac{n}{3} - |S| \;.
\end{aligned}
$$

Combining these inequalities, we get

$$|S|^2 + |S| - \frac{n}{3} \;\geq\; 0 \;,$$

and $|S|$ must be at least as big as the positive root of this quadratic:

$$
\begin{aligned}
|S| \;&\geq\; \frac{-1 + \sqrt{1 + \frac{4n}{3}}}{2} \\
&>\; \frac{-1 + \sqrt{\frac{4n}{3}}}{2} \\
&=\; \frac{k}{\sqrt{3}} - \frac{1}{2} \;.
\end{aligned}
$$

Homework 5 Solutions

1. (a) For every edge (u, v) in G, compute the residual capacity from u to v using the formula $r(u, v) = c(u, v) - f(u, v)$, where c is the capacity function. Also compute the residual capacity $r(v, u)$ in the opposite direction. If $r(u, v)$ is zero, then do not put the edge (u, v) into G_f. Otherwise, put the edge (u, v) into G_f with capacity $r(u, v)$. Do the same for (v, u). All the relevant computations can be done in $O(m)$ time since we spend at most constant time for each edge.

   (b) A minor modification of the algorithm of Exercise 3, Homework 3 does it. The only difference is that we are seeking paths of maximum bottleneck capacity instead of minimum length. Here is the algorithm:

   ```
   X := {s};
   P(s) := nil;
   for each x ∈ V − {s} do
           D(x) := r(s, x);
           P(x) := s
   end for;
   while X ≠ V do
           let x ∈ V − X such that D(x) is a maximum;
           X := X ∪ {x};
           for each edge (x, y) ∈ E_f such that y ∈ V − X do
               if min(D(x), r(x, y)) > D(y) then
                       P(y) := x;
                       D(y) := min(D(x), r(x, y))
               end if
           end for
   end while
   ```

2. Let every edge in G have unit capacity and find a maximum flow f^* in G. Then there exist k edge-disjoint paths from s to t if and only if $|f^*| \geq k$: certainly if there exist k edge-disjoint paths, then $|f^*| \geq k$ by pushing one unit of flow along each path. Conversely, if $|f^*| \geq k$, then we can repeatedly find a path flow from s to t with unit flow as in the proof of Lemma 17.4, then remove the edges along this path and repeat. With each iteration the flow value decreases by one, so at least k paths are found.

3. Make G a directed graph by replacing each undirected edge $\{u, v\}$ with two directed edges (u, v) and (v, u). The capacities on these directed edges will be the same as those on the corresponding original edge. Find a maximum flow from s to t in this network and compute the residual graph of this flow. Take A to be the set of vertices reachable from s in the residual graph, and let B be the rest. By the Max Flow-Min Cut Theorem, this

cut has minimum weight in the network. It is also a minimum cut for the original undirected graph because any edge between A and B has the same weight in both graphs.

Homework 6 Solutions

1. Gale and Shapley were the first to investigate the stable marriage problem and gave this solution in 1962 [36].

   Let $r_g(b)$ be g's ranking of b, $r_b(g)$ be b's ranking of g. Let B be the set of boys and G be the set of girls, $n = |B| = |G|$. If M is a partial matching, let $B_M = \{b \mid \exists g\ (b, g) \in M\}$ and $G_M = \{g \mid \exists b\ (b, g) \in M\}$. Let $M(b) = g$ if $(b, g) \in M$, undefined if no such g exists. Let $M(g) = b$ if $(b, g) \in M$, undefined if no such b exists. Execute the following program:

   ```
   M := ∅;
   while |M| < n do
           g := arbitrary element of G − G_M;
           b := element of B with r_g(b) maximum and either
               (i) b ∉ B_M
               (ii) b ∈ B_M and r_b(g) > r_b(M(b));
           if (i), set M := M ∪ {(b, g)};
           if (ii), set M := (M − {(b, M(b))}) ∪ {(b, g)}
   end while
   ```

   The following invariants are maintained by the **while** loop:

   - M is stable;
   - if $r_g(b) \geq r_g(M(g))$ then $b \in B_M$.

   The algorithm halts in $O(n^2)$ iterations of the **while** loop because the quantity
   $$\sum_{b \in B_M} r_b(M(b))$$
   increases by at least one each time.

2. Ford and Fulkerson solved this problem by reducing it to a network flow problem and then applying the Max Flow-Min Cut Theorem [34].

   In a bipartite graph $G = (U, V, E)$, the size of any matching is at most the size of any vertex cover, since all matched edges must have at least one endpoint in the cover. To show that this bound is attained, we construct a flow network H with vertices $U \cup V \cup \{s, t\}$ and edges
   $$\{(s, u) \mid u \in U\} \ \cup \ E \ \cup \ \{(v, t) \mid v \in V\} .$$

   The edges of E are directed from U to V in H. We give the edges of E infinite (or sufficiently large finite) capacity, and all other edges capacity 1. Let S, T be a minimum s, t-cut in H. This cut has finite capacity, since it is bounded by the capacity of the cut $\{s\}, (U \cup V \cup \{t\}) - \{s\}$, which is $|U|$. Therefore, no edge in E can cross from S to T, since those edges have infinite capacity. Thus each edge in E either

- has both endpoints in S,
- has both endpoints in T, or
- crosses from T to S.

In any of these three cases, the edge is incident to an element of the set

$$(T \cap U) \ \cup \ (S \cap V) \,,$$

so this set forms a vertex cover of G. Moreover, the capacity of the cut S, T is the size of this set, which is also the maximum flow value in H by the Max Flow-Min Cut Theorem. In Lecture 18 we argued that the size of the maximum matching in G is the value of a maximum flow in H.

3. Suppose first that G has a matching in which every vertex of U is matched. Let S be a subset of U. For every vertex $s \in S$, the vertex that s is matched to appears in $N(S)$. Since no two vertices in S are matched to the same vertex in V, we have $|N(S)| \geq |S|$.

Conversely, suppose G does not have a matching in which every vertex of U is matched. By the König-Egerváry Theorem, there exists a vertex cover C of G containing fewer than $|U|$ vertices. Let $S = U - C$. All vertices adjacent to vertices S must be in $V \cap C$, otherwise C would not be a vertex cover; *i.e.*, $N(S) \subseteq V \cap C$. Then

$$
\begin{aligned}
|N(S)| \ &\leq \ |V \cap C| \\
&= \ |C| - |U \cap C| &&\text{since } U \text{ and } V \text{ are disjoint} \\
&< \ |U| - |U \cap C| \\
&= \ |S| &&\text{since } S \text{ is defined to be } U - C.
\end{aligned}
$$

Thus there exists an $S \subseteq U$ such that $|N(S)| < |S|$.

Hall's theorem is sometimes called the Marriage Theorem because it tells us whether all U vertices can be "married" to a V vertex of their own.

4. Let d be the degree of the vertices in the regular bipartite graph $G = (U, V, E)$. The total number of edges is

$$d \cdot |U| \ = \ d \cdot |V| \,,$$

thus $|U| = |V|$; therefore any matching that uses all the vertices in U will be a perfect matching in G. By Hall's Theorem, it suffices to show that $|S| \leq |N(S)|$ for any $S \subseteq U$. For an arbitrary subset S of U, consider the subgraph of G induced by $S \cup N(S)$. There are exactly $d \cdot |S|$ edges in this subgraph, since every vertex in S has degree d. Similarly, this subgraph has no more than $d \cdot |N(S)|$ edges, because no vertex in $N(S)$ has degree larger than d. Thus

$$d \cdot |S| \ \leq \ d \cdot |N(S)| \, .$$

It follows that $|S| \leq |N(S)|$.

One of the reasons that matching theory is interesting is because of beautiful min-max theorems like the König-Egerváry Theorem and Hall's Theorem. Lovász and Plummer's book [75] provides extensive coverage of matchings for those who want to learn more about them. Papadimitriou and Steiglitz [85] and Lawler [70] also discuss important algorithmic and theoretical aspects of matchings.

Homework 7 Solutions

1. (a) We reduce the general CNFSat problem to the restricted problem in
       which variables are allowed at most three occurrences to show that
       the restricted problem is NP-hard. Given the CNF formula $\mathcal{B}$, let x
       be a variable with exactly m occurrences in $\mathcal{B}$. Let $x_1, x_2, \ldots, x_m$ be
       m new variables. Replace the ith occurrence of x with x_i and append
       the CNF formula

$$(\neg x_1 \vee x_2) \ \wedge \ (\neg x_2 \vee x_3) \ \wedge \ \cdots \ \wedge \ (\neg x_m \vee x_1)$$

   which is equivalent to the chain of implications

$$x_1 \ \rightarrow \ x_2 \ \rightarrow \ x_3 \ \rightarrow \ \cdots \ \rightarrow \ x_m \ \rightarrow \ x_1 \,.$$

   This will force all the x_i to have the same truth value in any satisfying
   assignment, and there are exactly three occurrences of each x_i. Do
   this for all variables in the original formula.

   The restricted problem is in NP, since it is a special case of the unre-
   stricted CNFSat problem. Therefore it is NP-complete.

   (b) If a variable x appears only positively (only negatively), then we can
       satisfy the clauses containing x by assigning x the value *true* (*false*),
       thus we might as well eliminate those clauses. The new formula is
       satisfiable iff the original one is.

   Suppose then that the variable x appears both positively and negatively. Since there are only two occurrences of x, there is one of each.
   If the occurrences are in the same clause, then that clause is true under any truth assignment, and we can eliminate it. If not, and if the
   two clauses contain no other variables, then we have reached a contradiction $x \wedge \neg x$ and there is no satisfying assignment. Otherwise,
   we apply the *resolution rule* of propositional logic: we combine the
   two clauses containing x, but throw out x itself. For example, if one
   clause is $x \vee y \vee z$ and the other is $\neg x \vee u \vee v$, then the new clause is
   $y \vee z \vee u \vee v$. Again, the new formula is satisfiable iff the original one
   was.

   We continue applying these rules until we see a contradiction $x \wedge \neg x$
   or we eliminate all of the variables. In the latter case, the formula is
   satisfiable.

   The resolution rule is a widely used proof procedure for propositional
   logic. It is known to require exponential time in the worst case when
   there are no restrictions on the number of occurrences of variables
   [47, 101]. Resolution, suitably extended to handle first-order formulas,
   forms the basis for many PROLOG implementations.

2. If the graph is not strongly connected, there is no TSP tour. Otherwise, we calculate the weight w^* of an optimal TSP tour as follows. Let $w(e)$ be the weight of edge e and let $d = \max_{e \in E} w(e)$. There exists a tour of weight at most $n^2 d$ consisting of minimum-weight paths between pairs of vertices (u_1, u_2), (u_2, u_3), ..., (u_n, u_1) placed end to end. Starting with $n^2 d$, perform a binary search to find w^*. This can be done in polynomial time, because we have to make only $O(\log(n^2 d)) = O(\log n + \log d)$ calls to our subroutine that tells whether there exists a TSP tour of weight k, and $\log d$ is the size of the binary representation of d.

Next we wish to determine the number of times each edge is traversed in some optimal tour. Note that these numbers are not unique; different tours may traverse an edge different numbers of times. Consider an operation in which we replace the edge $e = (u, v)$ with the graph D_k pictured below right, where k is the number of extra vertices. In the example shown, $k = 5$.

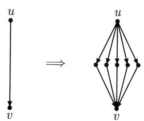

We give each of the edges in D_k weight $w(e)/2$. Any tour in the new graph gives rise to a tour in the old graph of the same weight. Conversely, any tour in the old graph that traverses e at least k times gives rise to a tour in the new graph of the same weight. Thus the weight of an optimal tour in the new graph is at least w^*, and strictly greater than w^* if all optimal tours in the old graph traverse e fewer than k times. Since no optimal tour of the old graph traverses e more than n times, if $k > n$ then the weight of the optimal tour in the new graph must be strictly greater than w^*.

Now, for each edge e in turn, we replace e with D_k, where k is as large as possible such that there still exists a tour of weight w^*. We discover k by binary search in the interval $0 \le k \le n$. When we are done, there is a tour of weight w^* in the resulting graph that traverses each edge exactly once (if not, some D_k could have been replaced by D_{k+1}). We find an Euler circuit in this graph, which will give rise to a TSP tour in the original graph of optimum weight w^*.

3. Let $\mathcal{B}$ be a CNF formula. We wish to produce an undirected graph $G = (V, E)$, integer k, and distinguished vertices $s_i, t_i, 1 \le i \le k$, such that there exist k vertex-disjoint paths connecting the s_i and t_i iff $\mathcal{B}$ has a satisfying truth assignment.

Let C be the set of clauses, let X be the set of variables, and let L be the set of occurrences of literals in $\mathcal{B}$. Let the set of vertices be

$$V = L \cup \{s_c, \, t_c \mid c \in C\} \cup \{s_x, \, t_x \mid x \in X\}$$

and take $k = |C| + |X|$. For $c \in C$, connect all occurrences of literals in c to s_c and t_c. For $x \in X$, connect all the positive occurrences of x in $\mathcal{B}$ in a single path, connect the negative occurrences of x in a single path, and connect one endpoint of each of these two paths to s_x and the other to t_x.

For example, consider the formula

$$\mathcal{B} = \underbrace{(x \vee \bar{y} \vee \bar{z})}_{c} \wedge \underbrace{(x \vee y \vee z)}_{d} \wedge \underbrace{(\bar{x} \vee y \vee \bar{z})}_{e}$$

with variables $X = \{x, y, z\}$ and clauses $C = \{c, d, e\}$. The construction produces the following graph:

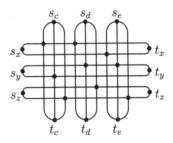

If $\mathcal{B}$ has a satisfying assignment, then for each $c \in C$, take the path from s_c to t_c of length two through some true literal of c, and for each $x \in X$, take the path from s_x to t_x through the false literals. These k paths are vertex-disjoint. Conversely, suppose there are k vertex-disjoint paths. The path from s_x to t_x, $x \in X$, must go through either all and only the positive occurrences of x or all and only the negative occurrences of x; any deviation would necessarily go through some s_c or t_c. Assign x *true* if the path from s_x to t_x goes through the negative occurrences of x and *false* if it goes through the positive occurrences of x. Since the paths are vertex-disjoint, the paths from s_c to t_c, $c \in C$, go through only true literals. Thus the truth assignment satisfies all clauses.

The problem is in NP since the disjoint paths can be guessed and verified in polynomial time.

Homework 8 Solutions

1. This problem is in *coNP* because its complement is in *NP*: we can guess a value for each variable and verify in polynomial time that the given expression does not vanish. We show *coNP*-hardness by showing that its complement is *NP*-hard using a reduction from CNFSat. Given a Boolean formula, we transform it into an algebraic expression that vanishes mod p for all variable assignments iff the original formula is unsatisfiable. We simulate the Boolean values *true* and *false* with 1 and 0 in $\mathcal{Z}_p$, respectively. If x is a variable of the Boolean formula, replace it with x^{p-1}. Replace each expression $\neg A$ by $1 - A$, $A \wedge B$ by AB, and $A \vee B$ by $A + B - AB$.

2. (a) The restricted problem remains in *NP*, so the difficult part is to show *NP*-hardness. We do this by reducing the undirected Hamiltonian circuit problem to TSP with the triangle inequality. Given an undirected graph $G = (V, E)$, we will construct a symmetric distance function $d : V \times V \to \mathcal{N}$ satisfying the triangle inequality such that G has a Hamiltonian circuit iff it has a TSP tour of length n. Let

$$d(u, v) = \begin{cases} 1 & \text{if } (u, v) \in E, \\ 2 & \text{if } (u, v) \notin E. \end{cases}$$

Then d obeys the triangle inequality trivially. A TSP tour in G that has length n must contain only edges of length 1. Thus it corresponds directly to a Hamiltonian tour in G.

(b) Actually, it is possible to find in polynomial time a tour that is no worse than 3/2 times the optimal tour by using an algorithm known as *Christofides' heuristic*. Our solution will only be guaranteed to be no more than twice the optimal solution, but it is important to understand how our solution works before looking at Christofides' algorithm, which uses matching. Papadimitriou and Steiglitz [85] discuss Christofides' heuristic for those interested in finding out more about it.

We will assume that distances are symmetric. First, we find a minimum spanning tree T. Next, we create a directed graph G by using two copies of each edge of T, one in each direction. Finally, we find an Euler circuit in G, which gives a TSP tour of weight twice that of the minimum spanning tree. Since every TSP tour contains a spanning tree of the original graph, the length of any TSP tour is at least as large as the weight of the minimum spanning tree. Therefore, the length of our Euler circuit is no more than twice the length of the optimal TSP tour.

Since the triangle inequality holds, we can convert the Euler circuit to a TSP tour of no greater weight in which vertices are visited only once: we merely skip over vertices previously visited.

3. Recall that if $G = (V, E)$ is not acyclic, its transitive reduction or Hasse diagram is not necessarily unique. The problem is in NP, since we can just guess a transitive reduction, verify that it is antitransitive (*i.e.*, that if (u, v) and $(v, w) \in E$ then $(u, w) \notin E$), take its transitive closure, and verify that this is the same as the transitive closure of E.

We show that the transitive reduction problem is NP-hard by exhibiting a reduction from the directed Hamiltonian circuit problem. The reduction from the vertex cover problem to the directed Hamiltonian circuit problem given in Lecture 24 produces a strongly connected graph, whether or not it has a Hamiltonian circuit. Thus the problem of determining whether a given strongly connected graph has a Hamiltonian circuit is also NP-hard. We now argue that a strongly connected graph H has a Hamiltonian circuit if and only if it has a transitive reduction with at most n edges. Note that the transitive closure of such a graph is the complete graph. If H has a Hamiltonian circuit, then the Hamiltonian circuit itself serves as a transitive reduction, and it has exactly n edges. Conversely, any transitive reduction of H must contain at least n edges, since it must enter every vertex at least once, since H is strongly connected. If it contains exactly n edges, then it enters every vertex exactly once, thus it must be a Hamiltonian circuit.

Homework 9 Solutions

1. We will use the concurrent-read exclusive-write (CREW) PRAM model with unit cost for integer operations and comparisons.

   Represent the dag G as an adjacency matrix A. Compute its reflexive transitive closure G^* either by computing $A^* = (I \vee A)^n$ in NC using parallel prefix, or more efficiently, using the relationship between matrix multiplication and transitive closure discussed in Lecture 5. Then sort the vertices by indegree in G^* using the algorithm of Miscellaneous Exercise 27. This gives a topological sort, since if there is a path from u to v in G, then vertex u has smaller indegree than v in G^*.

2. If G has an odd cycle, then it must have an odd simple cycle (one with no repeated vertices), because any odd cycle that is not simple is composed of two smaller cycles, one of which must be odd. Therefore, to check for an odd cycle, we need only check for a path of odd length at most n from a vertex back to itself. The kth power of the adjacency matrix A of G tells us the paths of length k in G. Using parallel prefix, we can compute all the odd powers of A up to n in NC and see if any of them contain a 1 on the main diagonal.

   This algorithm is NC, but it is not very efficient in its use of processors. We can save a factor of n processors by observing that we only have to check the diagonal of A^k for some odd k greater than $n - 1$. If there is an odd cycle of shorter length, we can extend it to one of length k by retracing an edge backwards and forwards. Thus we can use matrix powering instead of parallel prefix.

   Another approach would compute the $*$ of a matrix A over a Kleene algebra consisting of four elements $\bot$, 0, 1, and $\top$, where the operations $+$ and $\cdot$ are given by

$+$	$\bot$	0	1	$\top$		$\cdot$	$\bot$	0	1	$\top$
$\bot$	$\bot$	0	1	$\top$		$\bot$	$\bot$	$\bot$	$\bot$	$\bot$
0	0	0	$\top$	$\top$		0	$\bot$	0	1	$\top$
1	1	$\top$	1	$\top$		1	$\bot$	1	0	$\top$
$\top$	$\top$	$\top$	$\top$	$\top$		$\top$	$\bot$	$\top$	$\top$	$\top$

   We set

   $$A_{ij} = \begin{cases} 0 & \text{if } i = j \\ 1 & \text{if } (i,j) \in E \\ \bot & \text{otherwise.} \end{cases}$$

   The element 0 in position ij of A^* means that there is an even-length path between i and j; 1 means there is an odd-length path; $\top$ means there are both (then the graph is not bipartite); and $\perp$ means i and j are in different connected components.

Here is a method due to Shiloach and Vishkin [93] that is much more efficient in its use of processors. First, find a spanning tree of G. This can be done in $O(\log n)$ time using $O(n + m)$ processors on a CRCW PRAM. Assign a parity 0 or 1 to each vertex according to its distance from the root; this too can be done using $O(n + m)$ processors in parallel, using the technique of *pointer doubling* (see Miscellaneous Exercise 25). Finally, check every edge of G to make sure that an edge does not join two vertices of the same color.

3. (a) The system is described by the following matrix-vector equation, illustrated here for the case $k = 5$.

$$
\begin{bmatrix}
0 & 1 & 0 & 0 & 0 & 0 \\
0 & 0 & 1 & 0 & 0 & 0 \\
0 & 0 & 0 & 1 & 0 & 0 \\
0 & 0 & 0 & 0 & 1 & 0 \\
a_5 & a_4 & a_3 & a_2 & a_1 & 1 \\
0 & 0 & 0 & 0 & 0 & 1
\end{bmatrix}
\cdot
\begin{bmatrix}
x_{n-5} \\
x_{n-4} \\
x_{n-3} \\
x_{n-2} \\
x_{n-1} \\
c
\end{bmatrix}
=
\begin{bmatrix}
x_{n-4} \\
x_{n-3} \\
x_{n-2} \\
x_{n-1} \\
x_n \\
c
\end{bmatrix}
\tag{10}
$$

$$
\begin{bmatrix}
x_0 \\
x_1 \\
x_2 \\
x_3 \\
x_4 \\
c
\end{bmatrix}
=
\begin{bmatrix}
c_0 \\
c_1 \\
c_2 \\
c_3 \\
c_4 \\
c
\end{bmatrix}
\tag{11}
$$

Raising the $(k + 1) \times (k + 1)$ matrix on the left hand side of (10) to the nth power and using (11), we obtain

$$
\begin{bmatrix}
0 & 1 & 0 & 0 & 0 & 0 \\
0 & 0 & 1 & 0 & 0 & 0 \\
0 & 0 & 0 & 1 & 0 & 0 \\
0 & 0 & 0 & 0 & 1 & 0 \\
a_5 & a_4 & a_3 & a_2 & a_1 & 1 \\
0 & 0 & 0 & 0 & 0 & 1
\end{bmatrix}^n
\cdot
\begin{bmatrix}
c_0 \\
c_1 \\
c_2 \\
c_3 \\
c_4 \\
c
\end{bmatrix}
=
\begin{bmatrix}
x_n \\
x_{n+1} \\
x_{n+2} \\
x_{n+3} \\
x_{n+4} \\
c
\end{bmatrix}
$$

It therefore suffices to compute the nth power of the matrix in (10). Represent this matrix as the sum $C + U$, where

$$
C =
\begin{bmatrix}
0 & 1 & 0 & 0 & 0 & 0 \\
0 & 0 & 1 & 0 & 0 & 0 \\
0 & 0 & 0 & 1 & 0 & 0 \\
0 & 0 & 0 & 0 & 1 & 0 \\
a_5 & a_4 & a_3 & a_2 & a_1 & 0 \\
0 & 0 & 0 & 0 & 0 & 1
\end{bmatrix}
$$

and

$$U = \begin{bmatrix} 0 & 0 & 0 & 0 & 0 & 0 \\ 0 & 0 & 0 & 0 & 0 & 0 \\ 0 & 0 & 0 & 0 & 0 & 0 \\ 0 & 0 & 0 & 0 & 0 & 0 \\ 0 & 0 & 0 & 0 & 0 & 1 \\ 0 & 0 & 0 & 0 & 0 & 0 \end{bmatrix}.$$

Note that $UC = U$ and $U^2 = 0$; from this it follows that

$$\begin{aligned} (C+U)^m &= C^m + C^{m-1}U + C^{m-2}U + \cdots + CU + U \\ &= C^m + D_m, \end{aligned} \tag{12}$$

where

$$D_m = (\sum_{i=0}^{m-1} C^i)U.$$

The matrix C is a block diagonal matrix consisting of a $k \times k$ companion matrix in the upper left and a 1×1 identity matrix in the lower right, thus Miscellaneous Exercise 22 applies.

Given C^m and D_m, we can obtain C^{2m}, C^{m+1}, D_{2m}, and D_{m+1} in time $O(k^2)$. For the first two we use Miscellaneous Exercise 22. For the last two, we have

$$\begin{aligned} D_{2m} &= C^m D_m + D_m \\ D_{m+1} &= C D_m + U. \end{aligned}$$

The product $C^m D_m$ is essentially a matrix-vector product, since all columns of D_m except the last are zero.

Thus we can compute D_n and C^n with at most $\log n$ matrix operations, each taking time $O(k^2)$ (the sequence of operations is determined by the binary representation of n). The desired power $(C+U)^n$ is given by (12).

For a different approach to this problem, see [109, 86, 45].

(b) With $O(k^\alpha)$ processors, we can multiply two $(k+1) \times (k+1)$ matrices in time $O(\log k)$ using a parallel version of Strassen's matrix multiplication algorithm. Thus the nth power of the matrix in (10) can be computed in time $O(\log k \log n)$ by repeated squaring.

Here is how we parallelize Strassen's algorithm. Recall that Strassen multiplies 2×2 matrices as follows:

$$\begin{aligned} &\begin{bmatrix} a & b \\ c & d \end{bmatrix} \cdot \begin{bmatrix} e & f \\ g & h \end{bmatrix} \\ &= \begin{bmatrix} s_1 + s_2 - s_4 + s_6 & s_4 + s_5 \\ s_6 + s_7 & s_2 - s_3 + s_5 - s_7 \end{bmatrix} \end{aligned}$$

where

$$
\begin{aligned}
s_1 &= (b-d)\cdot(g+h) \\
s_2 &= (a+d)\cdot(e+h) \\
s_3 &= (a-c)\cdot(e+f) \\
s_4 &= h\cdot(a+b) \\
s_5 &= a\cdot(f-h) \\
s_6 &= d\cdot(g-e) \\
s_7 &= e\cdot(c+d)\ .
\end{aligned}
$$

We can first compute the quantities $b-d$, $g+h$, $a+d$, $e+h$, $a-c$, $e+f$, $a+b$, $f-h$, $g-e$, and $c+d$ in parallel, then compute $s_1,\ldots,s_7$ in parallel from these, and finally the four entries of the product from the s_i in parallel.

Now we apply this technique inductively. Given a pair of $k \times k$ matrices, we wish to build an NC circuit to compute their product. We break each matrix up into four submatrices of size roughly $\frac{k}{2} \times \frac{k}{2}$, and assuming that we have already constructed circuits to compute the sum and product of $\frac{k}{2} \times \frac{k}{2}$ matrices, we can use those circuits in the calculation of the $k \times k$ product exactly as in the 2×2 case described above.

Let $P(k)$ and $T(k)$ be, respectively, the number of processors (size of the circuit) and the time (depth of the circuit) necessary to to multiply two $k \times k$ matrices by this method. These quantities satisfy the recurrences

$$
\begin{aligned}
P(k) &= 7P(\frac{k}{2}) + O(k^2) \\
T(k) &= T(\frac{k}{2}) + O(1)
\end{aligned}
$$

since we need $O(k^2)$ processors and $O(1)$ time to add two $k \times k$ matrices. These recurrences give

$$
\begin{aligned}
P(k) &= O(k^{\log 7}) = O(k^{2.81\cdots}) \\
T(k) &= O(\log k)\ .
\end{aligned}
$$

For more details, see [44].

(c) Let y be an indeterminate and consider the generating function

$$
x(y) = \sum_{i=0}^{\infty} x_i y^i
$$

where the x_i are the solution to the recurrence. Multiplying $x(y)$ by y^i shifts the coefficients i positions; using this trick, we can encode the linear recurrence as a single equation involving shifts of $x(y)$ as follows. Let

$$
\begin{aligned}
p(y) &= a_1 + a_2 y + a_3 y^2 + \cdots + a_k y^{k-1} \\
q(y) &= c_0 + c_1 y + c_2 y^2 + \cdots + c_{k-1} y^{k-1} \\
r(y) &= (p(y) - a_k y^{k-1})(q(y) - c_{k-1} y^{k-1}) \bmod y^k .
\end{aligned}
$$

(The coefficients of $r(y)$ can be computed in time $O(\log k)$ with $2k$ processors using FFT.) Then

$$
\begin{aligned}
x(y) &= a_1 y (x(y) - (c_0 + c_1 y + \cdots + c_{k-2} y^{k-2})) \\
&\quad + a_2 y^2 (x(y) - (c_0 + c_1 y + \cdots + c_{k-3} y^{k-3})) \\
&\quad + a_3 y^3 (x(y) - (c_0 + c_1 y + \cdots + c_{k-4} y^{k-4})) \\
&\quad + \cdots \\
&\quad + a_{k-1} y^{k-1} (x(y) - c_0) \\
&\quad + a_k y^k x(y) \\
&\quad + c y^k (1 + y + y^2 + \cdots) \\
&\quad + c_0 + c_1 y + c_2 y^2 + \cdots + c_{k-1} y^{k-1} \\
&= y p(y) x(y) - r(y) + \frac{c y^k}{1 - y} + q(y) ,
\end{aligned}
$$

therefore

$$
\begin{aligned}
x(y) &= \frac{(q(y) - r(y))(1 - y) + c y^k}{(1 - y)(1 - y p(y))} \\
&= \frac{u(y)}{1 - y v(y)} \tag{13}
\end{aligned}
$$

where

$$
\begin{aligned}
u(y) &= (q(y) - r(y))(1 - y) + c y^k \\
v(y) &= 1 + p(y) - y p(y) .
\end{aligned}
$$

Expanding the denominator of (13) in an infinite series, we get

$$
x(y) = u(y) \sum_{i=0}^{\infty} y^i v(y)^i ,
$$

and since we are only interested in computing the first n terms, we might as well truncate the series and compute instead

$$
\begin{aligned}
\hat{x}(y) &= u(y) \sum_{i=0}^{n-1} y^i v(y)^i \tag{14} \\
&= \frac{u(y)(1 - y^n v(y)^n)}{1 - y v(y)} . \tag{15}
\end{aligned}
$$

We take Fourier transforms and use componentwise operations. In particular, to get the transform of $y^n v(y)^n$, we raise the transform of $yv(y)$ to the nth power componentwise, and to get the transform of $\sum_{i=0}^{n-1} y^i v(y)^i$, we divide the transform of $1 - y^n v(y)^n$ by the transform of $1 - yv(y)$ componentwise. There is one glitch: suppose that at a root of unity ω^j, we find that $\omega^j v(\omega^j) = 1$, so that we cannot do the division in (15) at the jth component. In that case, we use (14) instead, observing that

$$\sum_{i=0}^{n-1} \omega^{ji} v(\omega^j)^i = n \ .$$

We need N^{th} roots of unity and a multiplicative inverse of N, where N exceeds the degrees of all polynomials involved, so that there will be no wrap; since $u(y)$ and $v(y)$ are each of degree at most k, the numerator of (15) is of degree at most $kn+k+n$, thus $N > kn+k+n$ suffices.

Homework 10 Solutions

1. (a) As shown in Lecture 36, the expected value of the random variable $\mathcal{E}(X_{n+1} \mid S_n)$ is

$$\mathcal{E}(\mathcal{E}(X_{n+1} \mid S_n)) = \mathcal{E}X_{n+1} .$$

This yields the recurrence

$$
\begin{aligned}
\mathcal{E}S_0 &= 0 \\
\mathcal{E}S_{n+1} &= \mathcal{E}(S_n + X_{n+1}) \\
&= \mathcal{E}S_n + \mathcal{E}X_{n+1} \\
&= \mathcal{E}S_n + \mathcal{E}(\mathcal{E}(X_{n+1} \mid S_n)) \\
&\geq \mathcal{E}S_n + \mathcal{E}(\epsilon(m - S_n)) \\
&= \epsilon m + (1 - \epsilon)\mathcal{E}S_n
\end{aligned}
$$

whose solution gives

$$\mathcal{E}S_n \geq m(1 - (1 - \epsilon)^n) .$$

(b)

$$
\begin{aligned}
\mathcal{E}S_n &= \sum_{i=0}^{m} i \cdot \Pr(S_n = i) \\
&= m \cdot \Pr(S_n = m) + \sum_{i=0}^{m-1} i \cdot \Pr(S_n = i) \\
&\leq m \cdot \Pr(S_n = m) + \sum_{i=0}^{m-1} (m - 1) \cdot \Pr(S_n = i) \\
&= m \cdot \Pr(S_n = m) + (m - 1) \cdot (1 - \Pr(S_n = m)) \\
&= m - 1 + \Pr(S_n = m) .
\end{aligned}
$$

Combining this inequality with (a), we obtain

$$\Pr(S_n = m) \geq 1 - m(1 - \epsilon)^n .$$

(c) Using (b),

$$
\begin{aligned}
\mathcal{E}f(S_n) &= 1 \cdot \Pr(S_n < m) + 0 \cdot \Pr(S_n = m) \\
&= 1 - \Pr(S_n = m) \\
&\leq m(1 - \epsilon)^n .
\end{aligned}
$$

Also, by definition of f,

$$\mathcal{E}f(S_n) \leq 1 .$$

Then for any ℓ,

$$
\begin{aligned}
\mathcal{E}R &= \sum_{n=0}^{\infty} \mathcal{E}f(S_n) \\
&\leq \sum_{n=0}^{\ell-1} 1 + \sum_{n=\ell}^{\infty} m(1-\epsilon)^n \\
&= \ell + m(1-\epsilon)^\ell \sum_{n=0}^{\infty} (1-\epsilon)^n \\
&= \ell + \frac{m}{\epsilon}(1-\epsilon)^\ell .
\end{aligned}
$$

Taking

$$
\ell = \left\lceil \frac{\log m - \log \epsilon}{-\log(1-\epsilon)} \right\rceil
$$

gives the desired bound.

2. Let $a_u = |A_u|$. It will suffice to show that for any subset $\mathcal{B}$ of $\mathcal{Z}_p$ of size $k \leq d$,

$$
\Pr(\bigwedge_{u \in \mathcal{B}} x_0 + x_1 u + x_2 u^2 + \cdots + x_{d-1} u^{d-1} \in A_u) = \prod_{u \in \mathcal{B}} \frac{a_u}{p} .
$$

But

$$
\begin{aligned}
&\Pr(\bigwedge_{u \in \mathcal{B}} \sum_{i=0}^{d-1} x_i u^i \in A_u) \\
&= \frac{1}{p^d} |\{(x_0, \ldots, x_{d-1}) \mid \bigwedge_{u \in \mathcal{B}} \sum_{i=0}^{d-1} x_i u^i \in A_u\}| \\
&= \frac{1}{p^d} \sum_{z_u \in A_u,\ u \in \mathcal{B}} |\{(x_0, \ldots, x_{d-1}) \mid \bigwedge_{u \in \mathcal{B}} \sum_{i=0}^{d-1} x_i u^i = z_u\}| .
\end{aligned}
$$

Consider the $k \times d$ linear system

$$
x_0 + x_1 u + x_2 u^2 + \cdots + x_{d-1} u^{d-1} = z_u , \quad u \in \mathcal{B} .
$$

This can be represented in matrix form as

$$
Ax = z
$$

where A is a $k \times d$ submatrix of a $d \times d$ Vandermonde consisting of all rows

$$
(1,\ u,\ u^2,\ \ldots,\ u^{d-1}) , \quad u \in \mathcal{B} .
$$

Since the Vandermonde is nonsingular, A is of full rank k. Its kernel is therefore a subspace of $\mathcal{Z}_p^d$ of dimension $d - k$, thus the affine subspace of solutions to $Ax = z$ also has dimension $d - k$. In $\mathcal{Z}_p$, any such subspace has p^{d-k} elements. Thus

$$\frac{1}{p^d} \sum_{z_u \in A_u,\ u \in B} |\{(x_0, \ldots, x_{d-1}) \mid \bigwedge_{u \in B} \sum_{i=0}^{d-1} x_i u^i = z_u\}|$$

$$= \frac{1}{p^d} \sum_{z_u \in A_u,\ u \in B} p^{d-k}$$

$$= \frac{p^{d-k}}{p^d} \sum_{z_u \in A_u,\ u \in B} 1$$

$$= \frac{1}{p^k} \prod_{u \in B} a_u \ .$$

3. The solution to this problem is very similar to the analysis of Luby's algorithm given in class. Recall from there that a vertex is *good* if

$$\sum_{u \in N(v)} \frac{1}{d(u)} \geq \frac{1}{3} \ .$$

Lemma A *For all good v, $\Pr(v \in U) \geq \frac{1}{9}$.*

Proof. If v has a neighbor u of degree 2 or less, then

$$\Pr(v \in U) \geq \Pr(v = t(u))$$
$$\geq \frac{1}{2} \ .$$

Otherwise $d(u) \geq 3$ for all $u \in N(v)$, and as in the analysis of Luby's algorithm, there must exist a subset $M(v) \subseteq N(v)$ such that

$$\frac{1}{3} \leq \sum_{u \in M(v)} \frac{1}{d(u)} \leq \frac{2}{3} \ .$$

Then

$$\Pr(v \in U)$$
$$\geq \Pr(\exists u \in M(v)\ v = t(u))$$
$$\geq \sum_{u \in M(v)} \Pr(v = t(u)) - \sum_{\substack{u,\, w\, \in\, M(v) \\ u \neq w}} \Pr(v = t(u) \wedge v = t(w))$$
$$\text{(by inclusion-exclusion)}$$
$$\geq \sum_{u \in M(v)} \Pr(v = t(u)) - \sum_{\substack{u,\, w\, \in\, M(v) \\ u \neq w}} \Pr(v = t(u)) \cdot \Pr(v = t(w))$$

(by pairwise independence)

$$\geq \sum_{u \in M(v)} \frac{1}{d(u)} - \sum_{u,w \in M(v)} \frac{1}{d(u)} \cdot \frac{1}{d(w)}$$

$$= \Big(\sum_{u \in M(v)} \frac{1}{d(u)} \Big) \cdot \Big(1 - \sum_{w \in M(v)} \frac{1}{d(w)} \Big)$$

$$\geq \frac{1}{3} \cdot \frac{1}{3} = \frac{1}{9} .$$

□

Lemma B   *For all v, $\Pr(v$ is matched $\mid v \in U) \geq \frac{1}{2}$.*

Proof. There are several cases, depending on the number of H-neighbors of v and the number of H-neighbors of each H-neighbor of v. The situation minimizing the likelihood of v being matched is

There are eight possibilities for the choices of favorites of u, v, w, all equally likely. Of these, four give matchings for v. Thus

$$\Pr(v \text{ is matched} \mid v \in U) \geq \frac{1}{2} .$$

□

Combining Lemmas A and B, the probability that any particular good vertex is matched is at least $\frac{1}{18}$. The remainder of the argument is exactly like the analysis of Luby's algorithm given in class.

Note that the proof of Lemma A required only pairwise independence and the proof of Lemma B required only 3-wise independence, thus using Exercise 2 the algorithm can be made deterministic.

Solutions to Miscellaneous Exercises

1. The set $\mathcal{I}_{max}$ is closed under subset, so axiom (i) of matroids is satisfied. To show (ii), let $I, J \in \mathcal{I}_{max}$ such that $|I| < |J|$; we wish to find $x \in J - I$ such that $\{x\} \cup I \in \mathcal{I}_{max}$.

Let $\hat{I}$ and $\hat{J}$ be elements of M extending I and J, respectively. Consider the set

$$E = (J \cup (S - \hat{J})) - I .$$

The cardinality of E is greater than that of $S - \hat{J}$. By Exercise 1a of Homework 1, E is dependent in the dual, therefore contains a cut C. Now C must intersect every maximal independent set including $\hat{J}$, so it must contain an element of $J - I$. Let x be such an element of minimal weight.

We argue now that for any element $y \in C - \hat{J}$, the weight of y is at least as great as that of some element of $C \cap J$. This will say that x is of minimal weight in C, which will allow us to apply the blue rule. Let D be the fundamental cycle of y and $\hat{J}$. By Lemma 3.7, $C \cap D$ contains an element z of J, and by Lemma 3.8, the colors of y and z can be exchanged in the coloring $\hat{J}, S - \hat{J}$ to obtain an acceptable coloring. But the weight of z cannot exceed that of y, otherwise $\hat{J}$ was not of minimal weight.

At this point we have given a cut C disjoint from I such that $C \cap J$ contains an element x of minimal weight among all elements of C. If we color I blue, then we can apply the blue rule with x and C. Since $I \subseteq \hat{I} \in M$, it follows from Lemma 3.9 that $I \cup \{x\}$ is also contained in an element of M, therefore $I \cup \{x\} \in \mathcal{I}_{max}$.

2. Determine for each $e \in E$ the sizes of the two connected components obtained by deleting e. This can be done in linear time by depth-first search, computing the values recursively. Orient the edge e in the direction of the smaller component. The resulting directed graph is a directed tree, since no vertex has indegree greater than 1: if (s, u) and (t, u) were both oriented toward u, and if $|S|$, $|T|$, and $|U|$ were the subtrees pictured,

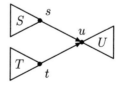

then

$$|S| \geq |T| + |U|$$
$$|T| \geq |S| + |U|$$

from which it would follow that $|U| = 0$, a contradiction.

Since we have a directed tree, there is a unique root r. The desired edge is the one from r to its largest subtree. To see this, let A, B, and C be the maximal proper subtrees of r, and let A be the one of maximum size. By the orientation of the edge from r to A,

$$|A| \leq \frac{n}{2} \leq \frac{2n+1}{3} \, .$$

Now $|B| \leq |A|$ and $|C| \leq |A|$, therefore $|B| + |C| \leq 2|A|$ and

$$
\begin{aligned}
n - 1 &= |A| + |B| + |C| \\
&\geq \frac{|B| + |C|}{2} + |B| + |C| \\
&= \frac{3(|B| + |C|)}{2} \, .
\end{aligned}
$$

It follows that

$$|B| + |C| + 1 \leq \frac{2n+1}{3} \, .$$

3. There are several reasonable approaches to this problem. Here is one involving Kleene algebra. Consider the structure

$$\mathcal{K} = (\mathcal{R} \cup \{\infty, -\infty\}, \ \min, \ +, \ ^*, \ \infty, \ 0)$$

where we extend the usual $+$ on $\mathcal{R}$ to $\mathcal{R} \cup \{\infty, -\infty\}$ by

$$
\begin{aligned}
\infty + a &= a + \infty = \infty, \ a \in \mathcal{R} \cup \{\infty, -\infty\} \\
-\infty + a &= a + (-\infty) = -\infty, \ a \in \mathcal{R} \cup \{-\infty\}
\end{aligned}
$$

and define * by

$$
a^* = \begin{cases} 0, & \text{if } a \geq 0, \\ -\infty, & \text{if } a < 0. \end{cases}
$$

A routine check of the axioms verifies that this structure is a Kleene algebra.

Let G be a directed graph with n vertices and real edge weights w, possibly negative. Form the $n \times n$ matrix A with $A_{uv} = w(u, v)$. If there is no edge (u, v), set $A_{uv} = \infty$. As shown in Lecture 7, the family of $n \times n$ matrices over $\mathcal{K}$ is again a Kleene algebra, and we can calculate A^* in time proportional to the time needed to multiply two $n \times n$ matrices over $\mathcal{K}$.

We claim that A_{uv}^* is the weight of the minimum-weight path from u to v, or $-\infty$ if there exists a path from u to v but no path is of minimum weight. As with the min, $+$ algebra discussed in Example 6.6, it can be argued by induction that A_{uv}^k gives the weight of the minimum-weight path of length k from u to v. Since $A^* = \inf_k A^k$, if there exists a minimum-weight path from u to v, and that path is of length k, then $A_{uv}^* = A_{uv}^k$.

It remains to argue that if there exists a path from u to v but no minimum-weight path, then the weights of paths between u and v are unbounded below, so that $A_{uv}^* = -\infty$. This argument is necessary, since it is conceivable that the weights of the paths from u to v approach some real lower limit without ever achieving it. We show that this cannot happen: if there is a path from u to v but no minimum-weight path, then there is a path from u to v that traverses some cycle of strictly negative weight, which can be traversed arbitrarily many times.

Under our assumption, there exists an infinite sequence $p_0, p_1, \ldots$ of paths from u to v such that p_i is a shortest (in terms of number of edges) path of weight strictly less than that of $p_0, p_1, \ldots, p_{i-1}$. The number of edges in these paths is unbounded, since for each k there are only finitely many paths with k edges. Let p_i be the first path in the list with at least n edges; then some vertex x must be repeated on p_i. The cycle that is traversed between the two occurrences of x on p_i must be of strictly negative weight, otherwise that cycle could be cut out of p_i to give a path of fewer edges and weight strictly less than that of $p_0, p_1, \ldots, p_{i-1}$, contradicting the minimality of p_i.

Another approach to this problem is to identify the vertices contained in negative-weight cycles and treat them separately. The solution to Miscellaneous Exercise 17(a) would presumably be useful in this regard. See [100] for more details about this approach.

4. (a) Call a schedule for a set of jobs A *safe* if no deadlines are violated. If A has a safe schedule, then so does any subset: simply delete the jobs not in the subset.

    Let A and B be two independent sets with $|A| < |B|$. Consider separate safe schedules for A and B. Assume without loss of generality that jobs are scheduled as early as possible with no gaps in the schedules. Let j be the job occurring latest in the schedule for B that is not in A. Let C be the set of jobs occurring after j in the schedule for B. Then $C \subseteq A$. Consider the following schedule for $A \cup \{j\}$: first schedule all the jobs in $A - C$ in the same order as in the schedule for A, then schedule j, then schedule C in the same order as in the schedule for B. This schedule is safe, since all elements of $A - C$ are scheduled no later than they were in A, and all elements in $\{j\} \cup C$ are scheduled no later than they were in B.

    (b) We use the greedy algorithm with the jobs sorted by penalty in decreasing order. The greedy algorithm produces a maximal independent set of maximum weight; these jobs can be scheduled safely. The remaining jobs are all scheduled after their deadlines and incur a penalty, but this penalty is a minimum. Since all maximal independent sets are of the same cardinality, we can do no better than this.

The sorting phase takes $O(n \log n)$ in general, or linear time if the penalties are small enough that bucket or radix sort can be used. The remainder of the algorithm can be implemented in time $O(n\alpha(n))$, where $\alpha(n)$ is the inverse of Ackermann's function, as follows.

Suppose that we are at some intermediate stage of the algorithm and have selected an independent set of jobs A. For $d \in \mathcal{N}$, define

$$\mu_A(d) \;=\; \text{the maximum number of jobs with deadline } d \text{ that could be added to } A \text{ without sacrificing independence.}$$

For example, $\mu_\emptyset(d) = d$. Then for any A,

$$\mu_A(0) \;=\; 0 \tag{16}$$
$$\mu_A(d) \;\leq\; \mu_A(d+1) \tag{17}$$
$$\leq\; \mu_A(d) + 1 . \tag{18}$$

The inequality (17) holds because if k jobs with deadline d can be safely added to A, then k jobs with any later deadline can be safely added to A. The inequality (18) holds because in any safe schedule for A and k additional jobs of deadline $d + 1$, $k - 1$ of the additional jobs must finish before time d, thus there is a safe schedule for A and $k - 1$ additional jobs of deadline d.

Properties (16), (17), and (18) say that the disjoint sets

$$\mu_A^{-1}(k) \;=\; \{d \mid \mu_A(d) = k\}$$

are intervals (contiguous sequences of natural numbers), and if the set $\mu_A^{-1}(k)$ is nonempty, then $\mu_A^{-1}(i)$ is nonempty for any $0 \leq i \leq k$.

We will use the union-find data structure to maintain the disjoint sets $\mu_A^{-1}(k)$. Consider a new job $j \notin A$ with deadline d_j. Then $A \cup \{j\}$ is independent iff $\mu_A(d_j) > 0$ iff $d_j \notin \mu_A^{-1}(0)$. Also, if $A \cup \{j\}$ is independent, then

$$\mu_{A\cup\{j\}}(d) \;=\; \begin{cases} \mu_{A\cup\{j\}}(d) - 1, & \mu_A(d) \geq \mu_A(d_j) \\ \mu_{A\cup\{j\}}(d), & \mu_A(d) < \mu_A(d_j) , \end{cases}$$

thus

$$\mu_{A\cup\{j\}}^{-1}(k)$$
$$= \begin{cases} \mu_A^{-1}(k), & k < \mu_A(d_j) - 1 \\ \mu_A^{-1}(k-1), & k > \mu_A(d_j) \\ \mu_A^{-1}(\mu_A(d_j)) \cup \mu_A^{-1}(\mu_A(d_j) - 1), & \text{otherwise.} \end{cases}$$

The sets $\mu_A^{-1}(k)$ will be linked in a list ℓ in order of increasing k. Initially, $\mu_A^{-1}(k) = \{k\}$, $0 \le k \le n$. To test for independence of $A \cup \{j\}$, where A is independent, we ask whether the set $\mathbf{find}(d_j)$ has a predecessor on the list ℓ. If not, $\mu_A(d_j) = \mu_A(0) = 0$ so $A \cup \{j\}$ is not independent. To insert the element j, we form the union of the set $\mathbf{find}(d_j)$ and its predecessor on the list ℓ.

5. The problem is in *coNP*, since its complement is in *NP*: we can guess a string of length n and check in polynomial time that it is not covered by any of the patterns.

   The problem is also hard for *coNP*, as the following reduction from (the complement of) CNFSat shows. Suppose we have a CNF formula $\mathcal{B}$ with n Boolean variables $x_1, \ldots, x_n$. Convert each clause c to a pattern σ_c of length n as follows:

   - if x_i does not appear in c, put $*$ in position i of σ_c.
   - if x_i appears positively in c, put a 0 in position i of σ_c.
   - if x_i appears negatively in c, put a 1 in position i of σ_c.

   A string of length n over $\{0,1\}$ represents a truth assignment to the variables $x_1, \ldots, x_n$ by assigning *true* to x_i if 1 appears in position i in the string, *false* if 0 appears in position i. Then σ_c covers exactly those strings corresponding to truth assignments that do not satisfy c. Therefore every string is covered by some σ_c iff every truth assignment falsifies some clause, *i.e.* iff $\mathcal{B}$ is unsatisfiable.

6. The problem is in *NP*, because we can guess a folding and compute its length in polynomial time. To show *NP*-hardness, we reduce the partition problem to it. Given an instance of the partition problem consisting of the weight function $w : \{1, 2, \ldots, n\} \to \mathcal{N}$, construct a ruler with $n + 4$ segments of length (in order)

$$N, \ \frac{N}{2}, \ w(1), \ w(2), \ \ldots, \ w(n), \ \frac{N}{2}, \ N$$

where N is very large (actually $N \ge \sum_{i=1}^{n} w(i)$ suffices), and let $k = N$. In order to fit, the endpoints of the two end segments of length N must line up vertically, and the two segments next to them of length $\frac{N}{2}$ must be folded back in. Thus we will get a fit if and only if the remainder of the ruler can be folded so that the inner endpoints of the $\frac{N}{2}$ segments line up vertically.

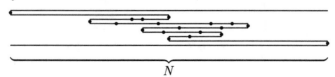

$$N$$

This can occur if and only if there exists a subset $S \subseteq \{1, 2, \ldots, n\}$ such that

$$\sum_{i \in S} w(i) \; = \; \sum_{i \notin S} w(i) \; ;$$

the sets S and $\{1, 2, \ldots, n\} - S$ correspond to the segments in the ruler pointing left and right, respectively.

7. Given a Boolean formula in CNF, perform the following operation on long clauses until every clause has at most three literals. First replace the clause

$$(x_1 \vee x_2 \vee x_3 \vee \cdots \vee x_k) \tag{19}$$

with

$$(y \leftrightarrow (x_1 \vee x_2)) \quad \wedge \quad (y \vee x_3 \vee \cdots \vee x_k) \tag{20}$$

where y is a new variable. The two formulas are equisatisfiable, and the number of satisfying truth assignments is the same, because the truth assignment to y is forced by the truth assignment to x_1 and x_2. The rightmost clause of (20) has one fewer literal than (19).

Next, replace the new clause

$$(y \leftrightarrow (x_1 \vee x_2))$$

with the equivalent formula

$$(\overline{y} \vee x_1 \vee x_2) \quad \wedge \quad (\overline{x}_1 \vee y) \quad \wedge \quad (\overline{x}_2 \vee y) \; .$$

This procedure gives a formula with at most three literals per clause.

It is possible to get exactly three distinct literals per clause as follows. Let x, y, and z be three new variables. Replace each deficient clause $(u \vee v)$ with $(u \vee v \vee \overline{x})$ and each deficient clause (u) with $(u \vee \overline{x} \vee \overline{y})$, and add the clauses (x), (y) and (z). The number of satisfying assignments is the same, since the new variables have to be *true* in any satisfying assignment. All clauses have exactly three literals except the three new ones. It now suffices to show how to express the conjunction $x\, y\, z$ in 3CNF. But

$$\neg(x\, y\, z) \quad \leftrightarrow \quad x\, y\, \overline{z} \vee x\, \overline{y}\, z \vee x\, \overline{y}\, \overline{z} \vee \overline{x}\, y\, z \vee \overline{x}\, y\, \overline{z} \vee \overline{x}\, \overline{y}\, z \vee \overline{x}\, \overline{y}\, \overline{z} \; ,$$

and a 3CNF representation of $x\, y\, z$ can be obtained by negating the right hand side and applying DeMorgan's law.

8. In the new representation, there will be a doubly linked list V of vertices. By "Given $u, \ldots$" we will mean, "Given a pointer to the list element for vertex u on the list $V, \ldots$" Each vertex u will point to a circular linked

list $\mathbf{adj}(u)$ of edges e such that $\mathbf{t}(e) = u$. By "Given $e,\dots$" we will mean, "Given the list element for e on the list $\mathbf{adj}(\mathbf{t}(e)),\dots$" The order on the circular list $\mathbf{adj}(u)$ will give the order θ. The edge e will point to $\theta(e)$, $\mathbf{t}(e)$ and $\bar{e}$; that is to say, the list element for e on $\mathbf{adj}(\mathbf{t}(e))$ will contain pointers to the list element for $\theta(e)$ on $\mathbf{adj}(\mathbf{t}(e))$, the list element for $\mathbf{t}(e)$ on V, and the list element for $\bar{e}$ on $\mathbf{adj}(\mathbf{t}(\bar{e})) = \mathbf{adj}(\mathbf{h}(e))$.

Given e, in constant time we can compute $\theta(e)$, $\bar{e}$ or $\mathbf{t}(e)$ by following a single pointer; and we can compute $\mathbf{h}(e)$ by following a pointer to $\bar{e}$ and then following the pointer there to $\mathbf{t}(\bar{e}) = \mathbf{h}(e)$. We can delete a given edge e in constant time by unlinking its list element from $\mathbf{adj}(\mathbf{t}(e))$ and unlinking the list element of $\bar{e}$ from $\mathbf{adj}(\mathbf{h}(e))$. We can delete a vertex u by first deleting all the edges on $\mathbf{adj}(u)$ as above and then unlinking u from V.

We now show how to obtain the new representation from the old one in linear time. The old representation consists essentially of the list V, for each u on V a pointer to an adjacency list $\mathbf{adj}(u)$ containing all edges e with $\mathbf{t}(e) = u$, and for each e on $\mathbf{adj}(\mathbf{t}(e))$ a pointer to $\mathbf{h}(e)$ on V. To calculate the pointers from e to $\mathbf{t}(e)$ in linear time, for each u scan the list $\mathbf{adj}(u)$ and append to each list element a pointer back to u.

It remains to calculate the pointers from e to $\bar{e}$. First produce for each vertex u an auxiliary adjacency list $\mathbf{aux}(u)$ with a list element for each e with $\mathbf{t}(e) = u$ and a pointer to $\bar{e}$. The lists $\mathbf{aux}(u)$ will contain the desired pointers but will not be in the correct order. The lists $\mathbf{aux}(u)$ are produced in linear time by initializing all $\mathbf{aux}(u)$ to the empty list, then scanning through all the lists $\mathbf{adj}(u)$ and for each e encountered appending a pointer to e to the front of the list $\mathbf{aux}(\mathbf{h}(e))$.

At this point each u points to two lists, $\mathbf{adj}(u)$ and $\mathbf{aux}(u)$, each with one entry for each edge e with $\mathbf{t}(e) = u$. The former list is in the correct order θ and the latter contains the $\bar{\ }$ pointers. We wish to consolidate them into a single list with both properties. For each u, execute the following two steps:

(a) Scan the list $\mathbf{aux}(u)$. For each e on the list, save the pointer to $\bar{e}$ in the list element for $\mathbf{h}(e)$ on V. The pointer to $\mathbf{h}(e)$ is available as $\mathbf{t}(\bar{e})$.

(b) Scan the list $\mathbf{adj}(u)$. For each e on the list, pick up the pointer to $\bar{e}$ from the list element for $\mathbf{h}(e)$ on V.

This procedure takes linear time, since each vertex and edge is visited a constant number of times.

9. Since $\bar{\ }$ and θ can be computed in constant time, the permutation $\theta^* = \theta \circ \bar{\ }$ can be computed in constant time. Construct a doubly linked list L of pointers to the list elements of all (directed) edges in the adjacency list

representation of G. While constructing L, store with each list element in G corresponding to an edge e a pointer to the list element in L corresponding to e. Repeat the following loop until L is empty. Let e be an arbitrary edge on L. Starting from e, successively compute θ^*, deleting each edge in succession from L and inserting it on a circular list C. Stop when we get back to e. Then C contains all edges in the cycle of θ^* containing e. Create a new vertex u in V^*, set $\mathbf{t}^*(e) = u$ for each edge e in C, and make C the adjacency list of u. When L is empty, set $\mathbf{h}^*(e) = \mathbf{t}^*(\bar{e})$ for each edge e. The pointers giving $^-$ are available from G.

10. As in Lecture 14, let n and n^* be the number of vertices and faces of G, respectively; let $m = |E|/2$, the number of undirected edges; let c be the number of connected components (orbits of E under the subgroup generated by θ and $^-$); and let $\theta^* = \theta \circ {}^-$. Note that the subgroup generated by θ and $^-$ is the same as the subgroup generated by θ and θ^*, since $^- = \theta^{-1} \circ \theta^*$.

Write θ as a product of disjoint cycles. Multiplying θ on the left by an involution $(a\ b)$ acts on θ as follows: if a and b are in different cycles of θ, then those two cycles are merged, and if a and b are in the same cycle, then that cycle is split. All cycles of θ not containing a or b are left intact. For example,

$$(1\ 5) \circ (1\ 2\ 3\ 4) \circ (5\ 6\ 7\ 8) = (1\ 2\ 3\ 4\ 5\ 6\ 7\ 8)$$
$$(1\ 5) \circ (1\ 2\ 3\ 4\ 5\ 6\ 7\ 8) = (1\ 2\ 3\ 4) \circ (5\ 6\ 7\ 8).$$

Here $(a_0\ a_1\ \ldots\ a_{n-1})$ is the permutation that maps a_i to $a_{(i+1) \bmod n}$, $0 \le i < n$, and fixes all other elements of E.

Let $\theta' = (a\ b) \circ \theta$. In terms of the graphs

$$G = (E, \theta, {}^-)$$
$$G' = (E, \theta', {}^-),$$

if the edges a and b have a common tail in G (*i.e.*, if a and b are in the same cycle of θ), then that tail is split into two vertices in G' as shown.

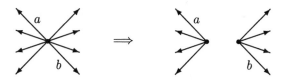

If a and b have different tails (*i.e.*, if a and b are contained in different cycles of θ), then the tails are merged in G'.

Note that

$$(\theta')^* \;=\; (\theta^*)' \;=\; (a\ b) \circ \theta^* \,,$$

so that these comments apply to the duals G^* and G'^* as well.

Write θ as a product of disjoint cycles

$$\theta \;=\; \theta_0 \circ \theta_1 \circ \cdots \circ \theta_{p-1} \,.$$

Each θ_i can be expressed as a product of $|\theta_i| - 1$ transpositions:

$$(a_0\ a_1\ \dots\ a_{k-1}) \;=\; (a_0\ a_1) \circ (a_1\ a_2) \circ \cdots \circ (a_{k-2}\ a_{k-1}) \,.$$

Thus θ can be expressed as a product of

$$\sum_{i=0}^{p-1} (|\theta_i| - 1) \;=\; 2m - p$$

transpositions. Let σ_i denote the product of the rightmost i transpositions in this list, and let G_i be the graph $(E,\ \sigma_i,\ ^-)$. Then σ_0 is the identity, which has $2m$ singleton cycles, and $\sigma_{2m-p} = \theta$, which has p cycles, so multiplication by the ith transposition taking σ_i to σ_{i+1} must combine two cycles into one. Thus G_{i+1} has one fewer vertex than G_i; *i.e.*, n decreases by one in each step.

Let the ith transposition be $(a\ b)$. Either

(i) a and b belong to different connected components of G_i;

(ii) a and b belong to the same component but different cycles of σ_i^*; or

(iii) a and b belong to the same cycle of σ_i^*.

In case (i), a and b belong to different cycles of σ_i^*, so c and n^* each decrease by one and $\chi(G_{i+1}) = \chi(G_i)$. In case (ii), n^* decreases by one and c remains the same, in which case $\chi(G_{i+1}) = \chi(G_i) + 2$. In case (iii), a and b belong to the same component of G_i and n^* increases by one. In this case, we claim that c remains the same, thus $\chi(G_{i+1}) = \chi(G_i)$. To see that c does not increase, it suffices to show that for any $d \in E$ there exists an η in the subgroup generated by σ_{i+1} and $^-$ such that $\eta(d) = \sigma_i(d)$; thus each orbit of the subgroup generated by σ_i and $^-$ is contained in an orbit of the subgroup generated by σ_{i+1} and $^-$.

If $\sigma_i(d) \notin \{a, b\}$, then

$$\begin{aligned}
\sigma_{i+1}(d) &= (a\ b) \circ \sigma_i(d) \\
&= \sigma_i(d) \ ,
\end{aligned}$$

so in this case we can take $\eta = \sigma_{i+1}$. Suppose now that $\sigma_i(d) = a$; the case $\sigma_i(d) = b$ is symmetric. Since a and b are in the same cycle of σ_{i+1}, there exists a k such that $\sigma_{i+1}^k(b) = a$. Let $\eta = \sigma_{i+1}^{k+1}$. Then

$$\begin{aligned}
\eta(d) &= \sigma_{i+1}^k(\sigma_{i+1}(d)) \\
&= \sigma_{i+1}^k((a\ b)\,(\sigma_i(d))) \\
&= \sigma_{i+1}^k(b) \\
&= a \\
&= \sigma_i(d) \ .
\end{aligned}$$

The reverse inclusion, which implies that c does not decrease, follows from a dual argument. (It is the dual argument that uses assumption (iii).)

11. We prove the harder direction ($\rightarrow$); the direction ($\leftarrow$) follows from a straightforward induction on the number of faces.

    Let σ_i and G_i be as in the solution to Miscellaneous Exercise 10. In that solution it was argued that $\chi(G_{i+1}) \geq \chi(G_i) \geq 0$ for all i. Since $G_{2m-p} = G$ and $\chi(G) = 0$, we have $\chi(G_i) = 0$ for all i.

    We proceed by induction on i. For the basis, σ_0 is the identity map and G_0 is the graph consisting of m connected components, each consisting of two vertices and an undirected edge. This certainly has a plane embedding consistent with σ_0.

    Now suppose G_i has a plane embedding consistent with σ_i. Let $(a\ b)$ be the ith transposition, so that $\sigma_{i+1} = (a\ b) \circ \sigma_i$. The tails of a and b in G_i are merged in G_{i+1}. Either

    (i) a and b lie in the same face of G_i, or

    (ii) a and b lie in different faces of G_i.

    In case (i), the tails of a and b can be merged across the common face of a and b. It is easily checked that the resulting embedding of G_{i+1} is consistent with σ_{i+1}.

    In case (ii), both n and n^* decrease by one in passing from G_i to G_{i+1}, so c must also decrease by one to maintain $\chi(G_{i+1}) = 0$. Thus a and b are in different connected components of G_i. By embedding on the sphere and changing the position of the North Pole, we can arrange the embedding of G_i so that a and b occur on the outer faces of their components, then merge the tails of a and b to obtain a plane embedding consistent with σ_{i+1}.

12. Instead of maximal cliques, take the complement graph and consider the maximal independent sets. Given a Boolean formula, construct a graph with a black vertex for each literal and a red vertex for each clause. Connect complementary literals and connect each clause to the literals it contains. Any maximal independent set M containing no red vertex contains exactly one of each pair of complementary literals and thus gives a truth assignment; moreover, it is a satisfying assignment, since every red vertex is connected to a vertex in M (otherwise M would not be maximal). Conversely, any satisfying assignment gives a black maximal independent set.

13. Given a partition problem (S, w), where S is the set of items, $n = |S|$, and $w : S \to \mathcal{Z}$ the weight function, let ℓ be an upper bound on the absolute values of weights of elements of S. Then for any subset $R \subseteq S$,

$$|w(R)| \;=\; \sum_{a \in R} |w(a)| \;\leq\; \ell |R| \; .$$

Thus, although there are $2^{|R|}$ subsets of R, there are only $2\ell |R| + 1$ weights these subsets can take on.

The following algorithm is quite reasonable if ℓ is sufficiently small. We calculate recursively the set of all possible weights of subsets of $R \subseteq S$. If $R = \{a\}$, the possible weights are 0 and $w(a)$. If $|R| \geq 2$, partition R into two disjoint sets R_1, R_2 of roughly equal size and recursively produce the data for R_1 and R_2. For each pair of weights w_1 and w_2 in the sets computed for R_1 and R_2, respectively, calculate $w_1 + w_2$ and record it in the set for R. Since w_1 is the weight of some subset of R_1 and w_2 is the weight of some subset of R_2, $w_1 + w_2$ is the weight of their union, which is a subset of R; moreover, every subset of R is obtained as such a union.

Since the weights of subsets of R_i lie between $-\ell |R_i|$ and $\ell |R_i|$, the calculation of all the weights $w_1 + w_2$ requires at most $O(\ell |R_1| \cdot \ell |R_2|)$ operations. This gives rise to the recurrence

$$T(n) \;=\; 2T(\frac{n}{2}) + O(\ell^2 n^2)$$

with solution

$$T(n) \;=\; O(\ell^2 n^2) \; .$$

Thus for partition problems with $\ell = \ell(n)$ a polynomial in n, $T(n)$ is also a polynomial in n.

14. Try $k = 2^{\lceil \log n \rceil}$, the smallest power of 2 greater than or equal to n. Recall that in the representation over $\mathcal{Z}_2[x]/x^n$, the binary-to-Gray operation amounts to multiplication by $x + 1$. We wish to show that $(x + 1)^k = 1$

and for all $0 \leq \ell < k$, $(x+1)^\ell \neq 1$; in other words, the order of $x+1$ in the group of invertible elements of $Z_2[x]/x^n$ is k. This will suffice to prove our result, since for any p, applying the binary-to-Gray operation k times gives $(x+1)^k p = p$, and for any $0 < \ell < k$, $(x+1)^\ell (x+1)^{k-\ell} = 1 \neq (x+1)^{k-\ell}$.

To show that $(x+1)^k = 1$, note that in $Z_2[x]/x^n$, squaring is a linear operation:

$$(p+q)^2 = p^2 + 2pq + q^2$$
$$= p^2 + q^2 ,$$

since $2 = 0 \pmod 2$. Thus

$$(x+1)^k = (x+1)^{2^{\lceil \log n \rceil}}$$
$$= (\cdots((x+1)^2)^2 \cdots)^2$$
$$= x^{2^{\lceil \log n \rceil}} + 1$$
$$= 1 ,$$

since $2^{\lceil \log n \rceil} \geq n$ and therefore $x^{2^{\lceil \log n \rceil}} = 0 \bmod x^n$. To show that no smaller power works, we use the fact that the order of $x+1$ must divide k, therefore it must be a power of 2. But for $m < \lceil \log n \rceil$ we have $2^m < n$, therefore

$$(x+1)^{2^m} = x^{2^m} + 1 \neq 1 .$$

15. (a) Consider the weighted 4-node widget A we used in Lecture 27 with the following adjacency matrix:

$$\begin{bmatrix} 1 & 1 & -1 & 0 \\ \frac{1}{2} & \frac{1}{2} & \frac{1}{2} & 0 \\ 0 & 0 & 0 & 1 \\ 1 & -1 & 0 & 0 \end{bmatrix}$$

The input nodes of the widget are 1 and 3 and the output nodes are 2 and 4. Note that $A_{34} = 1$ and everything else in the row and column containing A_{34} is 0. This says that every cycle cover of nonzero weight must contain the edge from 3 to 4 of weight 1. We might just as well collapse 3 and 4 into one node. The resulting widget is

$$\begin{bmatrix} 1 & 1 & -1 \\ \frac{1}{2} & \frac{1}{2} & \frac{1}{2} \\ 1 & -1 & 0 \end{bmatrix} \tag{21}$$

with input nodes 1 and 3 and output nodes 2 and 3. The desired behavior is summarized by the following equations, analogous to those presented in the lecture for the four-node widget. As before, $A(i; j)$

denotes the submatrix of A obtained by deleting row(s) i and column(s) j.

$$\text{perm } A(3;3) = \text{perm } A(2;1) = \text{perm } A(2,3;1,3) = 1$$
$$\text{perm } A(3;1) = \text{perm } A(2;3) = \text{perm } A = 0 \ .$$

A quick calculation shows that all these properties are satisfied by (21).

(b) To be used in this construction, any widget must have two distinct input vertices and two distinct output vertices, because there are good cycle covers containing two input edges and two output edges. Thus in any two-node widget, both nodes are input nodes and both are output nodes. The relevant equations are then

$$\text{perm } A(1;1) = \text{perm } A(2;2) = \text{perm } A(1,2;1,2) = 1$$
$$\text{perm } A(2;1) = \text{perm } A(1;2) = \text{perm } A = 0 \ .$$

The first line implies that $A_{11} = A_{22} = 1$. The first two equations of the second line imply that $A_{12} = A_{21} = 0$. Thus A must be the identity matrix. But then perm $A = 1$, so the last equation is violated.

16. (a) We first apply depth- or breadth-first search to determine whether the graph is 2-colorable (say with cyan and magenta) and find the connected components. If it is not 2-colorable, then no schedule exists. If it is, then we must decide for each connected component whether to schedule the cyan vertices of that component at time 0 and the magenta vertices at time 1 or vice versa so that there are at most m vertices in all scheduled at any one time. This is a partition problem with small weights and can be solved in polynomial time by the method of Miscellaneous Exercise 13.

(b) The problem is equivalent to the following graph coloring problem: given an undirected graph, can the vertices be colored with t colors so that no two adjacent vertices receive the same color and each monochromatic set is of cardinality at most m? The ordinary k-colorability problem discussed in Lecture 21 reduces to this problem trivially by taking $m = n$. Therefore the problem is NP-hard. It is also easily seen to be in NP, since a solution can be guessed and verified in polynomial time.

17. (a) The problem of detecting negative cycles is made easier by the following lemma.

Lemma *A vertex u is contained in a negative-weight cycle iff some vertex in the strong component of u is contained in a simple negative-weight cycle.*

Proof.

($\rightarrow$) If the negative-weight cycle containing u is simple, we are done. Otherwise there is a repeated vertex x on the cycle, and x is in the strong component of u. The cycle can be decomposed into two strictly smaller cycles containing x, at least one of which must have negative weight. By induction, there is a simple negative-weight cycle containing an element of the strong component of x, which is also the strong component of u.

($\leftarrow$) Let x be a vertex in the strong component of u contained in a simple negative-weight cycle. Combining the cycle through u and x with sufficiently many trips around the negative-weight cycle through x, we obtain a negative-weight cycle through u. $\square$

Every simple cycle of negative weight is of length at most n. Thus we can test for the existence of such a cycle by testing for the existence of any negative-weight cycle of length at most n. We can do this in polynomial time by examining the diagonal elements of $(I + C)^n$, where C is the weighted adjacency matrix and I is the identity matrix over the min,+ Kleene algebra.

(b) The problem is in *NP*, since we can guess a simple path and verify that it has negative weight in polynomial time.

To show *NP*-hardness, we reduce the Hamiltonian circuit problem to this problem. Given a graph $G = (V, E)$ with $|V| = n$, pick a vertex u and split it into two vertices v, t with no edge between. Each of v, t is connected to the other vertices of G in the same way u was. Let s be a new vertex and add an edge of weight $n - 1$ from s to v. Weight the remaining edges -1. The new graph has $n + 2$ vertices. Any path from s to t must begin with the edge from s to v of weight $n - 1$, therefore must traverse at least n other edges in order to be of negative weight. In order to be simple, it can traverse at most n other edges. Thus a simple negative weight path from s to t is of length exactly $n + 1$ and contains a simple path from v to t of length n. This gives rise to a Hamiltonian circuit in the original graph.

18. (a) Every maximal matching M can be extended to an edge cover C by adding an extra edge for each unmatched vertex. Each such extra edge must connect the unmatched vertex to a matched one, otherwise M was not maximal. Thus $|C| + |M| = |V|$.

Conversely, every minimal edge cover C contains a matching M by choosing one edge from each connected component of C. Each component of C consists of a vertex with edges radiating out from it; if a component had more than one vertex of degree greater than one, we could remove an edge and still have a cover. The number of components of C is $|M|$, and again, $|C| + |M| = |V|$.

We have shown that for every maximal M there is a C with $|C|+|M| = |V|$ and for every minimal C there is an M with $|C|+|M| = |V|$. Thus an edge cover of minimum cardinality can be obtained by extending a matching of maximum cardinality as described above.

(b) Find a maximum matching and take the vertex cover to be the set of matched vertices. This is a vertex cover, since any edge not covered could have been added to the matching. It is at most twice the size of a minimum vertex cover, since every vertex cover must contain at least one endpoint of each matched edge.

These algorithms can be implemented in time $O(m\sqrt{n})$ using the algorithm of Micali and Vazirani [80, 105].

19. As shown in Lecture 26, G has a cycle cover iff the permanent of its adjacency matrix is nonzero. Let G' be a bipartite graph whose bipartite adjacency matrix is the same as the (nonbipartite) adjacency matrix of G. Then G has a cycle cover iff G' has a perfect matching, so we can use any one of the fast algorithms given in class for maximum matching.

We can also go directly from an adjacency list representation of G to an adjacency list representation of G' in linear time without constructing the common adjacency matrix: duplicate the entire adjacency list representation of G and make the pointers in the edge lists in each copy to point to the other copy.

20. First find a maximum matching M in time $O(m\sqrt{n})$ using the Hopcroft and Karp algorithm. If there is a deficient set, then Hall's Theorem says that there is at least one free vertex $x \in U$. Starting from x, build a Hungarian tree of all vertices reachable from x along alternating paths. Cut each path off when a vertex that has been seen before is encountered. Let R be the set of vertices reachable from x in the Hungarian tree. Let $D = U \cap R$. We will show that D is a minimal deficient set.

First we claim that every element of R besides x is matched. There are certainly no free vertices in $R \cap U$ except x, since each such vertex is first seen immediately after traversing an edge in M. If there were a free vertex v in $R \cap V$, then the path from v back to x would be an augmenting path, contradicting the maximality of M. Moreover, for every matched vertex in R, its mate is also in R. Thus $|N(D)| = |D| - 1$ and D is deficient.

To show that D is minimal, we show that for any element $y \in D$, there is a matching in which all elements of D except y are matched; thus no proper subset of D is deficient. If $y = x$, we can take the matching M. Otherwise, y is matched in M. Change the status of all edges on the alternating path from y back to x through the Hungarian tree. This unmatches y and matches x. All other elements of D remain matched.

21. First we extend Menger's Theorem slightly.

Lemma *Let S be any set of k vertices of a connected undirected graph $G = (V, E)$. The following are equivalent:*

(i) G is k-connected;

(ii) any pair of vertices is connected by at least k vertex-disjoint paths;

(iii) for any vertex $s \in S$ and any vertex $v \in V$, s and v are connected by at least k vertex-disjoint paths.

Proof. The implication (i) → (ii) is given by Menger's Theorem and (ii) → (iii) is trivial.

To show (iii) → (i), let U be any set of $k - 1$ vertices. At least one element $s \in S$ is not in U, and for any other vertex v not in U, by (iii) there is a path from s to v avoiding U. Thus the removal of U does not disconnect G.   □

We will show how to test whether a given s and t are connected by k vertex-disjoint paths in time $O(km)$. By the lemma, we only need to do this for kn pairs of vertices. This gives an overall time bound of $O(k^2mn)$.

To test whether s and t are connected by k vertex-disjoint paths, we adapt the max flow algorithm of Edmonds and Karp. First we replace each edge with two directed edges, one in each direction, then give them all capacity 1. Then we split each vertex v into two vertices v' and v'' with an edge from v' to v'' of capacity 1. All edges that were directed into v are directed into v' and all edges that were directed out of v are directed out of v''.

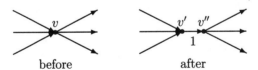

The value of an integral max flow from s to t in this graph will be the maximum number of vertex-disjoint paths from s to t. This follows from the Max Flow-Min Cut Theorem and the splitting of vertices that prevents more than one unit of flow to pass through any interior vertex.

However, we do not need to find a max flow, but only to check whether it is at least k. This can be done by performing k augmenting steps of the Edmonds-Karp algorithm, calculating new level graphs as necessary. The time to calculate all the level graphs is at most $O(km)$ and the time to do all the augmenting steps is at most $O(km)$.

22. Let e_i be the row vector with a 1 in position i and 0 elsewhere. For $1 \le i \le k$, the ith row of C_p is the first row of C_p^i; that is,

$$e_i C_p \ = \ e_1 C_p^i \ .$$

Then for any $m \ge 1$, the ith row of C_p^m is the first row of C_p^{m+i-1}:

$$
\begin{aligned}
e_i C_p^m \ &= \ e_i C_p C_p^{m-1} \\
&= \ e_1 C_p^i C_p^{m-1} \\
&= \ e_1 C_p^{m+i-1} \ .
\end{aligned}
$$

For any row vector $x = (x_1, \ldots, x_k)$, $x C_p$ can be computed in time $O(k)$:

$$x C_p \ = \ (-a_0 x_k, x_1 - a_1 x_k, x_2 - a_2 x_k, \ldots, x_{k-1} - a_{k-1} x_k) \ . \tag{22}$$

Thus we can compute any product $A C_p$ in time $O(k^2)$. Now given a power C_p^m of C_p, we can square it in time $O(k^2)$ as follows. First compute the row vector

$$e_1 C_p^{2m} \ = \ (e_1 C_p^m) C_p^m \ .$$

This takes time $O(k^2)$ and gives the first row of C_p^{2m}. Compute the remaining rows of C_p^{2m} by successively multiplying by C_p on the right. This takes time $O(k^2)$ by (22). We can compute C_p^n with at most $\log n$ operations of squaring and multiplying by C_p; the sequence of operations is determined by the binary representation of n.

23. Let $r = \operatorname{rank} A$ and let A' be an $n \times r$ submatrix of A of full rank r. Let B be an $n \times (n-r)$ matrix spanning $\ker A$. As argued in Lecture 40, $\operatorname{rank}(RA)^2 = \operatorname{rank} RA = \operatorname{rank} A$ iff the matrix $[RA'|B]$ formed by juxtaposing RA' and B is nonsingular. Thus

$$\Pr(\operatorname{rank}(RA)^2 = \operatorname{rank} RA = \operatorname{rank} A) \ = \ \sum_{S \in \mathcal{S}} \Pr(RA' = S) \ ,$$

where the sum is over the set $\mathcal{S}$ of all $n \times r$ matrices of full rank r such that $[S|B]$ is nonsingular.

We claim that RA' is a random[1] $n \times r$ matrix. To see this, let D be any nonsingular $n \times n$ matrix agreeing with A on the columns A'. Then

$$RA' \ = \ (RD)' \ ,$$

where $(RD)'$ denotes the $n \times r$ submatrix of RD obtained by deleting the same columns that were deleted from A to get A'. Since the map $R \mapsto RD$

---

[1]A *random matrix* is a matrix with each entry chosen independently and uniformly at random from the field. If the matrix is $k \times m$, then all q^{km} possible matrices are equally likely.

is a bijection and R is a random matrix, so are RD and $(RD)'$. Therefore for any $n \times r$ matrix S,

$$\Pr(RA' = S) \; = \; \Pr((RD)' = S) \; = \; \frac{1}{q^{nr}} \; .$$

We now calculate the size of $\mathcal{S}$. Note that a subspace of k^n dimension m has q^m elements, since every element is a linear combination of m basis elements, and there are q^m ways to choose the coefficients of the linear combination. We wish to count the number of ways of choosing an $n \times r$ matrix S of full rank whose columns avoid the subspace of dimension $n - r$ spanned by the columns of B. There are $q^n - q^{n-r}$ ways to choose the first column of S to avoid this subspace; once that column is chosen, there are $q^n - q^{n-r+1}$ ways of choosing the second column to avoid the linear span of B and the first column already chosen; and so on. After all but one column are chosen, there are $q^n - q^{n-1}$ ways to choose the last column. Thus there are in all

$$(q^n - q^{n-r}) \cdot (q^n - q^{n-r+1}) \cdots (q^n - q^{n-1}) \; = \; \prod_{i=1}^{r}(q^n - q^{n-i})$$

ways of choosing S, and this number is $|\mathcal{S}|$. Combining all the above equations, we have

$$\Pr(\operatorname{rank} (RA)^2 = \operatorname{rank} RA = \operatorname{rank} A)$$
$$= \sum_{S \in \mathcal{S}} \Pr(RA' = S)$$
$$= \frac{|\mathcal{S}|}{q^{nr}}$$
$$= \prod_{i=1}^{r}(1 - \frac{1}{q^i}) \; .$$

24. (a) To show that the problem is *coNP*-hard, we give a reduction from the pattern covering problem of Miscellaneous Exercise 5. Let P be a given set of patterns $p \in \{0, 1, *\}^n$. We show how to construct in polynomial time a set of terms T such that T is a cover of the ground terms over $\{f, a, b\}$ iff P is a cover of $\{0, 1\}^n$.

Let

$$F_n(x_1, \ldots, x_n) \; = \; f(x_1, f(x_2, \cdots f(x_{n-1}, x_n) \cdots)) \; .$$

Let $0' = a$ and $1' = b$. We will encode a string $d_1 d_2 \cdots d_n \in \{0, 1\}^n$ by the term $F_n(d_1', \ldots, d_n')$. Let S be the set of all terms of this form; i.e.,

$$S \; = \; \{F_n(d_1', \ldots, d_n') \mid d_1 d_2 \cdots d_n \in \{0, 1\}^n\} \; .$$

We will take $T = T_0 \cup T_1$, where T_0 will cover exactly the terms not in S, and T_1 will cover all terms in S iff P is a cover of $\{0, 1\}^n$. The set T_0 consists of all terms of the form

- $F_i(x_1, \ldots, x_{i-1}, a)$, $1 \leq i \leq n - 1$
- $F_i(x_1, \ldots, x_{i-1}, b)$, $1 \leq i \leq n - 1$
- $F_n(x_1, \ldots, x_{i-1}, f(y, z), x_{i+1}, \ldots, x_n)$, $1 \leq i \leq n$.

The terms (a) and (b) cover all ground terms not covered by F_n, and the terms (c) cover all ground terms covered by F_n that are not in S. Now, for each pattern $p = p_1 p_2 \cdots p_n \in \{0, 1, *\}^n$, let t_p be the term $F_n(p'_1, \ldots, p'_n)$, where

$$
p'_i = \begin{cases} a, & \text{if } p_i = 0, \\ b, & \text{if } p_i = 1, \\ x_i, & \text{if } p_i = * . \end{cases}
$$

The set of ground terms in S covered by $F_n(p'_1, \ldots, p'_n)$ is exactly the set of all ground terms $F_n(d'_1, \ldots, d'_n)$ such that $d_1 d_2 \cdots d_n \in \{0, 1\}^n$ is covered by p. We therefore take

$$
T_1 = \{t_p \mid p \in P\} .
$$

(b) We would like to guess a ground term and verify in polynomial time that it is not covered by T. The major difficulty here is that there are infinitely many ground terms. We need to know that if there exists a ground term that is not covered by T, then there is one of polynomial size. This will allow us to guess that term by a sequence of polynomially many nondeterministic binary choices.

For convenience, we view terms as functions labeling the nodes of the infinite binary tree with f, a, b, variables in X, or $\bot$. Formally, a term t is a map

$$
t : \{L, R\}^* \rightarrow \{f, a, b\} \cup X \cup \{\bot\}
$$

such that for all $\alpha \in \{L, R\}^*$, the following are equivalent:

- $t(\alpha) = f$
- $t(\alpha L) \neq \bot$
- $t(\alpha R) \neq \bot$

and such that $t(\alpha) \neq \bot$ for at most finitely many α. For example, the term $f(f(a, b), b)$ is represented by the map

$$
\begin{aligned}
\epsilon &\mapsto f \\
L &\mapsto f \\
LL &\mapsto a \\
LR &\mapsto b \\
R &\mapsto b \\
\text{everything else} &\mapsto \bot .
\end{aligned}
$$

Let t/α denote the subterm of t rooted at α:

$$t/\alpha(\beta) = t(\alpha\beta) .$$

Now let T be the given set of terms. Let

$$
\begin{aligned}
A_t &= \{\alpha \mid t(\alpha) \neq \perp\} \\
A &= \bigcup_{t \in T} A_t \\
\widehat{A} &= A \cup \{\alpha L, \alpha R \mid \alpha \in A\} .
\end{aligned}
$$

The set A_t is a set of paths, but it can be thought of as the binary tree obtained by ignoring labels on the nodes of t. The set A can be thought of as the tree obtained by superimposing the trees A_t, $t \in T$, on one another. The set $\widehat{A}$ can be thought of as the tree obtained from A by sprouting two new shoots out of each leaf.

Assume $|T| \geq 2$ (the only singleton cover is $\{x\}$). Let $n = \sum_{t \in T} |A_t|$ (a measure of the size of the problem). Then $|A| < n$ and $|\widehat{A}| - |A| = |A| + 1 \leq n$. Let M be the set of ground terms t such that A_t is the complete binary tree of depth $\log \log 2n$. There are at least $2n$ terms in M, one for each assignment of a and b to the $\log 2n$ leaves, and each term in M is of size $2 \log 2n$.

We claim now that if T covers all ground terms of size at most $n + 2n \log 2n$, then it covers all ground terms. To see this, suppose that T covers all ground terms of size at most $n + 2n \log 2n$, and let t be an arbitrary ground term. Associate with each $\alpha \in \widehat{A} - A$ a *unique* term $u_\alpha \in M$ such that $u_\alpha \neq t/\beta$ for any $\beta \in A$. Since $|M| \geq 2n$, $|A| \leq n$, and $|\widehat{A}| - |A| \leq n$, there are enough terms in M to do this. Let t' be a new term obtained from t by replacing all subterms t/α for $\alpha \in \widehat{A} - A$ with u_α. In other words,

- for $\alpha \in A$, set $t'(\alpha) = t(\alpha)$;
- for $\alpha \in \widehat{A} - A$ such that $t(\alpha) \neq \perp$, set $t'(\alpha\beta) = u_\alpha(\beta)$ for all $|\beta| \leq \log \log 2n$;
- for all α not assigned in (a) or (b), set $t'(\alpha) = \perp$.

From the construction of t', it is clear that

$$|A_{t'}| \leq |A| + |\widehat{A} - A| \cdot 2 \log 2n \leq n + 2n \log 2n ,$$

so by assumption t' is a substitution instance of some term $s \in T$.

We claim that t is a substitution instance of s as well. Certainly, if all the variables of s are distinct, then t is a substitution instance of s, since t and t' agree on all elements of A. Now suppose for a contradiction that there exist strings α and β such that $s(\alpha) = s(\beta) \in$

X (thus $\alpha, \beta \in A$) and $t/\alpha \neq t/\beta$. Then there exists a string γ such that

$$t(\alpha\gamma) \;=\; t/\alpha(\gamma) \;\neq\; t/\beta(\gamma) \;=\; t(\beta\gamma) \,.$$

We may assume without loss of generality that neither $t(\alpha\gamma)$ nor $t(\beta\gamma) = \bot$; otherwise, we can find a prefix of γ such that this is true, and take γ to be that prefix instead. We have three cases:

- If both $\alpha\gamma, \beta\gamma \in A$, then $t'(\alpha\gamma) \neq t'(\beta\gamma)$, since t and t' agree on A. This contradicts the fact that t' is a substitution instance of s.

- If $\alpha\gamma \notin A$ and $\beta\gamma \in A$, let γ' be a prefix of γ such that $\alpha\gamma' \in \widehat{A}-A$. Then $\beta\gamma' \in A$. Either $t/\beta\gamma'$ is entirely contained in A (in the sense that for all $\delta \in A_{t/\beta\gamma'}$, $\beta\gamma'\delta \in A$), in which case $t'/\beta\gamma' = t/\beta\gamma'$; or there exists a δ such that $\beta\gamma'\delta \in \widehat{A} - A$ and $t(\beta\gamma'\delta) \neq \bot$, in which case $t'/\beta\gamma'\delta = u_{\beta\gamma'\delta}$. In either case $t'/\alpha\gamma' = u_{\alpha\gamma'} \neq t'/\beta\gamma'$, again contradicting the fact that t' is a substitution instance of s.

- If $\alpha\gamma \notin A$ and $\beta\gamma \notin A$, let γ' be a prefix of γ such that $\alpha\gamma' \in \widehat{A}-A$ and $\beta\gamma' \in \widehat{A}$ (or vice versa—assume the former). If $\beta\gamma' \in A$, then we revert to the previous case. Otherwise, both $\alpha\gamma', \beta\gamma' \in \widehat{A} - A$. Then

$$t'(\alpha\gamma') \;=\; u_{\alpha\gamma'} \;\neq\; u_{\beta\gamma'} \;=\; t'(\beta\gamma') \,,$$

again contradicting the fact that t' is a substitution instance of s.

Since all three cases lead to a contradiction, we conclude that t is a substitution instance of s. Since t was arbitrary, T is a cover.

Thus to determine whether there exists a ground term not covered by T, we need only guess one of size at most $n + 2n \log 2n$ and check that it is not covered by any $s \in T$. This can easily be done in nondeterministic polynomial time.

25. This problem can be solved with n processors in $O(\log n)$ time. We associate a processor with each vertex. The processor associated with vertex v will calculate a pointer $\mathbf{next}(v)$ to the successor of v in the preorder traversal. If v is not a leaf, then $\mathbf{next}(v)$ is its leftmost child. If v is a leaf, then $\mathbf{next}(v)$ is the leftmost right sibling of $d(v)$, where $d(v)$ is the lowest ancestor of v that is not the rightmost child of its parent. If no such $d(v)$ exists, then v is the last vertex in preorder and has no successor.

To compute the $\mathbf{next}$ pointers of leaves in logarithmic time, we use the technique of *pointer doubling*. Initially, each vertex v sets

$$\mathbf{d}(v) := \begin{cases} \text{parent } (v) & \text{if } v \text{ is the rightmost child of its parent;} \\ v & \text{if } v \text{ is not the rightmost child of its parent or } v \text{ is the root.} \end{cases}$$

Each vertex v then iterates the operation $\mathbf{d}(v) := \mathbf{d}(\mathbf{d}(v))$ $\log n$ times. This must be done synchronously in parallel. At this point $\mathbf{d}(v) = d(v)$ if $d(v)$ exists, or the root if not. If so, the leaf v sets $\mathbf{next}(v)$ to the leftmost right sibling of $\mathbf{d}(v)$.

We now have a list $\mathbf{next}$ of all vertices in the correct order. It remains to compute the preorder number of v for each v. This is the number of vertices appearing on the list $\mathbf{next}$ before v. This can be done in $\log n$ stages with parallel prefix addition, using pointer doubling (*i.e.*, $\mathbf{next}(v) := \mathbf{next}(\mathbf{next}(v))$) to calculate the address to send the next message in each stage.

26. (a) To test whether G is outerplanar and to find an outerplane embedding if one exists, we add a new vertex v and an edge from v to all other vertices, then use the Hopcroft-Tarjan planarity test [52] to test whether the resulting graph G' is planar and find a plane embedding if so. This can be done in linear time. If G is outerplanar, then G can be embedded with all vertices on the outer face, so embedding v in the outer face allows v to be connected to all other vertices without crossing; thus G' is planar. Conversely, if G' is planar, then it can be embedded with v adjacent to the outer face; then deleting v and its incident edges gives an outerplane embedding of G.

(b) There always exists a $\frac{1}{3}$-$\frac{2}{3}$ separator of size 2. To find it, we first find an outerplane embedding as in part (a).

We then triangulate the interior faces. This can be done by traversing each interior face, adding an edge from the first vertex on the face to every other vertex on the face it is not already connected to. (We know from part (a) which face is the exterior face: it is the one that contained v.)

We then compute the plane dual of G using Miscellaneous Exercise 9, but we omit the vertex corresponding to the outer face of G and all incident edges. The resulting graph is a tree T, because any cycle would contain a vertex of G not on the outer face.

Exercise 2 can then be used to find an edge e in T whose removal disconnects T into two disjoint subtrees with no more than $\frac{2f+1}{3}$ vertices each, where f is the number of vertices in T (= number of interior faces of G). The desired separator consists of the endpoints of the dual edge of e.

27. (a) Let the data elements be $a_1, \ldots, a_n$. Assign n^2 processors to compare every element with every other element. For all i, j, $1 \leq i, j \leq n$, let

$$A_{ij} \;=\; \begin{cases} 1 & \text{if either } a_i < a_j \text{ or } (a_i = a_j \text{ and } i < j) \\ 0 & \text{otherwise.} \end{cases}$$

The $n \times n$ matrix A can be produced by the n^2 processors in one step. The matrix A determines the sorted order: for all i, the number of 1's in the ith row of A is the position of i in sorted order. Computing the ith row sum of A takes $O(\log n)$ time and $O(n)$ processors in parallel, or $O(\log n)$ time and $O(n^2)$ processors to compute all the row sums. Once the position of an element in sorted order is computed, that element is stored in the proper element of the output array. This takes one step with n processors, assuming random access to the output array.

(b) We use parallel mergesort. Each of n processors is assigned to a different input element. The set of elements is split into two sets of roughly equal size which are then sorted recursively in parallel. We then merge the two sorted arrays in $O(\log n)$ time with n processors as described below. We obtain the recurrence

$$T(n) \;=\; T(\frac{n}{2}) + O(\log n)$$

giving a running time of

$$T(n) \;=\; O((\log n)^2) \; .$$

We now show how to merge two sorted arrays in time $O(\log n)$. Let S, T be the two sorted arrays of size m and n, respectively. We have $m+n$ processors at our disposal, each assigned to a different element. First we find the medians x and y of S and T, respectively. This takes one step. Then compare x and y; say without loss of generality $x \leq y$. Split each of S and T into three arrays

$$
\begin{array}{ll}
S_0 = \{z \in S \mid z \leq x\} & T_0 = \{z \in T \mid z \leq x\} \\
S_1 = \{z \in S \mid x < z \leq y\} & T_1 = \{z \in T \mid x < z \leq y\} \\
S_2 = \{z \in S \mid y < z\} & T_2 = \{z \in T \mid y < z\}
\end{array}
$$

in one step. Note that each S_i is at most half the size of S and each T_i is at most half the size of T. For each $0 \leq i \leq 2$ in parallel, merge S_i and T_i recursively with the $|S_i| + |T_i|$ processors assigned to S_i and T_i. Let U_i be the array obtained by merging S_i and T_i, $0 \leq i \leq 2$. Now store U_0, U_1, and U_2 in an array end-to-end. The processor associated with the ith element of U_0 stores its element in position i of the output array; the processor associated with the ith element of U_1 stores its element in position $|U_0| + i$ of the output array; and the processor associated with the ith element of U_2 stores its element in position $|U_0| + |U_1| + i$ of the output array. This takes constant time in parallel. We obtain the recurrence

$$T(n) \;=\; T(\frac{n}{2}) + O(1)$$

giving a parallel time bound of

$$T(n) \;=\; O(\log n)$$

for the merge.

Parallel sorting is a topic of intense current interest. There are much more efficient NC algorithms known for sorting than the ones given here. To mention a few: Ajtai, Komlos, and Szemeredi [5] give a sorting network of depth $O(\log n)$ and $O(n)$ linear width; Cole [20] gives a CREW PRAM sorting algorithm that runs in time $O(\log n)$ on n processors; Bilardi and Nicolau[12] give an EREW PRAM bitonic sorting algorithm that runs in time $O((\log n)^2)$ on $n/\log n$ processors.

28. (a) We first show that the product of two circulant matrices is again a circulant matrix. A matrix C is circulant iff, when the columns are rotated one position to the left and then the rows are rotated up, we get C back; in terms of permutation matrices,

$$P^{-1}CP \;=\; C \,,$$

where

$$P \;=\; \begin{bmatrix} 0 & 0 & \cdots & 0 & 1 \\ 1 & 0 & \cdots & 0 & 0 \\ 0 & 1 & \cdots & 0 & 0 \\ \vdots & \vdots & \ddots & \vdots & \vdots \\ 0 & 0 & \cdots & 1 & 0 \end{bmatrix} \,.$$

Then AB is circulant if A and B are, since

$$P^{-1}ABP \;=\; P^{-1}APP^{-1}BP \;=\; AB \,.$$

While we are at it, let us show that the inverse of a circulant matrix, if it exists, is circulant:

$$P^{-1}A^{-1}P \;=\; (P^{-1}AP)^{-1} \;=\; A^{-1}.$$

We can easily compute the first row of AB in $O(\log n)$ time with n^2 processors, since each element of the first row is an inner product and can be computed in $O(\log n)$ time with n processors. Since AB is circulant, we need only rotate the first row to get the other rows. This takes constant time with n^2 processors.

(b) Let $a = (a_0, a_1, \ldots, a_{n-1})$ and $b = (b_0, b_1, \ldots, b_{n-1})$. Let $c(a)$ denote the unique circulant matrix with first row a; thus $c(a)_{ij} = a_{j-i}$. In [3, pp. 256–257], it is stated that the vector $F_n^{-1}(F_n a \cdot F_n b)$ is the *positive wrapped convolution* of a and b:

$$F_n^{-1}(F_n a \cdot F_n b) \tag{23}$$

$$= \left(\sum_{i=0}^{n-1} a_i b_{-i}, \sum_{i=0}^{n-1} a_i b_{1-i}, \sum_{i=0}^{n-1} a_i b_{2-i}, \ldots, \sum_{i=0}^{n-1} a_i b_{n-1-i}\right). \tag{24}$$

(Subscripts in (24) are taken modulo n.) It can be shown by a direct calculation that this is the first row of the matrix product $c(a) \cdot c(b)$; thus

$$c(a) \cdot c(b) \;=\; c(F_n^{-1}(F_n a \cdot F_n b)). \tag{25}$$

The vector $F_n^{-1}(F_n a \cdot F_n b)$ can be computed in time $O(\log n)$ with n processors by doing two Fourier transforms, a componentwise vector product, and an inverse Fourier transform.

Since the proof of (24) is omitted from [3], we supply one here. Let f and g be polynomials of degree at most $n - 1$ with coefficients a and b, respectively. As shown in Lecture 35, under the Fourier transform, multiplication of polynomials modulo $x^n - 1$ becomes componentwise vector product:

$$fg \bmod x^n - 1 \;=\; F_n^{-1}(F_n f \cdot F_n g). \tag{26}$$

Modulo $x^n - 1$, we can equate monomials x^i and $x^{i \bmod n}$. This allows us to take superscripts as well as subscripts modulo n. Doing so, we get the following calculation:

$$fg \bmod x^n - 1 \;=\; \sum_{i=0}^{n-1}\sum_{j=0}^{n-1} a_i b_j x^{i+j}$$

$$= \sum_{i=0}^{n-1}\sum_{k=0}^{n-1} a_i b_{k-i} x^k$$

$$= \sum_{k=0}^{n-1}\left(\sum_{i=0}^{n-1} a_i b_{k-i}\right)x^k.$$

Thus the coefficient of x_k in $fg \bmod x^n - 1$ is $\sum_{i=0}^{n-1} a_i b_{k-i}$, the kth element of the positive wrapped convolution of a and b. This and (26) give (24).

Algebraically, what is really going on here is that the circulant matrices form an n-dimensional subalgebra of the n^2-dimensional algebra of $n \times n$ matrices, and this subalgebra is isomorphic to the subalgebra of diagonal matrices via the map

$$C \mapsto F_n^{-1} C F_n \ .$$

Moreover, if $d(a)$ denotes the diagonal matrix with diagonal a, then

$$F_n^{-1} c(a) F_n \ = \ d(F_n a) \ . \tag{27}$$

This can be established by a direct calculation, using the property

$$\sum_{j=0}^{n-1} \omega^{ij} \ = \ \begin{cases} n \ , & \text{if } i \equiv 0 \bmod n \\ 0 \ , & \text{otherwise} \end{cases}$$

where ω is a primitive n^{th} root of unity: the i, ℓ^{th} element of $F_n^{-1} c(a) F_n$ is

$$\frac{1}{n} \sum_{j=0}^{n-1} \sum_{k=0}^{n-1} \omega^{-ij} a_{k-j} \omega^{k\ell} \ = \ \frac{1}{n} \sum_{m=0}^{n-1} \sum_{k=0}^{n-1} \omega^{-i(k-m)} a_m \omega^{k\ell}$$

$$= \ \sum_{m=0}^{n-1} a_m \omega^{im} \left(\frac{1}{n} \sum_{k=0}^{n-1} \omega^{(\ell-i)k} \right)$$

$$= \ \begin{cases} \sum_{m=0}^{n-1} a_m \omega^{im} & \text{if } i = \ell \\ 0 & \text{if } i \neq \ell \end{cases}$$

which is also the i, ℓ^{th} element of $d(F_n a)$.

(c) The first row of the inverse of $c(a)$ can be calculated by taking the Fourier transform of a, inverting all the elements of the resulting vector, and transforming back. In other words,

$$c(a)^{-1} \ = \ c(F_n^{-1}((F_n a)')) \ ,$$

where b' is the vector obtained from b by inverting all the elements. This follows immediately from the isomorphism $c(a) \mapsto d(F_n a)$ discussed in part (b) above, but in case you did not have the patience to wade through all that, here is a more direct argument. If $(F_n a)'$ exists, then by (25),

$$c(a) \cdot c(F_n^{-1}((F_n a)')) \ = \ c(F_n^{-1}(F_n a \cdot F_n(F_n^{-1}((F_n a)'))))$$

$$= \ c(F_n^{-1}(F_n a \cdot (F_n a)'))$$

$$= \ c(F_n^{-1}(1, 1, 1, \ldots, 1))$$

$$= \ c(1, 0, 0, \ldots, 0))$$

$$= \ I \ ,$$

thus $c(a)$ and $c(F_n^{-1}((F_n a)'))$ are inverses. Conversely, if the inverse $c(a)^{-1}$ exists and b is its first row, then

$$
\begin{aligned}
c(F_n^{-1}(1,1,1,\ldots,1)) &= c(1,0,0,\ldots,0)) \\
&= I \\
&= c(a) \cdot c(b) \\
&= c(F_n^{-1}(F_n a \cdot F_n b)) \ ,
\end{aligned}
$$

by (25). Therefore

$$
F_n a \cdot F_n b \;=\; (1,1,1,\ldots,1) \ ,
$$

so $(F_n a)'$ exists and is equal to $F_n b$. The entire operation can be done in time $O(\log n)$ with n processors using the fast Fourier transform.

Circulant matrices have numerous applications in geometry, differential equations, and mechanics. To find out more about them, see Davis' book [27].

29. For permutation $\sigma \in S_n$, define

$$
t(\sigma) \;=\; \prod_{i=1}^{n} T_{i,\sigma(i)} \ .
$$

Then

$$
\det T \;=\; \sum_{\sigma \in S_n} (-1)^{\mathrm{sign}(\sigma)} t(\sigma) \ .
$$

Let E_n be the set of permutations in S_n with only even cycles.

Lemma

$$
\det T \;=\; \sum_{\sigma \in E_n} (-1)^{\mathrm{sign}(\sigma)} t(\sigma) \ .
$$

Proof. We will show that the contributions of permutations σ containing odd cycles cancel each other out. Suppose σ contains an odd cycle ρ, and let $\tau = \sigma \rho^{-1}$. Then $\sigma = \tau \rho = \rho \tau$ (disjoint cycles commute). Consider the permutation $\tau \rho^{-1}$. Then

$$
t(\tau \rho^{-1}) \;=\; -t(\tau \rho) \ ,
$$

since $\tau\rho^{-1}$ changes the signs of an odd number of factors of $t(\tau\rho)$. For example, if $\rho = (1\,3\,7\,4\,6)$ and $\tau = (2\,5)$, then $\rho^{-1} = (6\,4\,7\,3\,1)$, and

$$
\begin{aligned}
t(\tau\rho) &= x_{25} \cdot -x_{25} \cdot x_{13} \cdot x_{37} \cdot -x_{47} \cdot x_{46} \cdot -x_{16} \\
t(\tau\rho^{-1}) &= x_{25} \cdot -x_{25} \cdot -x_{46} \cdot x_{47} \cdot -x_{37} \cdot -x_{13} \cdot x_{16} \\
&= -t(\tau\rho) \,.
\end{aligned}
$$

Moreover, $\text{sign}(\tau\rho) = \text{sign}(\tau\rho^{-1})$, since

$$
\begin{aligned}
(\tau\rho^{-1})^{-1}\tau\rho &= \rho\tau^{-1}\tau\rho \\
&= \rho^2
\end{aligned}
$$

which is even, thus $\tau\rho$ and $\tau\rho^{-1}$ are either both even or both odd. Thus the permutations containing odd cycles ρ and ρ^{-1} can be paired up so that their contributions $(-1)^{\text{sign}(\sigma)}t(\sigma)$ to $\det T$ cancel. This assignment can be repeated for other permutations σ not containing ρ but containing another odd cycle. Thus we are left with the permutations containing even cycles only.   □

(a) If the multivariate polynomial $\det T$ is not identically 0, then by the Lemma there must exist a permutation σ containing even cycles only such that $t(\sigma) \neq 0$. But then σ gives a perfect matching by taking alternate edges around the cycles. Conversely, let M be a perfect matching. Assign $x_{uv} = 1$ for $(u, v) \in M$ and $x_{uv} = 0$ otherwise. Under this substitution, there is exactly one σ with $t(\sigma) \neq 0$, namely the one corresponding to M, thus $\det T$ with this substitution is nonzero. Therefore $\det T$ is not identically 0.

(b) Select a random assignment α to the x_{uv} from a set of size 2^n. By Corollary 40.2, the probability that $\det T(\alpha) = 0$ is 1 if $\det T$ is identically 0 and at most $\frac{n}{2^n}$ if not. Thus with a probability of error at most $\frac{n}{2^n}$ we can determine whether G has a perfect matching.

(c) For each edge in succession, test whether the graph with edge e removed has a perfect matching using the above procedure. If so, then delete e from G. With high probability, we are left with the edges of a perfect matching.

Bibliography

[1] L. M. Adleman and M.-D. A. Huang. Primality testing and two-dimensional Abelian varieties over finite fields. preprint, University of Southern California, February 1988.

[2] A. V. Aho, M. R. Garey, and J.D. Ullman. The transitive reduction of a directed graph. *SIAM J. Comput.*, 1:131–137, June 1972.

[3] A. V. Aho, J. E Hopcroft, and J. D. Ullman. *The Design and Analysis of Computer Algorithms*. Addison-Wesley, 1975.

[4] R. K. Ahuja, J. B. Orlin, and R. E. Tarjan. Improved time bounds for the maximum flow problem. *SIAM J. Comput.*, 18:939–954, 1989.

[5] M. Ajtai, J. Komlos, , and E. Szemeredi. An $O(n \log n)$ sorting network. *Combinatorica*, 3:1–9, 1983.

[6] N. Alon, L. Babai, and A. Itai. A fast and simple randomized parallel algorithm for the maximal independent set problem. *J. Algorithms*, 7:567–583, 1986.

[7] C. R. Aragon and R. G. Seidel. Randomized search trees. In *Proc. 30th Symp. Foundations of Computer Science*, pages 540–545. IEEE, 1989.

[8] E. Bach. *Analytic methods in the analysis and design of number theoretic algorithms*. MIT Press, Cambridge, Mass., 1985.

[9] P. W. Beame, S. A. Cook, and H. James Hoover. Log depth circuits for division and related problems. In *Proc. 25th Conf. Foundations of Computer Science*, pages 1–6. IEEE, October 1984.

[10] C. Berge. Two theorems in graph theory. *Proc. National Acad. Sci.*, 43:842–844, 1957.

[11] S. Berkowitz. On computing the determinant in small parallel time using a small number of processors. *Information Processing Letters*, 18:147–150, 1984.

[12] G. Bilardi and A. Nicolau. Adaptive bitonic sorting: an optimal parallel algorithm for shared-memory machines. *SIAM J. Comput.*, 18(2):216–228, April 1989.

[13] Béla Bollobás. *Extremal Graph Theory*. Academic Press, 1978.

[14] J. A. Bondy and U. S. R. Murty. *Graph Theory with Applications*. North Holland, 1976.

[15] A. Borodin, J. von zur Gathen, and J. Hopcroft. Fast parallel matrix and gcd computations. *Information and Control*, 52(3):241–256, 1982.

[16] I. Borosh and L. B. Treybig. Bounds on positive integral solutions of linear diophantine equations. *Proc. Amer. Math. Soc.*, 55:299–304, 1976.

[17] W. Brown and J. F. Traub. On Euclid's algorithm and the theory of subresultants. *J. Assoc. Comput. Mach.*, 18:505–514, 1971.

[18] A. L. Chistov. Fast parallel calculation of the rank of matrices over a field of arbitrary characteristic. In *Proc. Conf. Foundations of Computation Theory*, volume 199 of *Lect. Notes in Comput. Sci.*, pages 63–69. Springer-Verlag, 1985.

[19] V. Chvátal. *Linear Programming*. Freeman, 1980.

[20] R. Cole. Parallel merge sort. In *Proc. 27th Symp. Foundations of Computer Science*, pages 511–516. IEEE, October 1986.

[21] J. H. Conway. *Regular Algebra and Finite Machines*. Chapman and Hall, London, 1971.

[22] S. A. Cook. The complexity of theorem proving procedures. In *Proc. 3rd Symp. Theory of Computing*, pages 151–158. ACM, 1971.

[23] S. A. Cook. The classification of problems which have fast parallel algorithms. In Karpiński, editor, *Proc. 1983 Symp. Foundations of Computation Theory*, volume 158 of *Lect. Notes in Comput. Sci.*, pages 78–93. Springer-Verlag, 1983.

[24] J. M. Cooley and J. W. Tukey. An algorithm for the machine calculation of complex Fourier series. *Mathematics of Computation*, 19:297–301, 1965.

[25] D. Coppersmith and S. Winograd. Matrix multiplication via arithmetic progressions. In *Proc. 19th Symp. Theory of Computing*, pages 1–6. ACM, May 1987.

[26] L. Csanky. Fast parallel matrix inversion algorithms. *SIAM J. Comput.*, 5:618–623, 1976.

[27] Philip J. Davis. *Circulant Matrices*. Wiley, 1979.

[28] E. W. Dijkstra. A note on two problems in connexion with graphs. *Numerische Math.*, 1:269–271, 1959.

[29] E. A. Dinic. Algorithm for solution of a problem of maximal flow in a network with power estimation. *Soviet Math. Doklady*, 11:1277–1280, 1970.

[30] J. Edmonds and R. M. Karp. Theoretical improvements in algorithmic efficiency for network problems. *J. Assoc. Comput. Mach.*, 19:248–264, 1922.

[31] J. R. Edmonds. A combinatorial representation for polyhedral surfaces. *Notices Amer. Math. Soc.*, 7:646, 1960.

[32] J. R. Edmonds. Matroids and the greedy algorithm. *Math. Programming*, 1:127–136, 1971.

[33] W. Feller. *An Introduction to Probability Theory and its Applications*, volume 1. Wiley, 1950.

[34] L. R. Ford, Jr. and D. R. Fulkerson. Maximal flow through a network. *Canad. J. Math.*, 8:399–404, 1956.

[35] M. L. Fredman and R. E. Tarjan. Fibonacci heaps and their uses in improved network optimization algorithms. In *Proc. 25th Symp. Foundations of Computer Science*, pages 338–346. IEEE, 1984.

[36] D. Gale and L. S. Shapley. College admissions and the stability of marriage. *Amer. Math. Monthly*, 69:9–14, 1962.

[37] Z. Galil. An $O(V^{5/3}E^{2/3})$ algorithm for the maximal flow problem. *Acta Informatica*, 14:221–242, 1980.

[38] Z. Galil and E. Tardos. An $O(n^2(m + n \log n) \log n)$ min-cost flow algorithm. *J. Assoc. Comput. Mach.*, 35:374–386, 1988.

[39] M. R. Garey and D. S. Johnson. *Computers and Intractibility: a Guide to the Theory of NP-Completeness*. W. H. Freeman, 1979.

[40] M. R. Garey, D. S. Johnson, and L. Stockmeyer. Some simplified *NP*-complete graph problems. *Theor. Comput. Sci.*, 1:237–267, 1976.

[41] A. V. Goldberg and R. E. Tarjan. A new approach to the maximum flow problem. *J. Assoc. Comput. Mach.*, 35:921–940, 1988.

[42] L. M. Goldschlager. The monotone and planar circuit value problems are logspace complete for *P*. *SIGACT News*, 9(2):25–29, 1977.

[43] R. Graham, D. Knuth, and O. Patashnik. *Concrete Mathematics: A Foundation for Computer Science*. Addison Wesley, 1989.

[44] A. C. Greenberg, R. E. Ladner, M. S. Paterson, and Z. Galil. Efficient parallel algorithms for linear recurrence computation. *Infor. Proc. Letters*, 15(1):31–35, 1982.

[45] D. Gries and G. Levin. Computing Fibonacci numbers (and similarly defined functions) in log time. *Infor. Proc. Letters*, 11(2):68–69, 1980.

[46] D. Gries, A. J. Martin, J. L. A. van de Snepscheut, and J. T. Udding. An algorithm for transitive reduction of an acyclic graph. *Science of Computer Programming*, 12(2):151–155, July 1989.

[47] A. Haken. The intractability of resolution. *Theor. Comput. Sci.*, 39:297–308, 1985.

[48] F. Harary. *Graph Theory*. Addison-Wesley, 1972.

[49] G. H. Hardy and E. M. Wright. *An Introduction to the Theory of Numbers*. Oxford, 1979.

[50] J. Hartmanis and J. Simon. On the power of multiplication in random access machines. In *Proc. 15th Symp. Switching and Automata Theory*, pages 13–23, 1974.

[51] J. E. Hopcroft and R. M. Karp. An $n^{5/2}$ algorithm for maximum matching in bipartite graphs. *SIAM J. Comput.*, 2:225–231, 1973.

[52] J. E. Hopcroft and R. E. Tarjan. Efficient planarity testing. *J. Assoc. Comput. Mach.*, 21:549–568, 1974.

[53] O. Ibarra, S. Moran, and L. E. Rosier. A note on the parallel complexity of computing the rank of order n matrices. *Information Processing Letters*, 11:162, 1980.

[54] S. L. Johnsson. Communication efficient basic linear algebra computations on hypercube architectures. Technical Report YALEU/DCS/RR-361, Yale University, September 1985.

[55] S. L. Johnsson and C.-T. Ho. Optimum broadcasting and personalized communication in hypercubes. *IEEE Transactions on Computers*, 38(9):1249–1268, 1989.

[56] N. Karmarkar. A new polynomial-time algorithm for linear programming. *Combinatorica*, 4:373–395, 1984.

[57] R. M. Karp. Reducibility among combinatorial problems. In R. E. Miller and J. W. Thatcher, editors, *Complexity of Computer Computations*, pages 85–103. Plenum Press, New York, 1972.

[58] R. M. Karp. On the complexity of combinatorial problems. *Networks*, 5:45–68, 1975.

[59] R. M. Karp and A. Wigderson. A fast parallel algorithm for the maximal independent set problem. In *Proc. 16th Symp. Theory of Computing*, pages 266–272. ACM, May 1984.

[60] L. G. Khachian. Polynomial algorithms in linear programming. *Zhurnal Vychislitelnoi Matematiki i Matematicheskoi Fiziki*, 20:53–72, 1980.

[61] S. C. Kleene. Representation of events in nerve nets and finite automata. In Shannon and McCarthy, editors, *Automata Studies*, pages 3–41. Princeton U. Press, 1956.

[62] D. E. Knuth. *The Art of Computer Programming: Fundamental Algorithms*, volume 2. Addison Wesley, 1973.

[63] D. C. Kozen. On induction vs. *-continuity. In Kozen, editor, *Proc. Workshop on Logics of Programs 1981*, volume 131 of *Lect. Notes in Comput. Sci.*, pages 167–176. Springer-Verlag, 1981.

[64] D. C. Kozen. On Kleene algebras and closed semirings. In Rovan, editor, *Proc. Math. Found. Comput. Sci. 1990*, volume 452 of *Lect. Notes in Comput. Sci.*, pages 26–47. Springer-Verlag, 1990.

[65] D. C. Kozen. A completeness theorem for Kleene algebras and the algebra of regular events. In *Proc. 6th Symp. Logic in Comput. Sci.*, pages 214–225. IEEE, 1991.

[66] J. B. Kruskal. On the shortest spanning subtree of a graph and the traveling salesman problem. *Proc. Amer. Math. Soc.*, 7:48–50, 1956.

[67] R. Ladner. The circuit value problem is logspace complete for P. *SIGACT News*, 7(1):18–20, 1975.

[68] R. E. Ladner and M. J. Fischer. Parallel prefix computation. *J. Assoc. Comput. Mach.*, 27(4):831–838, 1980.

[69] S. Lang. *Algebra*. Addison Wesley, second edition, 1984.

[70] E. L. Lawler. *Combinatorial Optimization: Networks and Matroids*. Holt, Rinehart, Winston, 1976.

[71] L. A. Levin. Universal sorting problems. *Problems of Information Transmission*, 9:265–266, 1973.

[72] D. Lichtenstein. Planar formulae and their uses. *SIAM J. Comput.*, 11(2):329–343, 1982.

[73] R. Lipton and R. E. Tarjan. Applications of a planar separator theorem. In *Proc. 18th Conf. Foundations of Computer Science*, pages 162–170. IEEE, 1977.

[74] L. Lovász. On determinants, matchings, and random algorithms. In Budach, editor, *Proc. Symp. on Fundamentals of Computing Theory*, pages 565–574, Berlin, 1979. Akademia-Verlag.

[75] L. Lovász and M. D. Plummer. *Matching Theory*. North Holland, 1986.

[76] M. Luby. A simple parallel algorithm for the maximal independent set problem. In *Proc. 17th Symp. Theory of Computing*, pages 1–10. ACM, May 1985.

[77] V. M. Malhotra, M. Pramodh-Kumar, and S. N. Maheshwari. An $O(V^3)$ algorithm for finding maximum flows in networks. *Information Processing Letters*, 7:277–278, 1978.

[78] K. Mehlhorn. *Data Structures and Algorithms 2: Graph Algorithms and NP-Completeness*. EATCS Monographs on Theoretical Computer Science. Springer-Verlag, 1984.

[79] A. R. Meyer and R. Ritchie. The complexity of loop programs. In *Proc. National Meeting*, pages 465–469. ACM, 1967.

[80] S. Micali and V. Vazirani. An $O(\sqrt{|V|} \cdot |E|)$ algorithm for finding maximum matchings in general graphs. In *Proc. 21st Symp. Foundations of Computer Science*, pages 17–27. IEEE, 1980.

[81] G. L. Miller. Riemann's hypothesis and tests for primality. *J. Comput. Syst. Sci.*, 13:300–317, 1976.

[82] K. Mulmuley. A fast parallel algorithm to compute the rank of a matrix over an arbitrary field. *Combinatorica*, 7(1):101–104, 1987.

[83] V. Ya. Pan. Strassen's algorithm is not optimal. In *Proc. 19th Symp. Foundations of Computer Science*, pages 166–176. IEEE, 1978.

[84] V. Ya. Pan. *How to multiply matrices faster*, volume 179 of *Lect. Notes in Comput. Sci.* Springer-Verlag, 1984.

[85] C. H. Papadimitriou and K. Steiglitz. *Combinatorial Optimization: Algorithms and Complexity*. Prentice-Hall, 1982.

[86] A. Pettorossi. Derivation of an $O(k^2 \log n)$ algorithm for computing order-k Fibonacci numbers from the $O(k^3 \log n)$ matrix multiplication method. *Infor. Proc. Letters*, 11(4):172–179, 1980.

[87] J. A. La Poutré. Lower bounds for the union-find and the split-find problem on pointer machines. In *Proc. 22nd Symp. Theory of Computing*, pages 34–44. ACM, 1990.

[88] W. Pugh. Skip lists: a probabilistic alternative to balanced trees. *Comm. Assoc. Comput. Mach.*, 33(6):668–676, June 1990.

[89] M. O. Rabin. Probabilistic algorithms for testing primality. *J. Number Theory*, 12:128–138, 1980.

[90] J. Renegar. A polynomial-time algorithm based on Newton's method for linear programming. *Math. Programming*, 40:59–93, 1988.

[91] R. L. Rivest and J. Vuillemin. On recognizing graph properties from adjacency matrices. *Theor. Comput. Sci.*, 3:371–384, 1976/77.

[92] J. T. Schwartz. Fast probabilistic algorithms for verification of polynomial identities. *J. Assoc. Comput. Mach.*, 27:701–717, 1980.

[93] Y. Shiloach and U. Vishkin. An $O(\log n)$ parallel connectivity algorithm. *J. Algorithms*, 3:57–67, 1982.

[94] D. Sleator and R. E. Tarjan. Self-adjusting binary trees. In *Proc. 15th Symp. Theory of Computing*, pages 235–245. ACM, 1983.

[95] D. D. Sleator. An $O(nm \log n)$ algorithm for maximum network flow. Technical Report STAN-CS-80-831, Stanford University, 1980.

[96] R. Solovay and V. Strassen. A fast Monte Carlo test for primality. *SIAM J. Comput.*, 6:84–85, 1977.

[97] V. Strassen. Gaussian elimination is not optimal. *Numerische Math.*, 13:354–356, 1969.

[98] E. Tardos. A strongly polynomial minimum cost circulation algorithm. *Combinatorica*, 5:247–255, 1985.

[99] R. E. Tarjan. A class of algorithms that require nonlinear time to maintain disjoint sets. *J. Comput. Syst. Sci.*, 18:110–127, 1979.

[100] R. E. Tarjan. *Data Structures and Network Algorithms*, volume 44 of *Regional Conference Series in Applied Mathematics*. SIAM, 1983.

[101] A. Urquhart. Hard examples for resolution. *J. Assoc. Comput. Mach.*, 34(1):209–219, 1987.

[102] P. M. Vaidya. An algorithm for linear programming which requires $O(((m + n)n^2 + (m + n)^{1.5}n)L)$ arithmetic operations. In *Proc. 19th Symp. Theory of Computing*, pages 29–38. ACM, 1987.

[103] L. G. Valiant. The complexity of computing the permanent. *Theor. Comput. Sci.*, 8:189–201, 1979.

[104] L. G. Valiant and G. J. Brebner. Universal schemes for parallel communication. In *Proc. 13th Symp. Theory of Computing*, pages 263–277. ACM, 1981.

[105] V. V. Vazirani. A theory of alternating paths and blossoms for proving correctness of the $O(\sqrt{|V|} \cdot |E|)$ general graph matching algorithm. Technical Report 89-1035, Cornell University, September 1989.

[106] J. Vuillemin. A data structure for manipulating priority queues. *Comm. Assoc. Comput. Mach.*, 21:309–314, 1978.

[107] D. J. A. Welsh. *Matroid Theory*. Academic Press, 1976.

[108] H. S. Wilf. *Algorithms and Complexity*. Prentice-Hall, 1986.

[109] T. C. Wilson and J. Shortt. An $O(\log n)$ algorithm for computing general order-k Fibonacci numbers. *Infor. Proc. Letters*, 10(2):68–75, 1980.

[110] A. C.-C. Yao. Monotone bipartite graph properties are evasive. *SIAM J. Comput.*, 17(3):517–520, 1988.

[111] R. E. Zippel. Probabilistic algorithms for sparse polynomials. In Ng, editor, *Proc. EUROSAM 79*, volume 72 of *Lect. Notes in Comput. Sci.*, pages 216–226. Springer-Verlag, 1979.

Index

Texts and Monographs in Computer Science

continued (from page ii)

Texts and Monographs in Computer Science

continued

Robert N. Moll, Michael A. Arbib, and A.J. Kfoury
An Introduction to Formal Language Theory
1988. X, 203 pages, 61 illus.

Helmut A. Partsch
Specification and Transformation of Programs
1990. XIII, 493 pages, 44 illus.

Franco P. Preparata and Michael Ian Shamos
Computational Geometry: An Introduction
1988. XII, 390 pages, 231 illus.

Brian Randell, Ed.
The Origins of Digital Computers: Selected Papers, 3rd Edition
1982. XVI, 580 pages, 126 illus.

Thomas W. Reps and Tim Teitelbaum
The Synthesizer Generator: A System for Constructing Language-Based Editors
1989. XIII, 317 pages, 75 illus.

Thomas W. Reps and Tim Teitelbaum
The Synthesizer Generator Reference Manual, 3rd Edition
1989. XI, 171 pages, 79 illus.

Arto Salomaa and Matti Soittola
Automata-Theoretic Aspects of Formal Power Series
1978. X, 171 pages

J.T. Schwartz, R.B.K. Dewar, E. Dubinsky, and E. Schonberg
Programming with Sets: An Introduction to SETL
1986. XV, 493 pages, 31 illus.

Alan T. Sherman
VLSI Placement and Routing: The PI Project
1989. XII, 189 pages, 47 illus.

Santosh K. Shrivastava, Ed.
Reliable Computer Systems
1985. XII, 580 pages, 215 illus.

William M. Waite and Gerhard Goos
Compiler Construction
1984. XIV, 446 pages, 196 illus.

Texts and Monographs in Computer Science